AF605834

KENJIRO NOMURA

AMERICAN MODERNIST

AN ISSEI ARTIST'S JOURNEY

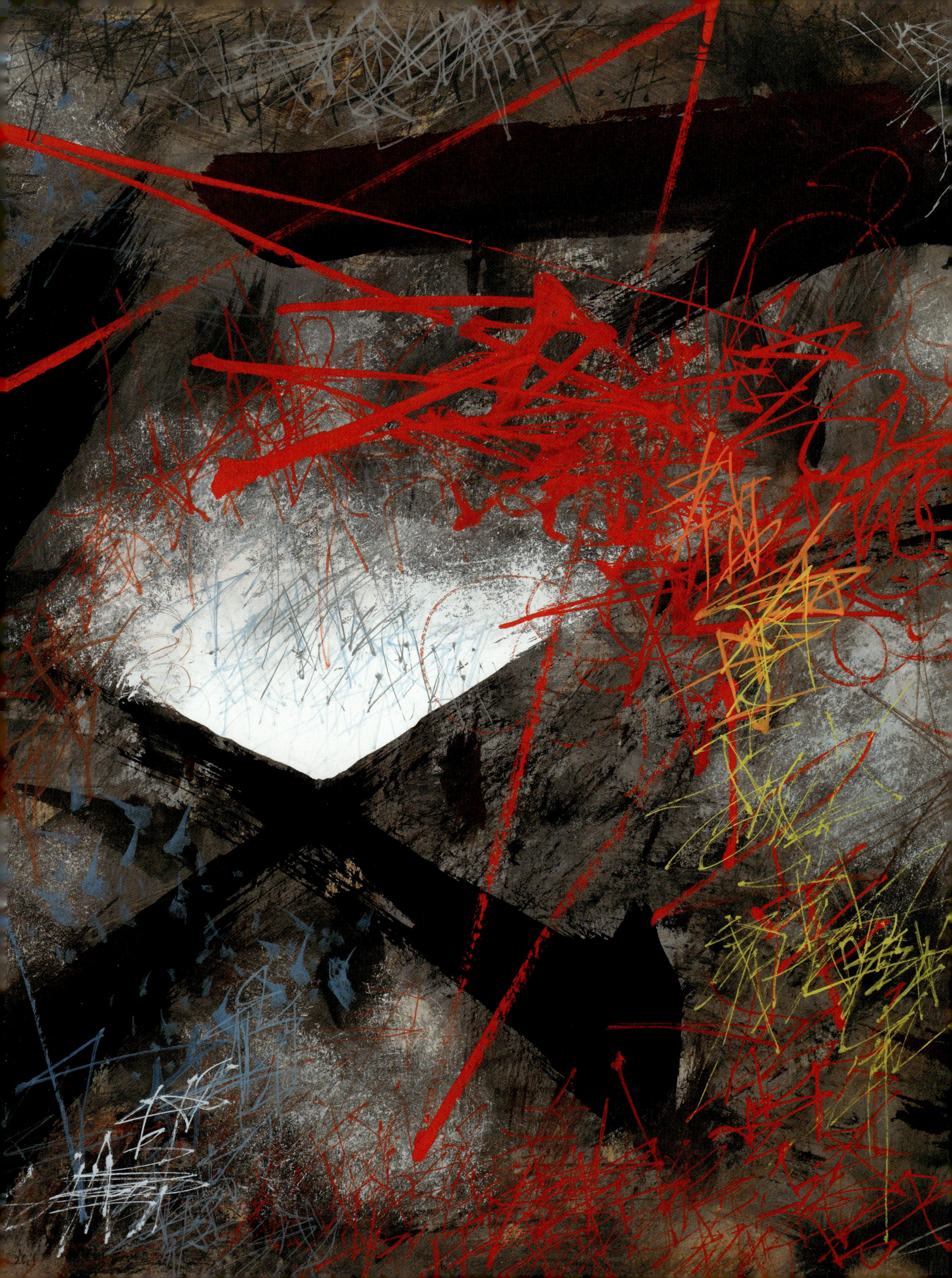

KENJIRO NOMURA

AMERICAN MODERNIST

AN ISSEI ARTIST'S JOURNEY

BARBARA JOHNS

FOREWORD BY
GAIL M. NOMURA

CONTRIBUTION BY
DAVID F. MARTIN

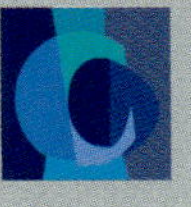

CASCADIA ART MUSEUM

DISTRIBUTED BY UNIVERSITY OF WASHINGTON PRESS

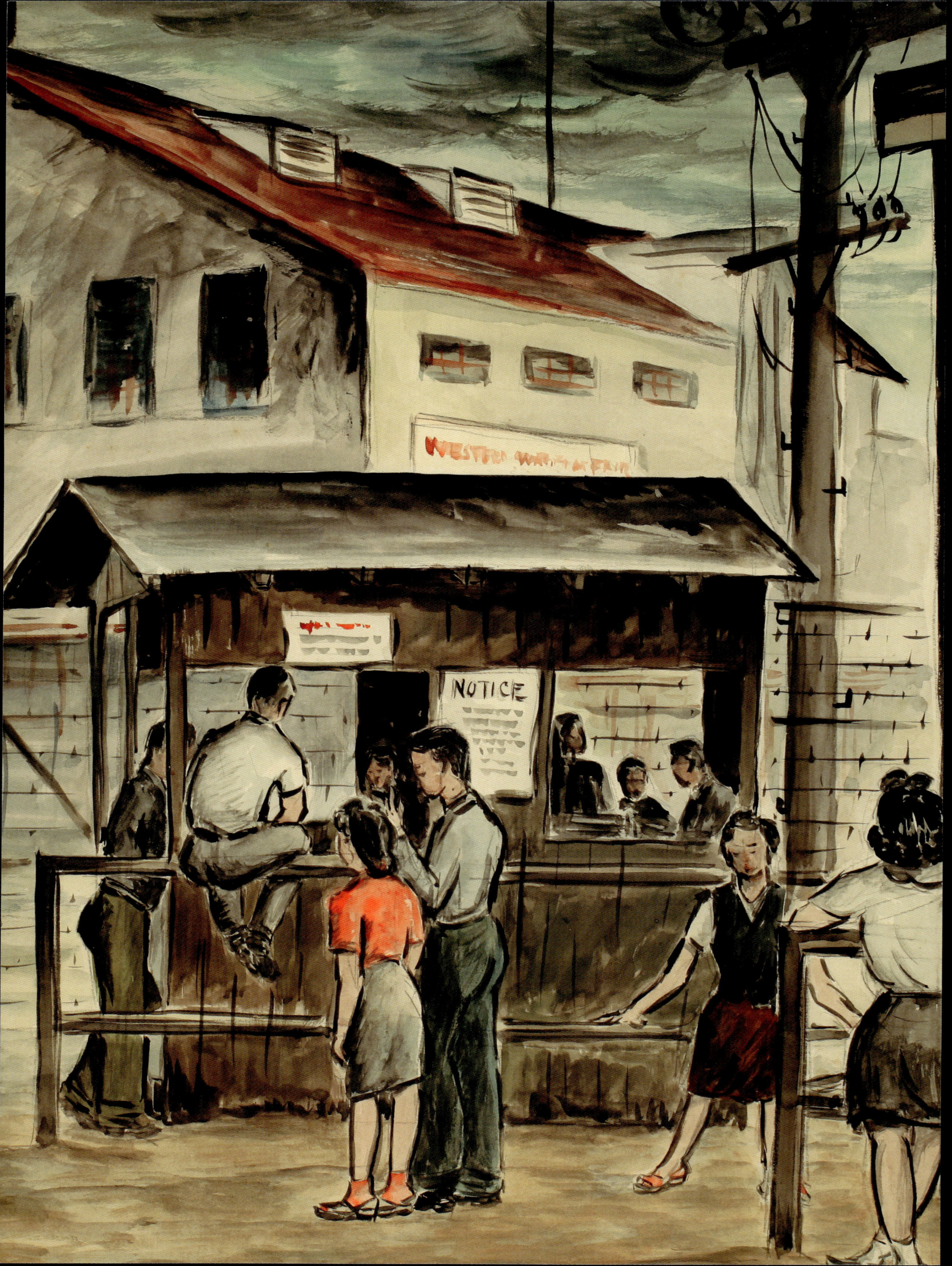
NOTICE

CONTENTS

Dedicated to Roger Daniels, mentor and friend,
whose encouragement has lit my way

FOREWORD
GAIL M. NOMURA

After reading my publication on Teiko Tomita (1896–1990), a Japanese immigrant woman poet in early twentieth-century Washington State, a prominent U.S. history professor questioned me about the literary life of the Issei, first-generation Japanese immigrants.[1] Because of the life of hardship that most Issei women lived, the historian asked me with incredulity and admiration when Tomita would have had the time to write poetry, which the historian had presumed was an art practiced by white elites who had the leisure time to pen poetry. I replied that Tomita composed her poems as she toiled in the fields and orchards during the day and committed them to paper and revised those poems late in the evening, when she had finished her field and domestic chores and her family was asleep. In fact, Tomita had written Japanese *tanka*, short poems of five-seven-five-seven-seven syllables, since she was a schoolgirl in Japan and continued to write and publish her *tanka* throughout her life in the United States. Japanese of all classes composed *tanka* and other poetry such as *senryū* and *haiku* in Japan and continued their art after they immigrated to the United States. Overcoming a life of often limited resources, anti-Asian discrimination, and exclusion from U.S. citizenship and other fundamental rights, they found joy and solace in their art and made the time to convey their vision and stories through their poems, just as Kenjiro Nomura (1896–1956), the subject of Barbara Johns's book, did through his paintings and drawings.[2] Teiko Tomita and Kenjiro Nomura were part of the vibrant artistic life of Issei in the literary, performing, and visual arts of the United States.

In pre–World War II Seattle Issei visual artists in particular received local, national, and international acclaim and support. In the 1920s Issei members of the internationally renowned Seattle Camera Club (SCC) exhibited in juried local, national, and international exhibitions, winning numerous prestigious awards. In the 1930s Seattle Issei painters also gained top regional and national recognition as American modernists, contributing to the defining of American art through their perspectives of the everyday life and built and natural landscapes of the communities in which they lived. These Issei artists were, on one hand, racially discriminated against and excluded from white society and yet, on the other, embraced and acclaimed in the arts by critics, judges, museums, and the arts community. Kenjiro Nomura was among the most prominent Issei painters in this prewar period. In 1935 the *Seattle Times* named Nomura as one of eight artists, and the only one of color, to have contributed significantly to the cultural life of Seattle.[3] Nomura was alone among his prewar Seattle Issei colleagues in regaining acclaim after World War II, in the 1950s.

However, though celebrated and recognized as an eminent American artist in the prewar period, with the outbreak of war with Japan in 1941, Nomura and more than 110,000 persons of Japanese ancestry were forcibly rounded up, removed from their homes, excluded, and incarcerated in inland government concentration camps, without charges and due process, solely on the basis of racial ancestry. Two-thirds of those incarcerated were U.S.-born citizen children and grandchildren of the Issei, and the other third were the Issei who were denied citizenship by race-based discriminatory naturalization laws, despite decades of productive life in the United States and the Issei's court challenges to these racist anti-Asian naturalization laws.[4] Allowed to bring only what he could carry to the camps, Nomura, in despair, burned a number of his paintings before his landlord offered to hold his remaining belongings for him.[5] But Nomura persevered in painting, drawing, and sketching in the camps. The resulting powerful images of the incarceration experience bear witness to this mass violation of civil liberties and serve as a visual record and a testament to the absolute need to preserve constitutional protections for all during national security crises.

In this, her fourth book about Seattle Issei artists, art historian Barbara Johns documents the importance of Kenjiro Nomura as an integral part of American cultural arts and contextualizes and analyzes his paintings and life history.[6] Through her in-depth research of Nomura, Johns brings a renewed public recognition of Nomura and the artistic achievements of Japanese American painters to the cultural life of Seattle and our nation. Issei painters brought fresh, new perspectives through their lens by virtue of being immigrants of color. Through their art, these artists provide keen insights into their sense of place and their perspectives of life in America and contribute to a richer understanding of the complex nature of American society and culture.

Today, there are troubling voices once again spewing hate-filled, anti-Asian, anti-immigrant, white supremacist, racist rhetoric supporting discriminatory policies and actions in the United States that resonate with the adversities faced by Nomura and other people of color. In her book on Kenjiro Nomura, Barbara Johns foregrounds the dignity and humanity of the artist of color behind the paintings and his resistance, agency, and resilience in meeting the challenges of becoming an acclaimed American artist. Through her sensitive telling of Nomura's story, Johns constructs a more inclusive and representative history of American art in Seattle and our nation, and in the process teaches that people of color are not apart but instead very much a part of the fabric of American culture.

MUSEUM FOREWORD

LINDSEY ECHELBARGER

Cascadia Art Museum is proud to present *Kenjiro Nomura, American Modernist: An Issei Artist's Journey*. This timely publication and exhibition tell the story of a Seattle Issei artist whose life and art have had little attention since his untimely death in 1956. Nomura was the first regional artist to have a solo exhibition at the newly opened Seattle Art Museum in 1933. That same year, he was included in a group exhibition at New York's Museum of Modern Art. His reputation was so significant that, in 1935, he was invited to join some of the most important artists of the state in the Group of Twelve. These painters included Northwest icons Morris Graves and Kenneth Callahan, as well as Ambrose Patterson and Walter F. Isaacs (the latter two headed the University of Washington School of Art for decades).

This book is written by the distinguished art historian Barbara Johns. Her compelling account illuminates Nomura's early rise as an artist followed by the tragic upending of his family and career when President Franklin Roosevelt's infamous Executive Order 9066 negatively altered the remainder of his life. His postwar success as a modernist abstract painter concluded a diverse and successful career.

This comprehensive overview of Nomura's life and art is Cascadia Art Museum's fifth publication. The museum's curator, David F. Martin, has contributed a chapter in this book to further elucidate Nomura's art in context with his regional contemporaries.

While a total of five books may not seem all that impressive when compared to the output of other museums, it is quite an accomplishment for a museum that is only five years old. When our dedicated group first gathered in 2014 to discuss the possibility of founding a new art museum focused on the early art of the Northwest, it was agreed that a publishing program to document our exhibitions would be an integral part of our mission. We feel strongly that Cascadia has a duty to add to the scholarship and intellectual body of knowledge of Northwest art history—a field that is characterized by a paucity of publications.

The Northwest art community owes Barbara Johns a hearty thank-you for her tireless efforts in shepherding this project to fruition and ensuring that Nomura's life and work are not forgotten. Further thanks are due to David F. Martin for his sensitive curation of the accompanying exhibition at the museum.

As Washington State's only cultural institution focusing exclusively on the early art of the Northwest, Cascadia Art Museum extends gratitude to the many generous donors (see page 171) for their support of this important publication and exhibition.

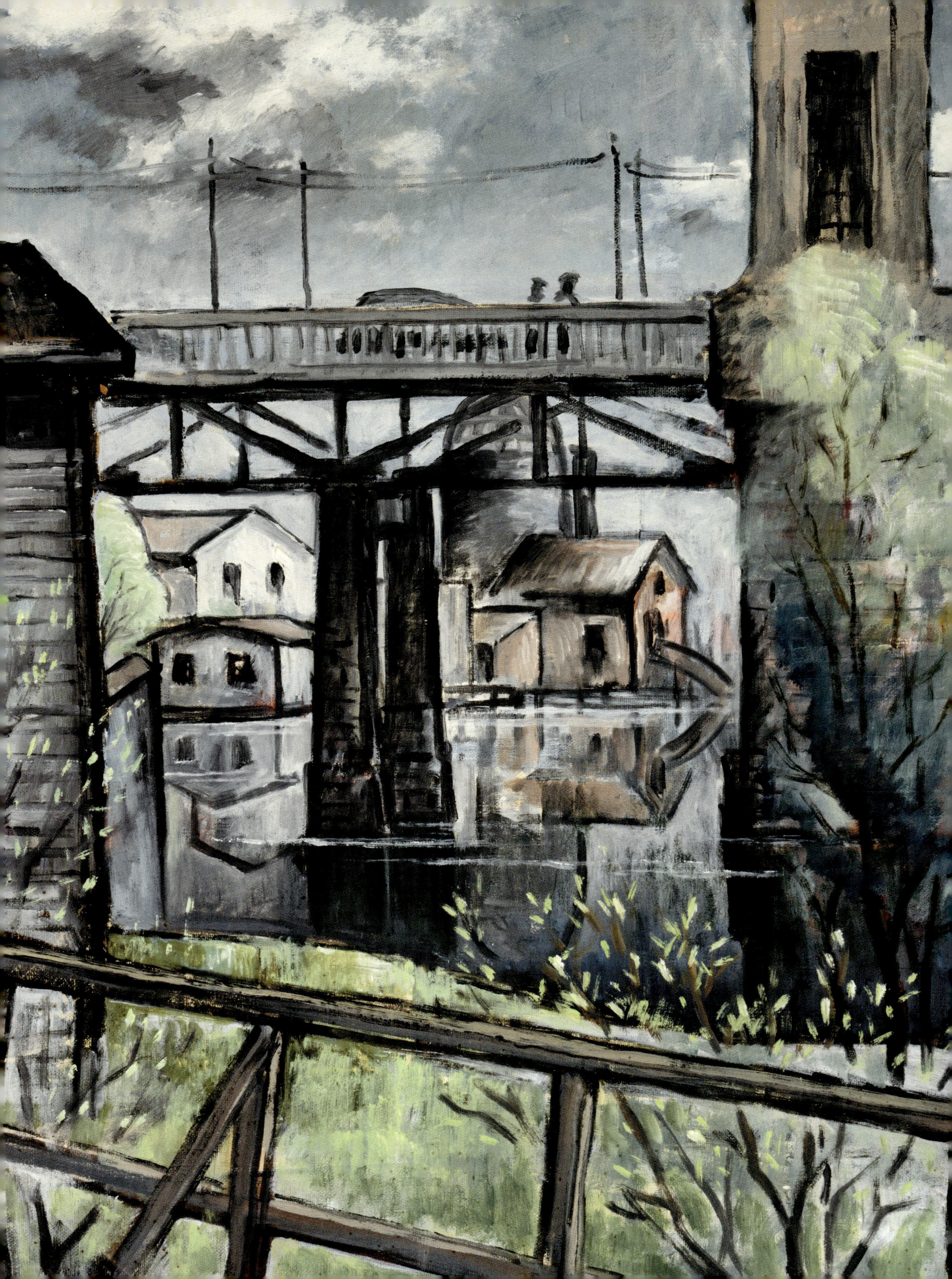

INTRODUCTION

New to Seattle some forty years ago, and new to my job as curatorial assistant in modern art at the Seattle Art Museum, I remember the pleasure of pulling out the racks in museum storage and finding strongly composed and beautifully crafted paintings in a 1930s American realist style. The paintings by Kenjiro Nomura (1896–1956) and Kamekichi Tokita (1897–1948) had seldom been exhibited in recent years.[1] In the next decade I had opportunities to exhibit them, to recommend them to others, and, after meeting Tokita's eldest son, Shokichi, to guide Tokita's papers to the Smithsonian's Archives of American Art.[2] Little did I guess that twenty-five years later I would undertake a study of these immigrant Japanese American artists and their colleagues.

Nomura, Tokita, and their fellow painter Takuichi Fujii (1891–1964) were the three most prominent Issei, or first-generation Japanese American, artists in Seattle before World War II. Their paintings were widely acclaimed in the Northwest and represented Washington State nationally. Incarcerated during the war together with 120,000 others of Japanese descent on the West Coast, each kept a record of his experience that provides a valuable Issei perspective.[3] I have previously written about Tokita and Fujii and now, with this study of Nomura, bring to completion an account of these three exceptional artists.

Spring, 1932
Detail of Fig. M.20

This is my fourth publication about Issei artists in Seattle and, counting a dissertation, the fifth book-length project. Each one has led me more deeply into Japanese American studies, a discipline that was new to me as a historian of modern American art. My study of Japanese America began with an invitation to organize an exhibition and write about the work of Paul Horiuchi (1906–1999), whose artistic career developed in Seattle after the war and continued nearly to the end of his life.[4] His work is better known than that of the older Issei artists, although his association with them dates to the 1930s. My subsequent book about Tokita was occasioned by the translation of the artist's wartime diary and brought the fullness of Tokita's artistic production and his diary to public attention for the first time.[5] While I was aware of the strong personal voice of the diary, I didn't yet understand the complexities of the situations and relationships he addresses. It is a remarkable, reflective document from an Issei perspective that deserves deeper study. My dissertation then addresses Nomura's, Tokita's, and Fujii's work of the 1930s, their peak years of recognition.[6] What followed was entirely fortuitous and opened the way to the most revealing of these recovery efforts, when I was introduced online to Fujii's grandson, Sandy Kita, then in the process of translating his grandfather's wartime diary. Neither the illustrated diary, which the historian Roger Daniels considers "the most detailed and informative work produced by an Issei prisoner in a War Relocation Authority camp," nor the artist's large collection of related artwork had been seen publicly.[7] These led to my book about Fujii.[8] And now, Nomura. To have been entrusted with the artists' stories by their families and to be able to put on record the artistic achievement of these Seattle Issei artists has been a gift of unanticipated magnitude.

Kenjiro Nomura

Born in Japan in 1896, Nomura came to the United States at the age of ten in the company of his parents. He spent his youth in the port city of Tacoma, Washington, and by the time he was twenty, lived in Seattle's Japantown and began attracting notice as an artist. He started a sign-painting business with a fellow artist, joining the many Issei entrepreneurs in the city, and they opened their shop as a gathering place for artists. Throughout the 1930s his paintings won recognition and awards. World War II brought a devastating blow: following Japan's attack on Pearl Harbor, and under mass exclusion orders, Nomura was forced from his home and confined under military guard in a remote, segregated camp. He continued to paint throughout his three and a half years' incarceration. Upon his release in 1945, he faced hardships that usurped any desire to paint. Eventually he resumed painting and developed a new abstract style that brought him recognition once again. In the last years of his life, he fulfilled a long-held desire to become a citizen in the country he had for decades considered his home.

Nomura, Tokita, and Fujii worked in the Western tradition of oil painting and were received as American modernists among the mainstream art community. Of the three, Nomura was the only one with formal training in Western art and held the longest record of exhibitions; he was the only one among them to regain recognition after the war.[9] Tokita died in 1948, and Fujii resettled in Chicago, where he was all but forgotten. Nomura's story is valuable for both the enduring quality of his artistic production and the extent of artwork that remains, from his student years until the end of his life, enabling us to see the full arc of his endeavor.

Nomura came of age artistically at a time when artists and critics sought to define an "American art" distinct from its European precedents. Framing the discussion was a conviction that the American experience was unique, that the nation, while young, had a traceable cultural heritage, and that its artists' role was to draw upon this material to create a distinctively American art. By 1930 that had come to be widely understood to be about local place and custom. Nomura's work was produced in this context. The late 1920s and 1930s were also an artistic coming-of-age for the young city of Seattle in the "farthest reach" of the United States, as the city's major art institutions took hold, despite the Depression, and helped anchor a growing community of artists.[10] Writing in local and national publications, the artist Kenneth Callahan (1905–1986) continually promoted painting that was more than "pretty pictures" as he made the case for modernism, urged reluctant viewers to open their minds, and supported its leading artists. Throughout the 1930s he was one of Nomura's most consistent and influential supporters.

Moreover, as an artist of Japanese descent, Nomura represented a cultural heritage that held great appeal to American and European artists. Since the West's forced reopening of Japan in the 1850s, Western artists, most notably the impressionists and post-impressionists, had begun to adopt stylistic elements of Japanese art. Contemporaneous spiritual movements embraced Eastern thought such as Buddhism in their quest for a syncretic, universal belief system, a universalist ideal that was foundational to much early twentieth-century non-objective or abstract art. The paintings that established Nomura's reputation display few of these tendencies explicitly, but in his person he embodied a direct connection for his contemporaries.

With the coming of World War II, Callahan became the spokesperson for a circle of painters who would become known as the "Northwest school." Senior among them was Mark Tobey (1890–1976), who had returned to Seattle after years abroad, an experienced, learned painter deeply interested in Asian art and philosophy. Amid wartime, discussions of Asian philosophical precepts were formative in the artists' search for a means of universalist expression. But as Tobey, Morris Graves (1910–2001), Callahan, and others gained increasing recognition in New York in the 1940s, Nomura and his colleagues were confined in remote concentration camps. They struggled to reestablish their lives in the immediate postwar years as a Northwest school was defined, with no mention of the Issei painters.[11] Nomura's eventual return to painting brought immediate recognition, but he did not live to develop the potential of his new work, nor did his name become part of the lexicon. It would be younger Asian American artists whom observers later welcomed into the ranks.

Nomura's biography and artistic production are presented here for the first time in the fullness of his accomplishment and framed by their historical and social context. An essay by David F. Martin discusses the artists with whom Nomura associated during his career. Nomura's artistic success stands in striking contrast to the circumstances of his life. His drive since youth to study painting and the early recognition his work received make evident a natural talent. His perseverance in painting throughout years of challenge and adversity show art-making to have been a sustaining life force. Before and after the war, his dedication to painting was a model to younger artists, and the public recognition of his work, an inspiration.

Sources

Foremost among the resources for this study are the many paintings and drawings that survive, although an unknown number were destroyed or lost during the war, and others lost with the vagaries of time. Five paintings are in the collection of the Seattle Art Museum, three acquired during the early 1930s and two more as a posthumous gift from his son. Four from the Depression-era Public Works of Art Project are in public institutions (including one of the Seattle Art Museum paintings). The Tacoma Art Museum is the major repository of the work from World War II. Most of his student and postwar artwork remains in the family, while some twenty pieces have been given to museums or are in private collections. This book is exceptionally generously illustrated to create a lasting record.

George Nomura (1930–2017), the artist's only son and offspring, was the guardian of his father's legacy and a valuable resource for his father's story and extended family history. He preserved Nomura's decades-long collection of artwork, initiated a memorial exhibition at the Seattle Art Museum in 1960, and in 1991 brought the wartime collection out of storage for its first public display at Seattle's Wing Luke Museum. He assigned descriptive titles to many pieces at the time, and his recollections provided the basis for the biographic account in the accompanying exhibition catalogue by June Mukai McKivor, Kenjiro's niece and George's cousin.[12] For nearly twenty years following the Wing Luke Museum exhibition, June McKivor and subsequently George and his wife, Betty, oversaw the wartime collection as it traveled throughout the region and to venues nationally. Betty was instrumental in cataloguing the large number of artworks in their possession and helping to preserve personal papers. In more recent years, David and I are fortunate to have had opportunities for extended conversations with George, which have added further detail to the account.

And yet, Nomura's story remains fragile. Regrettably, George's death shortly after this project was proposed has meant the loss of direct personal memories. Betty died in 2020 as the manuscript neared completion. Moreover, there are no letters or diary to provide a first-person voice that reveals more of the individual. Aside from the course of events and the evidence of artwork, there is little to tell us about the thoughts and worldview of its maker. In this, an account of his life differs from that of his colleagues Tokita and Fujii, each of whom left a diary of his experience during the mass incarceration of Japanese Americans.[13] While these first-person documents pertain to a period of crisis in the artists' lives, they give insight into the individual character, cultural mindset, and practical manner of coping. Nomura's life story shows him to be an industrious and resilient person striving to overcome meager resources, limited opportunity, and major losses. Shokichi Tokita, Kamekichi Tokita's son, remembers him as friendly and personable, a man who used to make his father laugh.[14] It is this positive, constructive outlook that characterizes much of his artwork, evident in his love of color and harmonious composition. It touches even that from the war. Throughout his life art was a motivating force, and perhaps at times a solace.

The history of Japanese America, and particularly the experience of World War II, is a large, ever-growing field of research as new scholarship supports deeper and more nuanced understanding, and it lays the foundation for this account. The histories of local ethnic Japanese communities in Tacoma and Seattle place Nomura more specifically, while documents such as ship manifests, census data, city directories, and museum records add personal details. Others' words in letters and oral histories lend immediacy. My own study of Nomura and his colleagues in the 1930s forms the basis of chapter 2. The voluminous records of the World War II–era War Relocation Authority, a civilian agency charged with the care and resettlement of incarcerated Japanese Americans, provide not only extensive reporting on the conditions in which Nomura was held but also details about his prewar and wartime-camp activities. While my use of this primary material is accurate to the best of my ability, the citation of some file locators unfortunately is incomplete; because of the 2020–2021 pandemic, I was unable to return to the National Archives for further research. Last but not least, this account builds upon the efforts of those who helped keep Nomura's memory alive in oral histories, essays, and exhibitions—especially George Tsutakawa, Martha Kingsbury, Mayumi Tsutakawa, June Mukai McKivor, and Kazuko Nakane.[15]

A few notes on terminology may be helpful to readers. People of Japanese ancestry in America name themselves by generation. *Issei* is the first, or immigrant, generation. *Nisei* is the second, their American-born children. A subgroup, *Kibei*, are Nisei who were sent to Japan in childhood, usually for education, and returned home to the United States. The naming continues with subsequent generations. Collectively, all are *Nikkei*.

During World War II, the U.S. government used euphemisms to mask the fact of forcibly removing and confining over one hundred thousand people based solely upon ethnicity. Two-thirds of them were American citizens; all were held without charge. "Internment," the commonly used term for this mass confinement, applies in the legal sense to the Issei leaders who were held separately in Department of Justice camps under terms of the Geneva Conventions. This account follows the example of many contemporary historians in using the terms "incarceration" and "inmates" to more accurately describe the majority experience of Japanese Americans held behind barbed-wire fences and under military guard.[16]

Today more than ever stories such as Nomura's remain relevant. In this time of increasing polarization and spread of falsehoods, their stories remind us how easily an entire group can be targeted, and that our democratic institutions are only as strong as our will to uphold them. And they remind us of the resilience of the human spirit to find a better way forward.

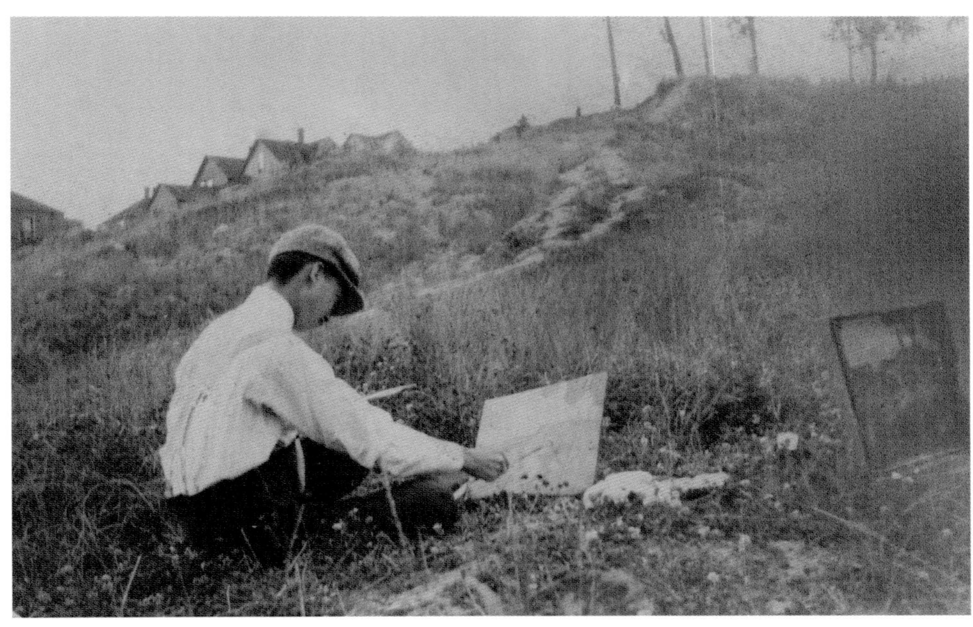

Nomura painting on a Seattle hillside, ca. 1916–1921
Nomura Estate

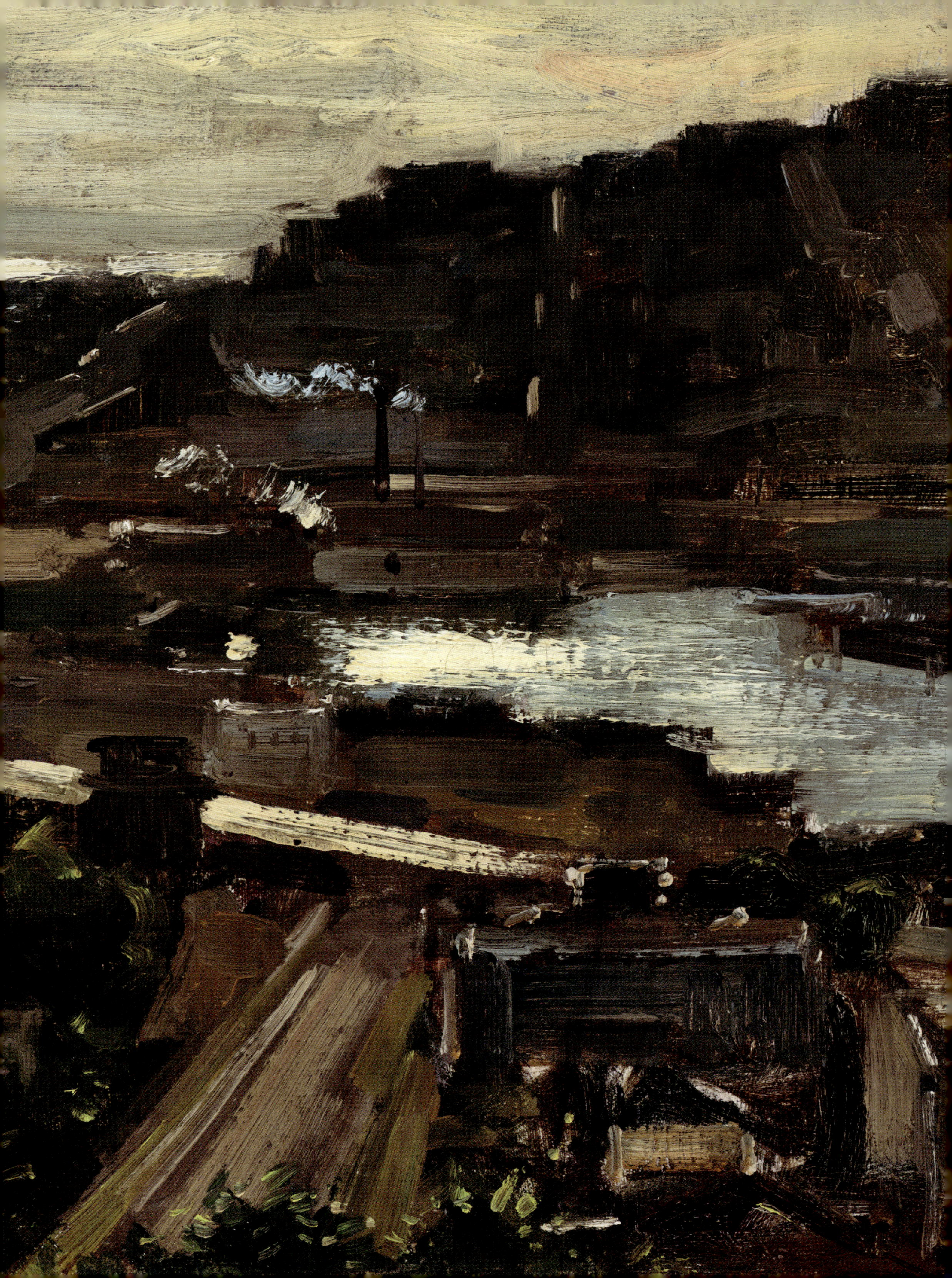

1.
THE IMMIGRANT

We can only imagine what it was like for ten-year-old Kenjiro Nomura to first sight Seattle on June 13, 1907. Together with his father, Harukichi Nomura, and his mother, Shiu, he had boarded the *Tosa Maru* in Yokohama fifteen days earlier. He must have heard stories about the land across the Pacific as long as he could remember, for it was his father's second journey. Now, as the *Tosa Maru* steamed into dock at Smith Cove, the young city rose on recently deforested hills above Puget Sound. Railroad tracks and two long docks lined the shore of Smith Cove, where the Great Northern Railway, the nation's second transcontinental railroad, stretched inland to the Great Lakes (fig. 1.1). The railroad baron and "empire builder" James J. Hill had bought six hundred acres of Smith Cove as he negotiated the first direct shipping service between Japan and the United States. Only in the past dozen years had steamships made the long, often rough trip through the North Pacific without the aid of auxiliary sails. The *Tosa Maru* from which Nomura and his family disembarked was part of the Nippon Yusen Kaisha, or NYK shipping line, Hill's partner in the venture. The family continued their journey thirty-five miles south to Tacoma, undoubtedly on Hill's train.

Untitled, 1916
Detail of Fig. 1.14

Youth in Japan

Kenjiro Nomura, the first child of Harukichi and Shiu Nomura, was born November 10, 1896, in the village of Mitsuya, part of present-day Ōgaki in Gifu Prefecture. One of the few prefectures without access to the sea, Gifu is in the center of Honshū island, as well as the geographic center of Japan, and has long been a crossroads. Mountains and steep valleys dominate its northern region, while the south, Nomura's birthplace, is a region of broad plains and rich waterways. For generations Nomura's family had been farmers, until Harukichi set a new path by becoming a tailor and entrepreneur.

Kenjiro represented the second generation to come of age in modern Meiji Japan. Throughout the rise of early Western imperialism, Japan resisted colonization and retained its sovereignty, effectively closing itself to the West for 250 years. The military rule of the Tokugawa shogunate had unified the country and established relative internal peace, economic growth, a cultural flourishing, and, in reaction to missionary efforts, a policy of foreign exclusion. As a means of maintaining order, Japanese society was divided into four hierarchical classes based upon Confucian ideals of moral purity, with samurai at the top, followed by peasant-farmers, artisans, and merchants. By the mid-nineteenth century, however,

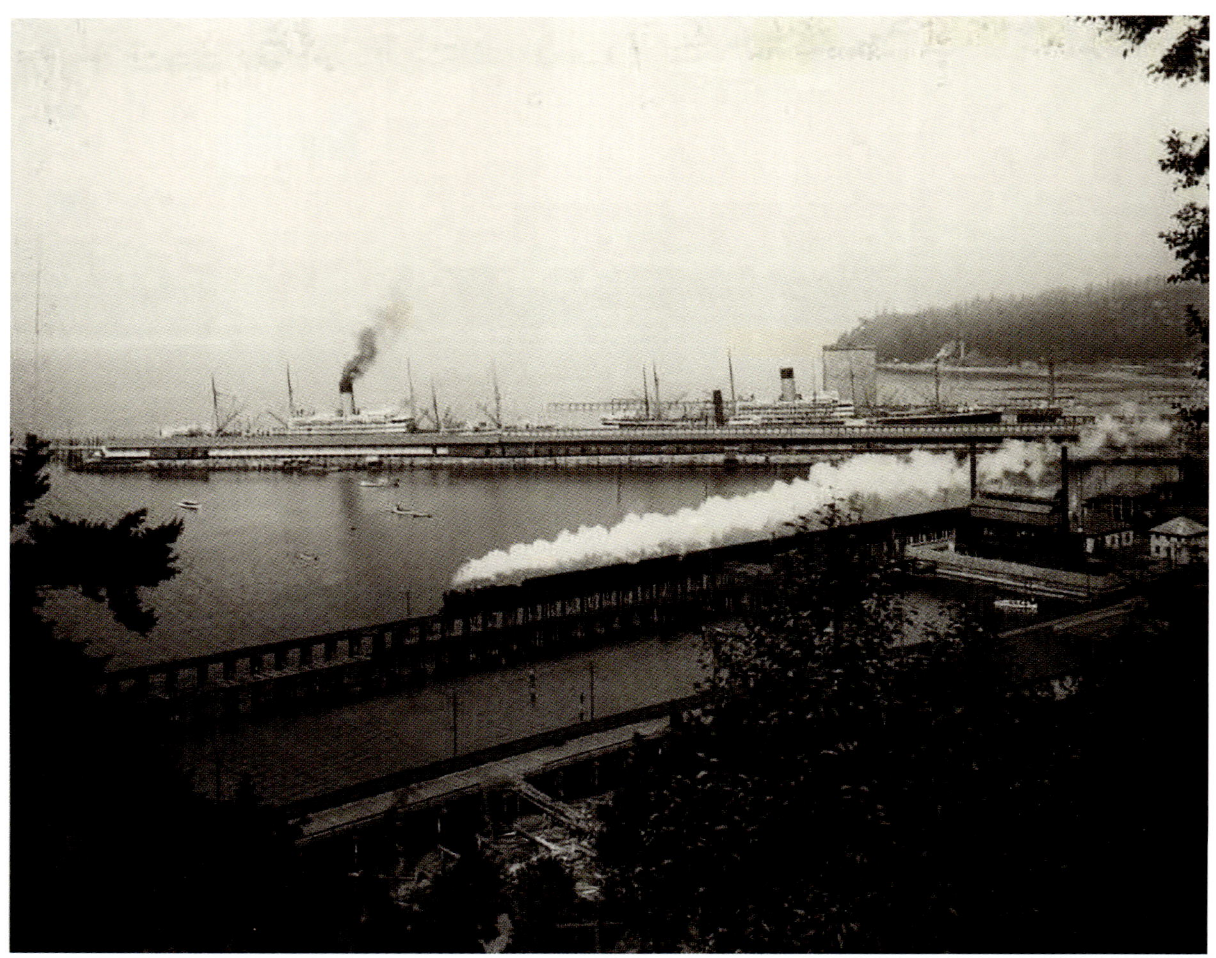

1.1
Great Northern train and ships at Smith Cove, ca. 1906
Photographer unknown
Museum of History and Industry, Seattle

The Great Northern Railway's *Oriental Limited* steams southward, and two Great Northern Steamship Company ocean liners, the *Dakota* and the *Minnesota*, stand at the dock.

there were growing challenges to Tokugawa control. Following American commodore Matthew Perry's landing in Edo Bay in 1853 and the imposition of unequal treaties upon Japan by the United States and Europe, a group of young, ambitious leaders of other clans, alarmed by Western intrusion, seized power in 1867. A year later they declared the restoration of the emperor, who took the name Meiji, "enlightened rule."

The Charter Oath issued in 1868 laid out a course to remold Japan by emulating selective practices of Western powers, with the intent to modernize Japan and withstand the West. The old class system, along with samurai privilege and landholdings, was dismantled, and Western knowledge was sought in the name of strengthening the foundation of the empire and building a modern nation-state. By the time of Nomura's birth, Japan had developed a constitutional government, a growing industrial base, extensive transportation and communications systems, universal education, and a modern army and navy. Within less than three decades the country had changed from a feudal agrarian society to a rising nation-state aspiring to parity with the West. Western learning dominated the upper grades of education, contributing to an expansive westward outlook. By the mid-1890s, Japan was also emerging as a major world power, demonstrated by its military victory over China in 1895, and another over Russia ten years later. The defeat of Russia was the first by an Asian power of a Western one in modern times, and it reinforced Japan's drive for equality with Western nations.[1] Harukichi Nomura exemplified the new generation freed of institutionalized class and occupational restrictions and whose ambition stretched across the Pacific to the West.

Japanese immigration to the Americas, like much of that from Europe, was driven by economic pressures as well as opportunity. The rapidity of modernization generated not only development but also severe inflation and internal conflict as the divide grew between urban and rural, progressive and conservative, those who benefited from the changes and those who did not. To ease pressure, the government initially allowed limited numbers to work abroad as contract laborers. Most workers came from Hiroshima, Yamaguchi, and other southern parts of Honshū, regions far from Tokyo that shared little of the benefit of modernization; few came from Gifu Prefecture, although all of Japan experienced some labor emigration once restrictions were lifted. Most workers were sojourners, or *desaki*, intending to make money and return home.

Harukichi Nomura was part of the drive to succeed abroad. He had demonstrated his independence in changing occupations from farmer to tailor, taking advantage of the Meiji lifting of Tokugawa-era restrictions that required a son to follow his father's work. His first journey across the Pacific in the 1890s was as a *desaki*, although there is conflicting evidence of his destination. He declared on the 1907 ship manifest that he had lived previously in Tacoma for about four and a half years.[2] The family story preserved by his grandson, George Nomura, tells of his venturing to Alaska before the great Klondike gold rush of 1898. He may have headed for the Juneau gold-mining district, where hard-rock mining was expanding in the 1880s and 1890s.[3] Whatever his destination, he established a tailoring business and when he had earned sufficient money, returned to Japan. At home in Mitsuya, Harukichi reestablished himself as a tailor, married young Shiu Sato, and soon had a son, Kenjiro.

Little is known about Kenjiro's early youth. He was the eldest, and for ten years, the only child of Harukichi and Shiu, who were twenty-eight and nineteen at his birth. The only clue to their economic well-being is a story recalled by Kenjiro's son, George, who years later recounted that his father felt fortunate compared to his classmates because he brought rice rather than the poor fare of barley in his school lunches.[4] Kenjiro attended school in Gifu from 1903 to 1907.[5] A nationalized system of education based upon American, French, and German administrative and curricula models had been among the first Meiji initiatives. Education was made mandatory through the sixth grade; Western learning was introduced progressively and dominated the upper grades. A shift came in 1890 when conservative pressure, reacting to the rapid infusion of Western learning and fearing loss of Japan's heritage, led to the Imperial Rescript on Education. The edict instated Confucian ethical principles governing the family and social harmony, such as filial piety and mutual obligation, which were fused with the Japanese virtues of patriotism and loyalty. This moral teaching became embedded in Japanese education beginning with the early grades and would be carried abroad during the period of American immigration. Kenjiro had four years of this modern, integrated schooling before his family left Japan for the United States.

Tacoma

Tacoma lies in south Puget Sound along the deep-water harbor of Commencement Bay, a name that promises new beginnings. In the near distance rises the majestic, glacier-topped Mount Rainier, whose indigenous name "Tahoma" the city adopted. To Tacoma's Japanese residents, it was their "Mount Fuji." Shunichi Otsuka, the author of an early

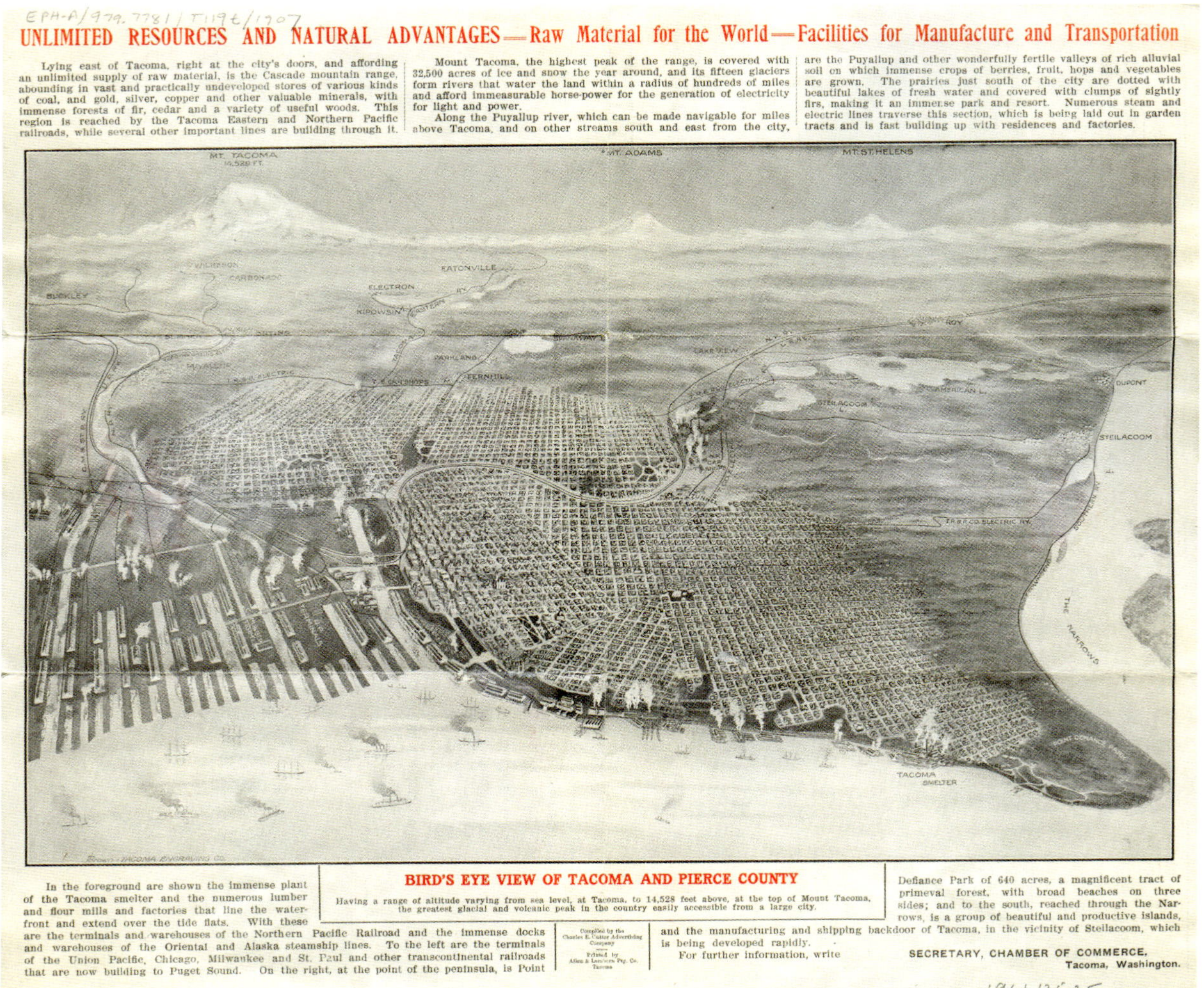

1.2
Bird's-eye view map, "Tacoma the Gateway to the Orient and Alaska: Traffic, industrial, and educational center of the Pacific Northwest," 1907
Published by W. J. Mead
Washington State Historical Society, 1961.125.25

history of the Japanese in Tacoma, declared, "There are those travelers who advocate travel to Suma and Akashi [sites associated with Noh theater]. I personally would rather tell of the beautiful shimmering sceneries around Commencement Bay."[6] He dates the first business established by a Japanese immigrant to 1886, only a year after an angry mob drove some two hundred Chinese residents out of the city. Lumber and shipping led the city's early economy. The Northern Pacific Railroad established a transcontinental terminus in Tacoma in 1887, linking the inlands to the port and spurring explosive growth in population and land speculation. Although the boom died with the nationwide Panic of 1893, Tacoma's role in Pacific trade, and especially trade with Japan, grew as rail capacity and steamship safety increased. The years 1898 and 1899 saw a jump in immigration from Japan as renewed Northern Pacific Railroad construction spurred the demand for labor and the number of shipping lines increased. Japanese labor contractors in Tacoma recruited as many as two thousand workers for the Northern Pacific, plus more for regional lines.[7] Otsuka writes of the time, "It was natural that many Japanese were drawn to Tacoma like an incoming tide and boldly took chances to start hotels, barber shops, bath houses, restaurants, etc., because of the sudden spurt of such activities."[8] This growth spurt occurred at the same time that the Klondike gold rush was drawing thousands of men through ports in Puget Sound, mostly through Seattle but many also through Tacoma, as its newspapers attest. The *Tacoma Daily Ledger* boasted of "Tacoma's supremacy on the sea": "Alaskan fleet large enough to handle the thousands of gold seekers who will outfit and start from here."[9] For six proud years, from 1894 to 1900, the city was home to the Japanese consulate until it was moved to Seattle. Japanese and Caucasian residents alike mourned its loss despite an ardent effort to retain it.

When the Nomura family arrived in 1907, they joined a Japanese immigrant community in Tacoma of about one thousand in a total city population that by 1910 would reach eighty-four thousand, more than doubling in a decade (making the ethnic Japanese slightly more than 1 percent).[10] The Gentlemen's Agreement was then under negotiation between the United States and Japan. Under the leadership of President Theodore Roosevelt, the executive-level agreement was a series of letters signed in 1907 and early 1908 that restricted labor immigration by limiting the types of passports issued by Japan. Business and professional persons like Harukichi were allowed, but no additional laborers, although those already in the United States could bring their immediate families. The agreement was intended both to quell rising anti-Japanese antagonism on the West Coast and to mollify Japan's desire to curb labor emigration.[11] There is no record of what drew the elder Nomura to Tacoma, but his bringing his family implies he intended to make a new home.[12] He would be one among many. The period around 1907 signaled a shift in Japanese immigration, when more people began to settle rather than return to Japan. The provision of the Gentlemen's Agreement that allowed wives spurred the rise of "picture brides" and a surge in the ethnic Japanese population; many committed to stay as they had children, who were American citizens by birth. The Japanese imperial government, determined that its subjects abroad reflect honor on Japan, implemented a policy urging

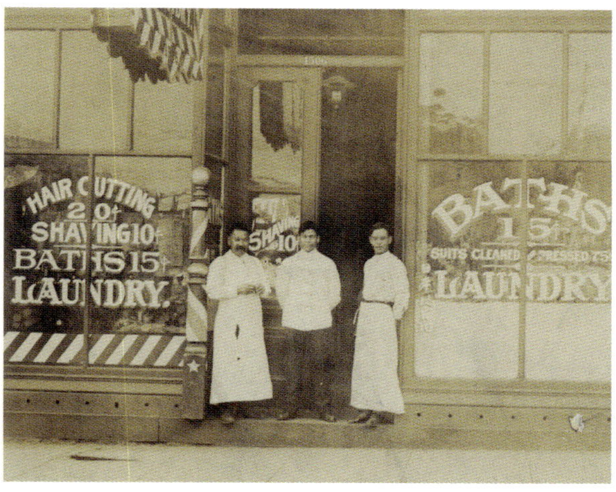

1.3
Barbershop, laundry, and bathhouse owned by N. Hayashi, 1506 South C Street, Tacoma, ca. 1910
Washington State Historical Society, 2009.20.16

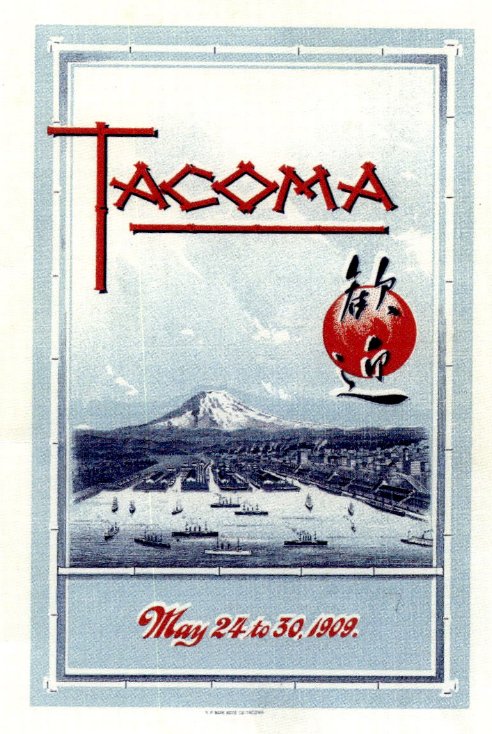

1.4
Menu, dinner by the citizens of Tacoma in honor of Rear Admiral Ijichi and officers of the Japanese training squadron, May 26, 1909, Hotel Tacoma, Tacoma, Washington
Washington State Historical Society, 1995.142.73

Admiral Ijichi was in Washington for the June 1 opening of the Alaska-Yukon-Pacific Exposition (AYPE) in Seattle, in which Japan featured prominently.

acculturation to deter the anti-Japanese factions that always threatened to erupt.

The Nomuras arrived in Tacoma in early summer and needed housing immediately. Three months later Shiu gave birth to a son, Shuji, the first of three American-born children. Two more sons would follow, Saburo in 1910, and Shoge in 1912 (figs. 1.5 and 1.6). They lived initially near Wright Park, where Harukichi opened a tailoring business. By 1909 they settled at Jefferson and South C Street in Tacoma's Nihonmachi, or Japantown, today the site of the University of Washington Tacoma campus. The house on Jefferson, shared with five other Nikkei, served as their home and place of business. They lived a short three blocks uphill from Pacific Avenue, where the Beaux-Arts Union Passenger Station was under construction and opened to fanfare in 1911.

Nihonmachi became a thriving district. The Ōsaka Shōsen Kaisha, or OSK, and other shipping lines regularly brought immigrants and goods from Japan. The *Tacoma Jiho* weekly newspaper provided news in Japanese, as did branch offices of three Seattle Japanese-language papers.[13] Tailoring was just one of many businesses that served and supported the Nikkei community. Sixty-three shops lined C Street in 1910, then the main artery, and more spread uphill from Pacific Avenue to Market Street and north and south between Eleventh and Seventeenth Streets.[14] They provided the whole variety of goods and services the community needed and catered to Caucasian customers as well. Harukichi steadily built a modest business. By 1911 he listed himself in the city directory as both a tailor and a merchant tailor, indicating he had the resources to stock the fabrics he used. The next year he advertised in boldfaced type: "Expert Ladies' and Gentlemen's Tailoring, Pressing, Cleaning, Repairing, Suits Made to Order." Nomura family portraits picture a handsomely dressed group. The Nikkei had reasons in addition to professional pride to dress well. The Japanese consul and the Japanese Association, responsible for overseeing the imperial mandate for acculturation, admonished immigrants to adopt American dress, learn English, educate their children, and excel in education and business.[15]

Although incipient racism was always present, relations between Tacoma's Euro-American majority and Japanese residents during the early years of the twentieth century were relatively calm.[16] White and Japanese civic and business leaders in West Coast ports were eager to cultivate trade with the equally ambitious empire of Japan. Tacoma and Seattle were among the West Coast cities that billed themselves as cosmopolitan centers as they vied for the title of "Gateway to the Orient" and highlighted their multi-ethnic populations in the process (see fig. 1.2 and 1.8).[17]

Kenjiro turned eleven in the fall of 1907. He attended elementary school for about six years, most or all of them at Central Elementary School nearby the family's home, and was placed in a special class for immigrant children. He was one of the oldest Japanese children in the school's district and, according to family stories, taunted by other students for his broken English. A photograph in an album he assembled as a young adult offers a poignant visual parallel to the family memory: three white boys lounge next to a large lion sculpture at the entrance to Wright Park, while the young Kenjiro stands alone on the path nearby (fig. 1.7).[18] For two years he also attended night school at the YMCA.[19]

In May 1912 the Japanese community celebrated the opening of the Tacoma Japanese Language School, where Japanese language, history, and ethics—the values and protocols carried by the parents from Japan—were taught in after-school hours to supplement public education. Nomura, then fifteen, was one of the oldest of the original thirteen students; his brother Shuji was among the youngest. The school was nonsectarian, rather than sponsored by a Buddhist temple or Christian church as most Japanese

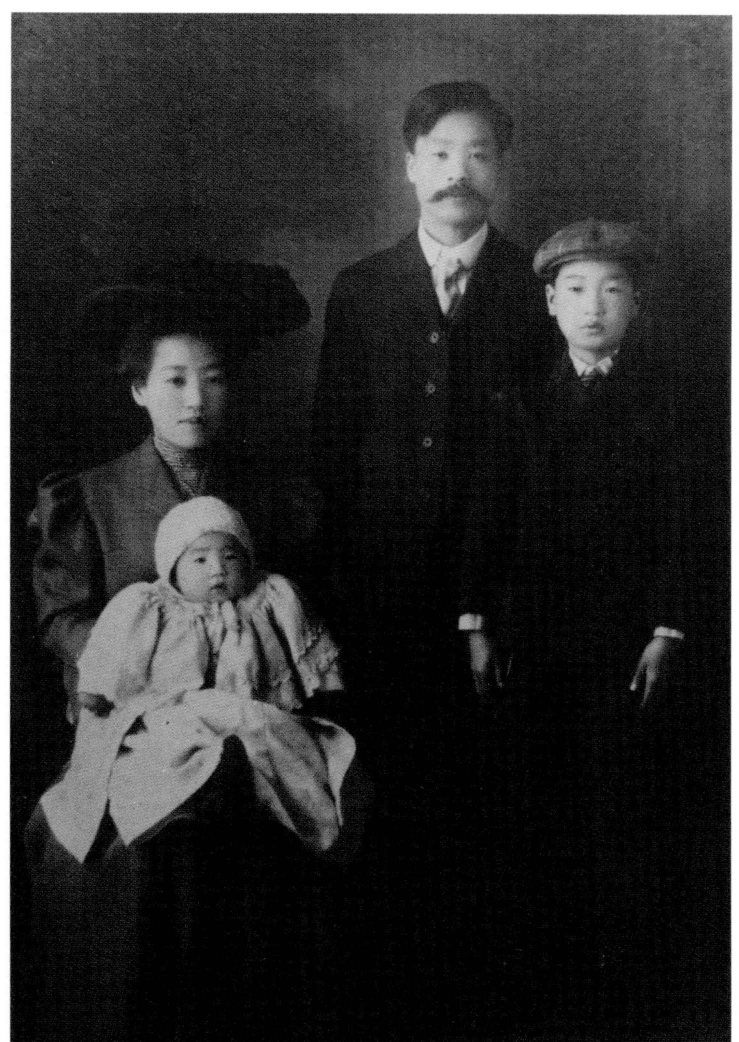

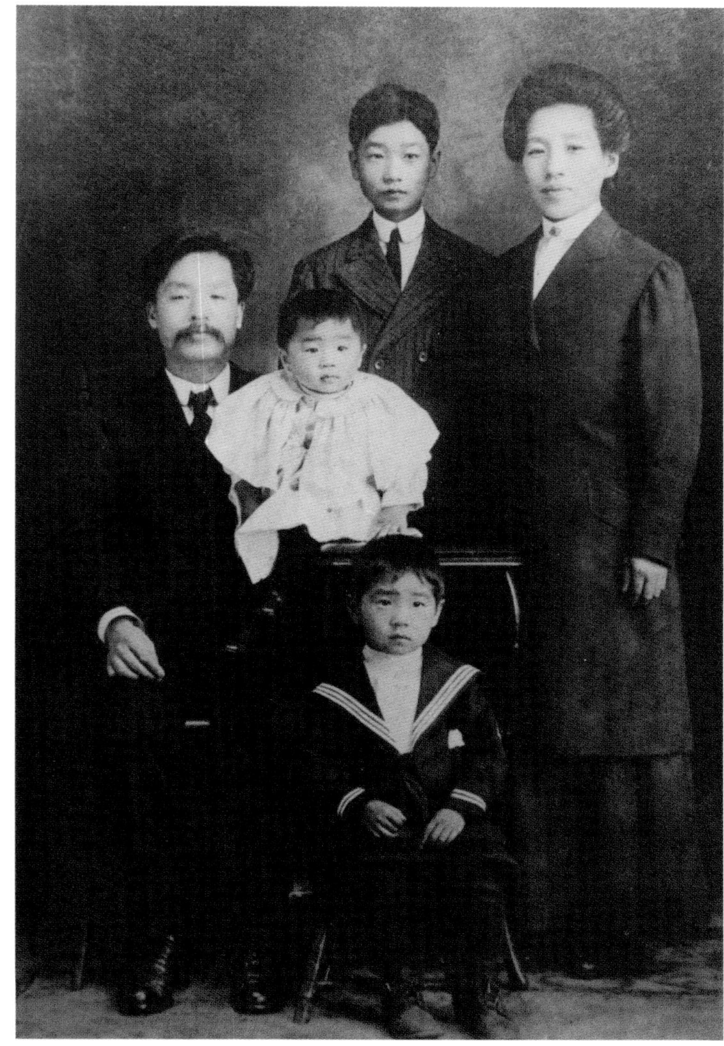

1.5
Nomura family, ca. 1908
Left to right: Shiu, Shuji, Harukichi, Kenjiro
Nomura Estate

1.6
Nomura family, ca. 1911
Left to right: Harukichi, Saburo, Shuji, Kenjiro (*standing*), Shiu
Nomura Estate

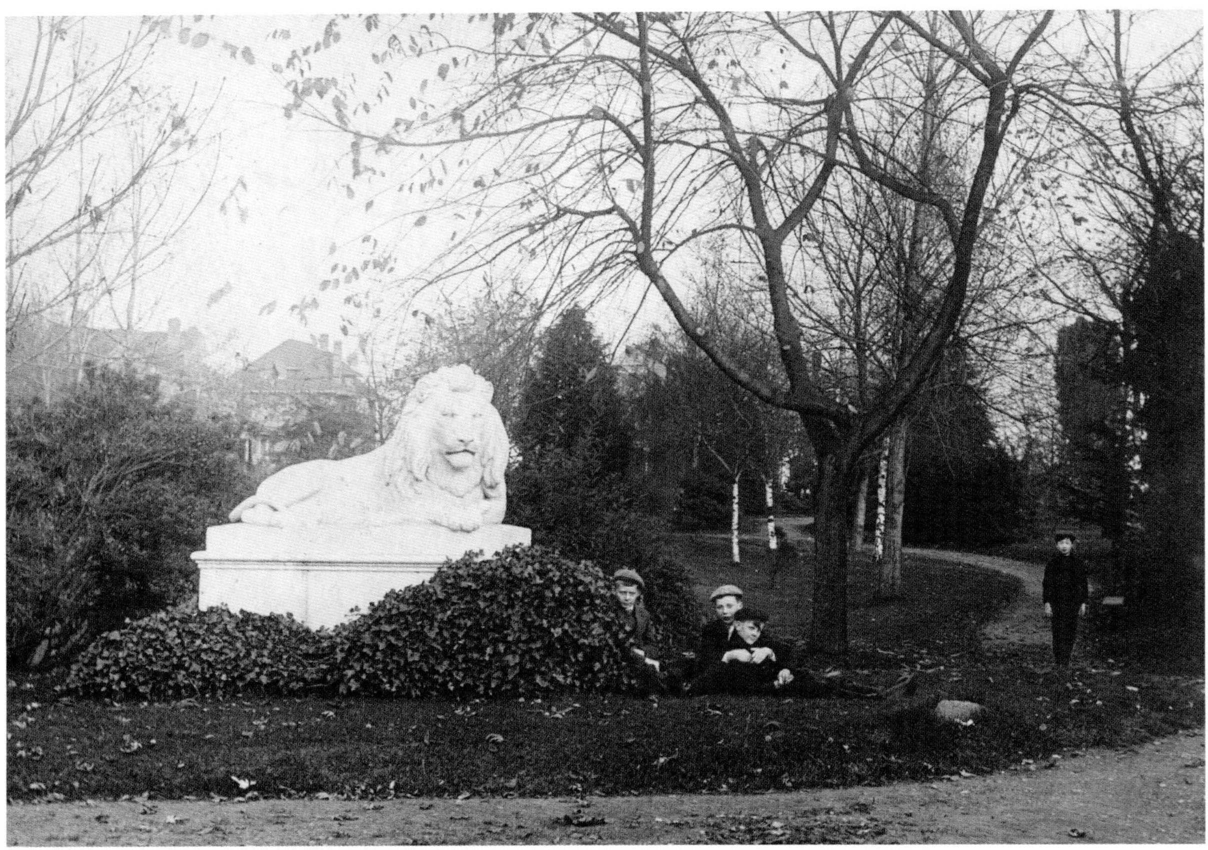

1.7
Nomura (*far right*) at Wright Park, Tacoma, ca. 1907–1912
Nomura Estate

language schools were. Parents paid two dollars a month toward the cost of rent and hiring two teachers, and they found excellent ones in Kuniko Yamasaki, an experienced and cultured teacher, and her husband, Masato Yamasaki, who became the principal. Both had been well educated in Japan and would remain foundational to the school until its closure in 1942. Both taught by personal example as well as formal instruction. As principal, Masato Yamasaki guided the development and philosophy of the school and served as a respected liaison with the mainstream community. Kuniko Yamasaki, known for her skill in calligraphy, would have offered Kenjiro a graphic skill and developing aesthetic sensibility that served him well in adulthood. It may have been at the school that his artistic drive was awakened.[20]

A significant change again redirected Kenjiro's life in 1913. When he had not yet turned seventeen, his parents returned to Japan with their three American-born children, a move attributed to his mother's homesickness. Too old to reenter school in Japan, he stayed in Tacoma alone. His parents gave him $10, the equivalent of about $270 today, to make his way. He left school at eighth grade and found a delivery job for a Japanese merchant, where he worked long, hard hours driving a horse and cart to deliver food and dry goods to rural Pierce County. He kept photographs of his family in Japan as his brothers matured and would retain lifelong contact with them.

Seattle

Sometime before his nineteenth birthday in 1915, Nomura moved to Seattle to make a new home.[21] He lived in Nihonmachi, almost certainly in a rooming house or one of the many Issei-managed workingmen's hotels. He became part of an ethnic community of some seven thousand immigrant- and American-born Japanese (about 2.5 percent of Seattle's population).[22] His first job in Seattle was selling, delivering, and stocking merchandise for a shopkeeper. In the summer of 1916, working through one of the Japanese labor contractors, he joined the seasonal crew at the Friday Harbor Packing Company's salmon cannery, located on San Juan Island in Washington's northwest corner.[23] World War I brought increasing demand for canned salmon and, with it, more opportunity for workers.[24] The summer seems to have been a coming-of-age period, for his photo album contains numerous pictures of Nomura, his friends, the cannery buildings, and the verdant, forested surroundings (fig. 1.9).

Seattle's Nihonmachi lay at the south end of the business district, centered on South Main and Jackson Streets and Fifth and Sixth Avenues, and extending up First Hill on the north, eastward along Jackson and southward into Rainier Valley. Like all immigrant communities, it shared the bonds of language and culture, but the Japanese community was bound also by its visible ethnic difference from white Seattle. And like other Japanese communities on the West Coast, it was bound by its high level of organization and particularized practices, many, such as the ethic of mutual obligation, brought from Japan and others developed in efforts to counter discrimination. "One of the striking characteristics of the Japanese in America," a sociologist observed in 1917, "is the thoroughness of their organization. . . . [T]he Japanese have been equaled by few, if any, of the European groups."[25] At the geographic and symbolic center of Nihonmachi was the Japanese consulate, representing the imperial government. Working alongside it was the Japanese Association, which watched over the community's daily affairs, provided services such as the issuance of documents, and headed the specialized trade associations that Nikkei were exhorted to join. Both offices were responsible to their respective headquarters in San Francisco and, in turn, to the imperial government.

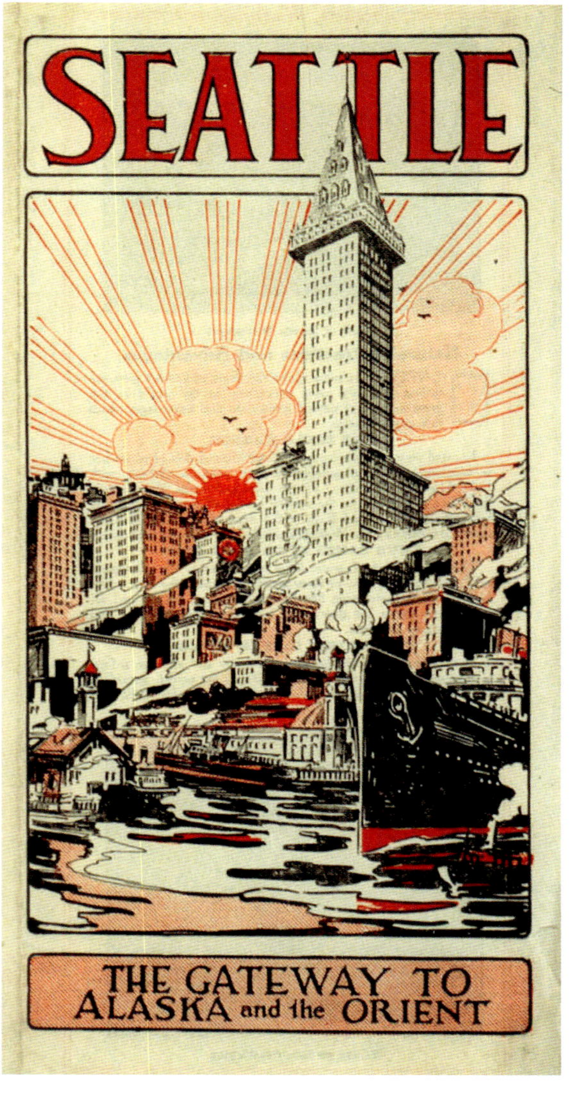

1.8
"Seattle—the Gateway to Alaska and the Orient," advertisement, 1913
Washington State Historical Society, 979.7771

The community shared the further bonds of an active intellectual and cultural life. Five Japanese-language newspapers were published in the 1920s, which were augmented in 1928 by the English-language *Japanese American Courier*. As many as three dozen magazines were locally published.[26] Artistic activities of many kinds—painting, poetry, music, dance, drama, flower arranging—were formalized, widely practiced means of self-expression among the Issei. Poetry groups flourished, the oldest formed in 1919, and several issued their own magazines. Members of

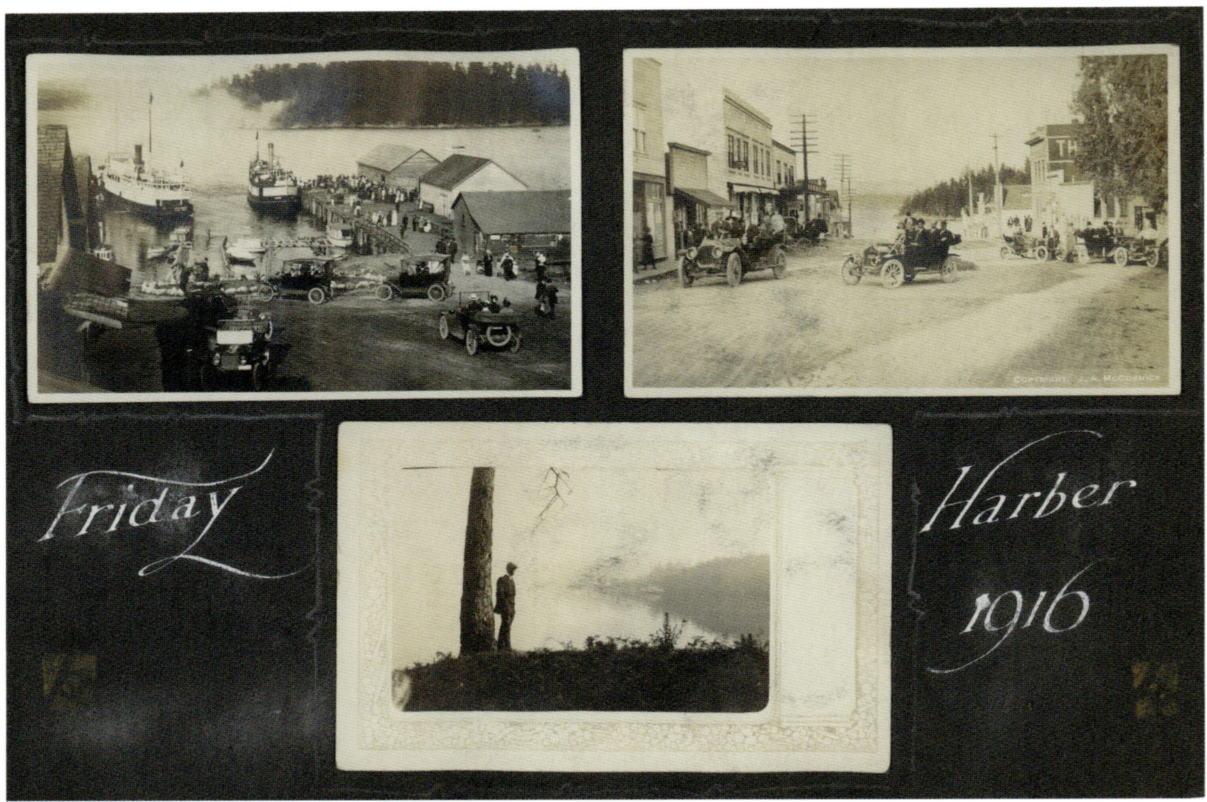

1.9
"Friday Harbor, 1916," page from Nomura's photo album
Nomura Estate

the Issei-founded Seattle Camera Club achieved international renown in the 1920s.[27] Noh, Kabuki, and contemporary Japanese drama appeared at the Nippon Kan Theater, the community's purpose-built cultural center, where Western as well as Japanese theatrical and musical productions, amateur and professional, regularly filled the theater. Nomura occasionally appeared in the amateur performances. He and other young painters in the 1920s were by then well known in the community for their contributions to its artistic vibrancy.

Seattle's Nikkei community, moreover, was distinguished by an exceptionally high level of entrepreneurship. Many small businesses provided basic goods and services to their fellow kinsmen as well as to other customers drawn to the low prices. Several large businesses operated internationally, notably the M. Furuya Company, which extended from trade and labor contracting to banking and real estate. The number of entrepreneurs reflects not only the Issei's determination but also the limited work opportunities available to them. Legally prevented from owning or leasing real property and spurned by most employers from all but menial jobs (as young adult Nisei would also find), they became their own bosses. In 1930, before the Depression hit hardest, there were some nine hundred business establishments, including professional offices such as physicians and lawyers, in the ethnic Japanese population of about eighty-five hundred.[28]

Yet for all its reputed social cohesion, the community was by no means homogeneous. Rifts and shifting relationships within the community resulted from differences in age, generation, education, economic and cultural status, religious affiliation, and personal relations to Japan. Such differences were further complicated by changing political relations between the United States and Japan. Individually and collectively, members of the ethnic minority community continually navigated their unstable relationship to the mainstream society.[29]

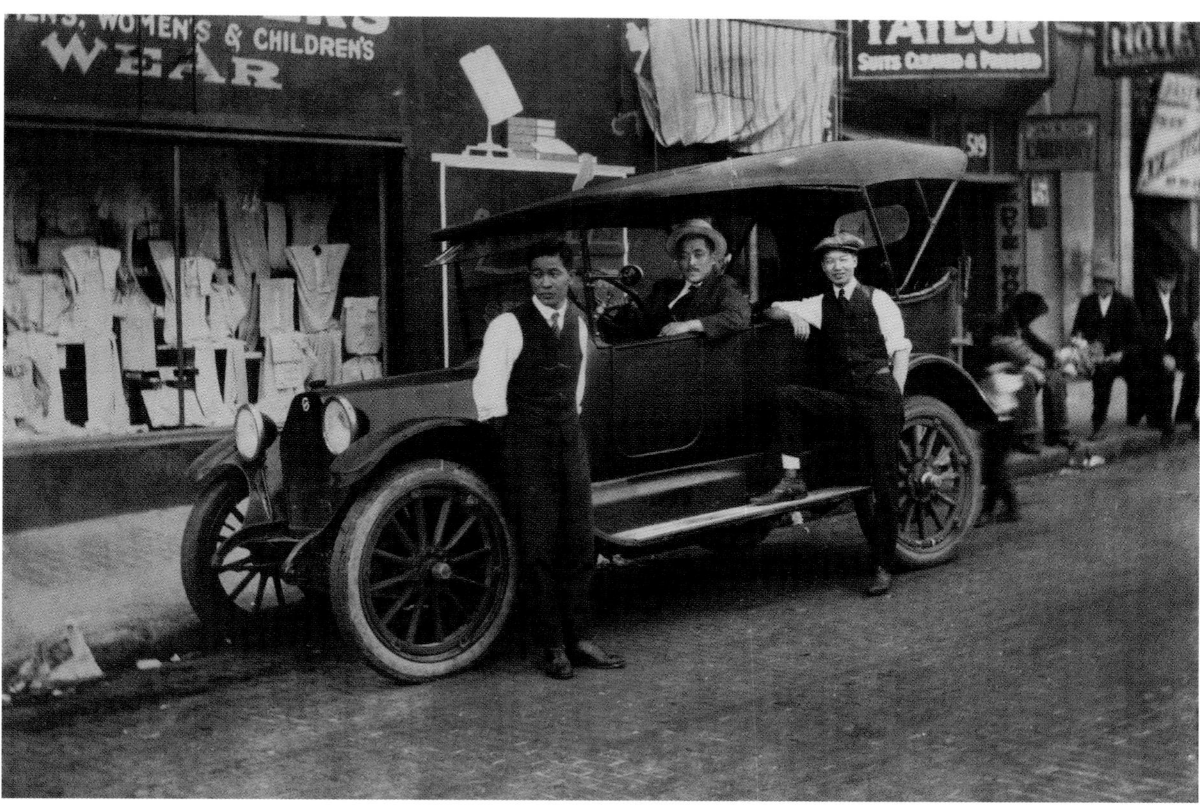

1.10
Nomura (*right*) and friends in Seattle's Nihonmachi, ca. 1920s
Nomura Estate

Nomura became one of Nihonmachi's entrepreneurs, a lineage following his father's footsteps. A July 1916 classified advertisement lists his seeking work as an "expert show card [window display] writer," indicating that he had begun to turn his skills in calligraphy to productive use.[30] By 1921 he could call himself a sign painter. He initially worked as an apprentice, most likely to Bungira Hirayama, who was the only Nikkei sign painter in the city at the time, and in 1922 he opened his own sign-painting business with a young artist, Show Toda.[31] They named their business Noto Sign Company for the two of them and within a year moved into a storefront at 216 Sixth Avenue South, on the steep hillside between Main and Washington Streets in the heart of Nihonmachi. When Toda left for other work in 1924, Kamekichi Tokita became Nomura's partner; they had no need to change the company name (fig. 1.11). The shop served as their place of business, their painting studio, a congenial meeting place for artists, and, until each married, their home. By 1931 they were the only sign-painting business in Nihonmachi. They produced illustrated signs and gold-leaf script on store windows, along with designs such as the banner for the *Japanese American Courier* and the backdrop for the Nippon Kan Theater. "These people were very busy, and much in demand by the Japanese merchants," the artist George Tsutakawa recalled. "They did beautiful work, these gold-leafed names of little banks and exchange [companies] and, well, all kinds of businesses."[32]

Becoming an Artist

Besides seeking employment, one of Nomura's first steps in Seattle was to begin study in 1915 with the artist Fokko Tadama (1871–1937) (fig. 1.13). Of Dutch-Indonesian ancestry, Tadama had been academically trained and painted professionally in Europe before immigrating to the United States in 1909. His studio on Capitol Hill was one of the two

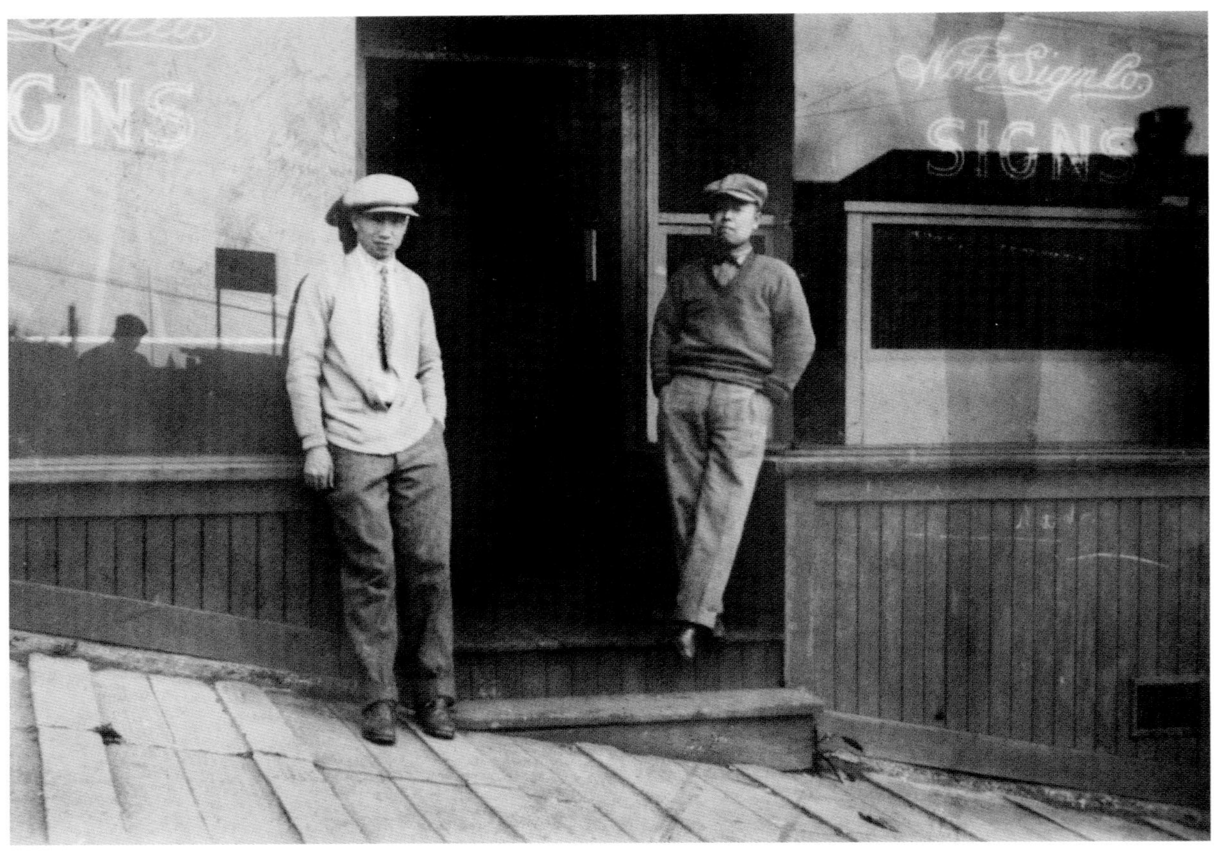

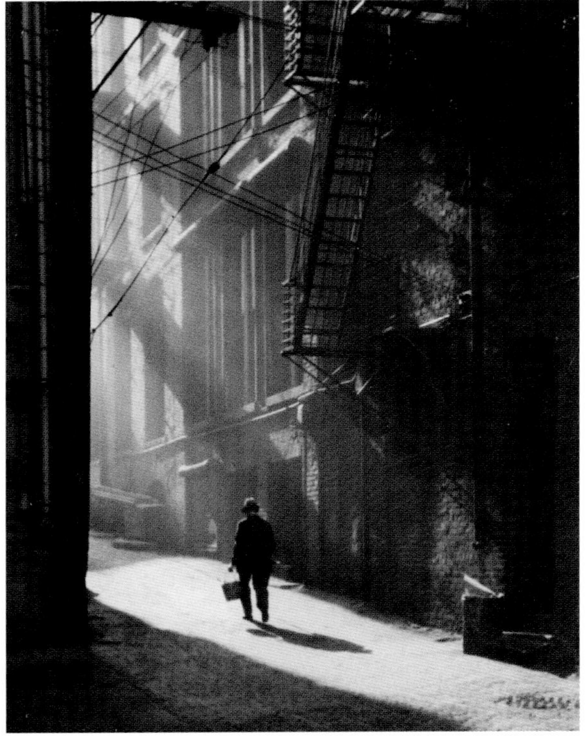

1.11
Nomura (*left*) and Kamekichi Tokita outside Noto Sign Company, 216 Sixth Avenue South, Seattle, ca. 1925–1930
Tokita papers, Archives of American Art, Smithsonian Institution

1.12
Kusatora Matsuki
Sunlight in the Morning, ca. 1929
Gelatin silver print, 10 x 8 in.
University of Washington Libraries, Special Collections, UW 29154

The modernist urban scenes of Matsuki and others in the Seattle Camera Club foretell those of Nomura and his colleagues.

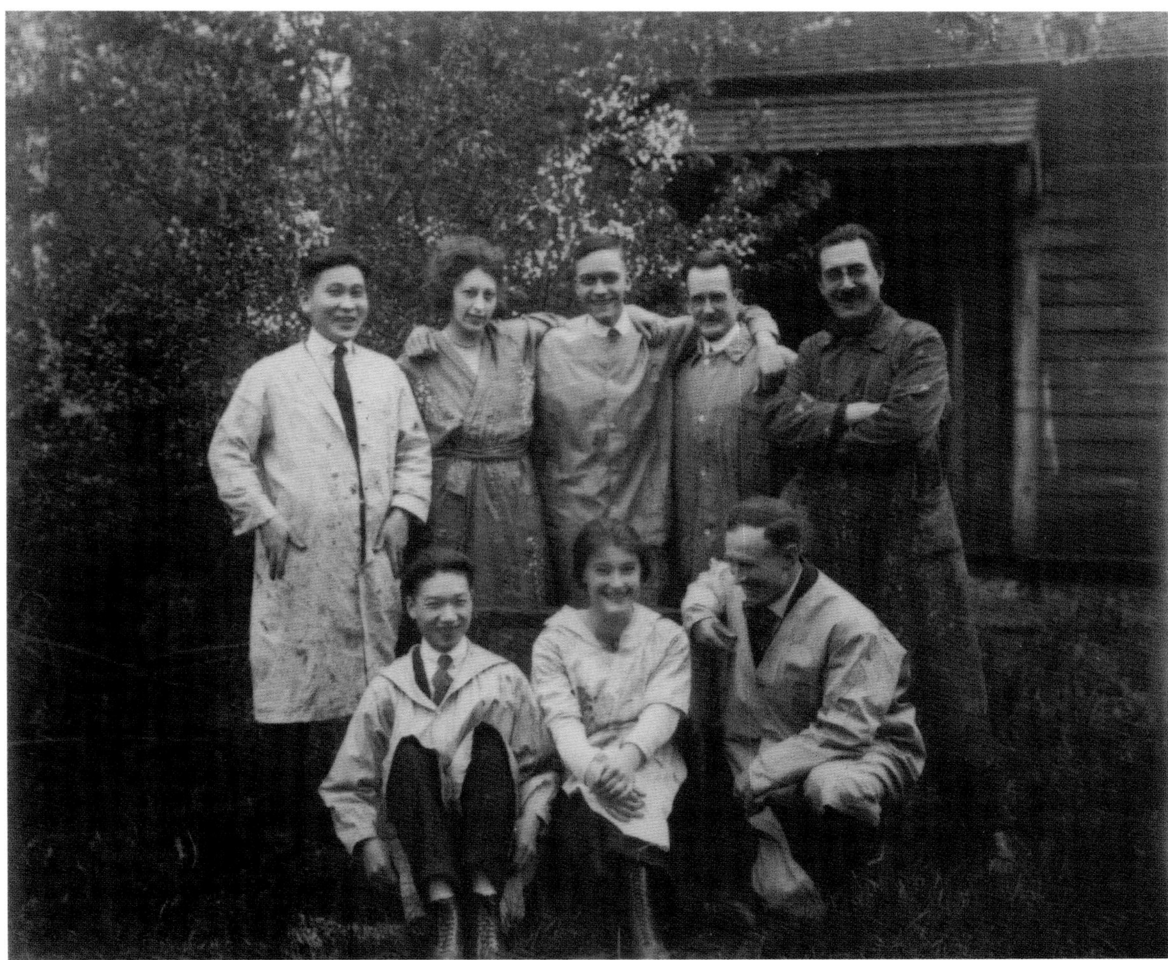

1.13
Soichi Sunami, photographer
Nomura (*seated left*) with Fokko Tadama (*standing right*) and students, including Sunami (*standing left*), ca. 1916
Courtesy of the Estate of Soichi Sunami

most frequented teaching studios in Seattle and was attended by several Issei, including Azo Nakagawa, Toshi Shimizu, and Yasushi Tanaka, all of whom had established exhibition records.[33] (See David F. Martin's essay, p. 117.) Photographs in Nomura's scrapbook—one of Shimizu painting in the field, another of the young Nomura and an unidentified older artist—indicate that these were important mentoring relationships.

Nomura must have shown exceptional aptitude. As early as October 1916 his paintings garnered notice when he exhibited in Nihonmachi along with the three more experienced Issei from the studio. The exhibition was billed as the first annual exhibition of the Japanese Art Association, both of which were organized by the Issei businessman and art supporter Tokusaburo Noto. Held at Fifth Avenue and Main Street, the exhibition featured "forty or fifty canvases" by the four painters, as well as several from artists in Portland and Canada.[34] It was a big enough event to be covered in the mainstream news and the *Town Crier*, the city's arts and culture magazine. A member of the Seattle Fine Arts Society, Adele M. Ballard, reviewed the exhibition in the magazine and noted with familiarity the work of Tanaka and Shimizu: "It is in a poorly-lighted store room the walls of which have been carefully covered with a light tan wrapping paper. But one overlooks such things while examining the canvases. Many of the paintings are pitched in a high key but on the whole some of the best canvases are in lower

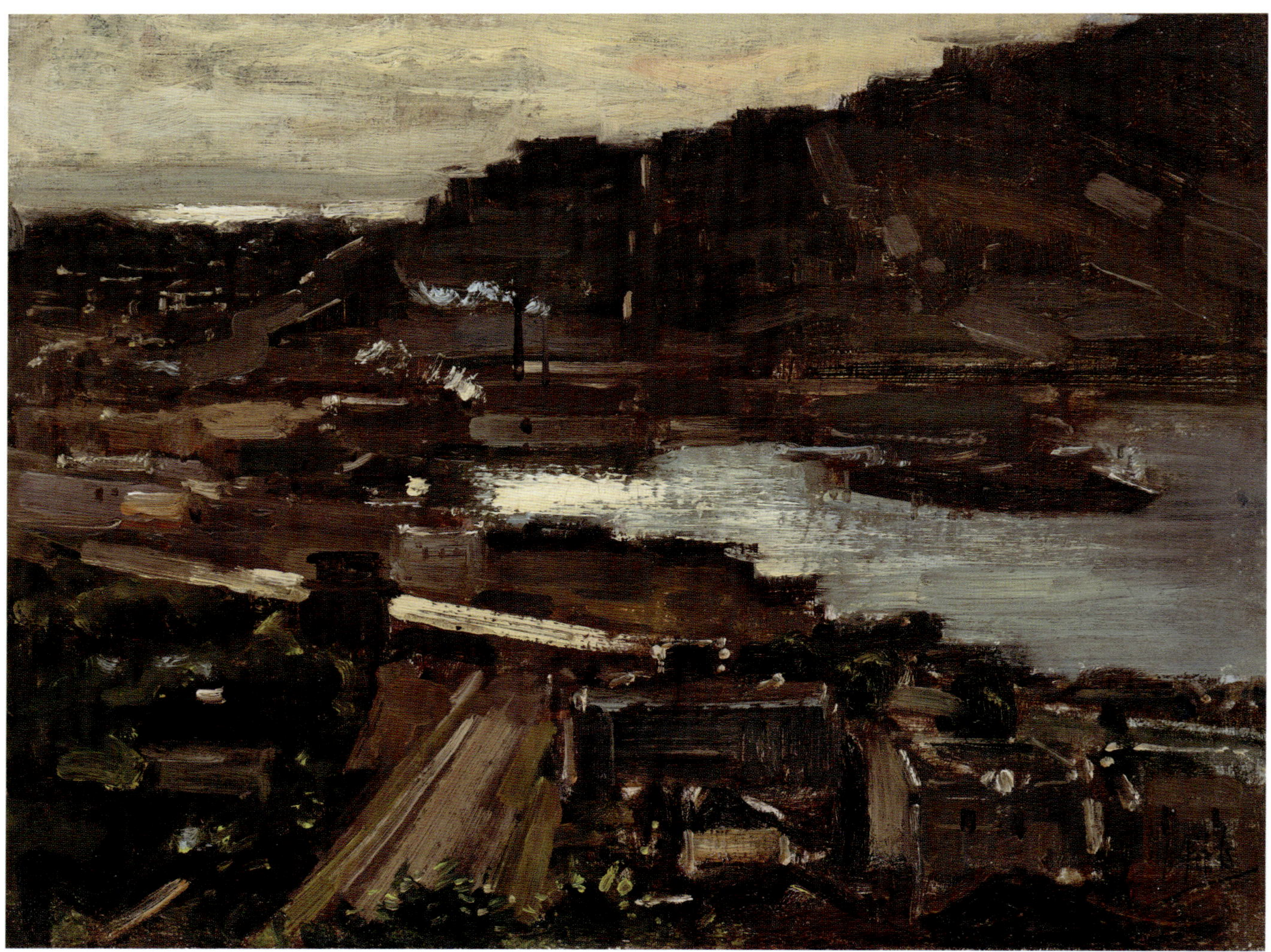

1.14
Untitled, 1916
Oil on canvas, 12¾ × 16⅝ in.
Private collection

tones."[35] Nomura's urban landscape paintings caught the attention of another, unnamed writer, who likened them to the maturity of those by Shimizu.[36] Japanese business leaders would continue to promote the community's artistic contribution to the city of Seattle.

Nomura studied in Tadama's studio until 1921. Tadama's own production was predominantly landscape, and his frequent subject was the shoreline, where he displayed his skill representing light on a watery surface and the graduated transition from land to water. His paintings are characterized by a plein air palette and impressionist-influenced brushwork and color; others display the close color harmonies and evocative mood of tonalism (see Martin, fig. M.4). From Tadama, Nomura would have learned not only the fundamentals of paint media, Western composition, perspective, and modeling but also the representation of light in oil paint, an interest that would pervade Nomura's landscapes in coming years. An early, dark-toned painting lushly rendered in oil looks across Lake Union westward toward Puget Sound; light reflects off the surface of both bodies of water and illuminates the edges of buildings, an approach that would inform his work in the 1930s (fig. 1.14). Titles of now-lost paintings by Nomura, such as *October Morn* (ca. 1923), *Reflection* (ca. 1925), and *A Bright Afternoon* (ca. 1926), evoke the poetic attitude and attention to qualities of light found in tonalism. Boats

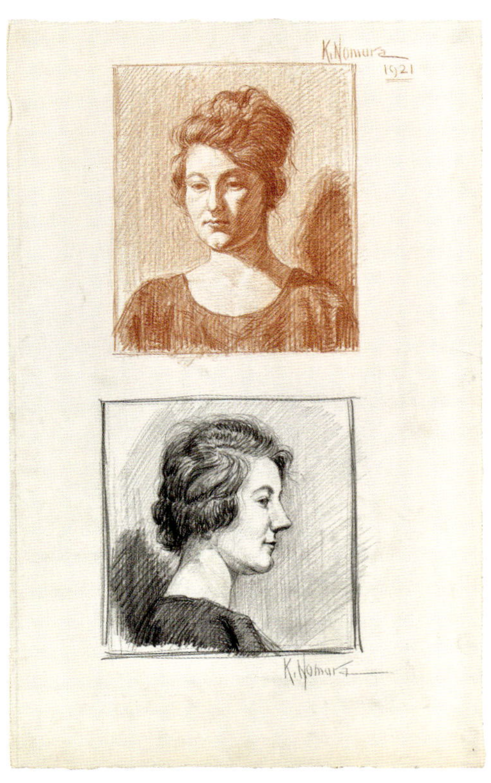

1.15
Studio models, 1921
Top, conte on paper; *bottom*, graphite on paper,
25 3/8 × 19 1/2 in.
Nomura Estate

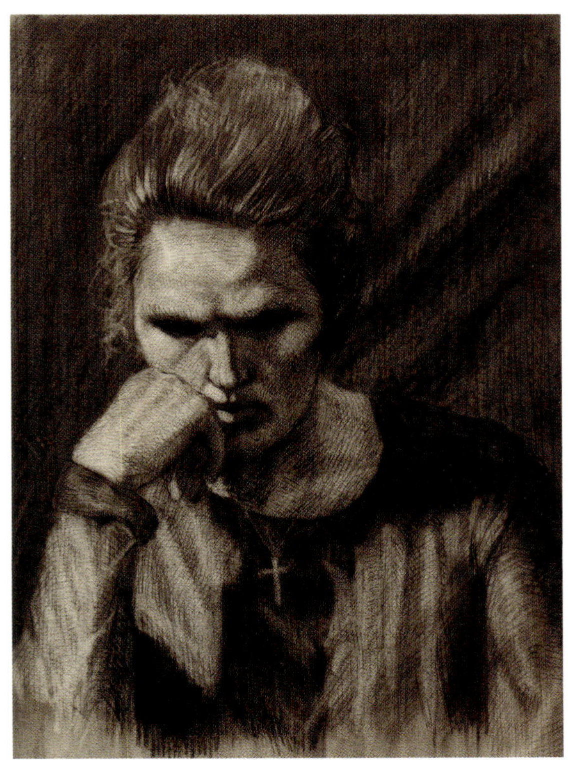

1.16
Face Study, 1919
Charcoal on paper, 25 × 19 in.
Nomura Estate

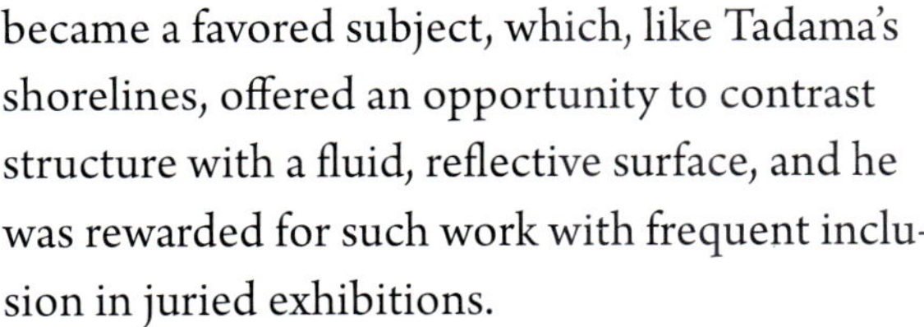

became a favored subject, which, like Tadama's shorelines, offered an opportunity to contrast structure with a fluid, reflective surface, and he was rewarded for such work with frequent inclusion in juried exhibitions.

Nomura also attended Tadama's classes in figure drawing at evening school at Broadway High School for four years, from 1919 to 1923.[37] His extant work portrays the female figure based upon studio models and perhaps fellow students, in some two dozen drawings of portrait heads, full figures, and nudes (figs. 1.15 and 1.16, and see fig. M.7). The drawing practice provided a solid complement to his study of oil painting and landscape.

Nomura's photo album from these early years offers more personal insight into his experience. Photographs picture Nomura in his artist's smock, fellow student artists, group portraits with Tadama, and Tadama posing formally in his

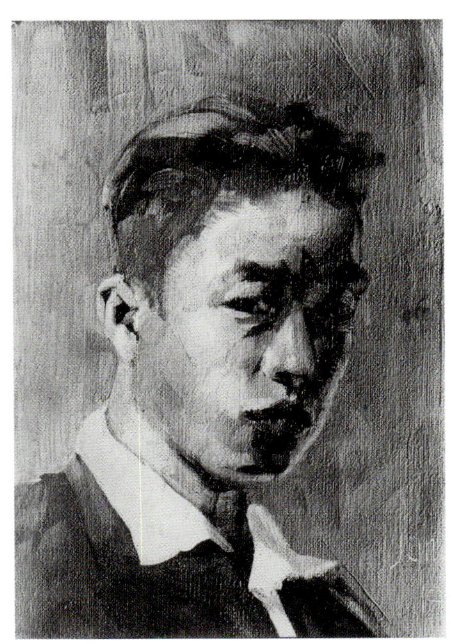

1.17
Self-portrait, undated
Reproduction in Nomura's photograph album
Nomura Estate

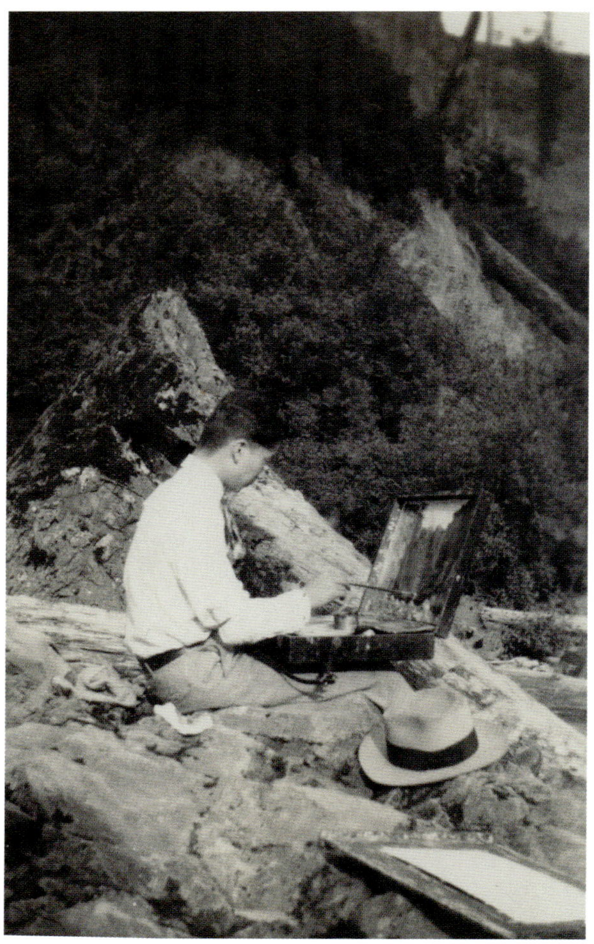

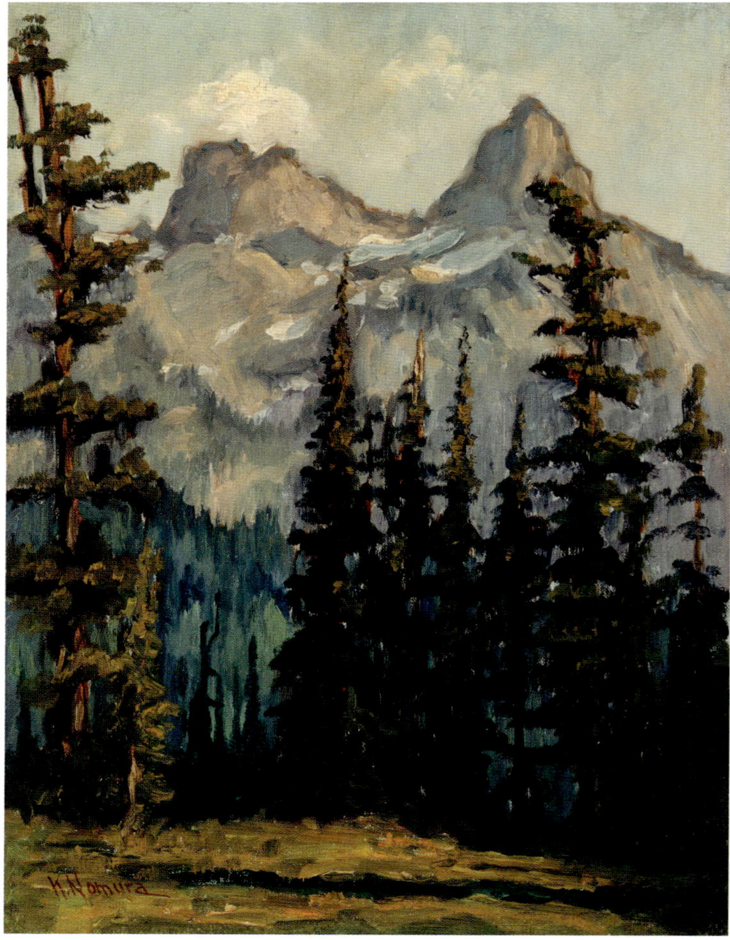

1.18
Nomura painting in the mountains, ca. early 1920s
Nomura Estate

1.19
Mountain Peaks, 1925
Oil on canvas, 17¾ × 14 in.
Collection of John and Annick Impert

smock (see figs. M.3, M.5, and M.6). They show a newly confident young man fully enjoying the company of his artist friends. Others show Nomura painting on a Seattle hillside, painting in a wooded landscape while several Nikkei watch, and on a painting field trip in the mountains, experiences that would shape his future practice more than the studio figures (fig. 1.18). A number of photographs picture mountain streams, beaches, and campsites, suggesting Nomura's delight in the natural environment.

Nomura first exhibited his work to a mainstream audience in the 1922 Northwest Annual Exhibition of Northwest Artists. The Northwest Annual, as it was commonly known, was a juried exhibition sponsored each year by the Seattle Fine Arts Society, a predecessor to the Seattle Art Museum, and was considered a measure of the artist's, and the region's, prowess. Issei artists had been represented since its formal beginning in 1914, when five of the thirty-one exhibiting artists were Issei.[38] Again Nomura's work gained notice. Art writer Madge Bailey identified Nomura as a former student of Tadama and characterized his entry, *Scow*, as "one of the best pieces in the exhibit." Alluding to Tadama's touch in praising Nomura's painting, she concluded, "It will be interesting to follow the development of the talent of this young artist."[39] Nomura exhibited three or four paintings in each of several subsequent annuals, typically landscapes and occasionally

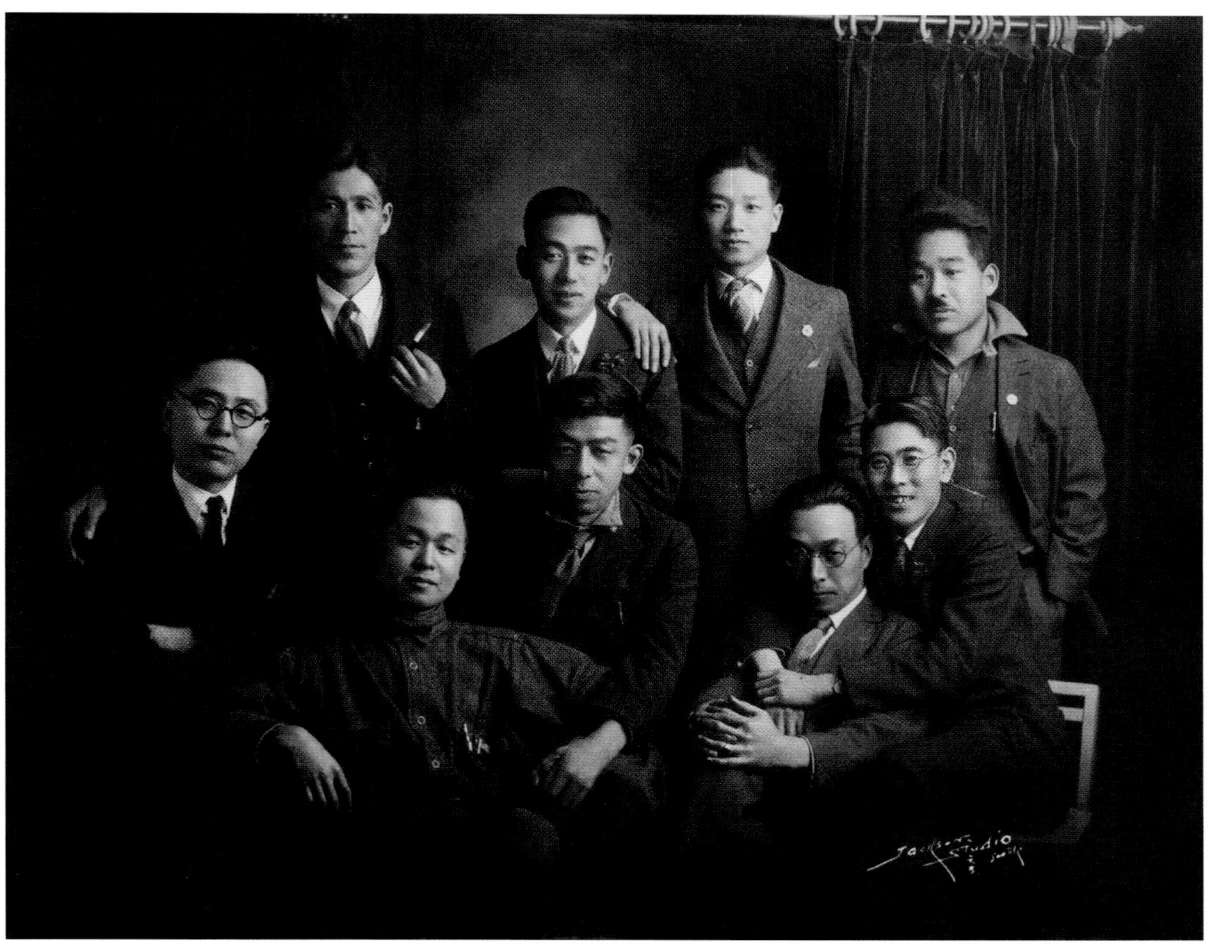

1.20
Young Issei men, ca. mid-1920s
Nomura (*standing second right*), Show Toda (*center*), and Kamekichi Tokita (*front left*)
Jackson Studio
Courtesy of Shokichi Tokita

a portrait. *Mountain Peaks,* the single extant landscape from this period, was selected for the 1925 Northwest Annual and displays carefully observed gradations of space and light stepping from foreground to mid-ground forest and distant mountains (fig. 1.19).

In 1924 a group of young Issei artists formed a group they called Shunjukai, or Spring and Autumn Club, for their semiannual exhibitions.[40] Their effort emulated the burst of artists' societies in Japan as artists in the late nineteenth and early twentieth centuries embraced Western painting. Shunjukai may be the subject of a mid-1920s photograph picturing well-dressed young Issei men, of whom only Nomura, Kamekichi Tokita, and Show Toda can be positively identified (fig. 1.20). A painting dated 1925 portrays a young man deep in concentration, perhaps a Shunjukai member (fig. 1.21).[41] A decade later, when Nomura and his friend Tokita were recognized as the preeminent Issei painters, an editor of the *Japanese American Courier* looked back and identified three waves of Issei artists' achievement and recognition: the first wave, the painters associated with the Tadama studio; the second, the young artists of Shunjukai; and the third, the mid-1930s, when Nomura and Tokita, and increasingly Takuichi Fujii, were the acknowledged leaders.[42] Nomura participated in all three.

Nomura's personal life flourished yet further in his meeting Fumiko Mukai. Born in 1908 in South Prairie, Washington, where her parents worked for the railroad, Mukai had been reared and educated in Japan, and at age fourteen returned to Washington—in generational terms, a Kibei. She attended public school in Seattle and in photographs of the time appears as an attractive and active young woman.

Soon a romance with Nomura blossomed, and in 1928 they married. Under U.S. law that assigned a woman her husband's citizenship, she forfeited her citizenship to marry Nomura, who as an immigrant from Japan was barred by federal law from naturalization. She would regain her rights as an American citizen only in 1931 when the forfeiture legislation was amended.[43] They honeymooned on a trip to Vancouver, British Columbia, and at home in Seattle enjoyed outings to the mountains and beaches with friends. In 1930 their first and only child, George Masaru Nomura, was born. The young family moved into an apartment at Twelfth Avenue and King Street, outside the Nihonmachi center but amid the activity of the Japanese American community. Nomura settled into a satisfying rhythm between home life and a business that allowed time and opportunity for his artistic aspirations.

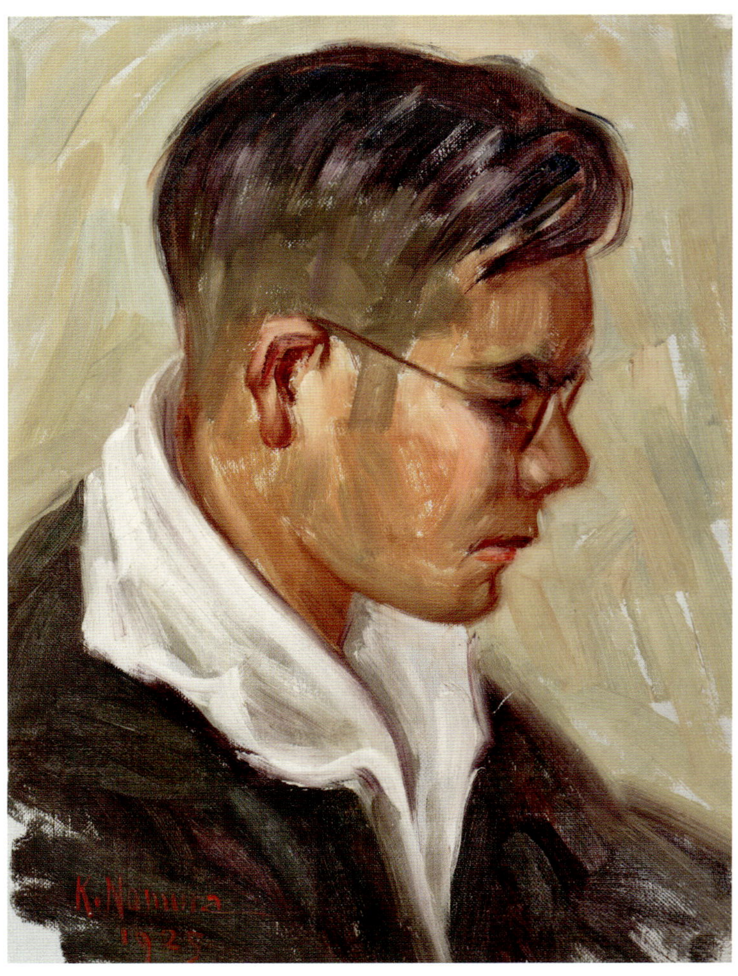

1.21
Portrait, 1925
Oil on canvas, 14¼ × 11¼ in.
Collection of Ashford Creek Pottery and Museum

1.22
Fumiko Mukai Nomura, wedding portrait, 1928
Nomura Estate

1.23
Fumiko, George, and Kenjiro Nomura, ca. 1932
Nomura Estate

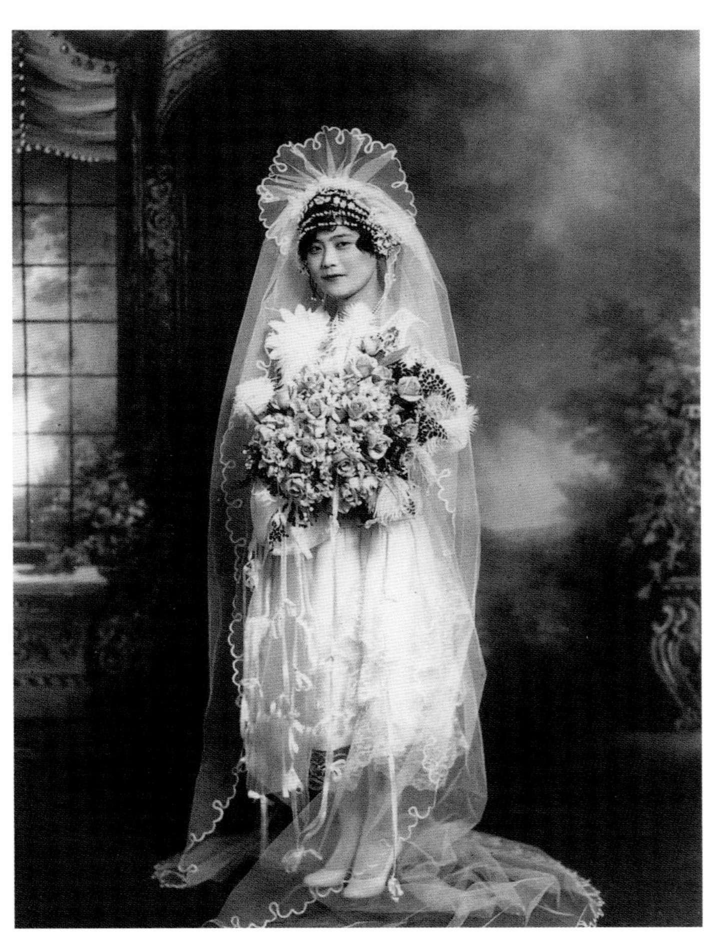

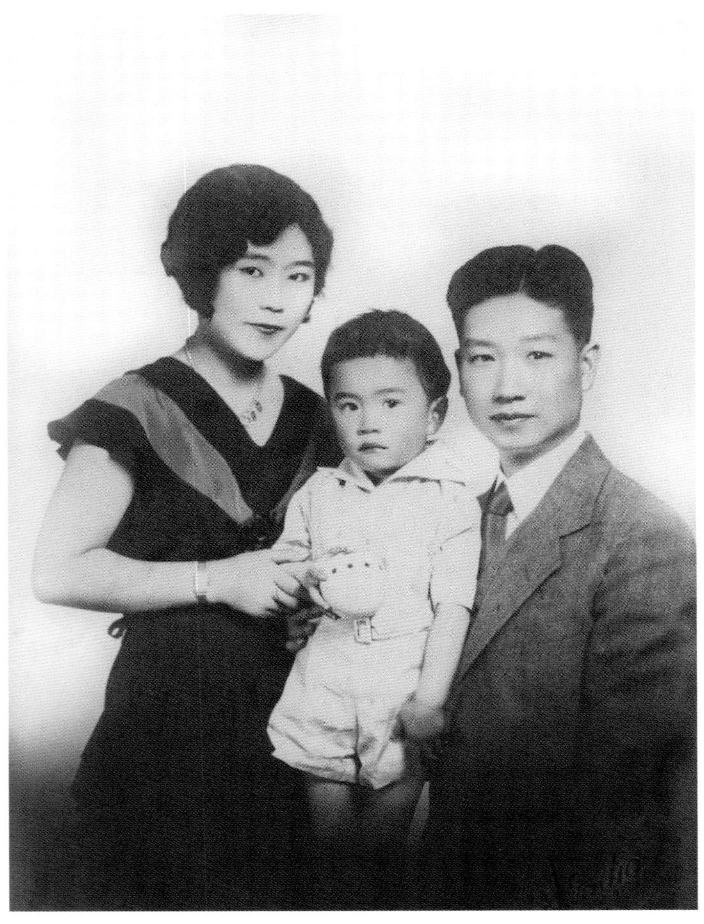

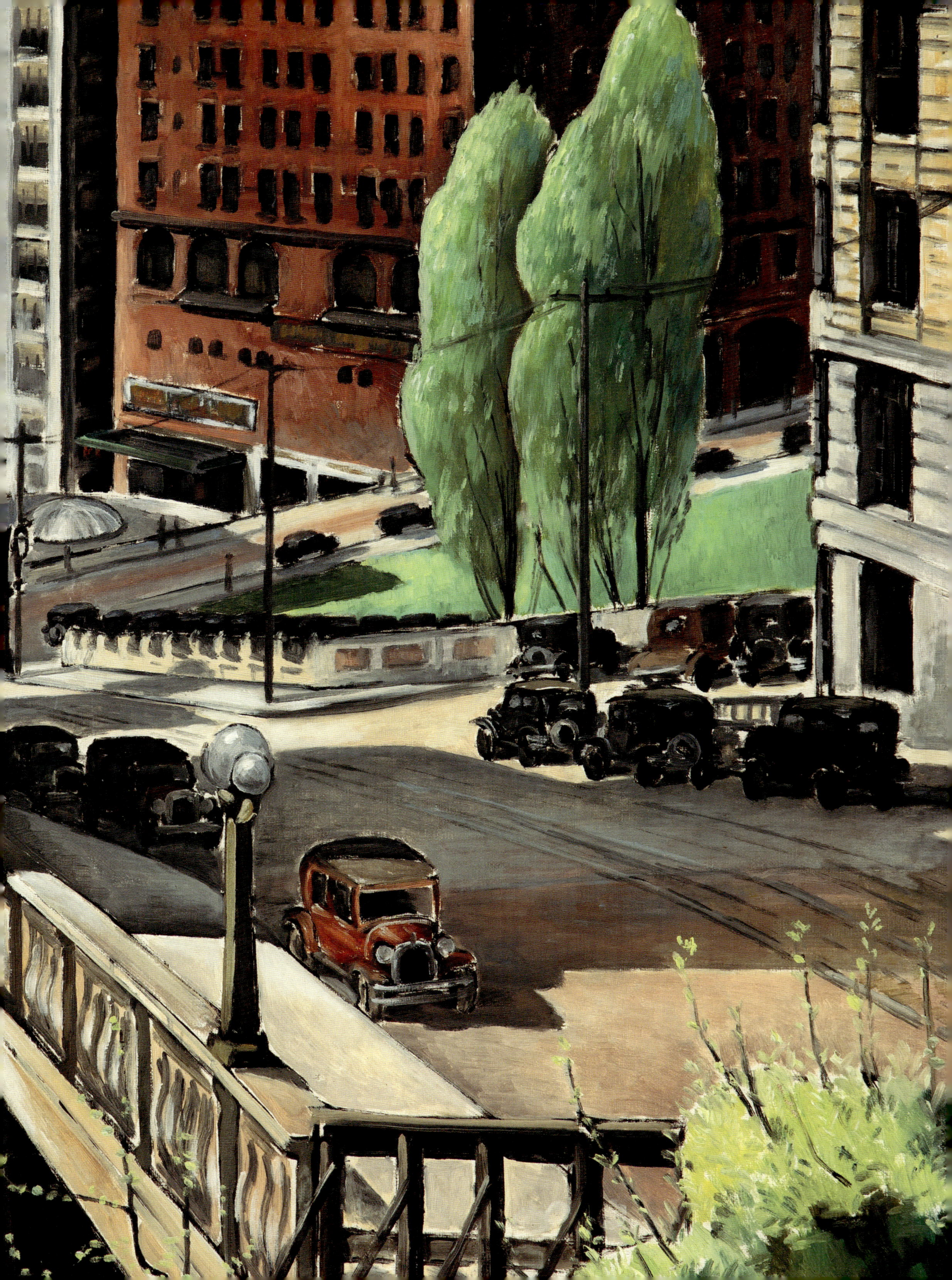

2.

THE ARTIST

The 1930s mark Nomura's maturation as an artist and his peak years of recognition. Between 1925 and 1930 he did not exhibit in Seattle, although he did so twice with distinction in the San Francisco Bay Area.[1] When he reentered Seattle exhibitions after a five-year hiatus in his home city, he presented a newly resolved painting style that gained immediate attention. His subject was the urban landscape and the working waterfront. The evocative titles are gone, replaced by brief generic labels of place rather than time of day, often so generic that they cannot be matched with certainty to extant paintings to which they might well apply. He would not produce figurative work again until World War II.

Nomura's *Fishing Boats* was selected for the Oakland Art Gallery's first annual exhibition for western artists in 1930.[2] He and Kamekichi Tokita were the only two artists from Seattle to be represented. "Competition is reported to have been keen, the jurors turning down 80 percent of the entries," reported the *Town Crier*.[3] Nomura's painting of boats at dock in Salmon Bay was featured in the *San Francisco Examiner* and subsequently shown in juried annuals in San Francisco and Seattle. An image exists today only in the newspaper reproduction, although a nearly identical composition by Tokita suggests how Nomura's painting would have appeared (figs. 2.1 and 2.2). The hull of a boat sweeps across the surface in a curved white plane, and above it rise the blocky cabins of other boats; below, angular planks of dock fill the lower register. Nomura's cropped and flattened composition reads simultaneously as image and construction. Its construction calls attention to the two-dimensional surface, the formal elements of painting, and the painting as object, process, and individual interpretation.

The Oakland exhibition, the *San Francisco Examiner* writer Gobind Behari Lal reported, was installed in categories of "conservative, radical, and liberal." Nomura's painting was displayed among the radicals and captioned in the newspaper illustration as "one of the new style oil paintings." While from a present perspective little about the painting seems radical, the label is a telling measure of standards at the time in the Bay Area and other regions of the country. Lal declared a prominent feature of the exhibition to be the mix of Eastern and Western influences, which he believed was "one of the stimulating signs and portents of the time." He found the mix most evident in the gallery of radical paintings. He identified Nomura as "Japanese-named

Yesler Way, 1934
Detail of Fig. 2.6

painter" and located *Fishing Boats* within the Western tradition, calling it "patently Occidental" with inflections of French modernism and Japanese-influenced color.[4] An immigrant himself, Lal offers a nuanced identification of Nomura and emphasizes the artist's agency in selecting influences among modernism's international borrowings.[5]

In coming years Nomura exhibited regularly at the annual juried exhibitions of the San Francisco Art Association, which were held at the California Palace of the Legion of Honor, and Seattle's Northwest Annual. His paintings continued to be noted favorably in the press. Significant recognition came in 1932, when *Street* won the Northwest Annual's first prize in oil painting, which carried with it the Katherine B. Baker Memorial Purchase Award (figs. 2.3 and 2.4). It was an honor that he would proudly cite in the years to come.[6] Additionally, his second submission that year, *Bridge*, won honorable mention (see fig. 2.9). Viewers agreed with the jurors' decision; his two entries together received the largest number of votes in a visitors' ballot. Nomura and his wife hosted a celebratory party for friends at the popular Gyokko Ken Café.

Prizewinners were customarily given a one-person exhibition the following year, but Nomura's award brought with it the double honor of a solo exhibition on the occasion of the Seattle Art Museum's formal opening in June 1933. Fourteen of his paintings hung in the new art deco building in Volunteer Park, where his work and a display of the museum collection were the only two exhibitions on view in the museum's first weeks. Attendance was exceptional, reportedly reaching twenty thousand on a Sunday, and fifteen to eighteen hundred on weekdays.[7] The exhibition was hailed in Nihonmachi. "Japanese N.W. Prize Winner's Art Shown as Park Museum Opens," a *Japanese American Courier* headline read; "Special Honor Given Him." To the *Taihoku Nippō* (Great Northern Daily News), he was "our artist."[8]

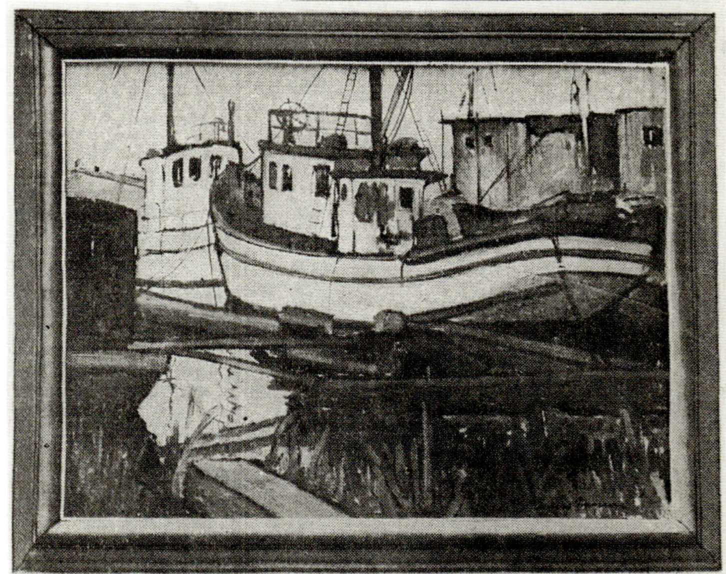
FISHING BOATS, by Kenjiro Nomura, is one of the new style oil paintings of merit at the Annual Exhibition of paintings and sculpture at the Oakland Art Gallery.

More than a hundred water and oil colors represent Western Artists' versatility at this show.

2.1
Nomura's *Fishing Boats* illustrated in *San Francisco Examiner*, April 6, 1930
Nomura papers, Nomura Estate

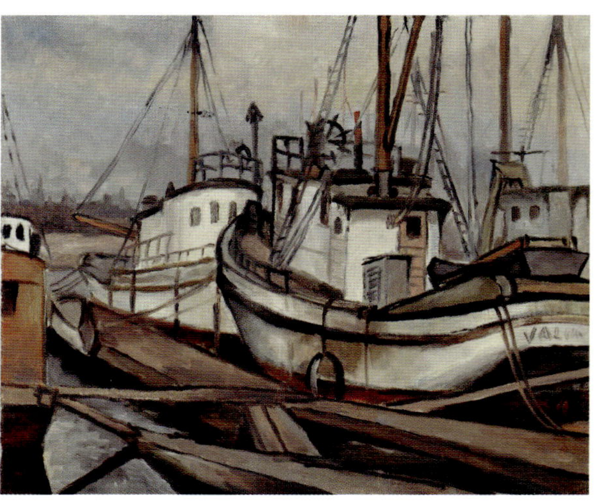

2.2
Kamekichi Tokita, untitled (fishing boats), ca. 1930
Oil on canvas, $18 \times 21\frac{3}{4}$ in.
Collection of Robert Tokita

Nomura's colleague Tokita had earlier been recognized with an award and a solo exhibition at the museum's predecessor, the Art Institute of Seattle (see fig. M.15). With Nomura's parallel rise, an editorial in the *Courier* declared their achievement to

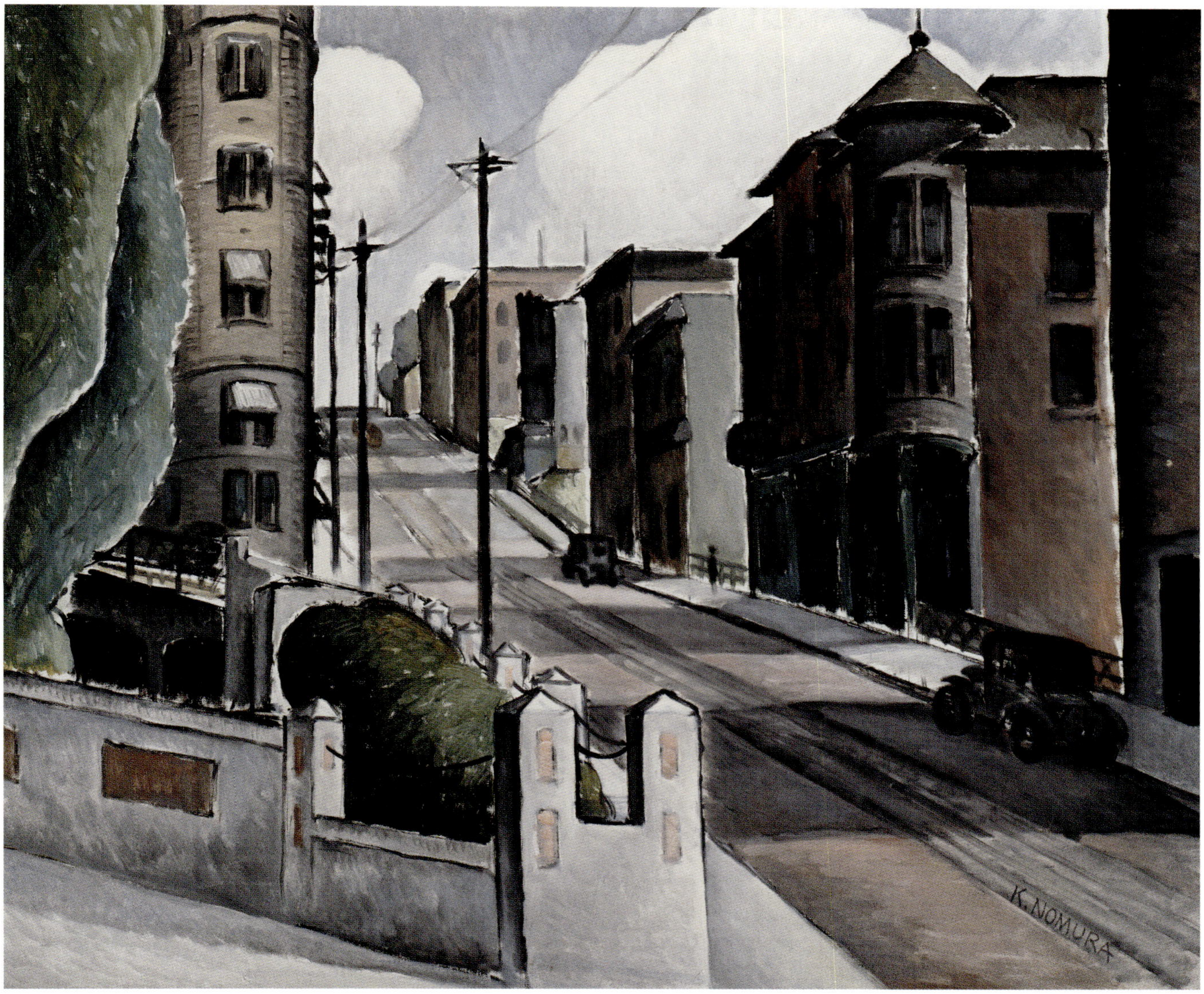

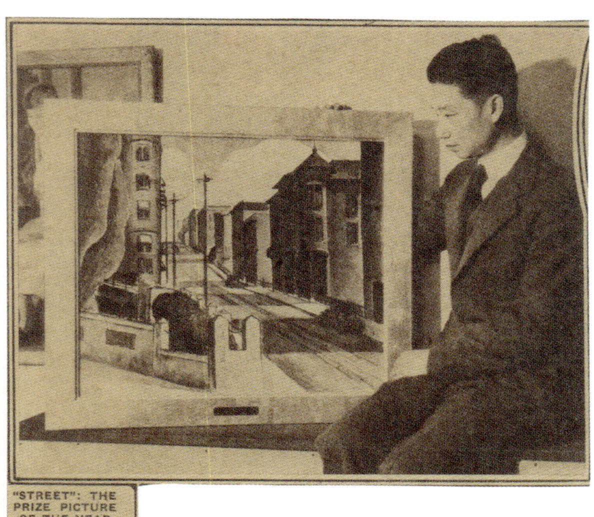
"STREET": THE PRIZE PICTURE OF THE YEAR BY A NORTHWEST ARTIST

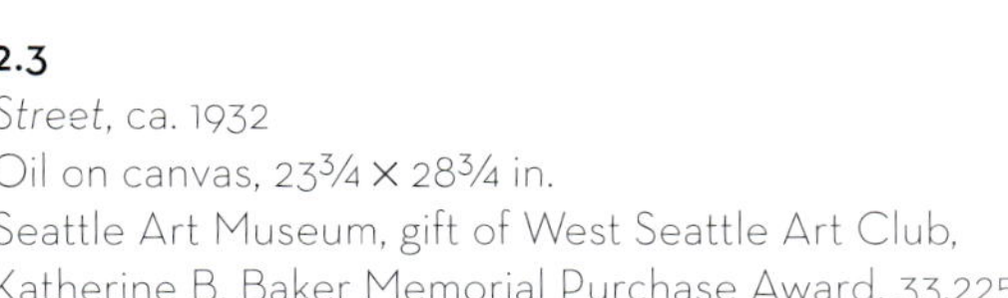

2.3
Street, ca. 1932
Oil on canvas, 23¾ × 28¾ in.
Seattle Art Museum, gift of West Seattle Art Club, Katherine B. Baker Memorial Purchase Award, 33.225

2.4
Nomura with his prizewinning painting
Seattle Times, October 23, 1932

reflect credit upon the entire Nikkei community: "These two men have done and are doing much to uphold the artistic recognition of the Japanese in the Northwest. . . . Tokita and Nomura are to be commended not only for the honors they have won for themselves, but also in the manner in which they have succeeded in combining artistically the two great cultural heritages."[9] As the annual's highest prizewinner, Nomura was named a juror for the 1933 Northwest Annual, the first person of Japanese ancestry to hold that role. This too was recognition he would cite in the future as evidence of his artistic standing.

Reviewing Nomura's exhibition for the *Seattle Times*, Kenneth Callahan named him "one of the leading progressive painters of Seattle."[10] Callahan praised his work in a feature article in the *Town Crier*: "Kenjiro Nomura's exhibition . . . brings to light a painter of surprising stature in one so young. . . . This, his first large exhibition, shows him to be a painter who has evolved a personal style and a definite mastery of his medium and subject." Emphasizing his point, he continued, "Nomura paints the old streets of Profanity Hill and the docks, seeing them with clear, unprejudiced and unsentimental eyes . . . ; details of the mass, form and color become part of the painting. Although a Japanese by birth, his art is essentially American and his own. In his delineation of forms and his lines, his ancestry can be seen, and that beauty of Japanese line is an asset in his work. There is nothing imitative in his painting and although Cézanne is a great master to him, he has derived from the Frenchman only in a technical sense." Callahan concluded emphatically, Nomura "is today one of the most important painters in the Northwest and will sometime achieve the recognition that is due him in other parts of America."[11] Rich in praise, Callahan's statement also reflects then-prevailing assumptions about ethnicity in ascribing "the beauty of Japanese line" to the artist's ancestry rather than an artistic decision.[12] Two years later, the chief editorial writer of the *Seattle Times*, James A. Wood, would name Nomura among eight artists (the only one of color) to have contributed significantly to the cultural life of the city.[13]

An Individual Style

Nomura's paintings of the 1930s are characterized by clearly constructed perspectival space and a rhythmic sequence of geometric shapes. In *Street*, buildings march up Yesler Way in alternating curves and planes. Their solidly modeled forms are outlined to define and simplify shape; the foliage is reduced to pattern and mirrored by the billowing clouds. The palette is rose-gray and green, a muted version of the red and green complements he favored in paintings of these years. Here and in other paintings, a clear light illuminates all pictorial elements and accentuates geometry and color. *Puget Sound* displays these features more strikingly (fig. 2.5). The brick-red buildings are framed by boldly patterned, luxuriant green foliage and the cool blues of water and sky. In the distance, sunlight radiates from beneath the clouds and reflects off the water to backlight the solid forms. The composition is replete with rhythmic repetitions that bring a satisfying harmony to the scene.

These are among a number of paintings that picture sites within the close vicinity of the Noto Sign Company, as Nomura and his artist-colleagues traced the neighborhood that they knew well. Their subjects are the streets, alleys, and pathways of everyday use, the places that defined their habitual patterns of passage and centered the Nikkei community in which they lived. At times they painted side by side to produce paintings that are nearly identical; others vary with individual artistic inclinations. *Yesler Way*, one of several from the perspective of the Yesler Way overpass, is a westward view on a sunny day that brings crystalline clarity to colors, shapes, and building details even as it crops the iconic Smith Tower (fig. 2.6). An untitled painting of Fourth Avenue

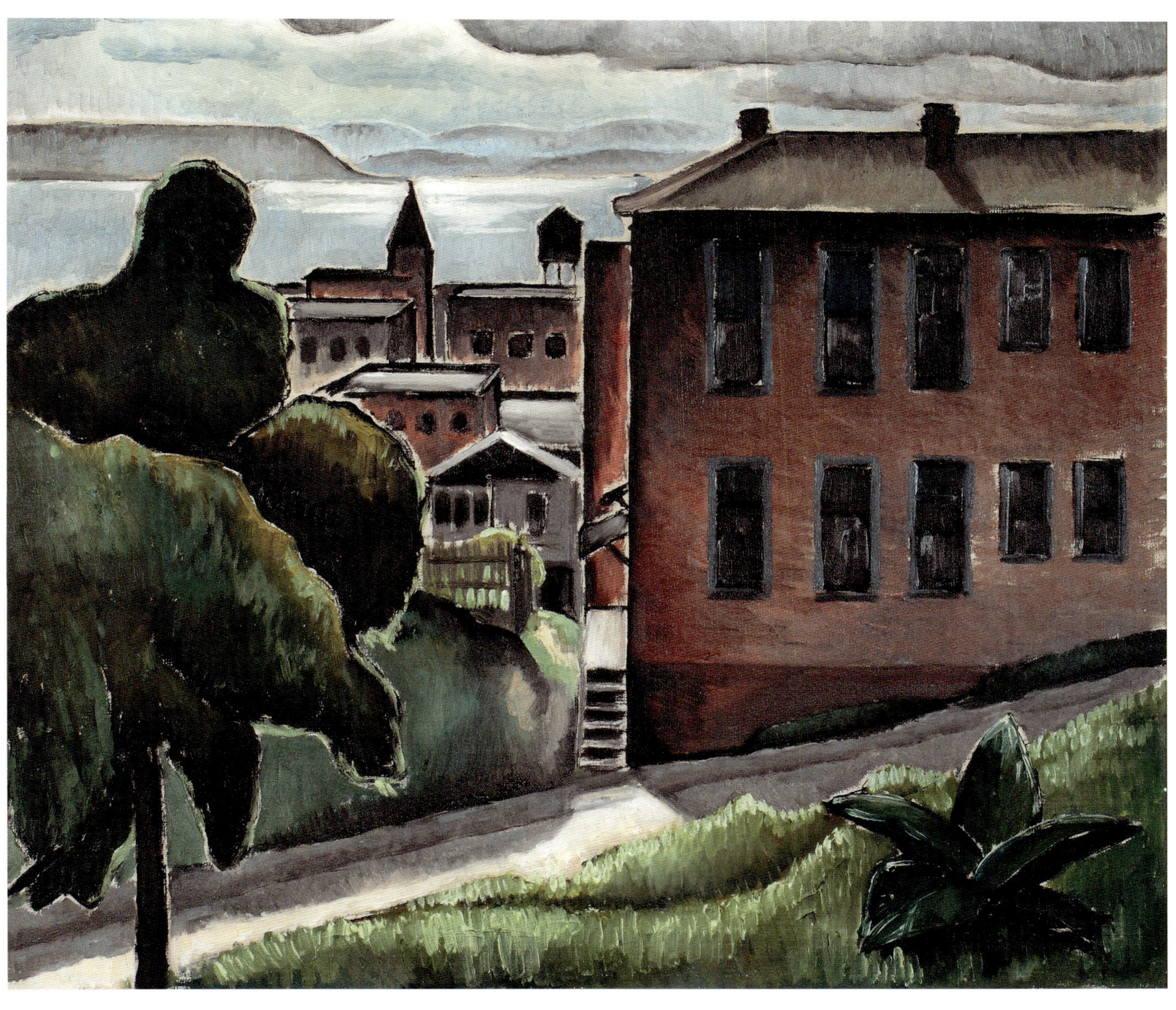

2.5
Puget Sound, ca. 1933
Oil on canvas, 19⅝ × 23¾ in.
Tacoma Art Museum, gift of Mr. and Mrs. Cyril A. Spinola, 1992.8

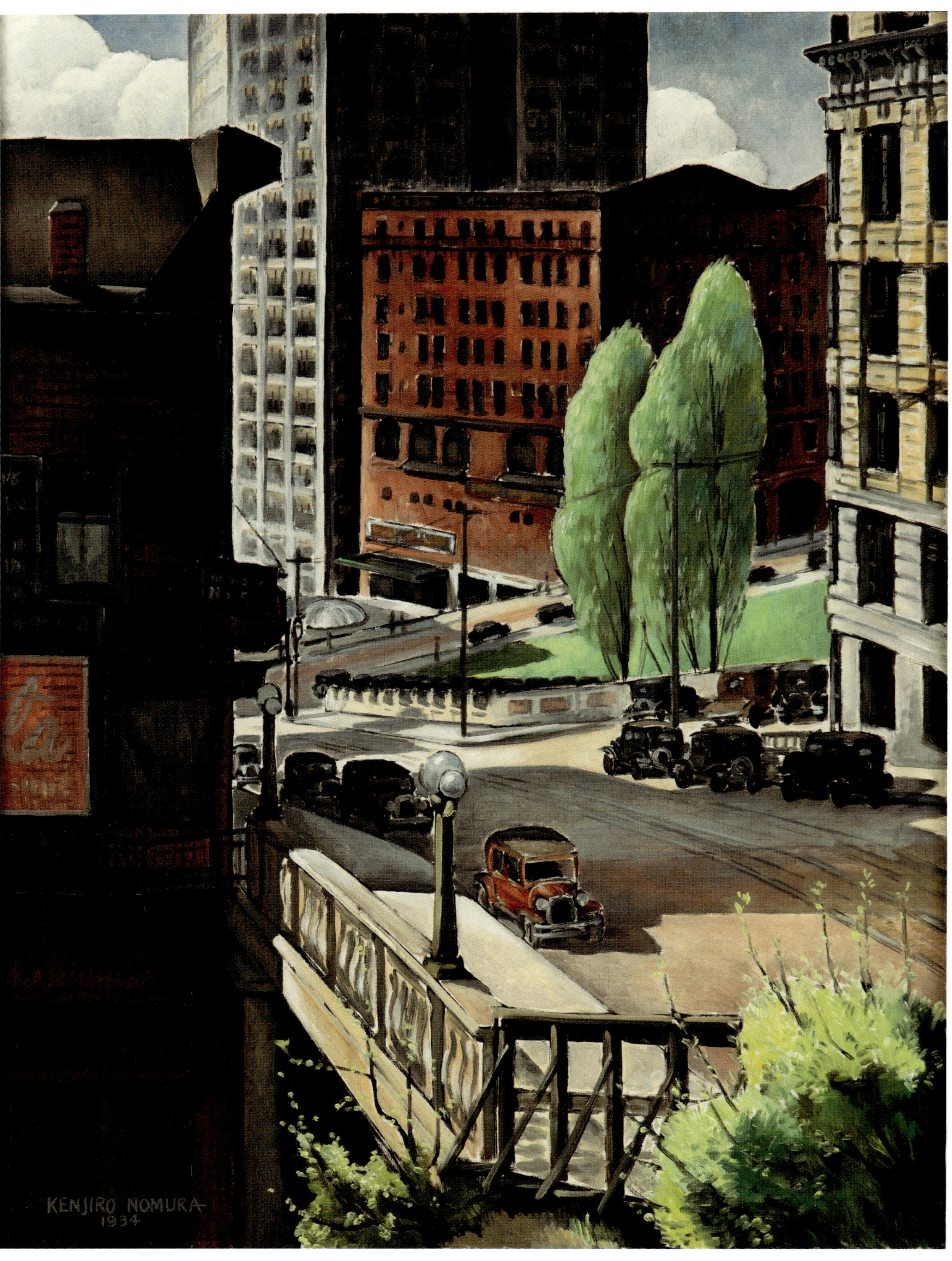
KENJIRO NOMURA
1934

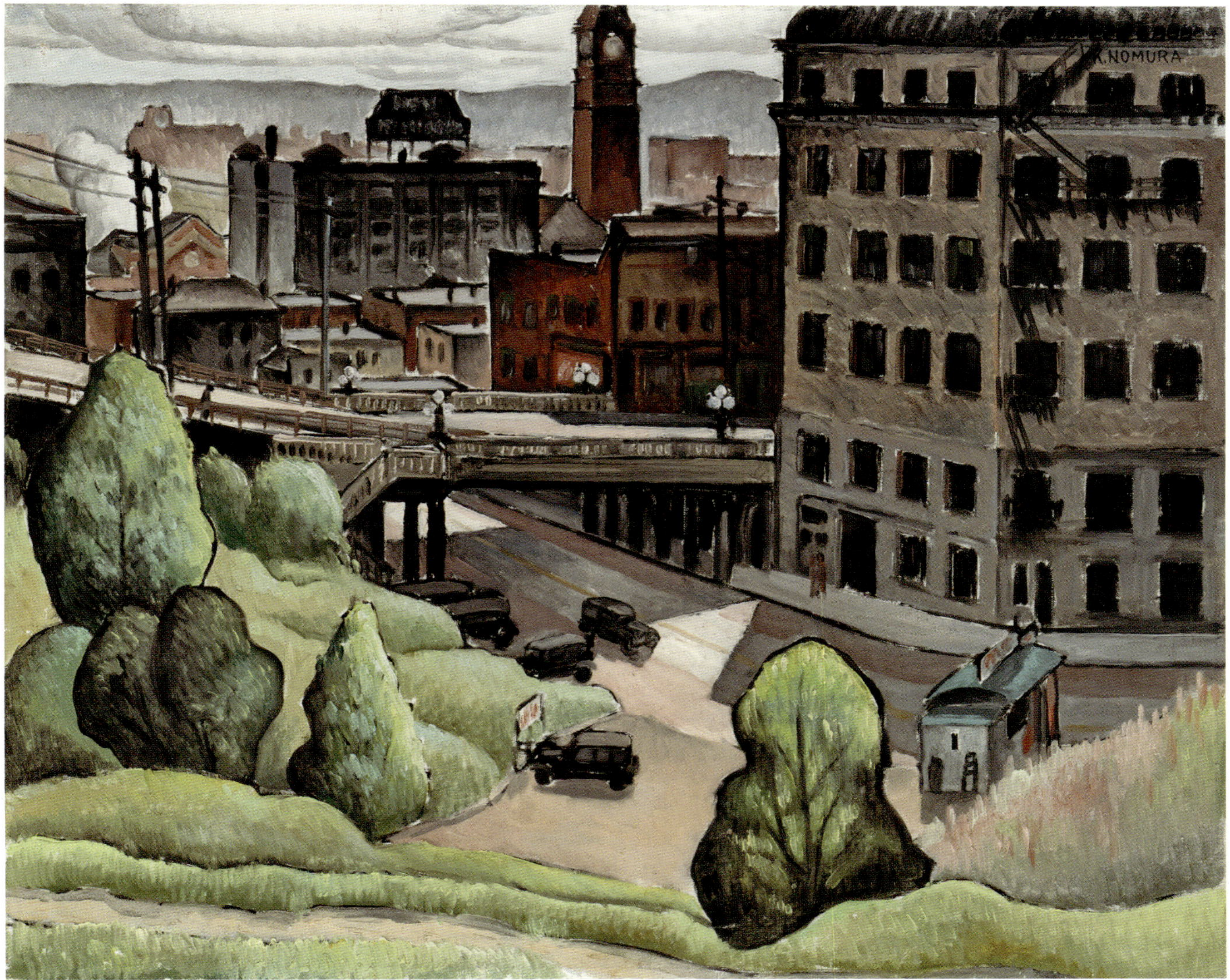

2.6
Yesler Way, 1934
Oil on canvas, 35 × 28 in.
Central Washington University, Public Works of Art Project, Washington State

2.7
Untitled (Fourth and Yesler), ca. early 1930s
Oil on canvas, 24 × 30 in.
Private collection

looks southward from First Hill (Callahan's "Profanity Hill") down onto Fourth Avenue and the overpass to buildings that recede into the distance; balancing the reds and grays of the buildings, patterned tiers of green foliage cascade down the foreground hillside (fig. 2.7). Yet another looks north across the railroad tunnel to the overpass and beyond to the red steeple of Our Lady of Good Help, a pedestrian-level view that portrays the density of the urban environment (fig. 2.8).

The city's waterways and bridges were another favorite subject. Nomura's paintings of the Spokane Street Bridge and the University Bridge are multifaceted compositions of structural elements, moving liquid surface, and reflected and refracted light (fig. 2.9 and see fig. M.20). *Bridge* adapts the closely cropped viewpoint favored by Tokita and is reiterated in a nearly identical painting by Fujii, signs of the artists' mutually supportive relationships. (Nomura's name is slyly signed on a bridge girder.) The paintings of bridges and such views as that of Fourth Avenue display another aspect

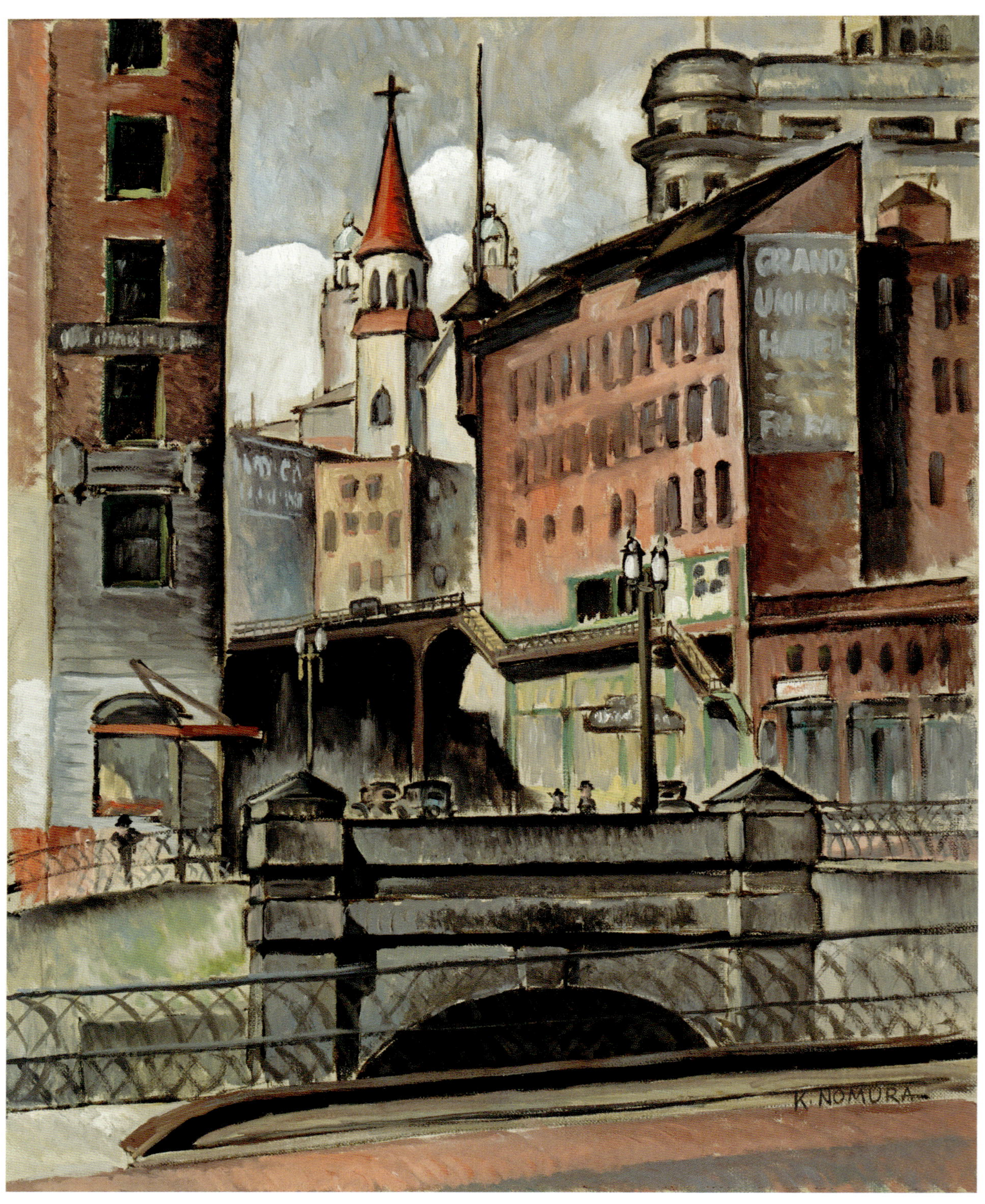

2.8
Untitled (Fourth Avenue railroad tunnel), ca. 1935
Oil on canvas, $28\frac{1}{2} \times 23\frac{1}{2}$ in.
Private collection, promised gift to Cascadia Art Museum.

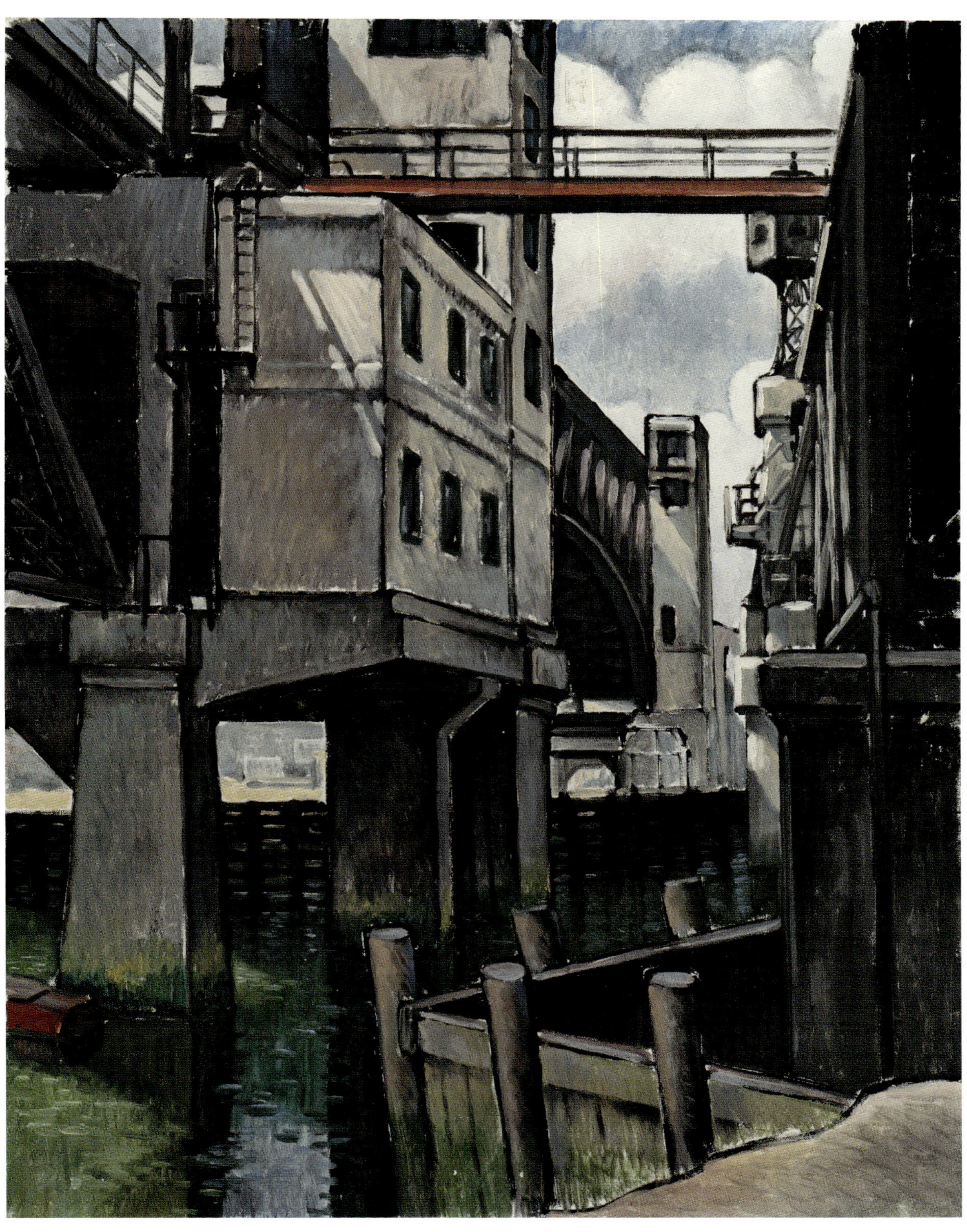

2.9
Bridge, ca. 1930
Oil on canvas, 30 × 24 in.
Wing Luke Museum, gift of Sean Callahan, 1991.073.003

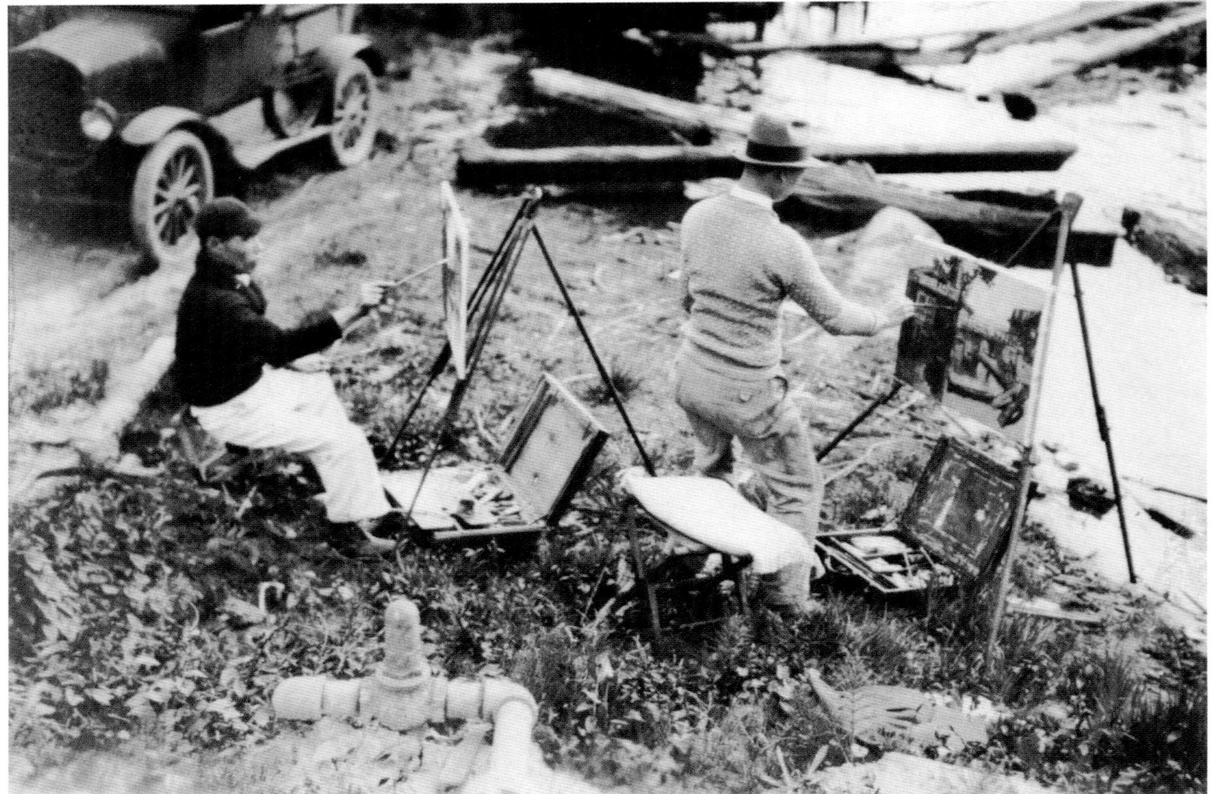

2.10
Takuichi Fujii (*left*) and Kenjiro Nomura (*right*), sketching trip, 1930s
Kamekichi Tokita papers, Archives of American Art, Smithsonian Institution

of Nomura's modernity in their focus on the urban infrastructure. Throughout Nomura's years living in Seattle, the city had been engaged in massive land-moving projects—lowering hills, cutting waterways, and filling in tidal lands. Not only the size of the projects but also the new technology used was record-setting.[14] Nomura's painted bridges span these man-made places, where new steel bridges opened to fanfare in 1930 and 1932. More than picturesque subjects, these and his paintings of the urban core show Nomura to be a keen observer of the city's development. These were also areas of the city where Nomura and his colleagues could paint without drawing unwelcome attention, and as they explored and returned to favorite areas, the pattern of their activity defined a territory of belonging.

The painters' Sunday sketching trips took them farther afield to the Duwamish waterway and the Green and White River valley south of Seattle. A new subject captured Nomura's interest in 1933 and 1934, when he produced a half-dozen paintings of barns. The valley area was home to many of the region's Japanese farm families who provided most of the city's produce; since early in the century, Issei farmers had dominated agricultural production there.[15] Rather than the truck farmers' modest sheds, Nomura was drawn to the architectonic forms of dairy barns, and he capitalized on their customary barn red. Issei farmers in the valley had learned dairying in the early twentieth century, becoming the major producers until most of them were driven out of business in the mid-1920s.[16] A few remained until World War II, although Nomura's paintings give no hint of the farmers' ancestry. *Red Barns* places the simplified volumetric building forms within a rhythmic field of green and blue-gray, where foliage steps back to blue hills and the moisture-laden clouds of a Northwest sky recede in parallel pattern (fig. 2.11). *The Farm*, produced a year later, is a similar view with less of

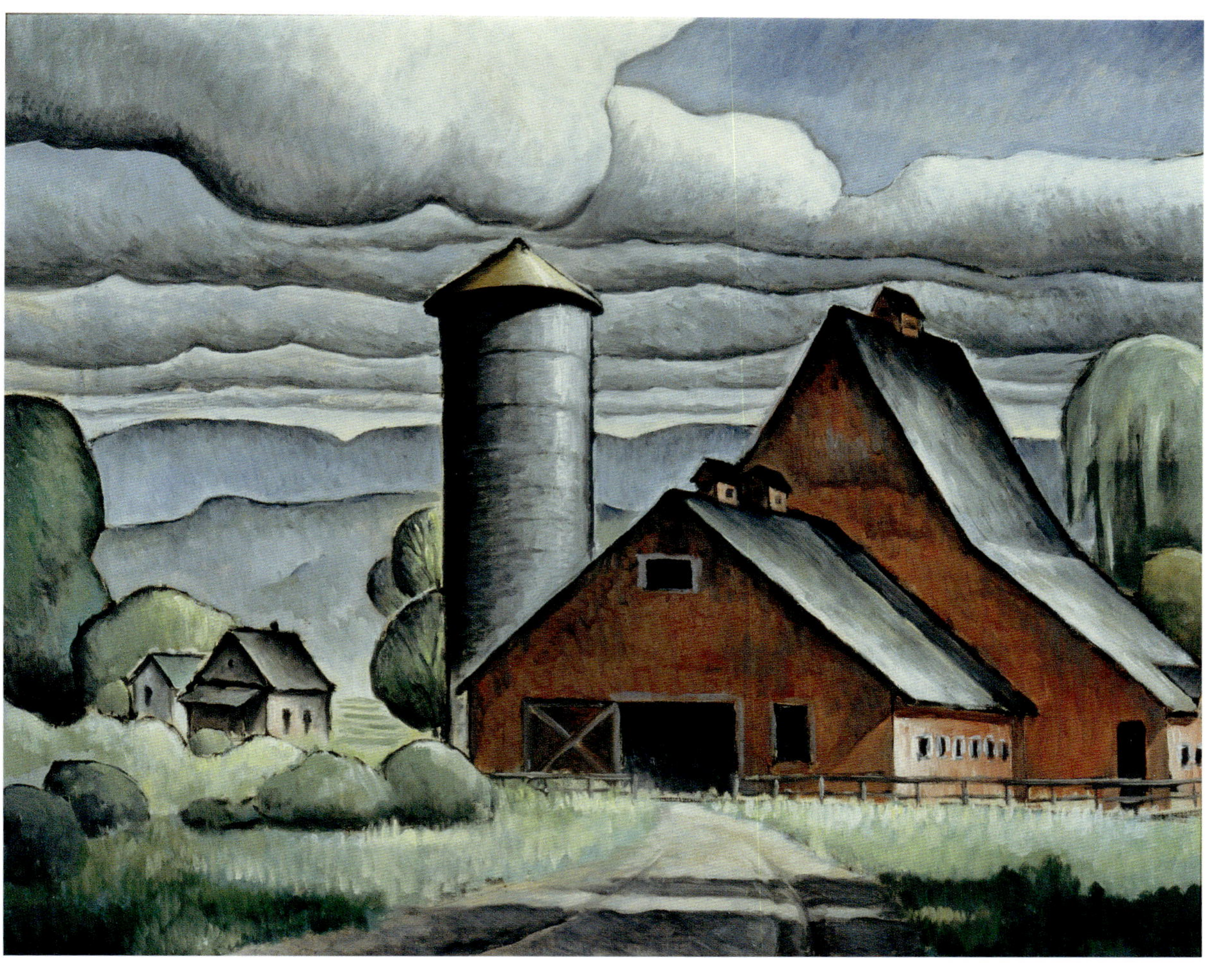

2.11
Red Barns, 1933
Oil on canvas, 28 × 36 in.
Seattle Art Museum, Eugene Fuller Memorial Collection, 33.224

2.12
Arima family on their farm, Christopher, Washington, ca. 1911
Photo: Kent Photography
White River Valley Museum Photograph Collection, PO-00210

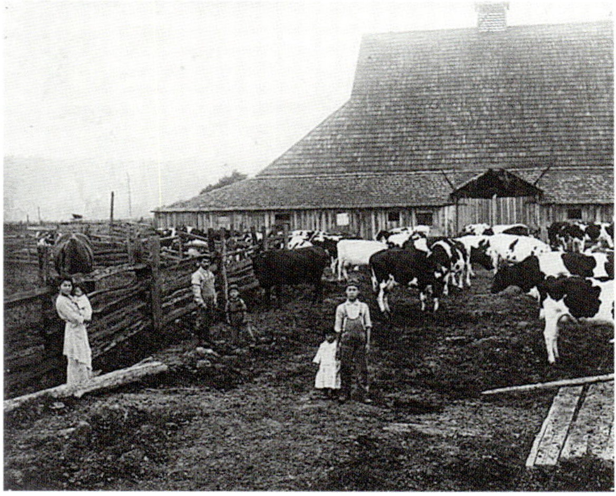

the stylized patterning and sharper, more revealing light (fig. 2.13). In these and many other paintings, Nomura displays a marked sensitivity to the character of the region's dramatic skies. Another, a bucolic composition of a barn and grazing cows titled *Washington Farm*, evokes the pristine rural idealism of Grant Wood, who had come to prominence as a leader of "American Scene" painting and whose work was widely published (fig. 2.14 and see fig. 2.20). All of Nomura's farm paintings, which were painted during dark years of the Depression, project scenes of pastoral beauty.

Institutional Support

Nomura's renewed public participation coincided with the growth of Seattle's art institutions, and from the time of his first reentry and throughout

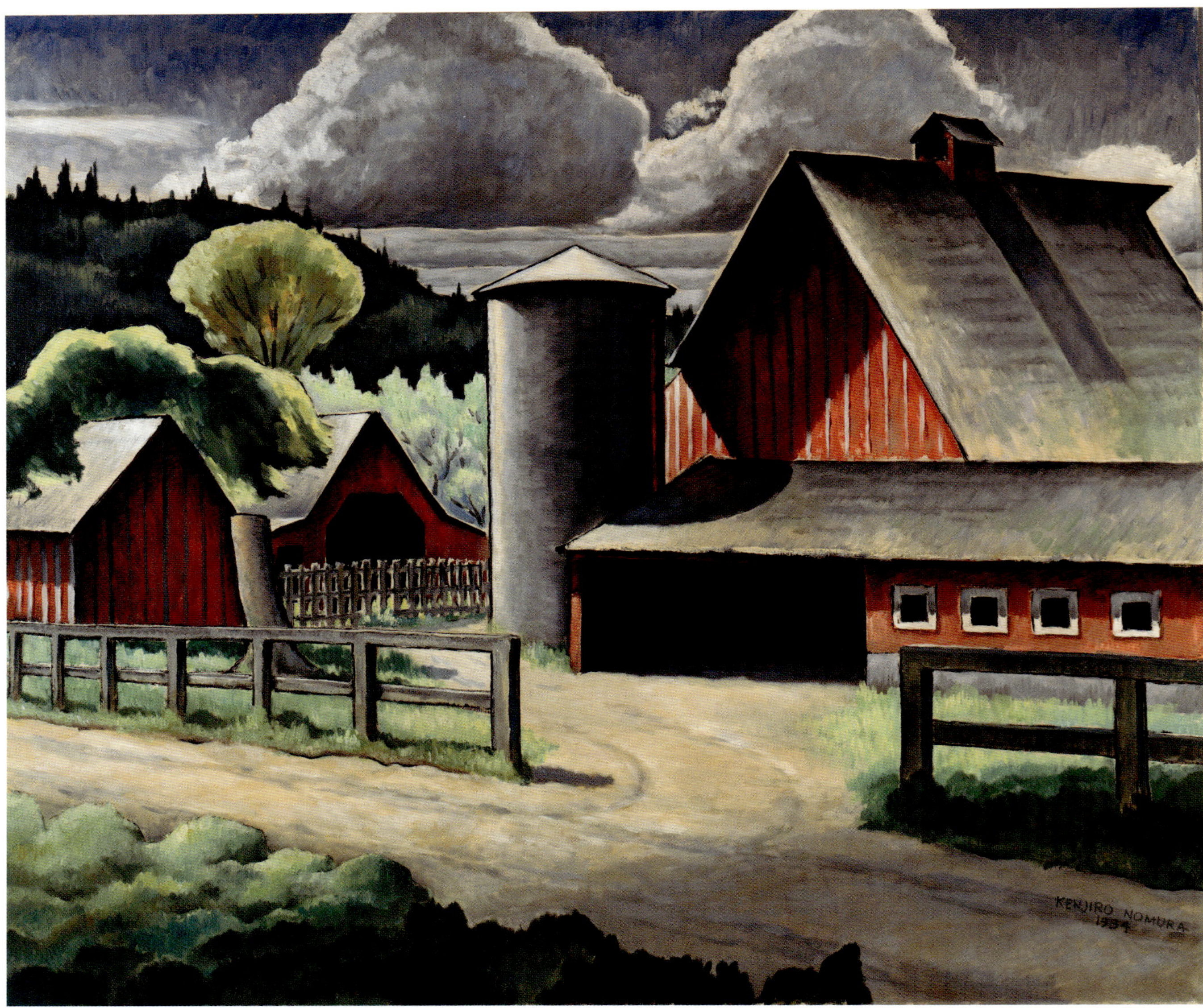

2.13
The Farm, 1934
Oil on canvas, 38¼ × 46⅛ in.
Smithsonian American Art Museum, transfer from the U.S. Department of Labor

the 1930s he received steady support from the leaders of the Art Institute of Seattle and its successor organization, the Seattle Art Museum.

The Art Institute of Seattle began in 1929 as a reorganization and renaming of the Seattle Fine Arts Society, signaling larger ambitions that aspired to the art institutes in Chicago, Pittsburgh, and Cleveland.[17] It moved into a gallery building at Horace C. Henry's home on Capitol Hill, which Henry had built to house his own collection before the construction of the Henry Gallery at the University of Washington.[18] There the institute's first professional director, John Davis Hatch Jr., launched an ambitious, wide-ranging program of exhibitions. His catholic interests and management style established the foundation of a newly vitalized and strengthened organization.[19] During most of Hatch's tenure, the president of the board was Dr. Richard E. Fuller, a geologist by education, a collector of Asian art, and the future donor and founding director of the Seattle Art Museum. Just as the city leadership invested in Asian trade, Asian art was a special focus of the Art Institute, one that Hatch underscored in reports and correspondence. The institute

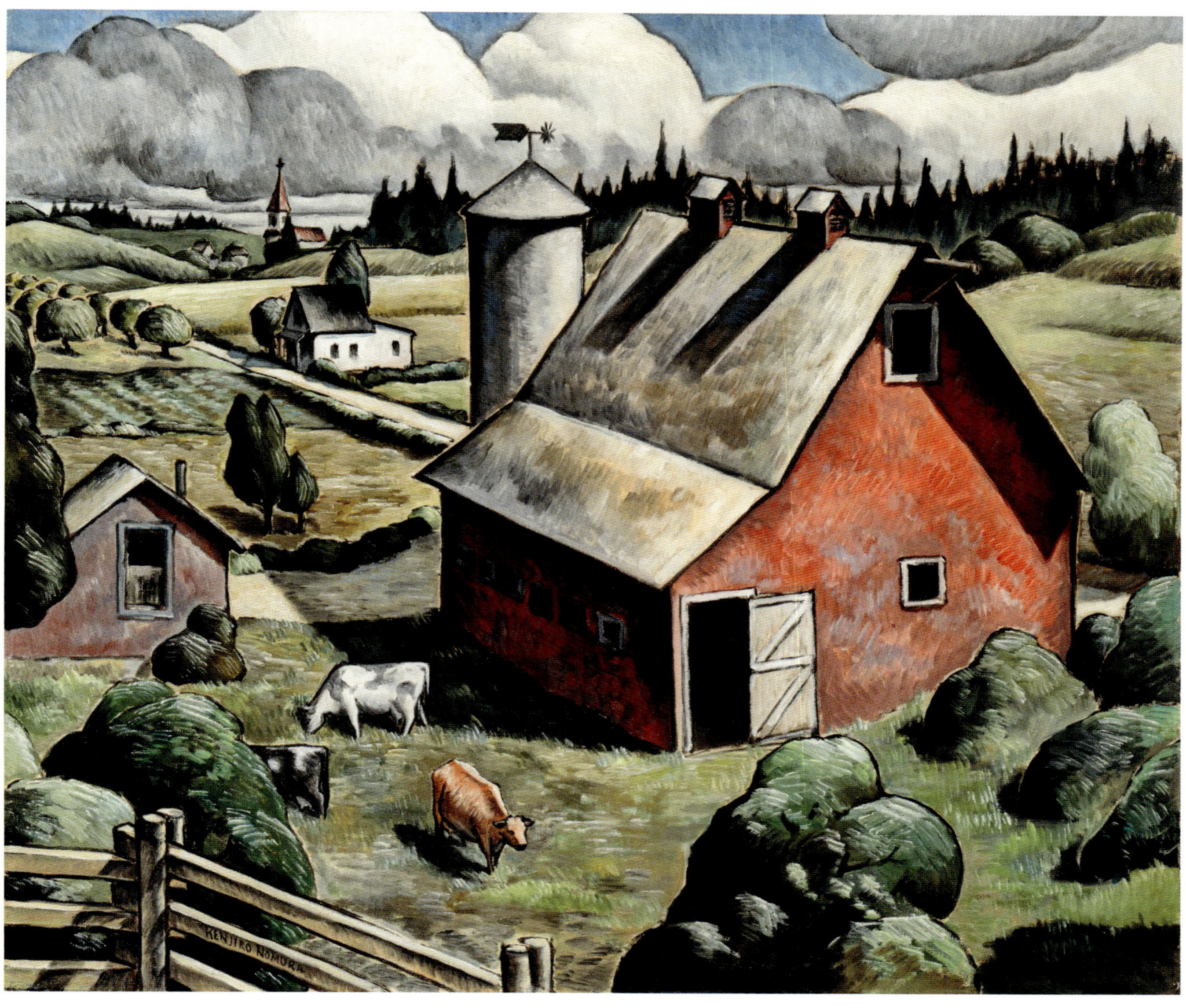

2.14
Washington Farm, ca. 1934
Oil on canvas, 27½ × 33½ in.
Collection of Lindsey and Carolyn Echelbarger, promised gift to Cascadia Art Museum

sponsored major surveys of Japanese, Chinese, and Indian and Indonesian art, organized in collaboration with the Japan Society, the China Club, the Far East Society, and the University of Washington Oriental Department.[20] Fuller was a leader among the organizers and a major lender to the exhibitions. The Japanese exhibition was called by visiting "authorities from various parts of the country" one of the finest they had seen.[21] All the objects on view were from local collections; of the sixty-two lenders, forty have Japanese surnames.[22] Business leaders in Nihonmachi were noteworthy in their support of cultural endeavors; as previously mentioned, Nomura had participated in the first Japanese Art Association exhibition in 1916, which was organized by a prominent Issei businessman. Hatch wrote the San Francisco artist Chiura Obata in 1931, "The Japanese colony here in the city . . . is quite an active group and has been endeavoring to make Seattle an art and cultural center for Japanese. I have a very large acquaintance among them and they have been interested in the activities of the Institute."[23]

In addition to the Northwest Annual, the Art Institute presented solo exhibitions for local,

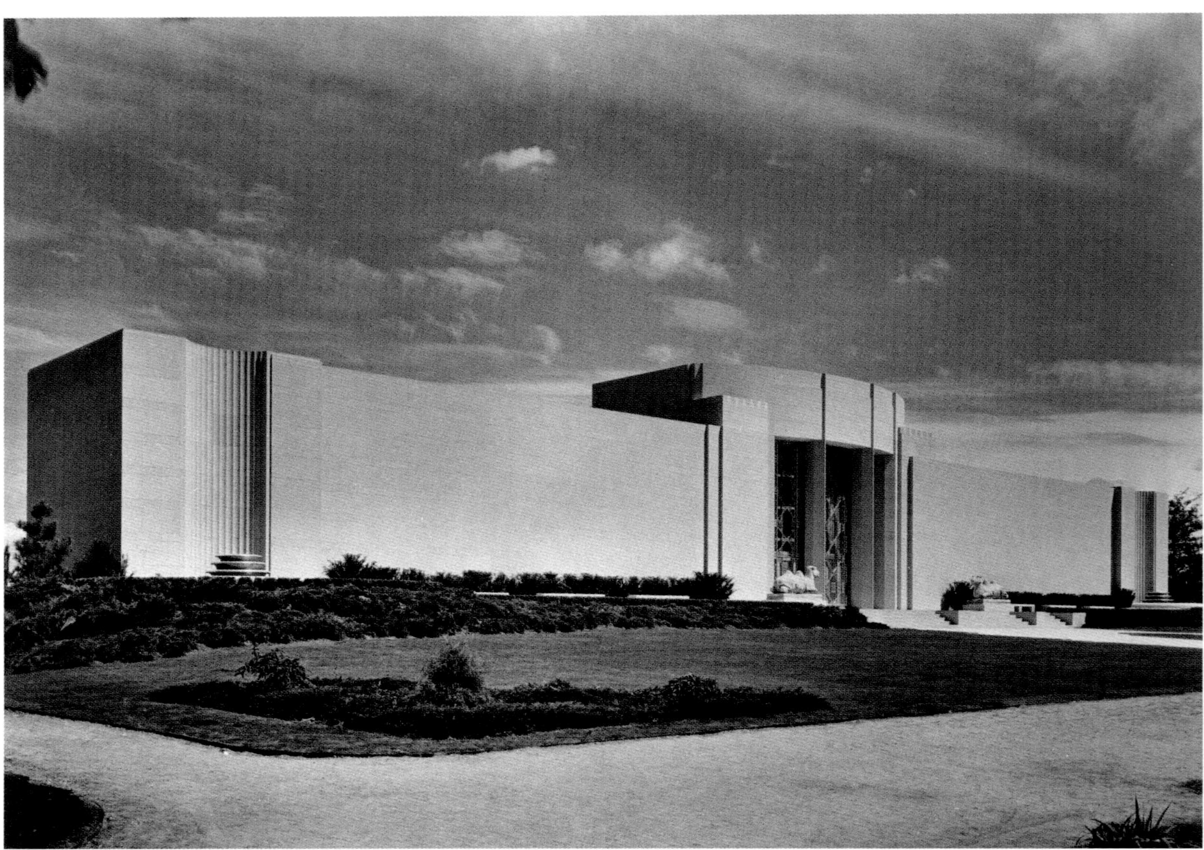

2.15
Seattle Art Museum, ca. 1933
Photo: H. C. Davidson
Special Collections, University of Washington Libraries, UW 5685

regional artists each month. Hatch also sought the help of colleagues in completing the exhibition schedule with conservative content to balance his own progressive interests, and he continually appealed for exhibitions of the best of contemporary American painting. He expressed strong support for Japanese American artists and hoped to organize a nationally representative exhibition, "a comprehensive showing of as many as 150 paintings . . . of the outstanding Japanese artists."[24] The exhibition was not realized but would have provided an important historic precedent. When Nomura, Tokita, and Fujii were selected for the 1931 San Francisco Art Association Annual, Hatch wrote director Spencer Macky that he "was pleased to see such a good representation from the Northwest, especially among the Japanese."[25]

The Seattle Art Museum opened in June 1933 in a building funded and given to the city by Fuller and his mother, Margaret E. MacTavish Fuller, and for the next forty years Fuller led the organization and provided most of its operating funds (fig. 2.15).[26] The museum opened with a substantial gift of Asian art from the Fullers, a selection of contemporary Seattle paintings, and Nomura's one-person exhibition. In his opening statement Fuller declared support for artists in the Northwest, saying, "I think that the encouragement of local art is one of the most important functions of any museum. We sincerely hope that the Seattle Art Museum will be an inspiration to local talent and, at the same time, will succeed in bringing their finest achievements to the recognition of the public."[27] He gave special honors to Nomura and Tokita in naming them Artist Life-Members of the museum in recognition that each had given paintings to the nascent collection; they were two of only three artists so recognized.[28] Building upon Hatch's network of connections,

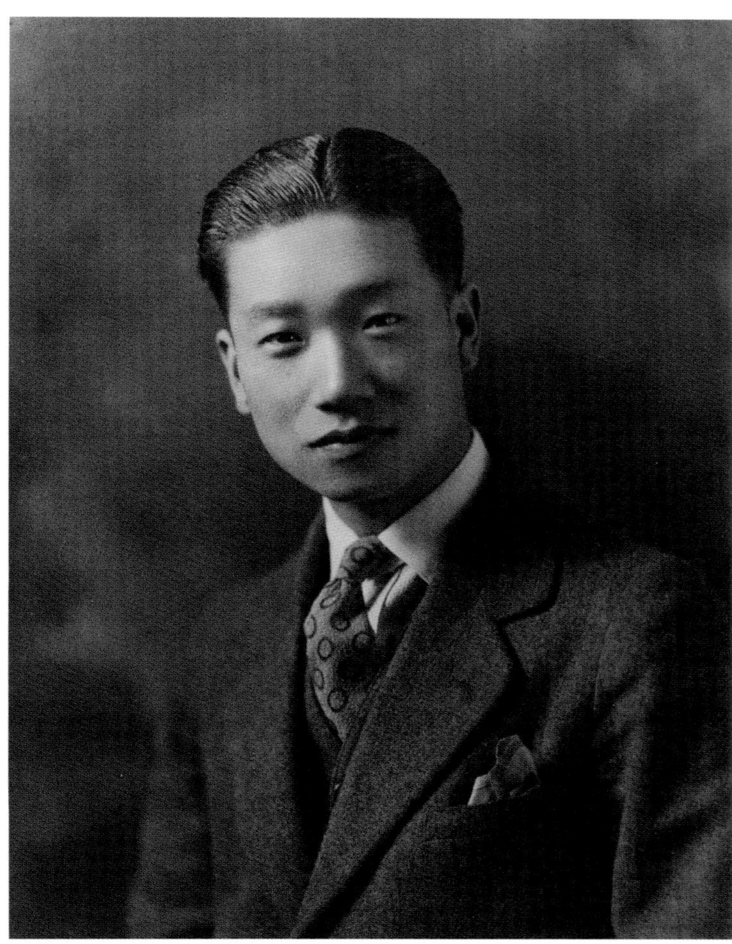

2.16
Kenjiro Nomura, 1930s
Nomura Estate

Fuller pursued a similarly balanced exhibition schedule, declaring that the museum would seek a mid-ground between the extremes of conservative and modern art.[29] Its monthly solo exhibitions continued the earlier practice and provided exceptional opportunity to the region's artists.

Fuller was encouraged in his support of the region's artists by Kenneth Callahan, who was not only a frequently exhibiting painter but also now the museum's deputy director, curator, registrar, and publicist. Having returned to his native Washington in 1928 after several years of travel and work abroad, he had quickly befriended older artists such as Mark Tobey and Ambrose and Viola Patterson. In 1930 he married Margaret Bundy, an editor of the *Town Crier*, and assumed responsibility for the art column. He became the predominant art writer in Seattle, an ardent advocate for modernism, and a consistent supporter of Nomura's, as well as Tokita's and Fujii's, work. He and Margaret made their home a gathering place for artists and acquired Nomura's *Bridge* for their own collection in the process of trading paintings with artists they admired (see fig. 2.9).[30] After becoming the publicist for the Seattle Art Museum, Callahan held a unique position as a fellow artist, a curator, and a writer and critic for the *Seattle Times* and national art magazines. For two decades he would be the primary voice in articulating a regional vision.

Unquestionably, artwork on view at the Art Institute of Seattle and the Seattle Art Museum provided Nomura a valuable resource. Hatch, the Art Institute director, described Nomura, Tokita, and Fujii talking among themselves when attending an exhibition of contemporary landscape paintings: "You will be pleased," he wrote the Canadian painter Fred Varley, "when I tell you that three Japanese painters, who are considered the most serious artists in Seattle, were in the galleries the other day and were particularly moved by your three or four latest pieces of the Indian country."[31] When the Seattle Art Museum opened, Asian art was the foundation of the collection and always on view; much of the history of Western art was represented in reproductions, then a common practice for regional museums. Signature paintings by American artists such as Charles Sheeler, Edward Hopper, and Georgia O'Keeffe, as well as smaller works by Pablo Picasso, Georges Braque, and other European modernists, appeared on singular occasions, but borrowing first-rate work remained a challenge in the far-northwest city. At any opportunity, works of art on exhibition provided Nomura firsthand experience with the painted object to compare and deepen his own practice.

Recognition came steadily following Nomura's first prize in 1932. He was among six

Seattle-area artists selected for the exhibition *Painting and Sculpture from 16 American Cities* at New York's Museum of Modern Art in 1933, and the only Issei among the national representation.[32] His selection was publicized in San Francisco's Japanese American press as well as in ethnic and mainstream Seattle papers; the San Francisco paper noted also his "singular honor" of having been selected a juror of the Northwest Annual.[33] Following the New York presentation, the Seattle Art Museum featured the six Seattle artists in an exhibition of American painting.

In 1934 Nomura and Tokita together with the Bay Area painters Masuta Narahara and Henry Sugimoto were the subjects of the exhibition *Oil Paintings by Four Japanese Artists of the West Coast.* The exhibition, which was organized jointly by the directors of the Seattle Art Museum and the California Palace of the Legion of Honor, opened in Seattle, traveled to the Legion of Honor in San Francisco, and toured West Coast cities. Again, the occasion was warmly greeted by newspapers in Seattle's Nihonmachi, which regularly noted the achievements of "our artists." The exhibition, one headline noted, was "sponsored by powerful patrons."[34] The *Berkeley (CA) Daily Gazette* hailed the San Francisco opening of the exhibition by "four of the most gifted Japanese artists living on the West Coast."[35] The organization of such an exhibition by two prominent mainstream institutions signaled exceptional acknowledgment of the Issei artists' achievement.

The same year, one of Nomura's paintings produced during the Public Works of Art Project of 1934 (discussion follows) was selected for exhibition at the Corcoran Gallery of Art in Washington, DC. In 1936 he, Tokita, and Fujii were among ten artists to represent Washington State in the *First National Exhibition of American Art* held at New York's Rockefeller Center, where they were three of only four artists of Japanese ancestry, and the only ones from the West.[36] Nomura, alone among them, was selected for the 1937 sequel. Culminating his prewar record, he, together with Callahan, Peter Camfferman, and Walter Isaacs, represented Washington at the Golden Gate International Exposition in 1939. In all these exhibitions but the Bay Area annuals and the Corcoran Gallery exhibition, Seattle Art Museum director Richard E. Fuller was a member of the local selection committee (he served ex officio on the Northwest Annual jury). Nomura wrote him at the time of the Golden Gate Exposition, "I am positive you are doing all this for me but I do not know how to express my appreciation. I can only say I thank you very much and please accept this simple words [*sic*] as my gratitude."[37]

Depression Years

While Nomura became established artistically during the 1930s, his personal life was buffeted by the larger events around him. His story, one shared by many, highlights the vulnerability of an immigrant marginalized by place of birth and ethnicity, one who is driven to succeed in his adopted homeland, and yet whose foothold on security and stability remains tentative. The years had begun with promise with his marriage to Fumiko and the birth of their son. The sign shop provided him a living and a congenial painting studio.

Only a few months before their son's birth, the stock market crash in October 1929 precipitated what became the Great Depression, bringing cataclysmic change to the material conditions and psyche of the country. In an accelerating contraction, industrial production fell 21 percent in 1930, five thousand banks closed between 1930 and 1932; by late 1933 twenty million people, one out of six Americans, were unemployed, and the U.S. gross national product was half what it had been in 1929.[38] The election of President Franklin D. Roosevelt brought a mandate and a new approach to economic stabilization and relief, the New Deal. Between 1934 and 1943, a battery of reform,

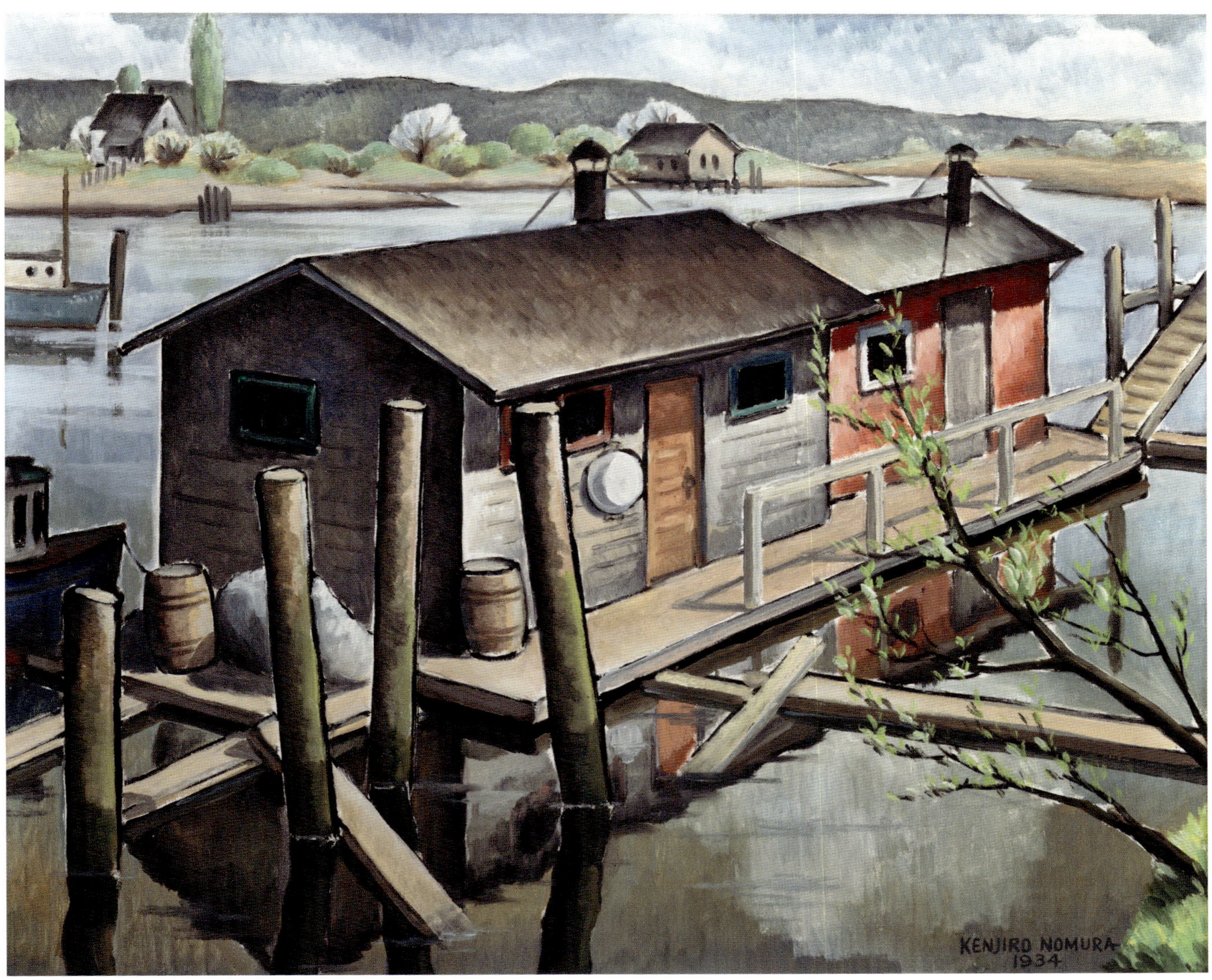

2.17
Houseboat, 1934
Oil on canvas, 21 × 26 in.
Longview Public Library, Public Works of Art Project, Washington State

relief, and recovery projects funneled billions of dollars into the economy.

The Depression hit the already marginalized Nikkei community particularly hard. Businesses experienced a severe downturn. From the perspective of the late 1930s, the Seattle-born sociologist S. Frank Miyamoto observed, "The depression has not dealt kindly with these shop-keepers; . . . the failure of the community's one bank, and the large movements of their population back to Japan, and even more to California, have drained a good part of the life-blood out of the community."[39] The period saw the local ethnic Japanese population decline from its peak of about eighty-five hundred in 1930 to seven thousand in 1940.[40]

Nomura's and Tokita's sign-painting business suffered along with many others, and in early 1934 the two of them found employment in the Public Works of Art Project (PWAP). The PWAP was a six-month trial program, the first of four federally funded initiatives that would support artistic endeavors in an unprecedented nationwide reach. Modeled on the Civilian Conservation Corps, it stressed living wages and eventually reached 3,749 people by providing employment varying from four weeks to six months. It offered a bright

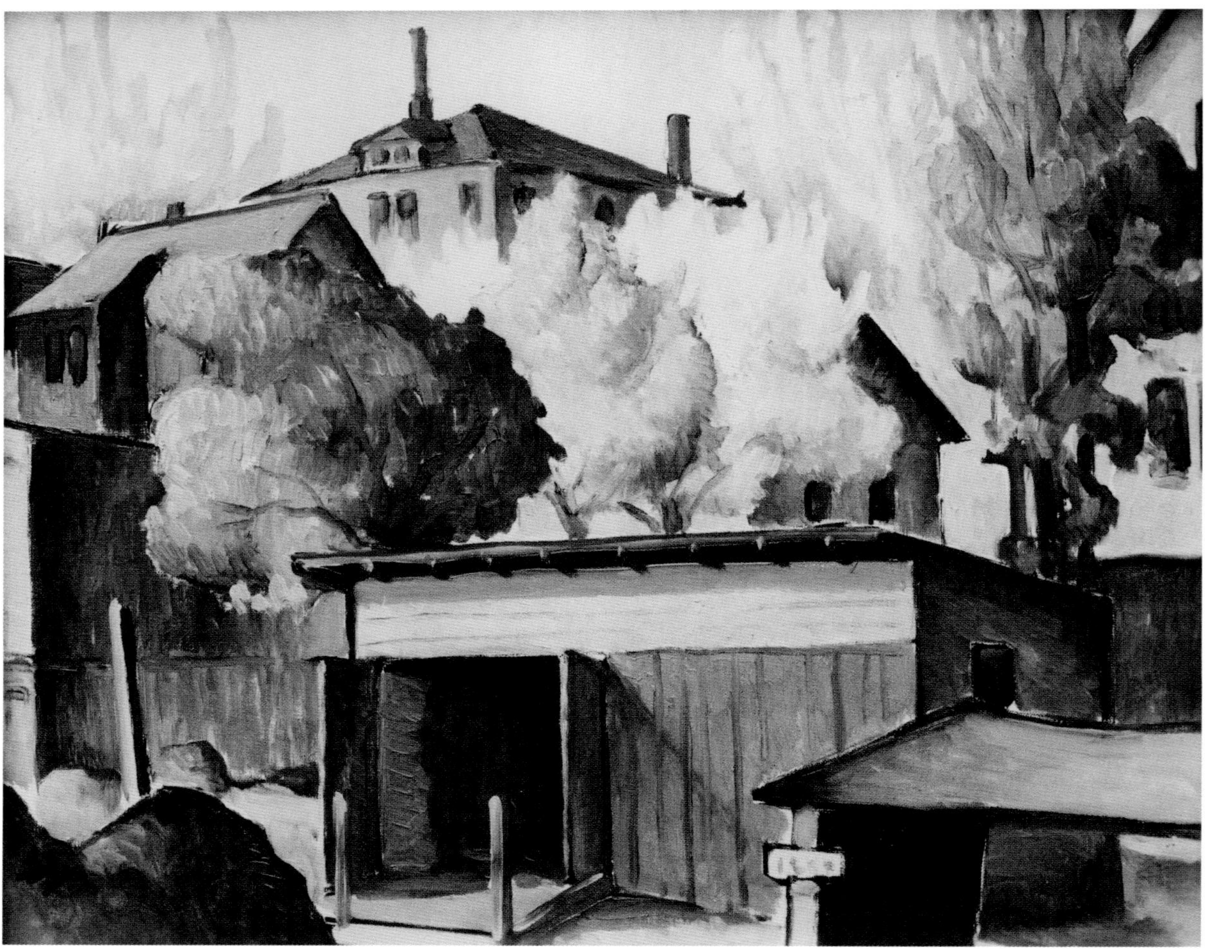

2.18
Alley, 1934
Photographic reproduction (original, oil on canvas, 28 × 36 in.)
Artist file, Emily Stimson Bullitt Library, Seattle Art Museum

The painting was produced during the PWAP and given to the Seattle Public Schools. Location unknown.

spot of opportunity for Nomura and Tokita, who were employed for four weeks in February in the top rank of artists and paid $38.25 per week. (Annualized, their salary would have exceeded the average annual income of American families.)[41] They were among seventeen artists in Washington to be chosen for group 1, the highest among three ranks, and the only ones of Japanese descent among the sixty Washington artists in the program.[42] Each produced six paintings, which were distributed to public institutions at the project's end, five within Washington State and one each to federal agencies in Washington, DC (figs. 2.17, 2.18, and see figs. 2.6 and 2.13). The salary enabled Nomura to buy canvas for the largest paintings of his lifetime production. As the program drew to a close, he received an invitation to the Corcoran Gallery of Art, where *The Farm* was selected for a nationally representative exhibition of the project's artwork and subsequently placed in the Department of Labor.[43] At the same time, *Yesler Way* was included in an exhibition of Washington artists' PWAP work at the Seattle Art Museum. The popular show drew lingering visitors "who left for other exhibits and went back again and again."[44]

Nomura and Tokita closed their sign shop the following year. Nomura and his wife had already moved to Seattle's Central District to run a small grocery, hoping to supplement their income, but that too failed. In the interval Nomura learned the dry-cleaning process from a neighbor, Taro

Nagafuchi, and with his new skill he opened his own shop, Stadium Cleaners.[45] Stadium Cleaners was one of a number of Issei-run dry cleaners in the Wallingford neighborhood, located north of the ship canal that connects Lake Union to Puget Sound.[46] He and Fumiko worked and lived in the same building. They became part of a dispersed but identifiable Nikkei community centered near Green Lake. Their son, George, attended the Green Lake Japanese Language School on Saturdays. Nomura was a "good citizen" of the greater Nikkei community; he joined the Japanese dry-cleaners trade association, made annual contributions to the Community Chest and the Red Cross, as the Japanese Association urged, and kept abreast of the news in *Taihoku Nippō* and the *Seattle Post-Intelligencer*. Gradually the couple gained financial stability, and by the early 1940s they could look ahead to buying a home.[47] They planned to do so in Fumiko's name, for under Washington's Alien Land Law, Nomura, an Issei, was barred from owning real property.[48] Their dream would vanish with the outbreak of war with Japan.

In later years, George remembered his father's pride in his entrepreneurial endeavors as he followed the path his own father had set. While Nomura would remain most closely identified with the sign-painting shop, he subsequently participated in each of the three main business sectors that Issei owner-managers dominated in Seattle: groceries, dry cleaning, and hotel management, which he attempted briefly after the war.[49]

Despite the uncertainties of the late 1930s, Nomura continued to paint. He and Tokita were among the Washington artists, and the only Japanese Americans, to exhibit with the Northwest chapter of the newly formed American Artists' Congress in 1937.[50] He continued to submit new work to the Northwest Annuals. Records, however, trace only a few paintings during the years from the shop's closure until World War II, and of these, only one extant painting, *Renton Bridge* (1938), can be dated with certainty to this time (see fig. M.2). In grayed tones of blue-green and rose, it pictures a flattened, compressed perspective of the Cedar River town. Unknowable at the time, the 1939 Golden Gate International Exposition, "A Pageant of the Pacific," would be Nomura's final honor of this period.

An American Modernist

From the first mention in the *San Francisco Examiner* in 1930, Nomura was identified as a modern, "patently" Western-style painter who successfully combined aspects of Western and Asian art. In the few direct references credited to him, Nomura speaks of his continual effort to progress as a painter, although he gives little hint of specific sources.

Nomura came of age artistically when defining an "American art" independently of European practice was a subject of active discussion. Around the time of World War I, some artists and writers began to view American art as something distinct from its European precedents, with its own sources and history. The argument was part of a larger discussion of the nation's political and cultural history, which would lead to new disciplines of American history and interdisciplinary American studies.[51] Questions of what was American and what was modern were bound inextricably, for, in progressive circles, to be American of one's time *was* to be modern. For some, the modern city, epitomized by New York, and the rapidly changing experience of time and space enabled by new modes of transportation and communication called for abstract forms of expression. For others, the American experience was to be found in the distinctiveness of place. Such artists as Georgia O'Keeffe, Marsden Hartley, Edward Hopper, and Charles Burchfield found their subjects in America's small towns and rural areas.

The idea of a distinctively American art spread throughout the 1920s, but what it looked

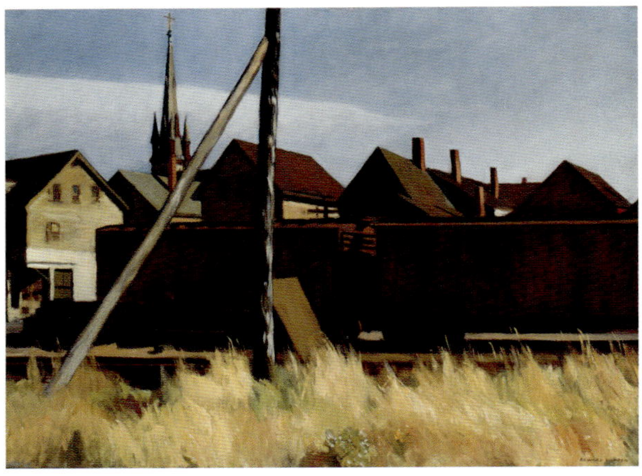

2.19
Edward Hopper, *Freight Cars, Gloucester*, 1928
Oil on canvas, 29 × 40⅛ in.
Addison Gallery of American Art, Phillips Academy, Andover, Massachusetts, gift of Edward Wales Root in recognition of the 25th Anniversary of the Addison Gallery, 1956.7 © 2020 Heirs of Josephine N. Hopper/Licensed by Artists Rights Society (ARS), NY

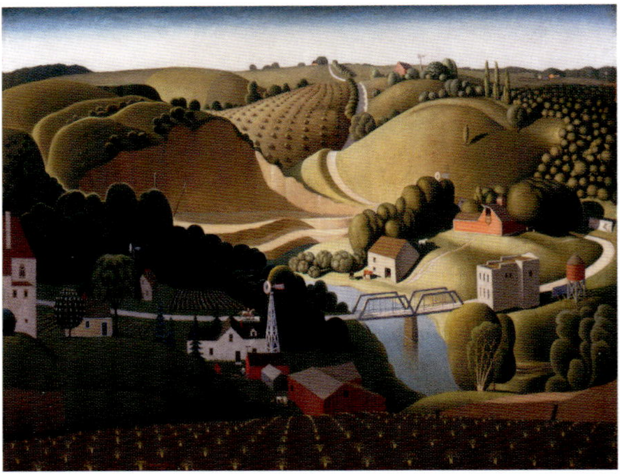

2.20
Grant Wood, *Stone City, Iowa*, 1930
Oil on wood panel, 30¼ × 40 in.
Joslyn Art Museum, gift of the Art Institute of Omaha, 1930.35. © 2020 Figge Art Museum, successors to the Estate of Nan Wood Graham/Licensed by VAGA at Artists Rights Society (ARS), NY

Wood's painting was illustrated in *Creative Art*, June 1932.

like remained a matter of frequent discussion found in art magazines and led by the eastern intelligentsia. As exemplified by Hopper and Burchfield, place could be represented by a "middle course" that was attentive to contemporary subject matter but retained naturalistic form, the "beauty in the everyday" (fig. 2.19). The simultaneous rise to national acclaim of Grant Wood, Thomas Hart Benton, and John Steuart Curry at the end of the decade and their emphasis on their midwestern roots and local culture brought their more literal regionalist style to widespread popularity (fig. 2.20). Such an approach was reinforced by Depression-era federal art programs to become the dominant mode of the 1930s.

Callahan continually made the case for "the painters who have attempted to see the Northwest as it really is, and not as California, the Mediterranean, or Paris." Artists' close contact with their environment, he asserted, "results in better work." He named "the two Japanese—Nomura with his 'Barn' and Tokita with his 'Drugstore' and 'Bridge,' all excellent paintings with definite relationship to this region and to the painters as individuals. They capture much of the real mood of the country, the earthy, vigorous, and low-toned character found here."[52]

For artists everywhere far from art centers, reproductions in magazines were an important source of information. A still life painting by Nomura, of which only a photograph remains, offers intriguing clues to Nomura's concerns (fig. 2.21). In tilted and flattened perspective, a guitar and apples on a patterned tablecloth speak clearly of French modernism in the lineage of Paul Cézanne and Pablo Picasso, and on the table is a February 1931 issue of the American magazine *Creative Art*. Published from 1927 to 1933, *Creative Art* was a liberally illustrated magazine covering a spectrum of visual arts, from painting and sculpture to architecture, "applied arts," stage design, and photography. Its cover and numerous articles on architecture and design display the patterned, streamline aesthetic of art deco. It frequently featured American artists considered to be on the forefront, giving them voice and visibility. Nomura could have learned a great deal from these and other magazine illustrations; his *Red Barns*, more than any other of his paintings, displays art deco's distinctive patterning (see fig. 2.11). Discussions

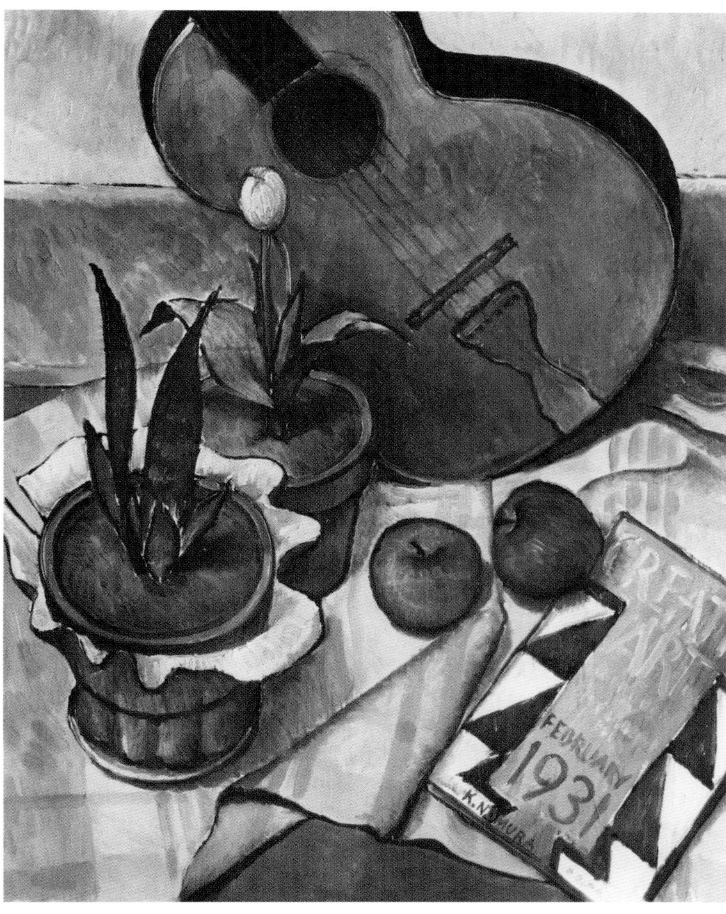

2.21
Still life, ca. 1931
Photographic reproduction
Location unknown; photograph Nomura Estate

about the intent, content, and style of American art appeared regularly in the magazines, together with reproductions of work by American painters to which his work shows closest affinity. One of the most widely exhibited and published artists of the time, Charles Burchfield, wrote in *Creative Art* that his own knowledge of art was largely limited to reproductions. Callahan would write of their importance to Seattle artists.[53]

Nomura's interest in Cézanne is evident in the still life painting and cited by Callahan in his review of Nomura's 1933 solo exhibition. It was an interest he shared with Tokita, his business partner and studio mate since the mid-1920s. Hints of their discussions can be found in Tokita's personal papers, which contain reproductions of historic and contemporary European, American, and Japanese painting, and the book *Modern French Painters,* published in 1923 and inscribed by Tokita in 1924. In the heavily annotated chapter on Cézanne, Tokita underlined the author Jan Gordon's statement that contemporary artists are "trying to free the eye from the prejudices imposed upon it" in favor of a new pictorial expression. Tokita bracketed a paragraph in which Gordon names Cézanne as the first to completely discard the picturesque; the author then describes the process of looking at a Cézanne landscape to understand its color harmony, rhythmic line, and spatial divisions and the relationships of forms that suggest spatial depth.[54] These qualities, although not Cézanne's method, could also describe Nomura's mature style of the 1930s. He and Tokita were serious students of historical and contemporary art as they sought to deepen their own practice. The younger artist George Tsutakawa recalled stopping by the Noto Sign Company to listen to their discussions: "I used to drop by after school or weekends, and those guys were always working, seven days a week. . . . [T]here were several young Japanese art students, as well as Chinese art students. . . . We'd sit there and talk about art. [Nomura and Tokita] were already very much in the art, and they were very knowledgeable. They had studied European art, American painting, and they were doing some very fine work." "They were very, very sincere," he emphasized, "very intent and hard working."[55]

Japanese and American

In 1935 Nomura was invited to join the newly formed Group of Twelve, organized by Callahan together with the University of Washington art professor Ambrose Patterson. The Group of Twelve, Callahan reported, aimed to represent "the best" painting in the region.[56] Of the twelve, three were Japanese American—Nomura, Tokita, and Fujii—and three were women; seven of the twelve were foreign-born.[57] The group functioned as an artists' cooperative, with members expected to help mount rotating exhibitions at the Penthouse Art Gallery atop Textile Tower at Seventh Avenue and Olive Way. Callahan energetically sought members' representation in the group's several exhibitions at the Tacoma Art Association (the predecessor of the Tacoma Art Museum) and the Seattle Art Museum, one of which traveled to Mills College in Oakland.[58] Its most enduring project was the publication of a small catalogue in 1937, *Some Work of the Group of Twelve*, which represents each of the twelve artists with the reproduction of a painting, a brief biography, and an artist's statement. It is one of the few documented statements of intent by Nomura, and the only ones by Tokita and Fujii. Nomura's reads:

> My desire in painting is to avoid the conventional art rules, so that I can be free to paint and approach Nature creatively. I have gradually and almost unconsciously been influenced by the work of early Japanese painters. Now realizing this influence, I am consciously trying to utilize those qualities that I want, such as color, line and simplicity of conception, in my own style of painting.
>
> Due to the great difference between the Western style of painting and the Japanese, the problem is a very difficult one, but I am devoting every effort to achieve this.[59]

The synthesis of artistic traditions that Nomura sought shares in a decades-long search by artists in the West and Japan as they aspired to a universal, modernist means of expression.[60] Drawing upon Western and Japanese sources, Nomura asserts his agency as an artist, "trying to utilize those qualities that I want . . . in my own style of painting." The characteristics of Japanese art that he names are abstract qualities, rather than a style. His artistic decisions are a matter of study, choice, and intention in the pursuit of deepening his means of creative expression.

Callahan and other reviewers emphasized the "occidental" character of Nomura's paintings as they tried to reconcile Nomura's American realist painting with his ethnicity. The same held true for Tokita and Fujii, who were typically named together with Nomura as "the Japanese." Critiques of their work shifted from a denial of any trace of Japanese influence, to a supposed identification of "racial" heritage visible in their work, and to the discernment of qualities such as line and color that reflect Japanese aesthetics. The question was unspoken, however, whether the presumed Japanese influence was determined by ancestry or represented a deliberate artistic choice. In reviewing Nomura's solo exhibition, Callahan is careful to point out that the artist's interest in Cézanne is "only in a technical sense," that is, it is incorporated into his paintings in an original rather than a mimetic way. At the same time, he declares that Nomura's "ancestry can be seen" in his use of line.[61] Lloyd Rollins, the juror of the 1933 Northwest Annual and the former director of San Francisco's California Palace of the Legion of Honor, is more bluntly deterministic in praising Nomura and Tokita for having "adapted themselves to the occidental world, yet maintained a definite racial quality."[62] Assertions of this kind were part of the period's understanding of "race," which encompassed varying definitions of difference, including nationality, ethnicity, or religion, and, with it, native intellectual and physical capacities. Callahan, while reflective of his time, seems genuinely to have tried to discern common aesthetic qualities in the three artists' work while, in doing so, he asserted their individuality.

To what extent Nomura's statement that he had "gradually and almost unconsciously been influenced by the work of early Japanese painters" is the result of his own study or reflects his accommodation of the mainstream view of his work, we cannot know. His statement makes clear, however,

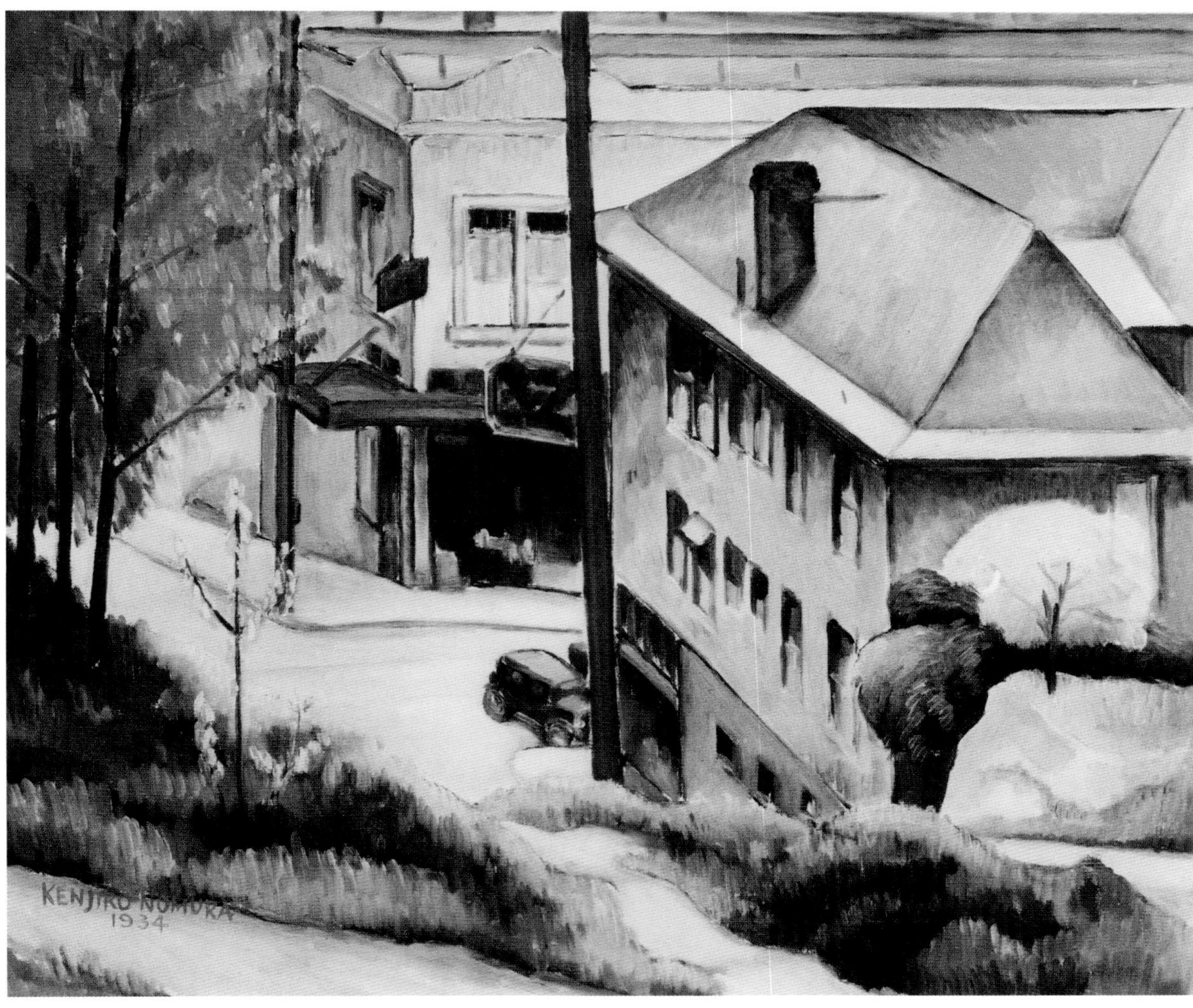

2.22
Street, 1934
Illustrated in *Some Work of the Group of Twelve* (Seattle: Dogwood Press, 1937)
Location unknown

that far from an artist whose practice was determined by his ethnicity, he was an inquiring, knowledgeable, and generative artist who transformed the places he knew into memorable works of art.

The painting illustrated in the Group of Twelve catalogue reinforces his statement (fig. 2.22). Titled *Street*, signed and dated 1934 and known today only in reproduction, it presents a strongly conceived and intimate view of Nihonmachi. A well-worn path leads from the foreground steeply downhill to a street corner of shops, their signs hanging over the sidewalk, where the dark accent of a utility pole anchors and draws one's attention to the corner. Activity is not visible but is implied in the details of the shop entry, the parked cars, and the curtained windows upstairs. The painting pictures a place of familiarity: a Japanese American community located in Seattle's hilly terrain; a community proud of its rich Japanese heritage and determinedly embracing opportunity in America and, in the process, creating a richly blended immigrant-American culture. The vision and strength of Nomura's work contributed significantly to the vibrancy and artistic leadership of Seattle's Japanese American community. Embraced by the mainstream as well as the Nikkei cultural community, his artwork brought credit to and helped substantiate the young region's artistic standing.

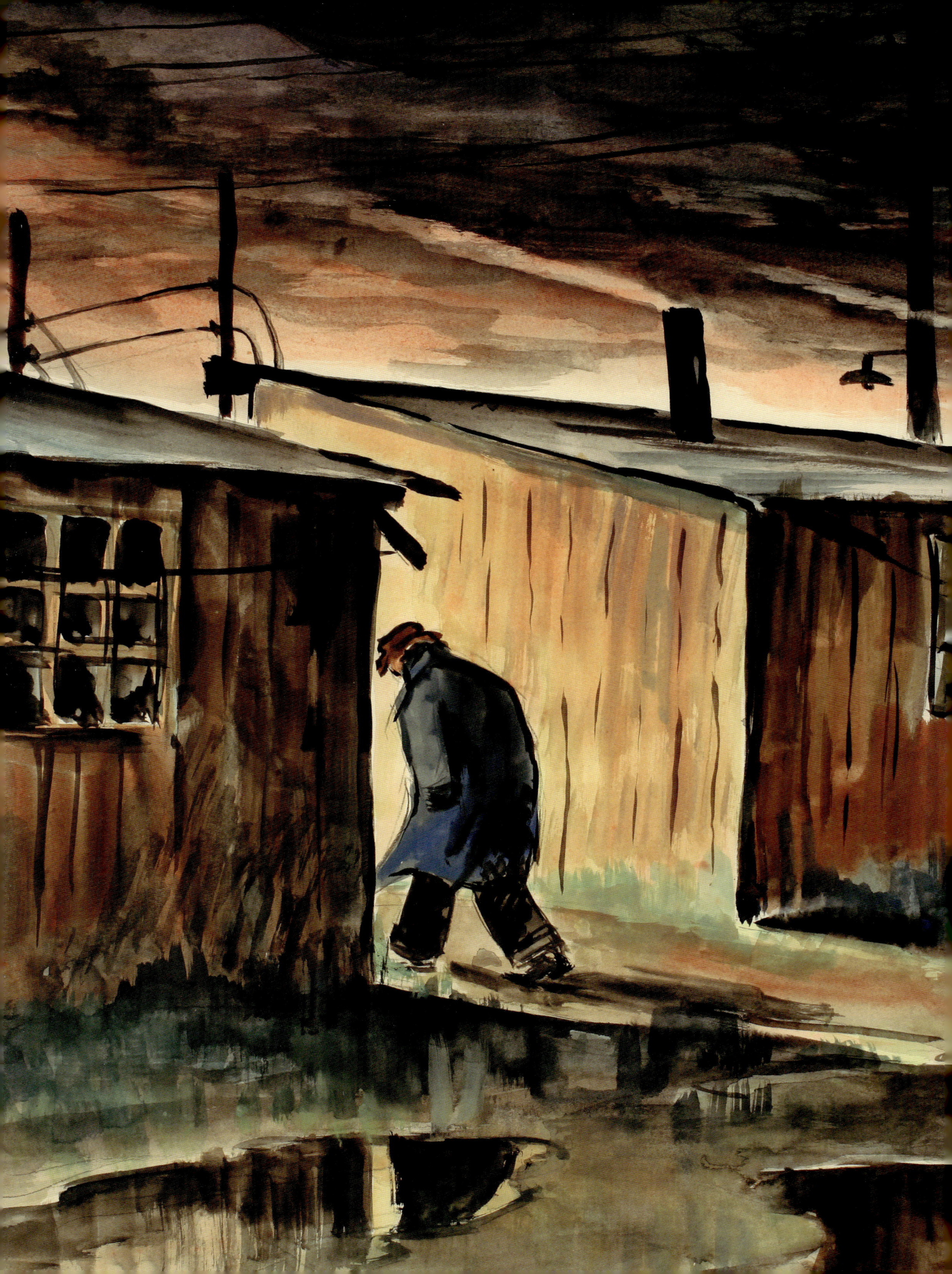

3.

THE WARTIME PRISONER

Tensions were mounting between the United States and Japan when Nomura's paintings were on display at the Golden Gate International Exposition in 1939. As much as Nomura, Tokita, and Fujii had enjoyed visiting the Callahans' home, they no longer did so. "We see Mr. Nomura occasionally, but the group has stopped calling socially," Margaret Callahan commented. "As the world's crisis grows, they seem to grow more guarded, more remote."[1] Once more, in 1940, Kenneth Callahan selected work by Nomura and three Issei colleagues for an exhibition of Northwest paintings at the Seattle Art Museum.[2] Fujii alone among them exhibited in the Northwest Annuals in 1940 and 1941.

Japan's attack on Pearl Harbor on December 7, 1941, brought abrupt and irrevocable change to the ethnic Japanese on the West Coast. "My heart is full to bursting," Tokita wrote in a diary he began that day. "In a moment, we have lost all the value of our existence in this society. Not only have we lost our value, we're unwanted. It would be better if we didn't exist."[3] That night, even before the United States' declaration of war, the Federal Bureau of Investigation (FBI) began arresting Issei community leaders: officers of the Japanese Association and the Japanese Chamber of Commerce, newspapers publishers, Japanese language school teachers, Buddhist priests, merchants who imported goods from Japan, anyone construed as having close connections to Japan. Governmental surveillance of the Nikkei community had begun as early as the 1920s and in 1939 tightened with the coordination of FBI and military intelligence activities, enabling the immediate arrests when war came.[4]

Barracks, 1942
Detail of Fig. 3.10

Regulations imposed on the Nikkei changed day to day. Bank accounts were frozen and then reopened, the FBI searched homes, cameras and shortwave radios were banned, Issei were registered as "enemy aliens," and in coming weeks, curfew and travel restrictions were imposed. Many businesses lost customers immediately; others like Nomura's dry-cleaning shop experienced little initial change.[5] While Nomura belonged to the Japanese dry-cleaners trade association, he was not a leader and not subject to early arrest and separation from his family.[6] Most oppressive was the fear and uncertainty. Increasingly it appeared that some measure would be taken to isolate the Issei, who were barred by federal law from naturalized citizenship and remained subjects of Japan.

Amid the political climate of escalating anti-Japanese racism, wartime propaganda, and

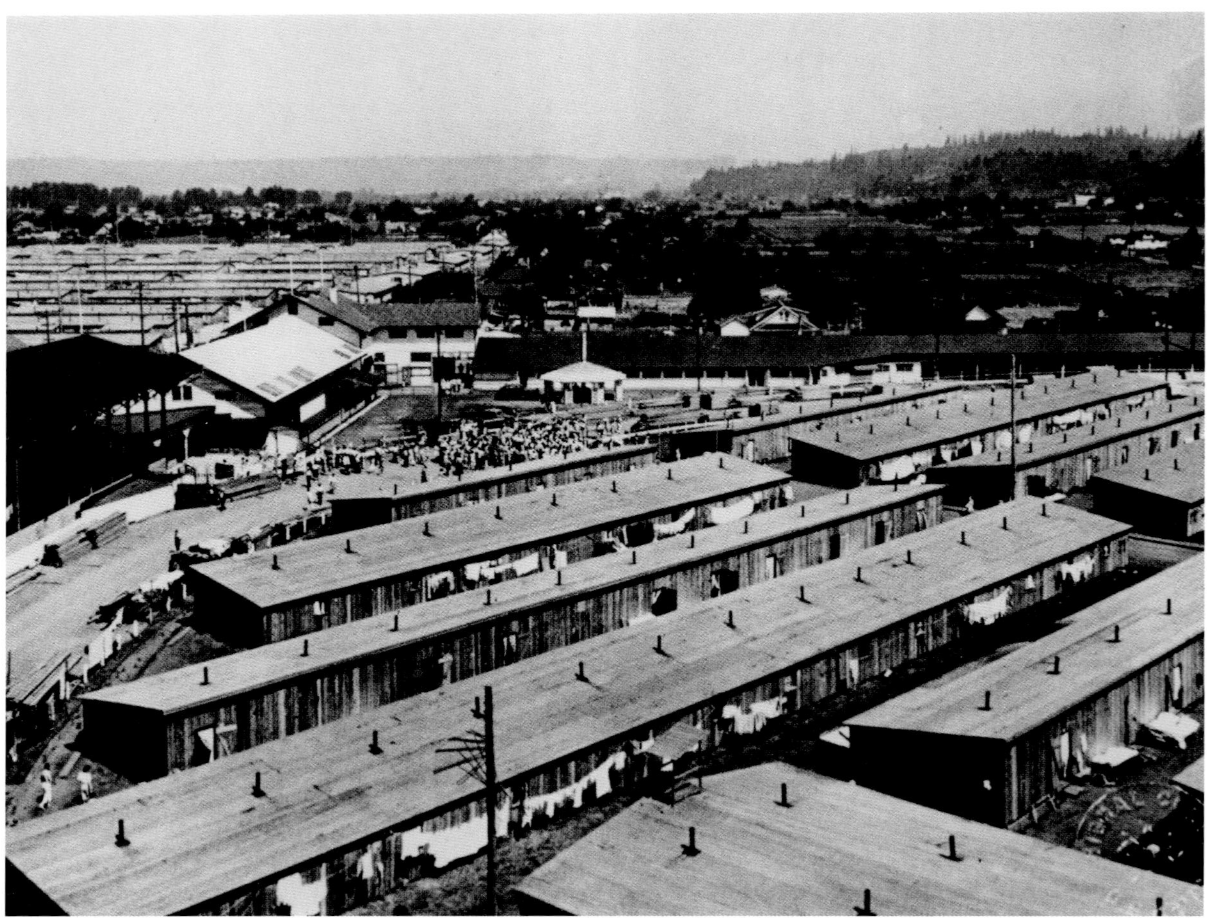

3.1
Puyallup Assembly Center, Washington, 1942. Denshō, https://encyclopedia.densho.org/sources/en-denshopd-i217-00021-1/, courtesy of Library of Congress Prints and Photographs Division

successive Japanese military victories in the Pacific, President Franklin D. Roosevelt signed Executive Order 9066 on February 19, 1942. The order authorized the army to establish military defense zones from which any persons could be excluded as deemed necessary. It targeted but did not name people of Japanese ancestry on the West Coast. For two months the advisability and constitutionality of such a measure had been intensely debated among the U.S. attorney general's office and top-ranking army officers, namely, Judge Advocate General Allen W. Gullion, his assistant Karl Bendetsen, and Western Defense commander Lieutenant General John L. DeWitt, until step-by-step the Department of Justice gave way to the military exclusionists.[7] When the army orders for the forced removal began a month later, they included "all persons of Japanese ancestry, aliens and non-aliens." "Non-aliens" masked the fact that two-thirds of the targeted persons were second- and third-generation, American citizens by birthright. Nomura registered his family with army authorities as required. He, Fumiko, and their twelve-year-old son, George, became known as numbers 10961A, B, and C for the duration of the war.

The first exclusion orders were issued on March 24 for Nikkei on Bainbridge Island, across Puget Sound from Seattle. Subsequent orders were issued by district throughout a West Coast exclusion zone that included the western halves of Washington and Oregon, all of California, and southern Arizona. Tokita wrote in his diary as he absorbed the news, "Relocation means that we have to throw away virtually everything we have worked for. We won't be able to earn a penny once we move. There will be no way to find a job either. Everywhere we go, Japanese are boycotted." He added days later, "Stores owned by Japanese have started desperately selling goods at give-away prices."[8] Orders were posted in Nomura's neighborhood on April 24 with instructions to report on May 1, bringing only the possessions each person could carry. Nomura, deeply upset, lit the burn barrel behind his shop and began to burn his paintings.[9] Their sympathetic landlord, John Morrison, agreed to store Nomura's personal belongings and what paintings remained and sell his dry-cleaning equipment. Although Nomura told him to keep the proceeds in exchange, Morrison personally delivered the money to him a few weeks later.[10]

Puyallup Assembly Center

Nomura and his family boarded a bus at Twenty-Second Avenue and East Madison Street in a caravan bound for Puyallup, thirty miles south of Seattle, where a temporary confinement site was hastily constructed on the Washington State Fairgrounds (fig. 3.1). The orders for mass removal had been issued so quickly that the government had no means of housing and caring for well over one hundred thousand people on a long-term basis.[11] Temporary detention camps were built on fairgrounds and racetracks, which were near urban population centers and provided acres of flat land and a modicum of infrastructure. Built under army orders in seventeen days and spread over the fairgrounds and adjacent parking lots, the Puyallup camp was divided into four sections by city streets, each part surrounded by a double row of barbed-wire fence.[12] Long rows of single-room barracks were built directly on newly scraped ground. From April 28 to May 16, seven thousand Nikkei from Seattle, parts of Pierce County, and Alaska climbed off buses and were herded into camp.[13]

The sight of barbed-wire fences and guard towers made real the fact of imprisonment (fig. 3.2). "What was I doing behind a fence like a criminal?" asked Monica Sone, a Nisei. "If there were accusations to be made, why hadn't I been given a fair trial? . . . Of one thing I was sure. The wire fence was real. I no longer had the right to walk out of it. It was because I had Japanese ancestors."[14] The army veiled the transgression in terms usually applied to rescue operations: the mass forced removal was "evacuation"; temporary detention sites were "assembly centers," and from there, Nikkei were to be resettled in "relocation centers." As a government brochure explained in 1942, an assembly center was "a convenient gathering point within the military area, where evacuees live temporarily while awaiting the opportunity for orderly, planned movement to a Relocation Center." The relocation center, it further explained, was "a pioneer community, with basic housing and protective services provided by the Federal Government."[15] Compounding the euphemisms, army publicists named Puyallup "Camp Harmony."

Nomura and his family were assigned to Area A, which held two thousand people. It was built on a parking lot across the street from the fairgrounds where the grandstand and exhibition halls stood. Two guard towers surveilled the area, and a machine gun pointed inward from the back side. Each family was assigned a single-room barrack, or "apartment," bare except for metal-frame cots and a wood-burning stove. From a distance, the barracks appeared to some like chicken coops; Fujii called his a "cattle stall."[16] Mess halls, latrines, showers, and laundry were communal. People stood in long lines for meals and basic needs, made all the more miserable by an exceptionally cold, wet spring (fig. 3.3). Crowded conditions and poor construction produced constant noise, chronic sanitation problems, and a profound loss of privacy. Communal life also put added pressure on the family. Deprived of homes and livelihood, fathers and mothers no longer provided for their family, and families no longer had the physical and

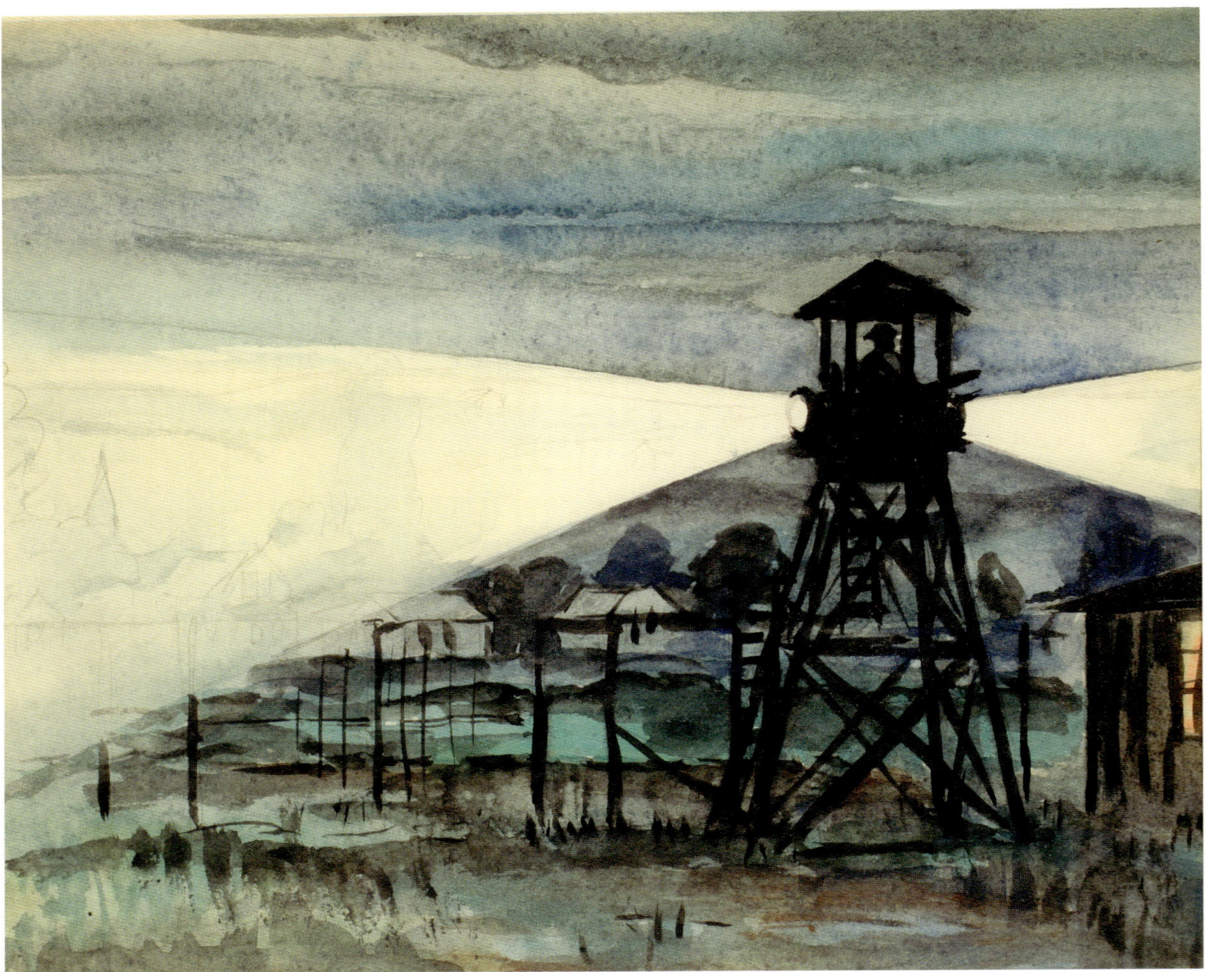

3.2
Guard Tower at Night, 1942
Watercolor and ink(?) on paper, 7¼ × 9½ in.
Tacoma Art Museum, George and Betty Nomura Collection, 2013.7.21

emotional center of the home. A Nisei woman remembered of her brother, "The family no longer had as great an influence on him as friends, because you no longer ate at home.... [A]ll you did was go back home to sleep."[17]

Generational difference played out in significant other ways as a result of wartime conditions. In the immediate aftermath of Pearl Harbor, leaders of the Japanese American Citizens League (JACL), a Nisei organization, had vigorously asserted their loyalty as American citizens. As plans for mass exclusion became a reality, the leader of the Seattle chapter, James Sakamoto, a co-founder of the JACL and the publisher of the *Japanese American Courier*, followed the national league's mandate in pledging cooperation with the government to demonstrate their loyalty. The Wartime Civil Control Administration (WCCA), the army agency charged with managing the removal and temporary confinement, pushed forward the Nisei to serve as intermediaries to the Nikkei community, of whom they had little knowledge.[18] A select group of JACL members under Sakamoto's leadership were sent in advance to Puyallup to prepare for the arrival of seven thousand people. While the WCCA supervised and surveilled the camp, the young adult Nisei administered and policed daily internal affairs.[19] They walked a narrow line carrying out the army's mandates and proving their loyalty to fellow Nikkei. For the Issei, whose customary community and familial authority had already been shaken by the loss of community leaders and further

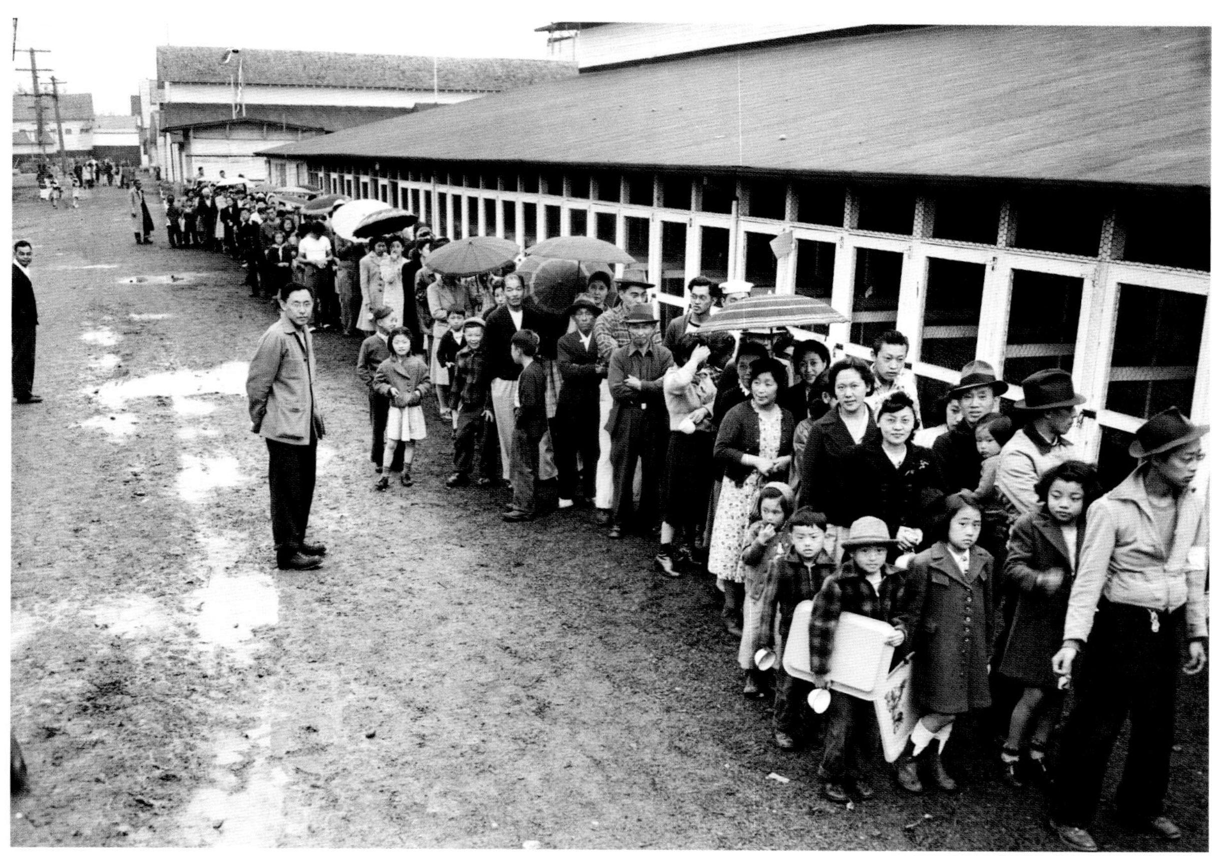

3.3
Incarcerees lined up in the rain at Camp Harmony, Puyallup, 1942
Seattle Post-Intelligencer Collection, Museum of History and Industry, Seattle, 1986.5.6681.3

undermined by the deprivation of home and livelihood, coming under the supervision of Nisei was yet another blow. Tensions would persist between generations, and between factions within generations, under the conditions of mass incarceration. The relationships were complex, varying with an individual's age, immigration history, family background, education, and urban or rural experience, and they changed with shifting conditions within the camps, the changing status of the war, and individual perceptions of the war's outcome.[20] Nomura depicts generational interaction in images of Puyallup that describe the shared communal life rather than divisive tension.[21]

Nomura joined a work crew as a sign painter, although there is scant record about his assignment. A WCCA memo reads simply, "Called sign-painter—no response."[22] His own paintings and drawings comprise a larger record of his experience of Puyallup. His attention to signage is represented in several paintings—in garbage can labels and "street" signs in the corridors between barracks. One sign reads "Sec. B," indicating he had permission to move from one area of the camp to another.[23]

Picturing His Experience

At Puyallup Nomura began what would become an extended visual record, his only extant personal record of this tumultuous time. He was among many of both generations who sought to give expression to the experience of incarceration. Because cameras were banned, art was a means to document experience and to express deep emotion.[24] Some were established artists; many were novices. Nomura's colleagues Tokita and Fujii were among the number who turned also to diaries and poetry.[25]

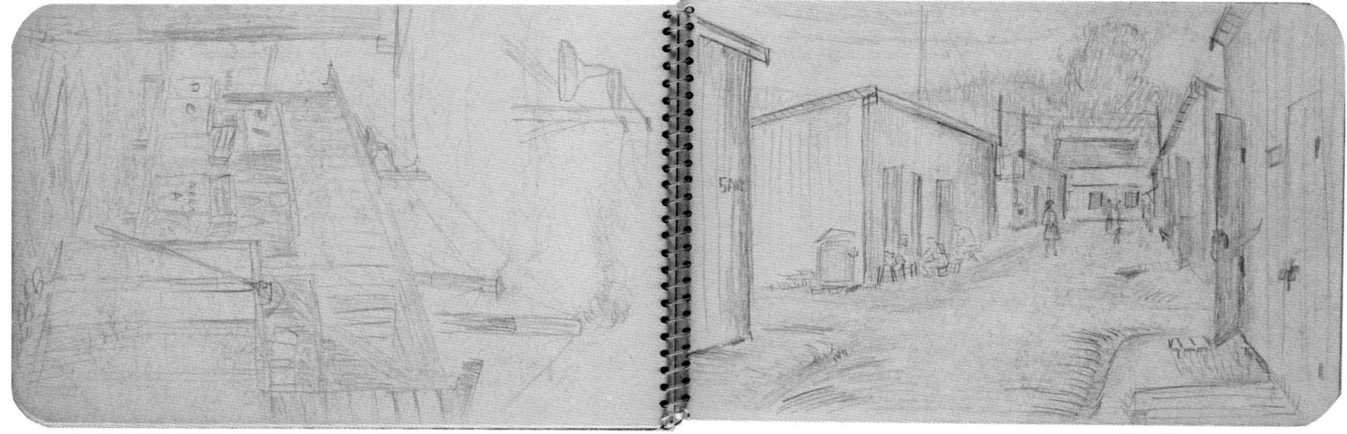

3.4
Bound sketchbook (Puyallup), 1942
Graphite on paper, 2 pages, each $4\frac{7}{8} \times 7\frac{3}{4}$ in.
Tacoma Art Museum, George and Betty Nomura Collection, 2013.24.2 A-CC

Art became an important organized program at Puyallup and all other camps, one of many activities designed to lift morale and fill the unstructured time. The largest and most prominent art programs were schools organized by Chiura Obata at the Tanforan Assembly Center south of San Francisco and by Obata and George Matsusaburo Hibi at the Topaz WRA center in Utah. Obata, a widely recognized Issei artist and a member of the art faculty at the University of California, Berkeley, persuaded army administrators of his purpose, drew upon his university contacts for supplies, and staffed the schools with experienced Nikkei artists and University of California art school graduates. As early as June 1942, artwork produced by inmates at Tanforan was exhibited in several Bay Area venues. Elsewhere, artists with yearslong experience started schools, led art programs, and exhibited their work outside camp.[26] While neither Puyallup nor Minidoka had established art schools, art programs flourished at both sites.

The program at Puyallup was part of the activities office, which was among the functions established by the center's Nisei leaders to manage daily internal affairs. A four-person team of young artists staffed the art department from a single-room office beneath the grandstand. They organized widely attended art and craft exhibitions, made scenery for theatrical productions, planned dances and a Bon Odori, the annual celebration of ancestors, and provided decorations for birthdays and weddings in an effort to personalize these occasions amid the pressures of mass confinement. Ed Tsutakawa felt himself lucky to be chosen as one of the team. Artists in camp were respected, he remembered, and paid at the highest, "professional" rate of nineteen dollars a month.[27] His position enabled him to pass from one area of camp to another and to requisition the finest art supplies for his own use. Given the job of organizing the first art exhibition at Puyallup, he visited Fujii to encourage his participation and surely must have encouraged Nomura as well.[28] There is no record but his artwork to indicate what Nomura might have exhibited.

Nomura's total extant wartime work comprises oil and watercolor paintings, pencil and ink drawings, and two small sketchbooks, altogether nearly one hundred discrete images. The paintings vary in formality, from some that are signed and dated to others that are loosely sketched. The more finished ones are characterized by their well-balanced construction and precise perspective that recall Nomura's formal training. Many of the drawings are preparatory sketches, although not all are realized in paintings.

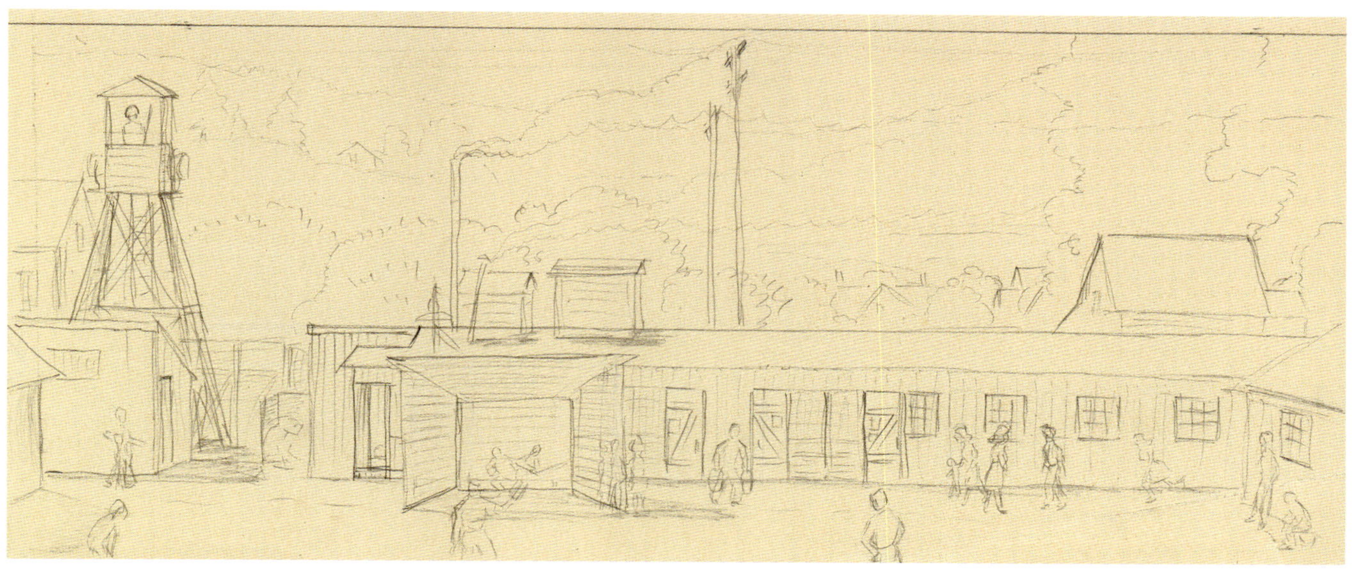

3.5
Untitled (Puyallup guard tower and service buildings), 1942
Pencil on paper, 9⅝ × 24 in., sheet 19 × 24 in.
Nomura Estate

Of his wartime production, nine watercolors and more than a dozen related pencil drawings picture Puyallup. Seven of the paintings are notably uniform: nineteen by twenty-four inches in the horizontal or vertical dimension, each a finished composition that is signed and dated. Figures animate the built landscape of the otherwise stark camp. Nomura's predilection for complementary colors pervades each composition: flashes of red details brighten the dull surroundings, an effect heightened by the green grass that sprouts beneath buildings and the blue-green sky overhead. At first glance, the color is deceptively cheerful, but it cannot dim the reality of incarceration. Granular details such as signage provide the specificity of place one knows from daily experience. Sketches in Nomura's notebook show his compositional development of the landscape and the figurative notation that populates the scenes (fig. 3.4). Despite their small size, the sketches are drawn in detail that adds immediacy to the subject.

Nomura's return to figurative subjects for the first time since his early years as an artist tells of the changed conditions in which he lived, amid crowded temporary buildings in a confined and controlled community (fig. 3.5). It is also a change from the "timelessness" of his landscape paintings that suggests a personal shift, a need to document the gravity and enormity of what he and the imprisoned Nikkei were experiencing. Their lives, particularly those of the Issei, who had struggled and worked to establish a home, would never again be the same; loss and insecurity seemed all that lay ahead. In his Puyallup images, Nomura grounds the figures in their specifically rendered built environment to record their new reality.[29]

Mess Hall (1942) is exemplary (fig. 3.6). The working end of the mess hall, where three women toil, fills the right half of the composition, and on the left, barracks recede out of sight. Garbage cans labeled "A" identify the section in which Nomura lived. A foreground figure directs the view down the corridor filled with people, among them, parents with small children. The milling crowd is a scene of activity with no focused action. What an image such as *Mess Hall* cannot represent is the constant noise produced by thousands of people crowded together. Masako Fujii, the young adult daughter of Takuichi Fujii, wrote in her first week at Puyallup that she had never experienced "such a crowd of Japanese people and so much noise at one time as in this place." "When I first arrived here, I felt as if I just landed in a bee hive crowded with bees with their perpetual buzzing."[30]

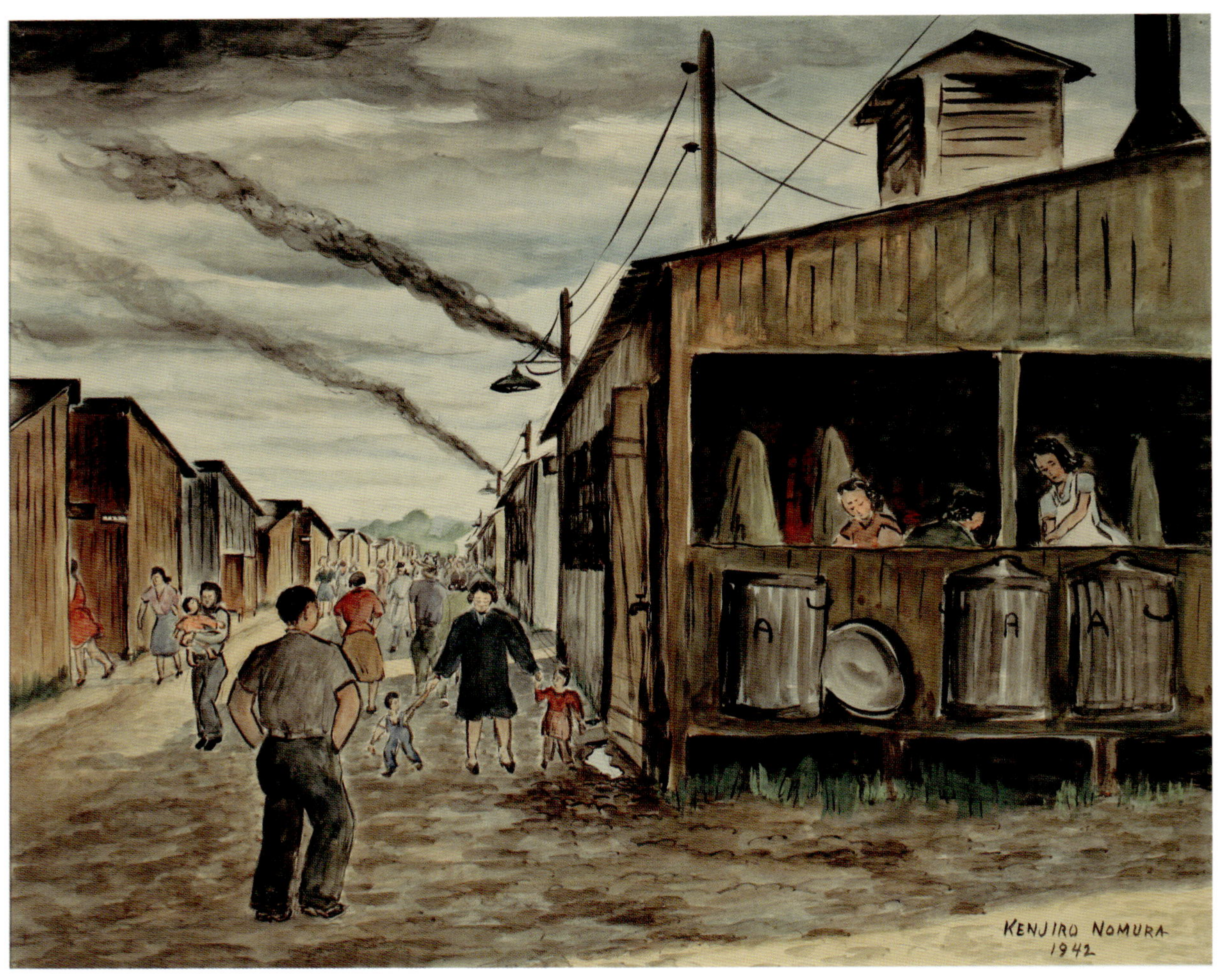

3.6
Mess Hall, 1942
Watercolor on paper, 19 × 24 in.
Tacoma Art Museum, George and Betty Nomura Collection, 2013.7.3

3.7
K-P, 1942
Watercolor on paper, 24 × 19 in.
Tacoma Art Museum, George and Betty Nomura Collection, 2013.7.4

3.8
Barber Shop, 1942
Watercolor on paper, 19 × 24 in.
Tacoma Art Museum, George and Betty Nomura Collection, 2013.7.7

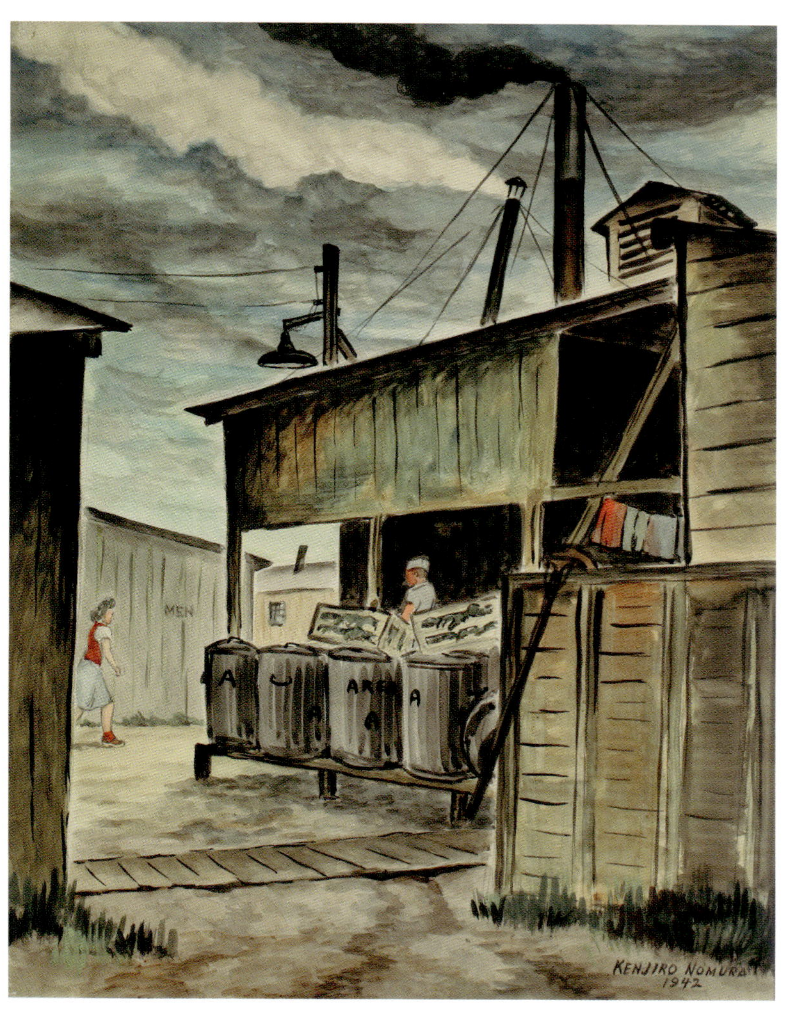
MEN
KENJIRO NOMURA
1942

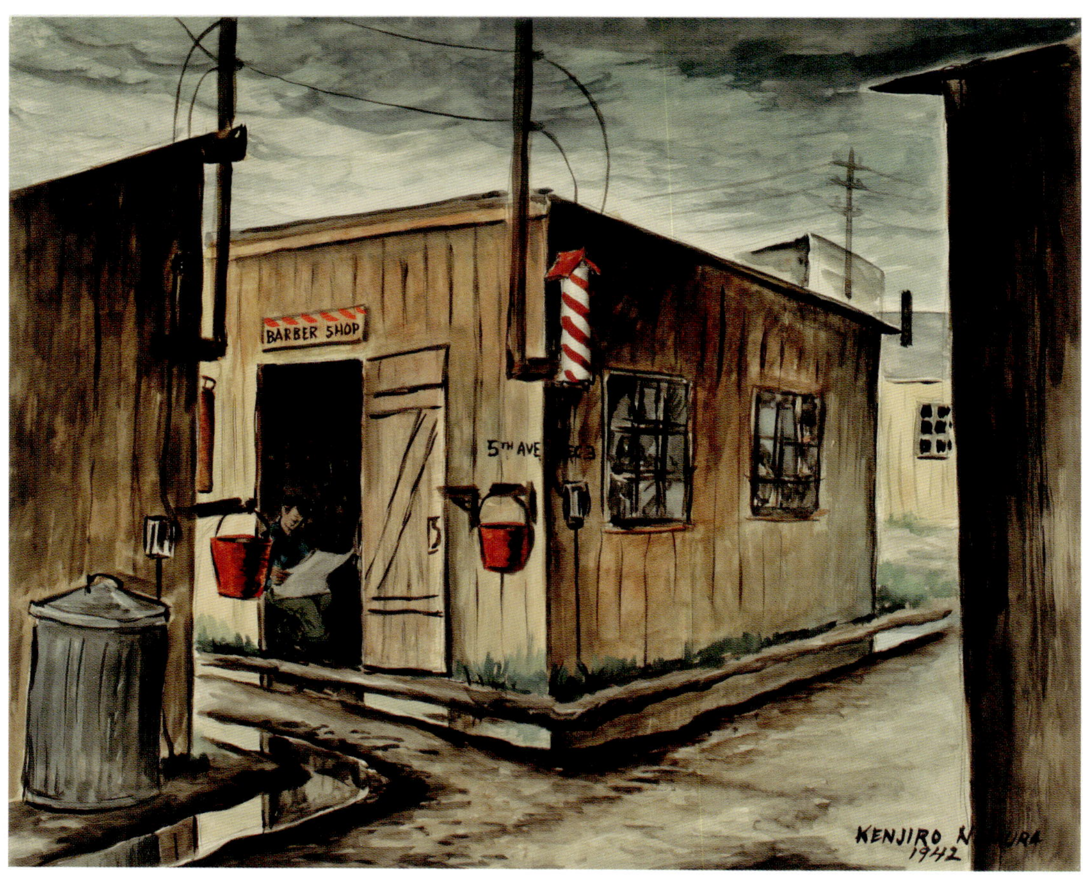
BARBER SHOP
5TH AVE
KENJIRO NOMURA
1942

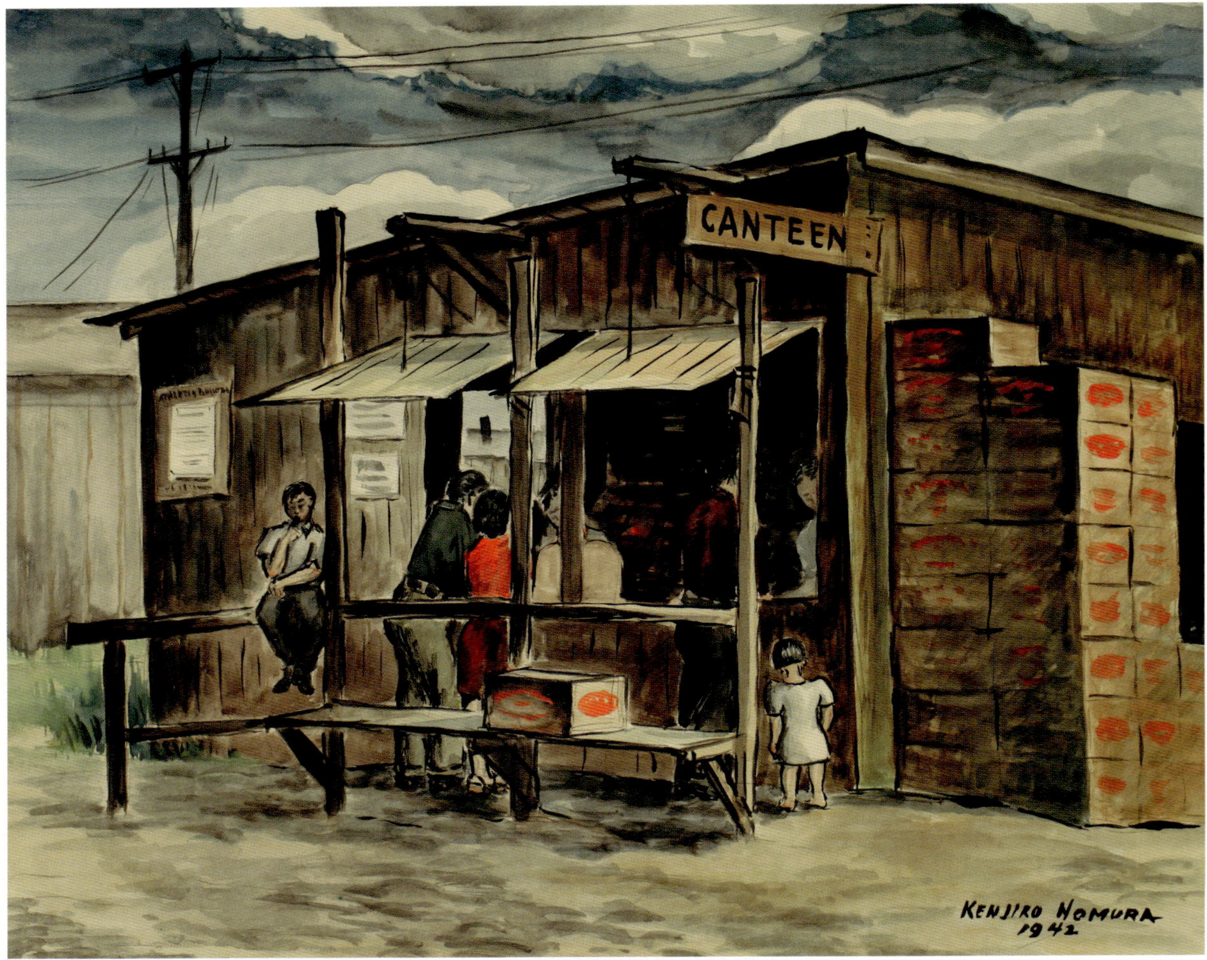

3.9
Canteen, 1942
Watercolor on paper, 19 × 24 in.
Tacoma Art Museum, George and Betty Nomura Collection, 2013.7.5

Together the Puyallup paintings build a selective picture of daily activities. A man in *Barber Shop* reads as he awaits customers, while outside his door, water-filled trenches along the path tell of the "torrential" rain that fell "unceasingly for days at a time" that year (fig. 3.8).[31] *Canteen* pictures a couple and two children lingering at the shop during its few open hours (fig. 3.9). Here Nomura's use of color is especially lively, with the bright red of the woman's dress repeated in the stacked shipping boxes, a scene that belies the spartan supplies available and the frustration of forced leisure. Similarly, *Main Gate* shows clusters of young people standing around the sentry station as they pass the time talking, while a soldier guards the gate, his back to the small gathering (fig. 3.11). Other paintings are unremittingly somber. In *Barracks* a man hunches against the wind as he walks between buildings on a dark, wet day (fig. 3.10). *Guard Tower at Night* is the darkest in content as well as hue (see fig. 3.2). Searchlights blanch everything in their path, and from the tower, a silhouetted soldier stands in surveillance.

The paintings suggest more than they reveal directly. The reality of fences, watchtowers, and machine guns was one of the first and most prominent impressions recorded contemporaneously and by survivors in later years.[32] *Main Gate* depicts young people socializing inside a barbed-wire fence that reaches over their heads. They are not only confined and guarded, as the soldier's presence makes clear, but also restricted in crossing

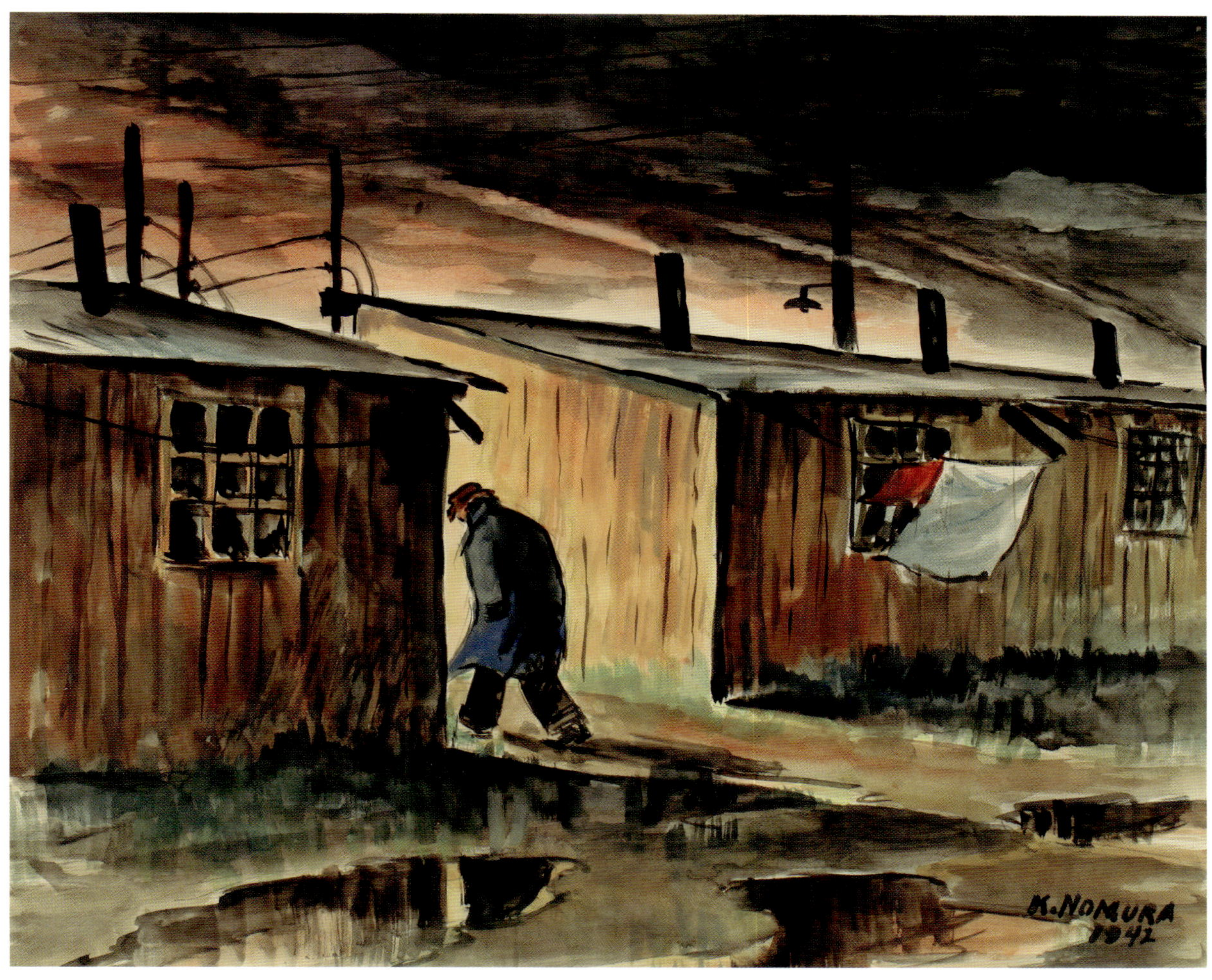

3.10
Barracks, 1942
Watercolor on paper, 19 × 24 in.
Tacoma Art Museum, George and Betty Nomura Collection, 2013.7.8

the street to Area D, which is represented by the large exhibition hall of the fairgrounds. Monica Sone, a Nisei the same age as Masako Fujii, stretches for humor in describing the experience of going to her job in camp: "Area D was just across the street from A, but we required armed chaperones to make the crossing. After the guard inspected our passes and counted noses, the iron gate yawned open for us, and we marched out in orderly formation, escorted fore and aft by military police."[33] Nomura's friend Takuichi Fujii pictures the scene more starkly in his illustrated diary. His drawing of the Area B gate is an unembellished view of an armed sentry marching along the gate in a site otherwise empty of people; the text reads, "This is the front gate. It was strictly guarded" (fig. 3.12). A subsequent entry shows a couple approaching the gate while a guard in dark glasses and holding a club towers over them, and in yet another, "What it looked like when I visited a friend living in Area A," a large cluster of people are dwarfed by the guard and the gate ahead.[34] Nomura, by comparison, presents a view that has become normalized. His image focuses on the dozen figures in variously relaxed postures who are spread across the painting within a sturdy framework of the sentry station, fence, and nearby buildings. Rather than fear or intimidation, the image connotes the passing of unstructured time that weighed heavily on the days in confinement.

The more intimate impact of incarceration is found in a watercolor sketch of a mother sitting with her small child in the gap between the fence

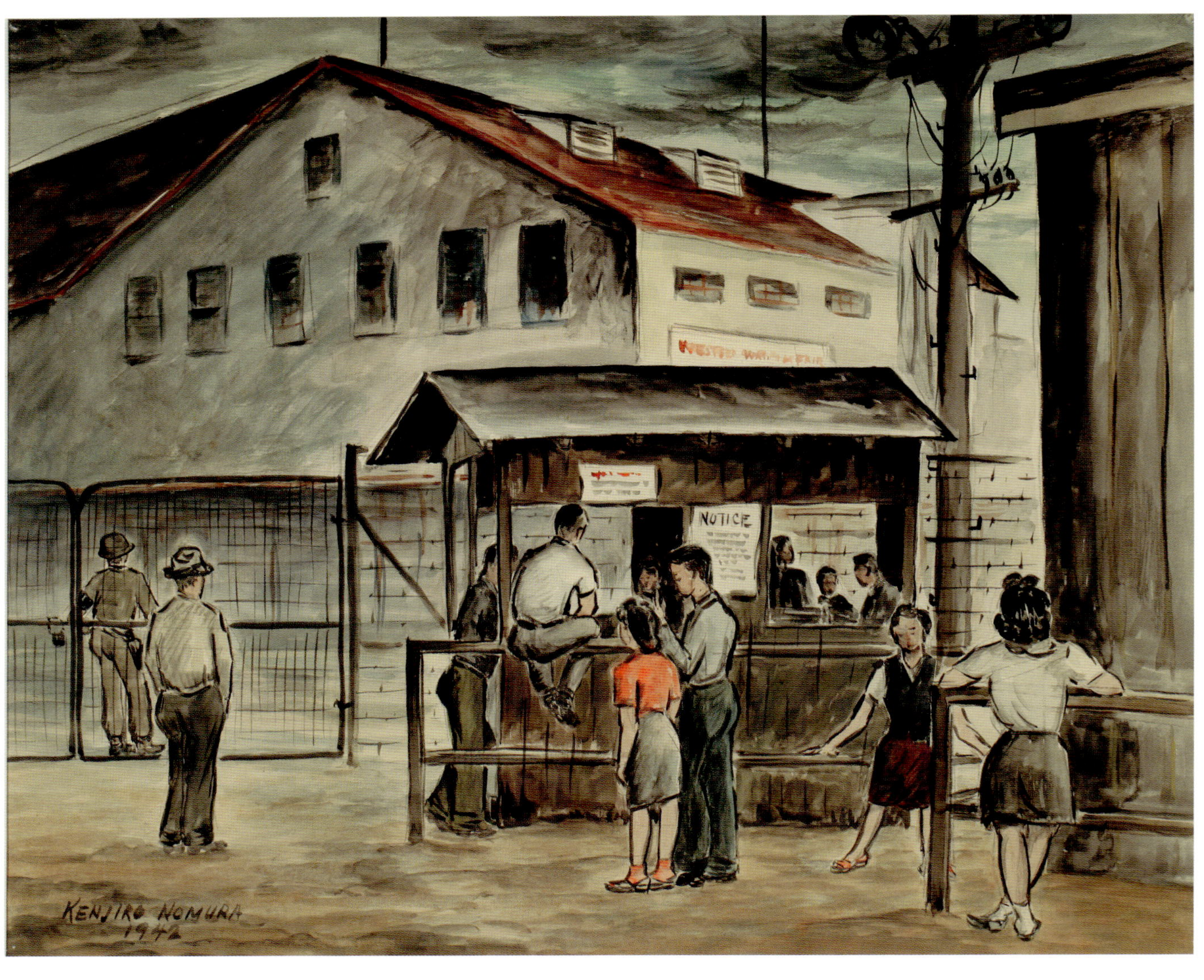

3.11
Main Gate, 1942
Watercolor on paper, 19 × 24 in.
Tacoma Art Museum, George and Betty Nomura Collection, 2013.7.6

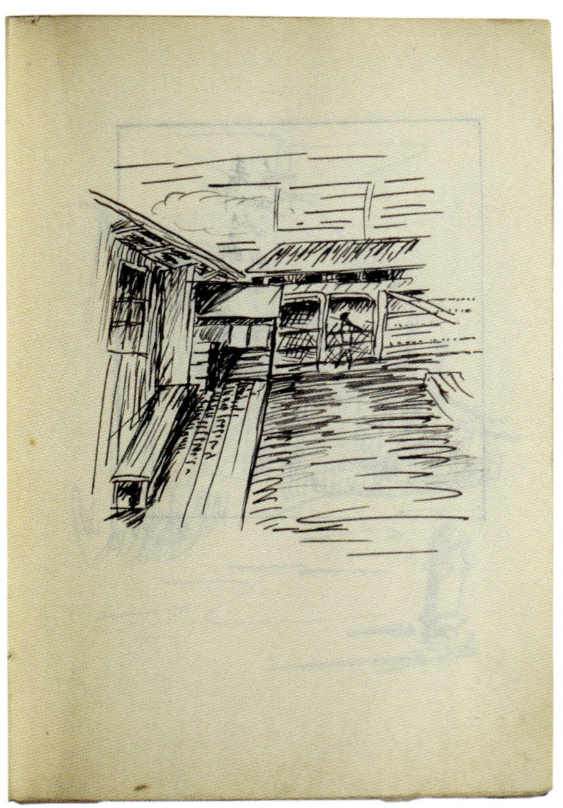

3.12
Takuichi Fujii, diary entry, 1942
Ink on paper, 8 × 5½ in.
Diary, Wing Luke Museum, gift of Ellen Ferguson

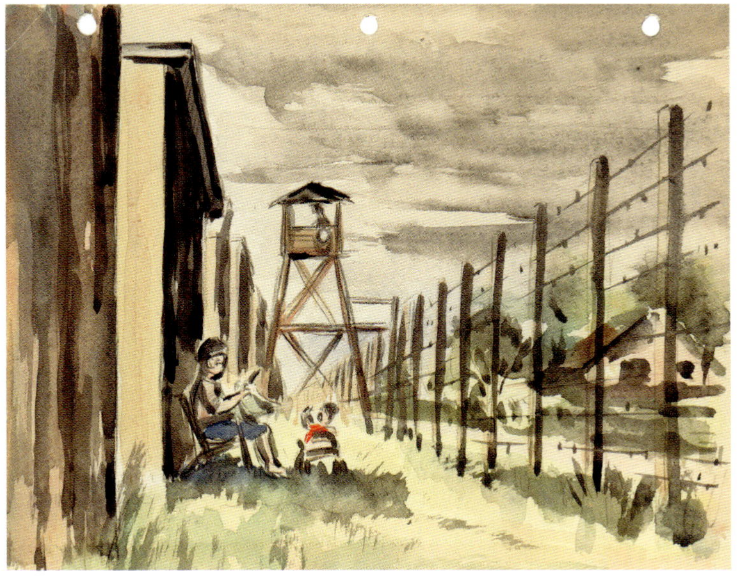

3.13
Untitled (woman and child by fence), 1942
Watercolor on paper, 8½ × 11 in.
Wing Luke Museum, gift of Pamela Waldron

and the barracks, while behind them a sentry in a guard tower surveils the camp (fig. 3.13). Visible through the fence is a house in free territory, a bitter comparison to her situation. Similarly, *Guard Tower at Night* pictures houses beyond the tower and fence, marking the thin but absolute line of authority that demarcates imprisonment and freedom. Sone's words again lend a voice to the image as she describes her first night experiencing the searchlight that Nomura features so prominently: "I was glad Mother had put up a makeshift curtain on the window for I noticed a powerful beam of light sweeping across it every few seconds. The lights came from high towers placed around the camp where guards with Tommy guns kept a twenty-four hour vigil."[35] As weeks passed, the enforced community settled into as much a routine as possible—the camp life that Nomura pictures. Temporary detention sites like Puyallup were the initial shock of incarceration that compelled the Nikkei's adaptation to the conditions of armed control and communal life and braced them for long-term confinement.[36]

One painting by Nomura is distinct from the others as a summary image of Puyallup, a montage of the individual scenes that he sketched and painted. The painting is prominently and precisely labeled, "Camp Harmony / Area A / Puyallup, Wash.," and in the corner above, "W.C.C.A. / Japanese Assembly Center / 1942" (fig. 3.14). The mess hall, canteen, barbershop, barracks, and guard tower are there, as is a bird's-eye view of row upon row of barracks as he would have seen them from the grandstand. The formality of the label together with the summary portrayal raises a question about Nomura's intent. Was it related to his assigned work, or was it a chance to display his skills at an art exhibition in camp? With only the slimmest clues about his job and none about his exhibition activity, we can only speculate about any intent other than the product of his creativity.[37]

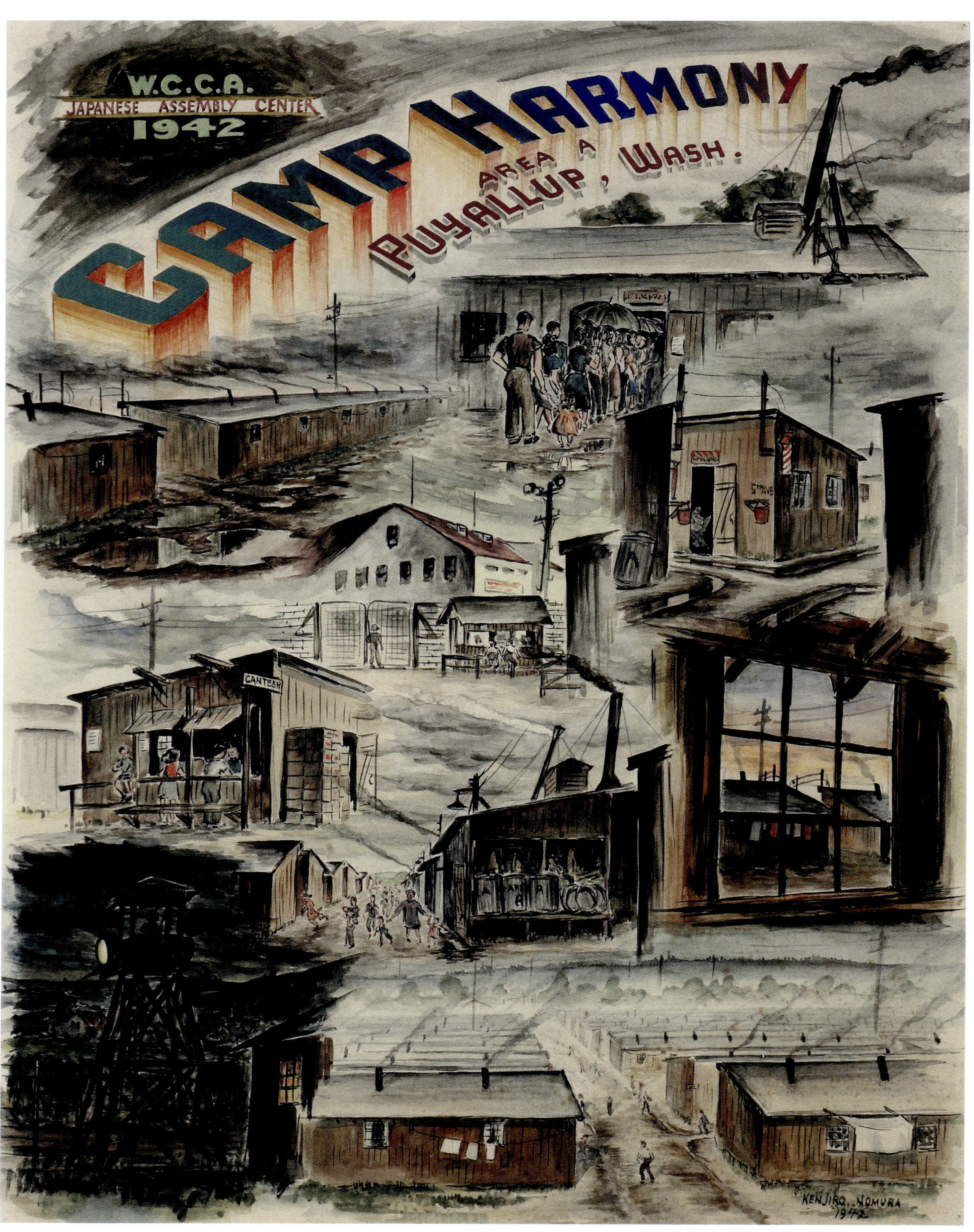
W.C.C.A.
JAPANESE ASSEMBLY CENTER
1942
CAMP HARMONY
AREA A
PUYALLUP, WASH.
CANTEEN
KENJIRO NOMURA
1942

Minidoka Relocation Center

The Nikkei knew from the beginning that their stay at the Puyallup fairgrounds was temporary, but only in early August did they learn that they would be sent to south-central Idaho, where a long-term encampment called the Minidoka Relocation Center was under construction (figs. 3.15 and 3.16). They would be colonists, they were told, making a community in the desert and bringing barren land to productivity. Through the camp newspaper they learned also that housing was still being built, four wells to serve the camp were not yet in operation, and plumbed facilities were only partly usable.[38] An advance group of two hundred Nisei volunteers left on August 9 to help prepare for the mass transfer of inmates from temporary detention sites in Puyallup and Portland. Between August 16 and September 13, trains carrying some five hundred people arrived nearly daily at Minidoka.

Nomura and his family packed once again and on September 2 boarded a train headed eastward. The trains were old, decommissioned ones returned to service; one rider thought hers must have been used "in the Civil War—it was that ancient, dirty, filthy, and rickety-rackety." After a stiflingly hot thirty-hour trip, the train stopped on a newly built spur, "right in the middle of the desert with nothing but sagebrush, no station stop or anything."[39] Nomura was among the passengers who had become ill from fatigue and motion sickness and were taken by ambulances from the train to the camp hospital.[40] All others were transferred under armed guard to buses for the last few miles to Minidoka.

Minidoka was built on 950 acres of high desert, federal reserve land, part of the 35,000-acre Gooding Reclamation District. Ancient volcanic flows had left an irregular and rocky landscape, and through it cut the North Canal of the Snake River. Temperatures in the high desert were extreme, ranging from 110 degrees Fahrenheit to 30 below zero. The Bureau of Reclamation had leased the land to the War Relocation Authority (WRA) with the understanding that it would be cultivated by camp labor. Diverting from the military-style grid of other WRA camps, Minidoka stretched in a three-mile-long arc along the canal, where thirty-seven blocks of barracks lay at angles to accommodate the terrain. Upon completion, it was a "sprawling sagebrush city" of six hundred buildings.[41] Construction of the camp required scraping off the vegetation that held the fine volcanic soil, which was further broken by the constant truck and tractor traffic. Dust storms were frequent, causing dense clouds of dust to rise hundreds of feet in the air and at times so darkening the day that work had to be stopped. Dust penetrated everything, and when rains came in the fall, it turned to mud.

Nomura was assigned to Block 28, Barrack 7-A. He posted a carefully scripted nameplate, "K. Nomura and Family," outside the door (fig. 3.17). Each block consisted of twelve barracks of six single-room living units, or "apartments," minimally constructed with tar-paper exterior and equipped with a coal-burning stove and an electrical outlet but no running water.[42] A recreation hall and a sanitation building with communal showers, laundry, and, eventually, latrines completed the block configuration. Next to Nomura's block stood one of the two water towers that were landmarks of the site, an image he would draw and paint often (fig. 3.18). The canal curved along the south; to the southwest were warehouses and, beyond, the administration area; to the north and east lay fields to be developed for agriculture. Here he would spend the next three years.

The site, as the Nikkei had been told, was still under construction when he and others arrived. Tractors continued to tear up the ground, raising frequent dust storms, and trenches lay open and roads were rutted from the heavy equipment.

3.14
Camp Harmony, 1942
Watercolor on paper, 24 × 19 in.
Tacoma Art Museum, George and Betty Nomura Collection, 2013.7.2

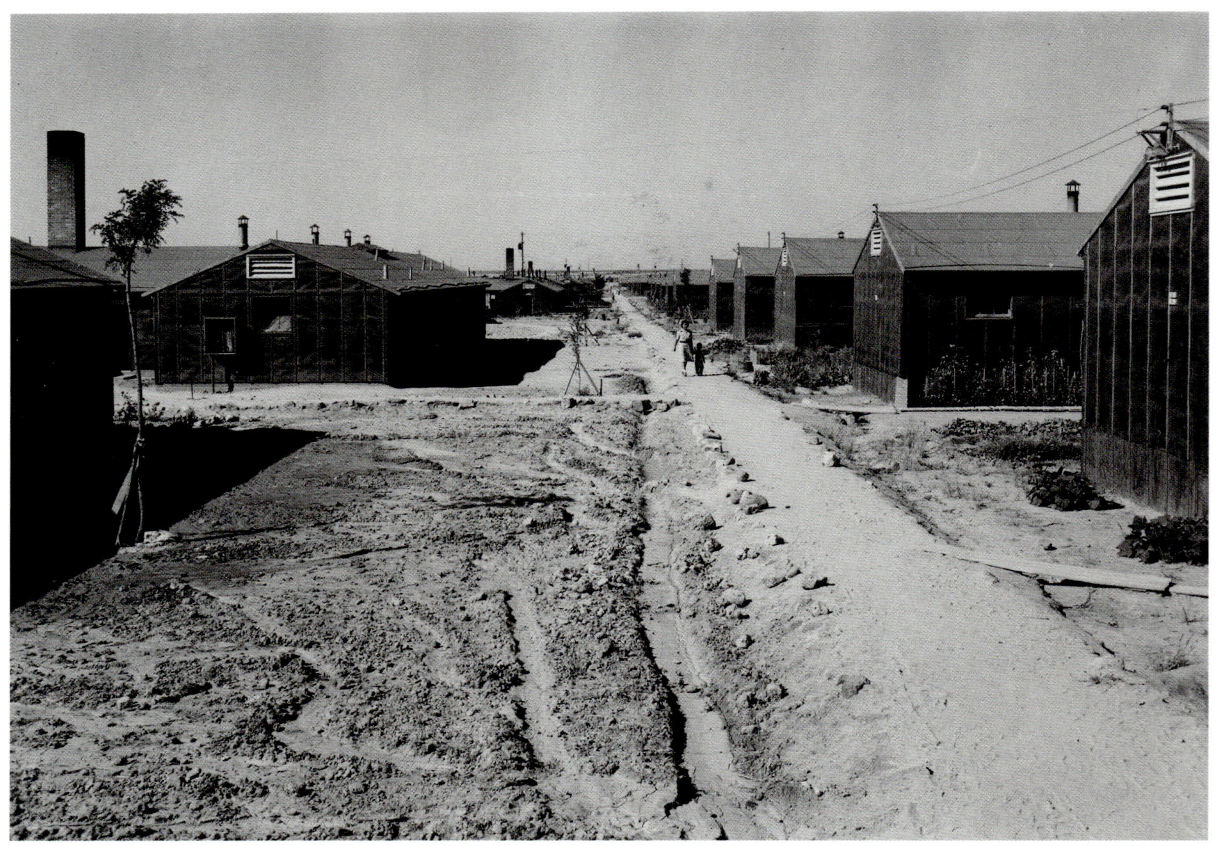

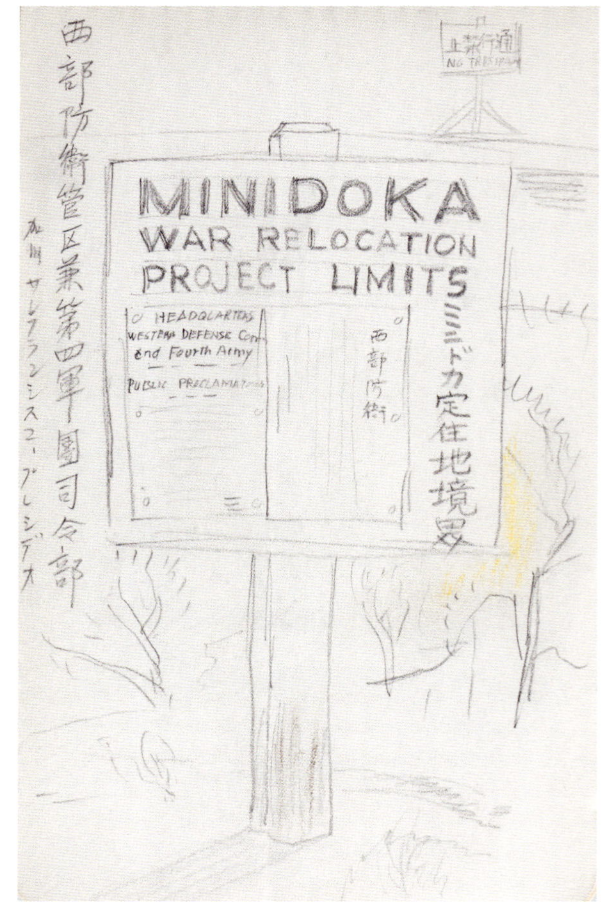

3.15
Minidoka Relocation Center, Idaho, August 1943
Denshō, https://ddr.densho.org/ddr-densho-37-424, courtesy of National Archives and Records Administration

3.16
Minidoka boundary sign, sketchbook, ca. 1942–1945
Graphite on paper, 7¾ × 4⅞ in.
Tacoma Art Museum, George and Betty Nomura Collection, 2013.24.2.A-CC

Incomplete housing left five hundred inmates in temporary quarters. All but a few blocks were without hot water, outhouses substituted for plumbed latrines, and only after temperatures dropped to freezing were potbellied stoves connected for heating. As they had at Puyallup, inmates gleaned lumber to furnish their units.

Minidoka was one of ten detention sites constructed and administered by the WRA. Unlike the army-staffed WCCA, the WRA was a civilian agency charged with the long-term confinement of Japanese Americans and their resettlement in areas distant from the West Coast.[43] Many of the WRA staff had come from the Bureau of Indian

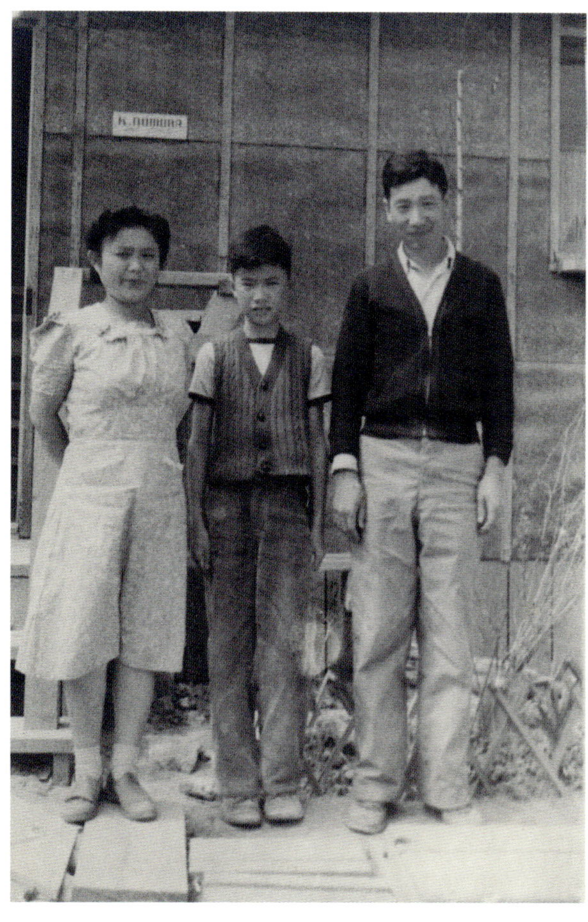

3.17
Fumiko, George, and Kenjiro Nomura, ca. 1942–1943
Nomura Estate

3.18
Hospital, 1944
Oil on paper, 5 × 8 in.
Japanese American National Museum, gift of George and Betty Nomura, 97.132.2

The tall chimney identifies the hospital.

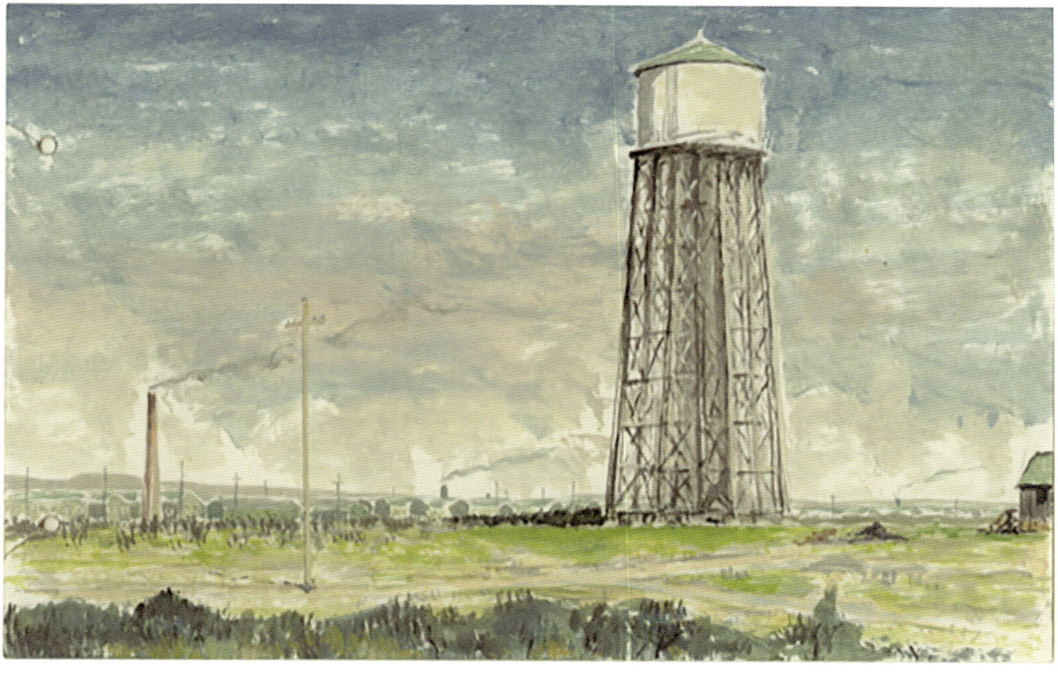

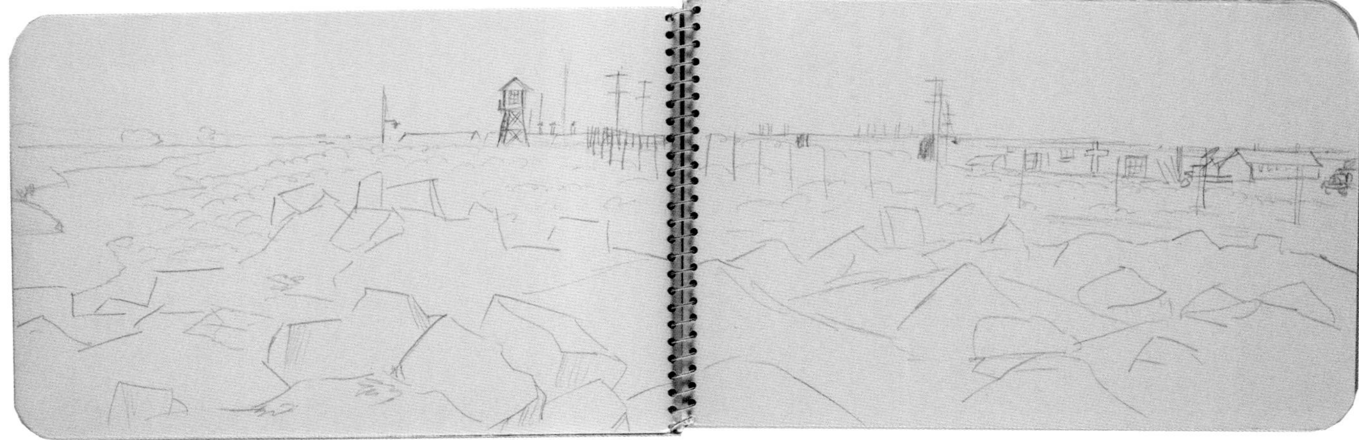

3.19
Bound sketchbook (Minidoka landscape with fence), ca. 1943
Graphite on paper, 2 pages, each 4⅞ × 7¾ in.
Tacoma Art Museum, George and Betty Nomura Collection, 2013.24.2.A-CC

Affairs and the social sciences, giving the agency a relatively sympathetic bias, but the administrative character of each camp, and the inmates' response to it, varied with the leadership.[44] The aim was to promote semi-self-governing communities under WRA supervision. The Issei, however, were still classified as "enemy aliens" and remained subordinate to Nisei. Tokita protested, "The American people in charge of this camp tell us that they are running the camp democratically. I think that's false. . . . They say 'election,' 'right to vote,' and 'democracy.' We don't understand what kind of democracy they are talking about. This is an internment camp. They want to make a distinction between citizens and non-citizens even though they put us all in here. That's absurd and unbelievable. I absolutely don't want to spend any of my time on this ridiculous so-called democracy."[45] Errors in policy and management both nationally and locally contributed to hostilities between inmates and the administration, and among factions of inmates. Minidoka differed from other WRA camps in its predominately urban population, mostly from Seattle and Portland, making it relatively homogeneous compared to others with more pronounced differences between rural and urban populations. While it was reputedly the most peaceful of the camps, tensions were always present in the segregated, confined community and would increase in later months with changes in nationally dictated regulations and the local administrative staff.

Tensions flared when, on orders from the Western Defense Command, a fence was erected around the camp in early November, a physical and highly symbolic barrier. "The residents are unanimous in possessing deep and bitter resentment against the fence," a WRA officer reported. "This feeling was accentuated by the fact that for three months before the fence was built the residents had felt they were on their honor and had cooperated with the local administration in staying within bounds" (figs. 3.19 and 3.20). That tension burst into outrage when the fence was briefly and without authorization electrified by the contractor, after inmates cut through the fence where it blocked their access to the fields.[46] The original aim of the WRA had been to settle West Coast Nikkei elsewhere in the country as quickly as possible, but governors of the western states had vigorously resisted any suggestion of settlement and agreed to the construction of "relocation centers" only if they were fenced and guarded concentration camps.[47] Eight guard towers were erected around Minidoka, although they were never manned. Incarcerees could venture beyond the boundary in daytime and had to

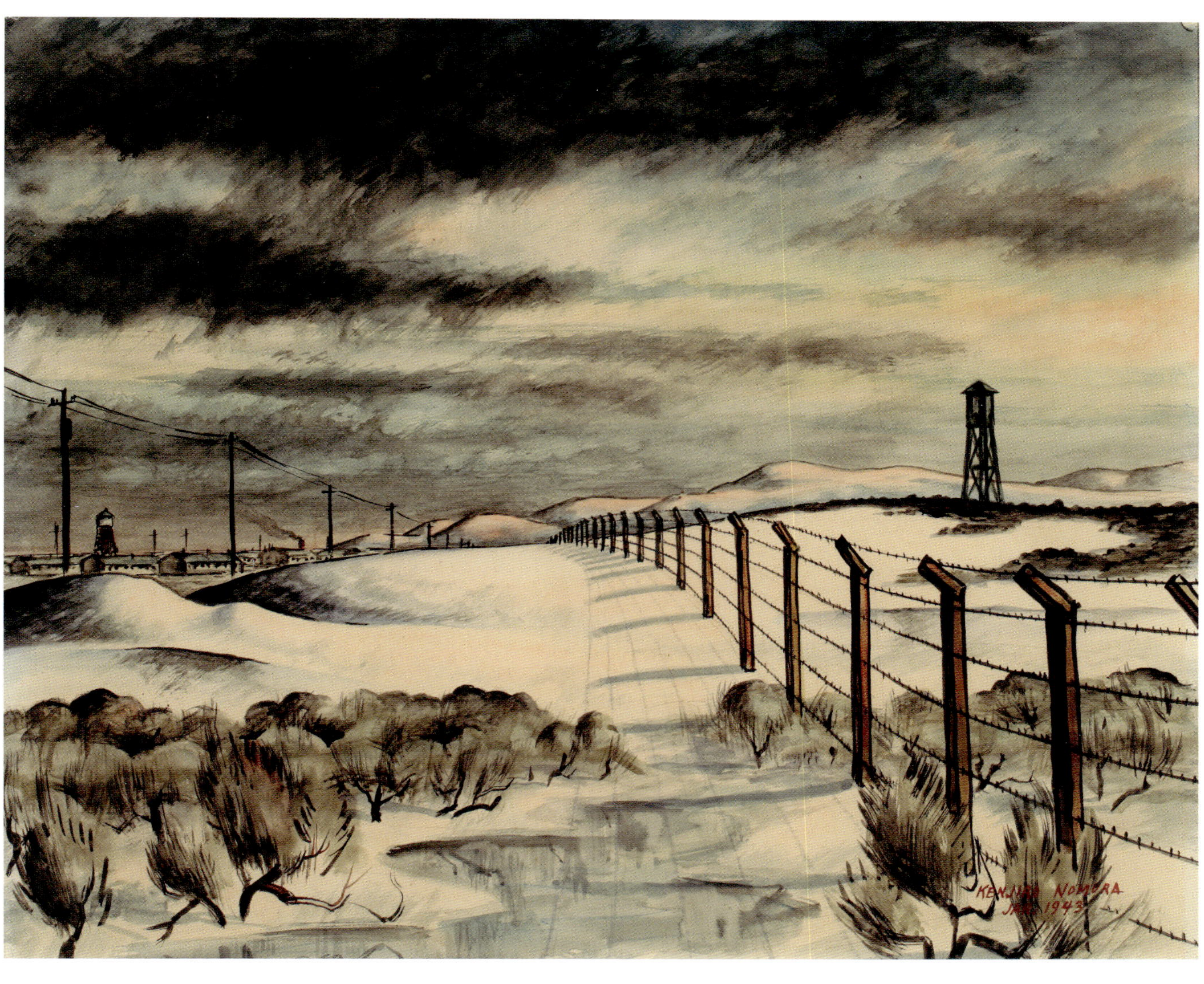

3.20
Guard Tower, 1943
Oil on paper, 19 × 24 in.
Tacoma Art Museum, George and Betty Nomura Collection, 2013.7.9

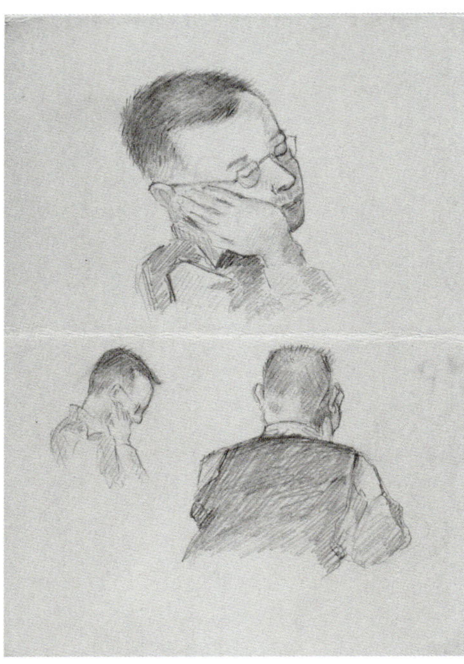

3.21
Untitled (Kamekichi Tokita), ca. 1943
Graphite on paper, 6⅞ × 5 in.
Tacoma Art Museum, George and Betty Nomura Collection, 2013.24.3.8

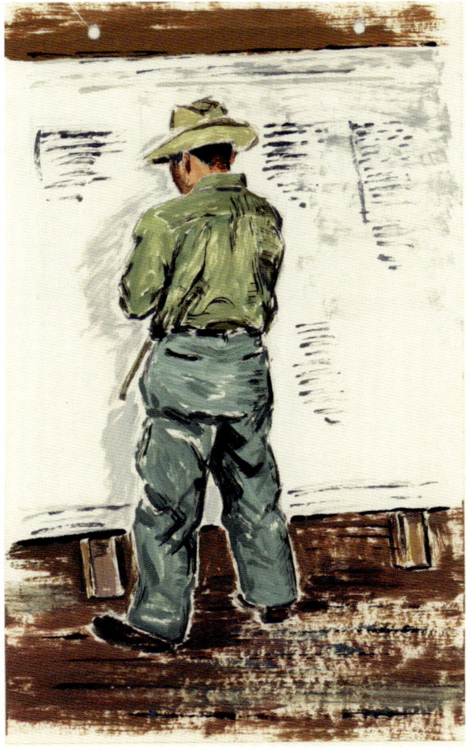

3.22
Untitled (Kamekichi Tokita painting the Honor Roll), ca. 1943–1944
Oil on paper, 8 × 5 in.
Tacoma Art Museum, gift of Barbara Johns in honor of Shokichi Tokita

return by sundown. In spring 1943 two and a half miles of the fence were removed to open access to agricultural land, but the remainder was an omnipresent reminder.

Within a month of his arrival Nomura began work as a sign painter, one of a team of about ten sign painters working in the carpenter shop. He also became a sanitary laborer, among the men called upon to maintain outhouse repair and to relocate them when necessary. Fumiko worked as a mess hall waitress.[48]

The carpenter shop was the first work unit of inmates to be established at Minidoka in mid-August, and for months remained the most active. The crew built office furniture for the administration and, later, school furniture.[49] Sign painting was also in high demand. The San Francisco headquarters of the Western Defense Command specified the types, number, and location of all perimeter as well as many interior signs. Signage, initially produced by the Army Corps of Engineers, was soon assigned to inmates.[50] Minidoka WRA staff supervised the work and activities divisions but put Nisei in charge of managing affairs, a structure similar to that in Puyallup, although this time without Sakamoto's leadership and with some Issei participation. Nomura worked for sixteen dollars a month, the rate for semi-skilled labor. His friend Tokita initially declined a request to work as a sign painter, declaring, "Working under a Nisei was the last thing I wanted to do," but by the next spring he too joined the crew.[51] The shop was in Warehouse 20 near the barbed-wire fence that ran along the canal. It served as a base for Nomura's artwork as he began making a record of his new surroundings. "There was a good spirit among the workers in the carpenter shop," a WRA officer noted, which extended to their organizing an exhibition of their products and "handiwork."[52] Several small pencil sketches

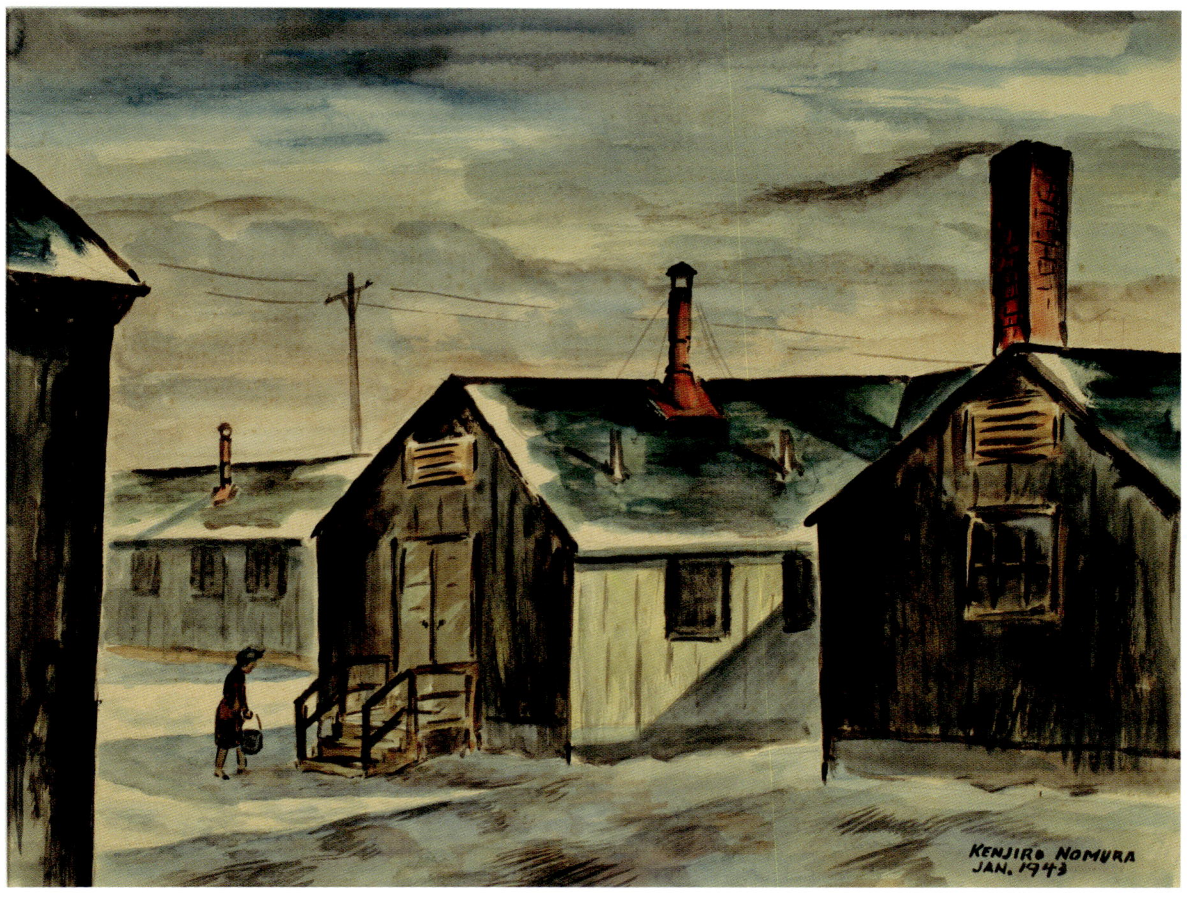

3.23
Laundry and Sanitation Building, January 1943
Watercolor on paper, 12 × 16 in.
Tacoma Art Museum, George and Betty Nomura Collection, 2013.7.11

picture Tokita and other men, perhaps sign painters (figs. 3.21 and 3.22). By the first of April 1943 the crew had produced 5,229 signs.[53]

A Visual Journal

Nomura's artistic production at Minidoka includes paintings, finished drawings, and sketches in oil, watercolor, ink, color pencil, and graphite. With the exception of a few pencil sketches, they are almost entirely of the built and natural landscape. Occasionally a lone figure or two inhabit the scene. The paintings range from three-by-four-inch watercolors to a commanding oil measuring twenty-four by thirty inches; the drawings vary from loose notation to precise renderings. A number are preliminary studies for larger works in oil or watercolor. A few drawings include the careful labeling of colors to be used, although comparable paintings, if any were made, are unknown.

The earliest dated painting is from January 1943, the first winter at Minidoka and an exceptionally cold one. A woman with a basket makes her way across the snow to shower or do laundry (fig. 3.23). In *Outhouse*, dated a month later, a man treads along a road framed by the clearly labeled men's outhouse, still in use in February (fig. 3.24). *Guard Tower* depicts an otherwise beautiful snowy landscape sliced by the barbed-wire fence that recedes out of sight (see fig. 3.20). Elsewhere, Nomura finds beauty in the graphic forms of sagebrush against the white ground or in the cool blue of ice on the canal (figs. 3.25 and 3.26).

The wide desert horizon and the rise and fall of landforms are transposed into rhythmic sequence in the landscapes. Together the landscapes mark his attention to the seasons and the

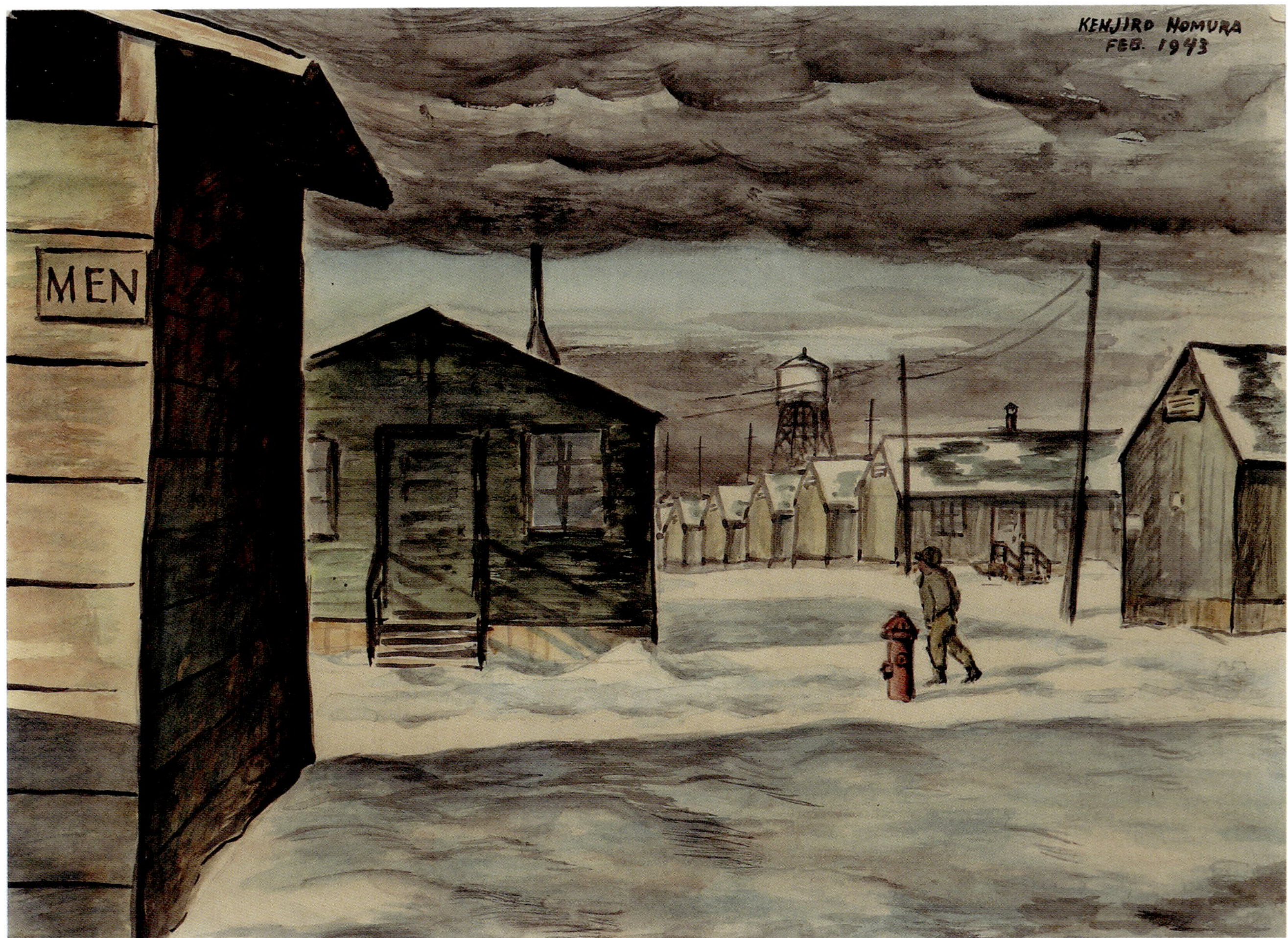

3.24
Outhouse, February 1943
Watercolor on paper, 12 × 16 in.
Tacoma Art Museum, George and Betty Nomura Collection, 2013.7.12

weather in a primitive rural environment where nature is intimately experienced every day. They trace Nomura's exploration of the camp in seeking subject matter, many in drawings that are not realized in finished paintings. The two water towers figure prominently as landmarks on the horizon and appear as subjects of detailed drawings. Other images portray the fence reaching toward the horizon. Some dozen drawings in pencil or crayon and watercolors as small as three by four inches focus on the natural landscape, making evident the uneven volcanic terrain, the vast plain, and the dramatic skies (figs. 3.27–3.29). Several picture the canal in different seasons. Numerous others depict the built environment: barracks rendered individually and in rows, the men's outhouse, the latrine and laundry building, the fire station, hospital, recreation hall, warehouses, root cellar, lumberyard, and gymnasium (figs. 3.30–3.33). *Barracks and Water Tower* (1943) is the most robustly composed of the Minidoka paintings (fig. 3.34). Rays of sunshine beam down from broken clouds, whose forms mirror the undulating landscape; a barrack garden fills the foreground corner. Nomura pictures a striking weather phenomenon of the desert, but here, what seems at first glance an image of optimism takes a different cast when one notes the figure carrying a gun.

The majority of these images are small; many are pencil drawings in two bound sketchbooks, one of them handmade. Large and small, they reveal the artist's sensitivity to the spatial, atmospheric, and social environment. The spatial and atmospheric

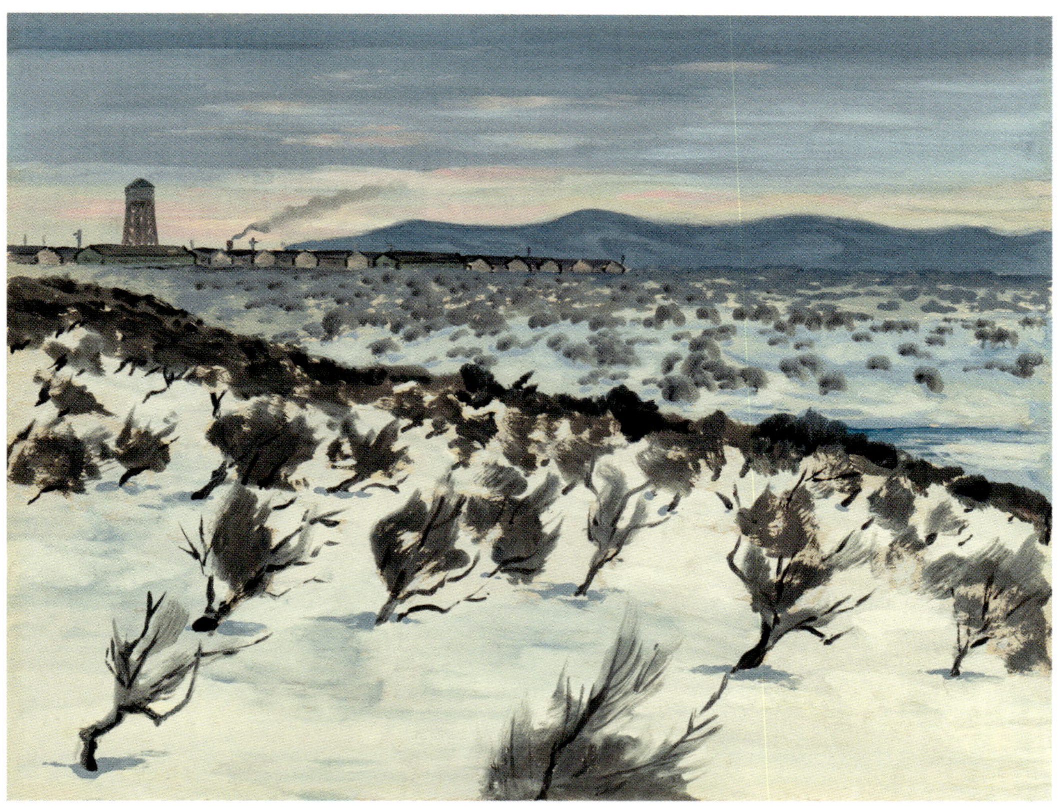

3.25
Untitled (sagebrush in snow), ca. 1943–1945
Oil on paper, 9 × 12 in.
Private collection

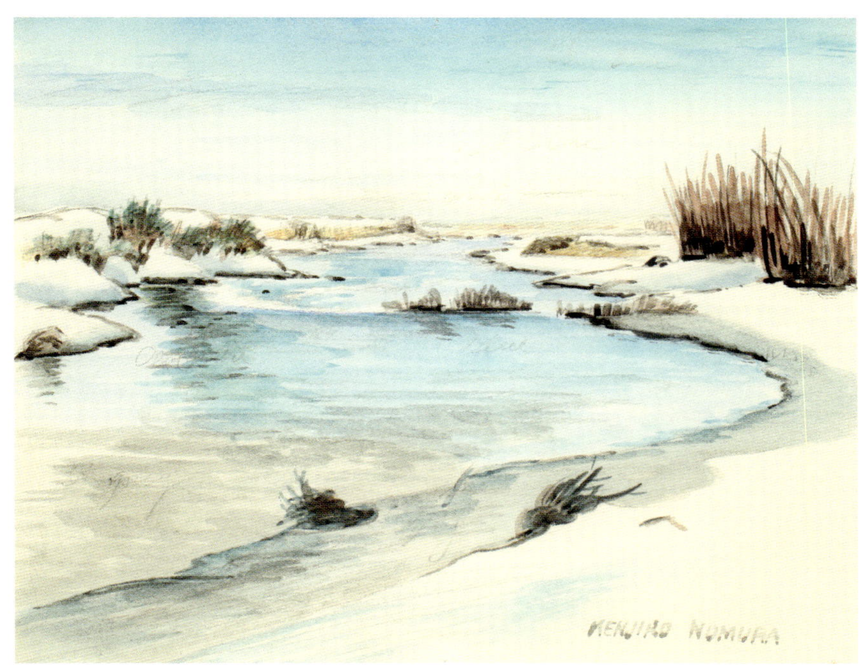

3.26
Canal, ca. 1943–1945
Watercolor on paper, 5 × 6 in.
Tacoma Art Museum, George and Betty Nomura Collection, 2013.7.20

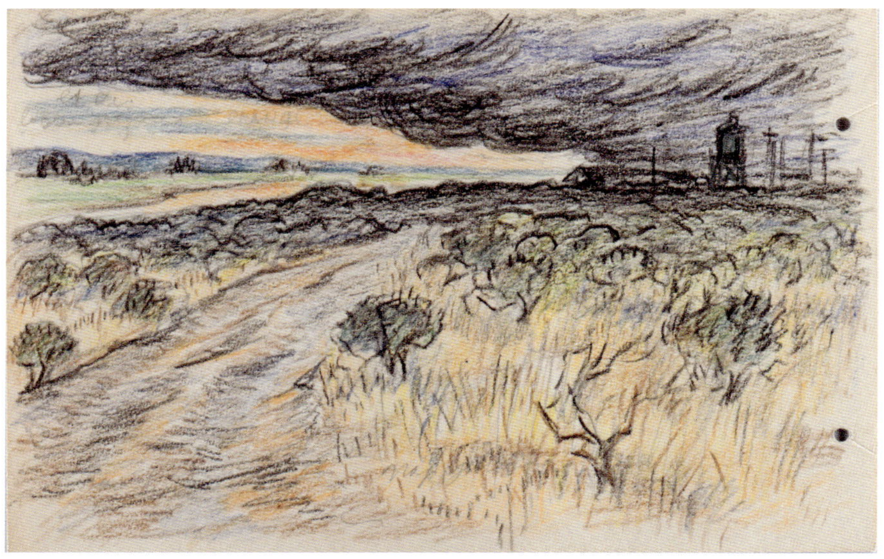

3.27
Untitled (rainstorm over Minidoka WRA Center), ca. 1943
Color pencil and graphite on paper, 5 × 8 in.
Tacoma Art Museum, George and Betty Nomura Collection, 2013.24.3.28

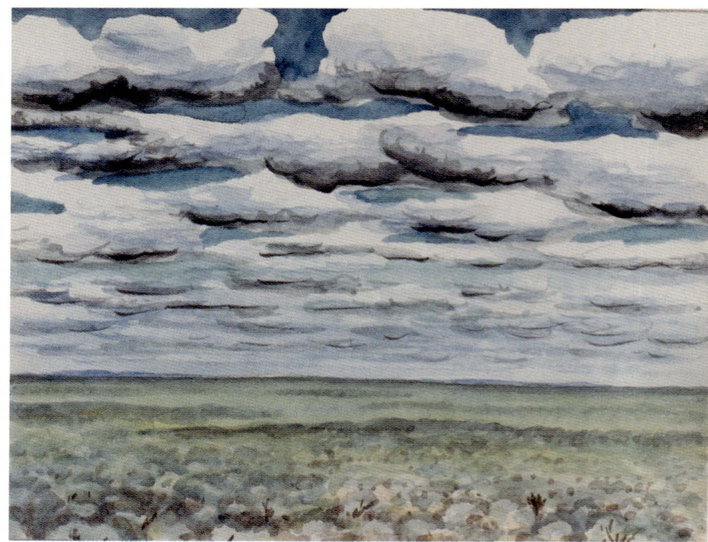

3.28
Sagebrush Land, 1943
Watercolor on paper, 4⅞ × 6¼ in.
Tacoma Art Museum, George and Betty Nomura Collection, 2013.24.3.5

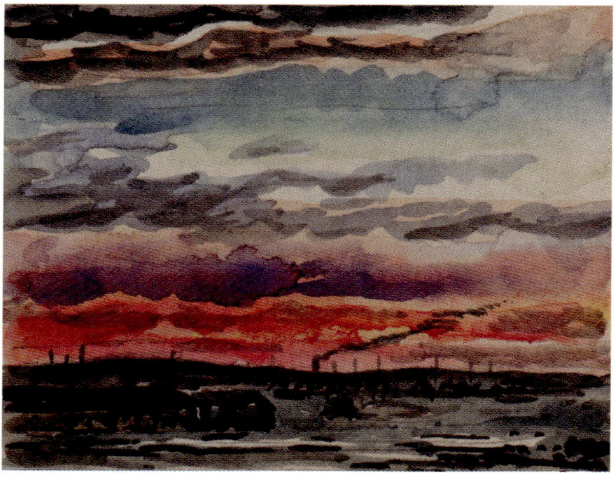

3.29
Sunset from Block 28 Looking over the School and Block 19, 1943
Watercolor and graphite on paper, 3 × 4 in.
Tacoma Art Museum, George and Betty Nomura Collection, 2013.24.3.1

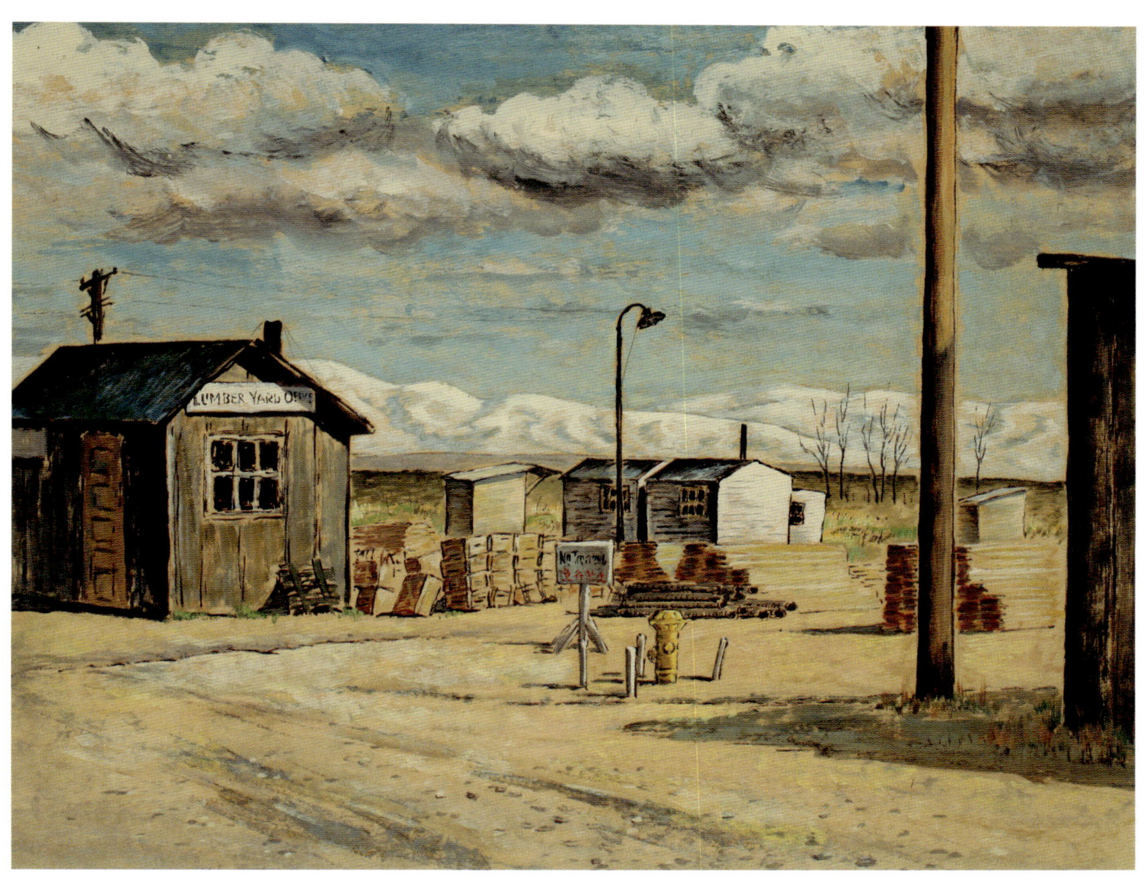

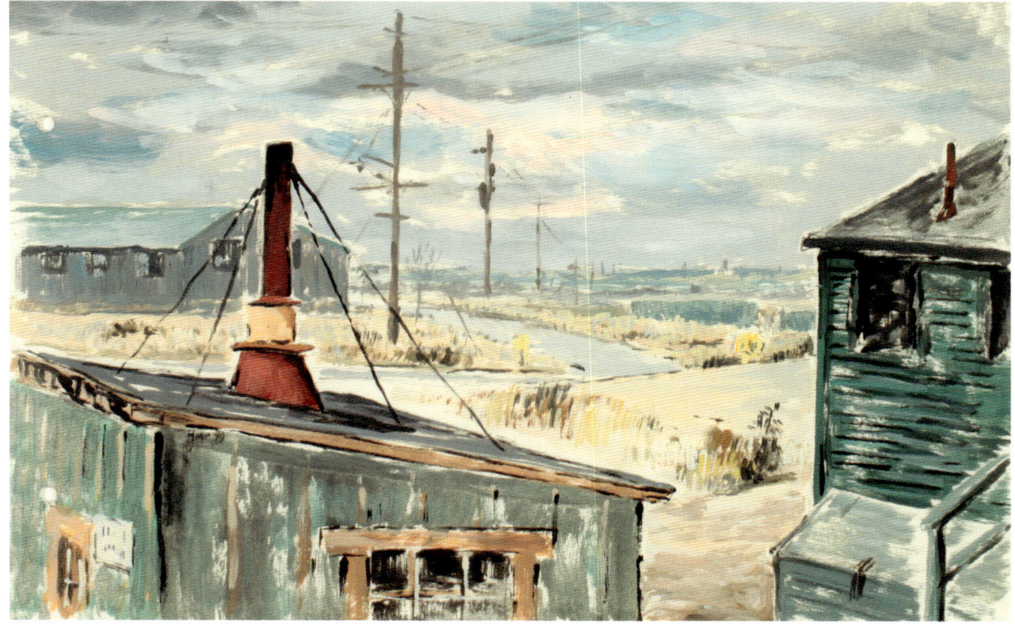

3.30
Lumberyard, ca. 1942–1945
Oil on paper, 12 × 16 in.
Tacoma Art Museum, George and Betty Nomura Collection, 2013.7.15

3.31
Barracks Window, ca. 1942–1945
Watercolor and ink on paper, 7¼ × 9½ in.
Tacoma Art Museum, George and Betty Nomura Collection, 2013.7.22

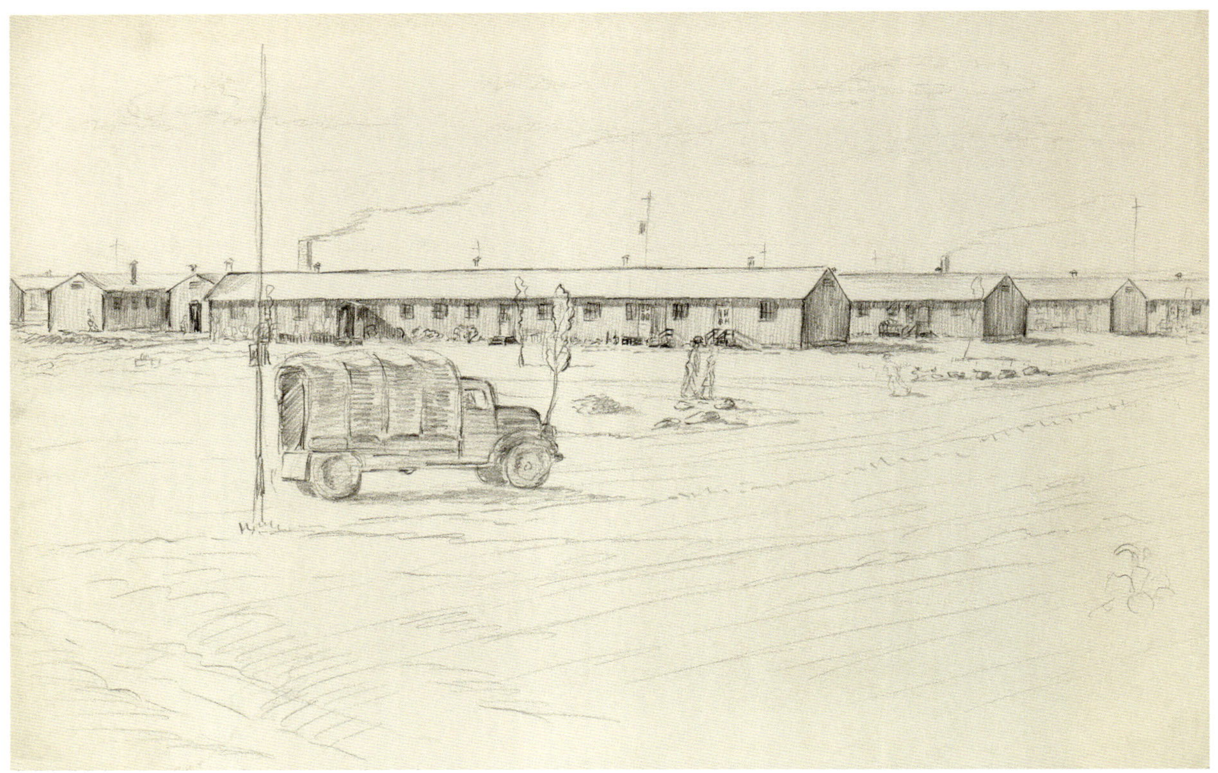

3.32
Untitled (Minidoka, barracks and truck), ca. 1943–1945
Graphite on paper, 12 × 19⅛ in.
Nomura Estate

characteristics are apparent in the inventory of buildings, the many views of barracks, and the canal and fields that surround them. The desert skies are as dramatically varied as the temperature, from the stark flatness of midday sun to black clouds and ruby sunsets. The social environment is more nuanced. In contrast to Puyallup, a person at Minidoka could be alone in a broad stretch of land. The size of the camp required inmates to walk long distances to a job, a relative's barrack-home, or obligatory administrative business. The desert itself dwarfed human activity. Moreover, the varied perspectives of the barracks or the water towers that marked the way trace Nomura's experience of the place, just as his paintings of his Seattle neighborhood defined a place of belonging.

Past Block 28, where the Nomura family lived, lay agricultural fields. The closest was the pea patch, which he rendered in watercolor and pencil drawings (figs. 3.36 and 3.37). His many images of cultivated fields show the accomplishment but not the effort of turning sagebrush land to productivity. The WRA planned that the camps would produce much of their own food and trade their surplus with one another. Minidoka was optimistically projected to yield seventeen thousand cultivated acres, but conditions meant that less than a tenth of that was achieved. Clearing the land of sagebrush

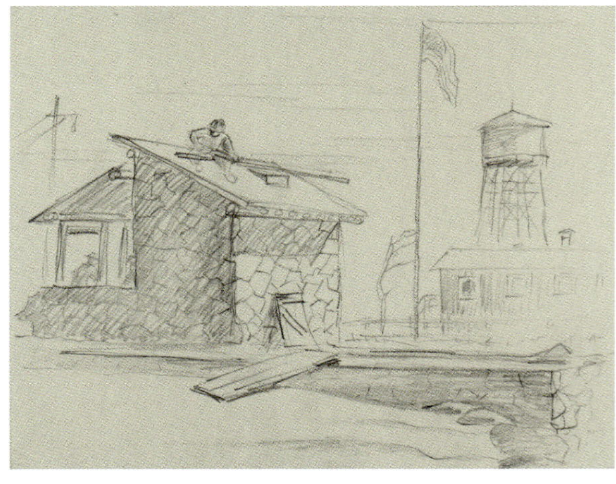

3.33
Building the Stone Gate, 1943
Graphite on paper, 4¾ × 6⅜ in.
Tacoma Art Museum, George and Betty Nomura Collection, 2013.24.3.4

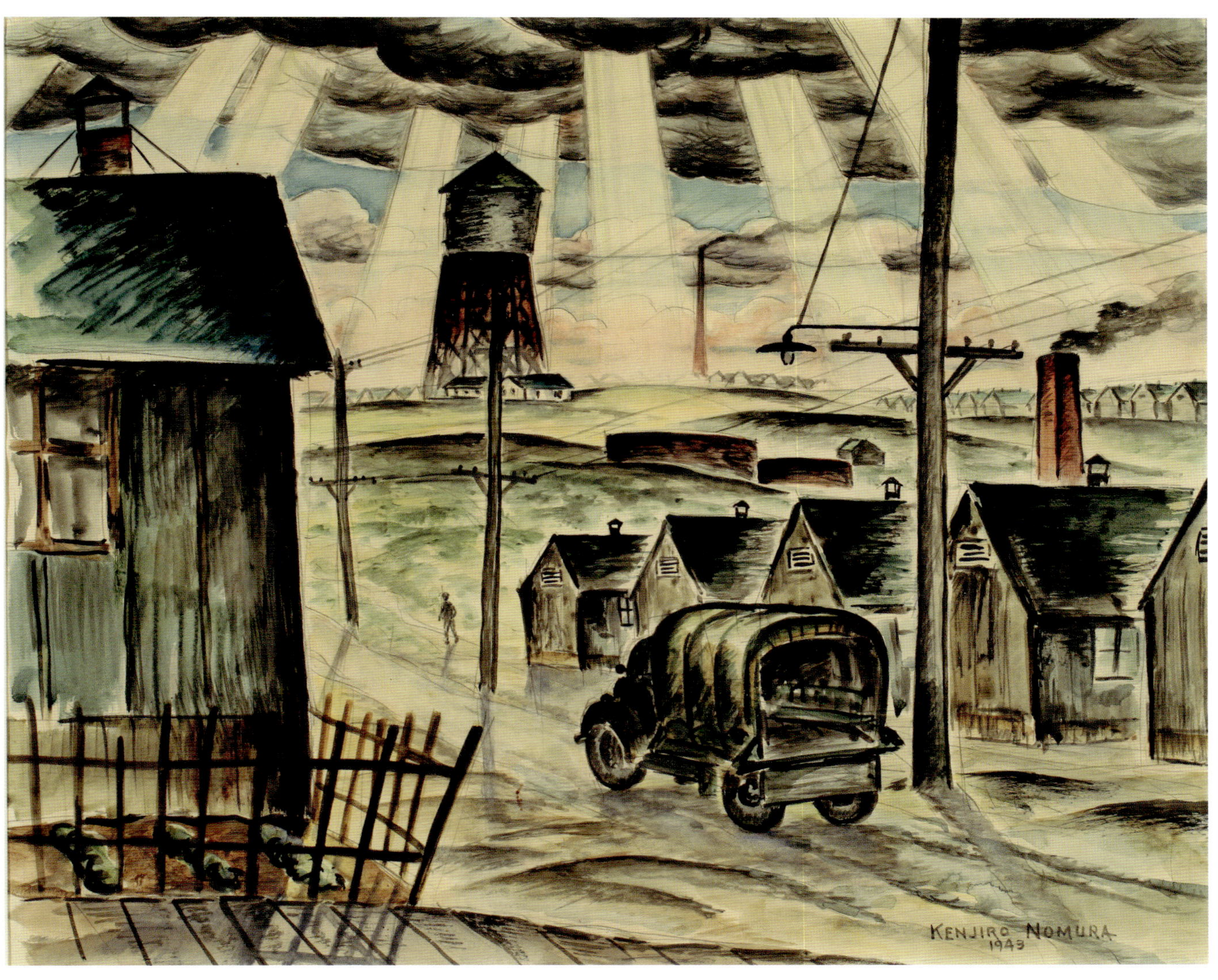

3.34
Barracks and Water Tower, 1943
Watercolor and ink on paper, 19 × 24 in.
Tacoma Art Museum, George and Betty Nomura Collection, 2013.7.10

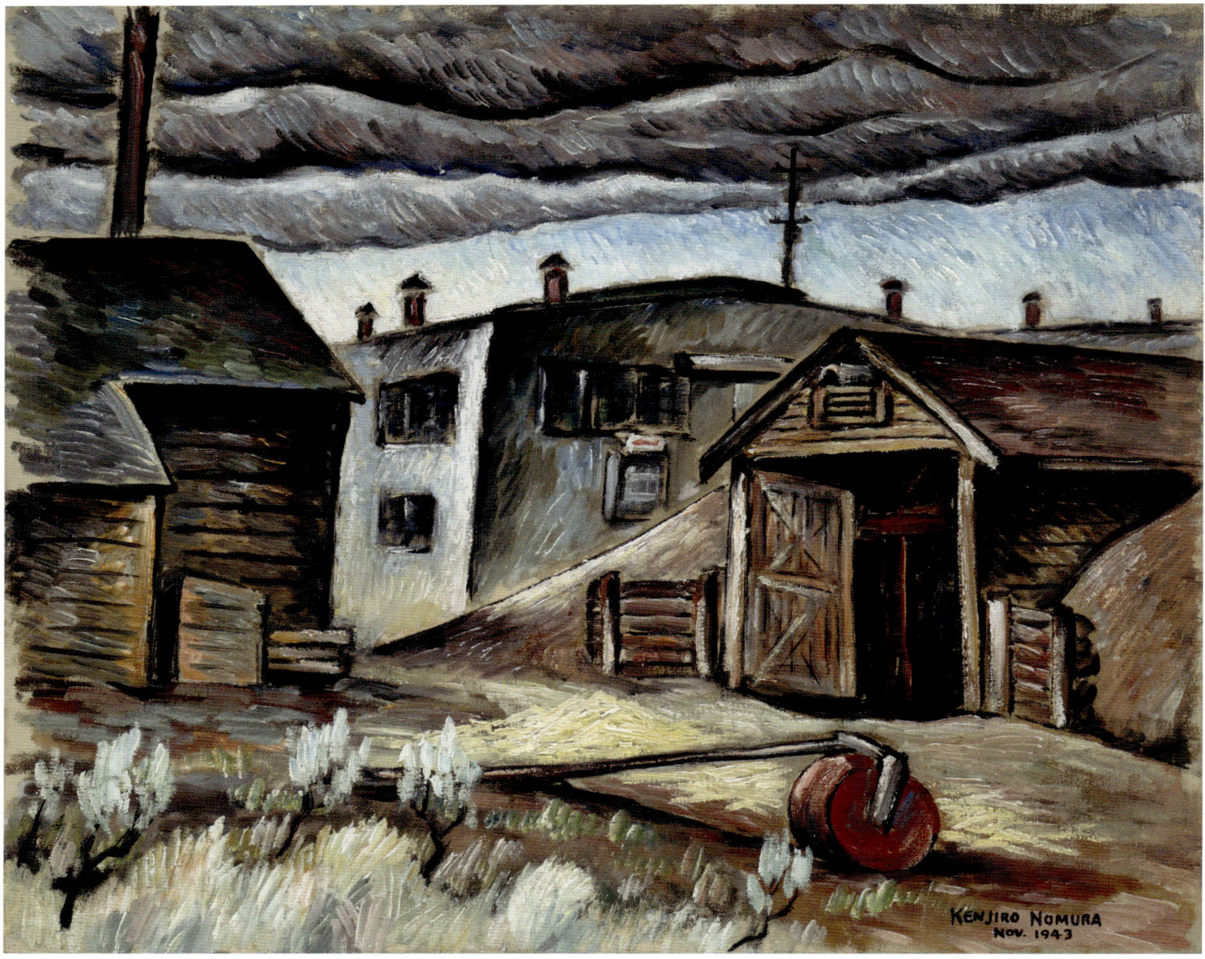

3.35
Untitled (root cellar), November 1943
Oil on canvas, 19 × 24 in.
Private collection

and lava rock outcroppings was a major challenge until a proper method was devised. Some forty-five miles of irrigation and drainage ditches fed the fields, much of them dug by hand. And yet despite inadequate equipment, the inexperience of the largely urban population, and the loss of manpower as young people were released from camp for school, work, or military service, the Nikkei produced more than two million pounds of produce in 1943 and over three million in 1944, supplying fresh food to the mess halls and feed for the chicken and hog farms.[54] They built a root cellar to hold the surplus (which stands today) and a pickling plant to make the preserved foods they favored (fig. 3.35). Nomura's *Truck Farm* of May 1943 is a rhythmic landscape of gently mounded terrain beneath clouds that mirror the land; an untilled section of old lava flow divides the fields that evoke fecundity with little hint of the labor involved (fig. 3.36).

The largest and one of the last of Nomura's wartime artworks is *Gymnasium*, an oil on canvas painting measuring twenty-four by thirty inches, signed and dated 1945, the year the high school auditorium-gymnasium—pictured in the background of Nomura's composition—was completed (fig. 3.38). Construction had been long planned by the inmates but was delayed by the unavailability of materials, labor disputes with the administration and among individuals, and the declining workforce as young people left the camp.[55] For two years the WRA had urged adult Nisei, and later Issei, to resettle for work or school east of the Western Defense Zone; at the same

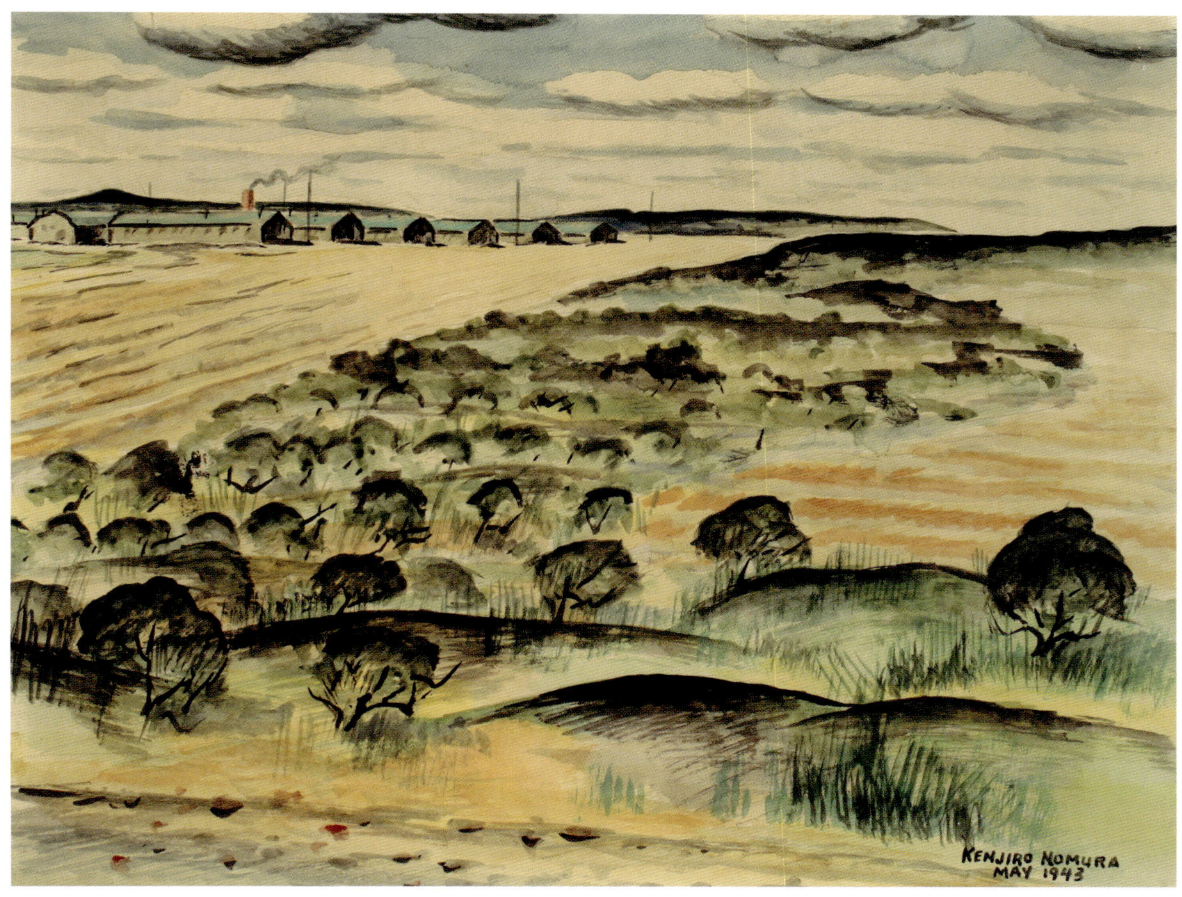

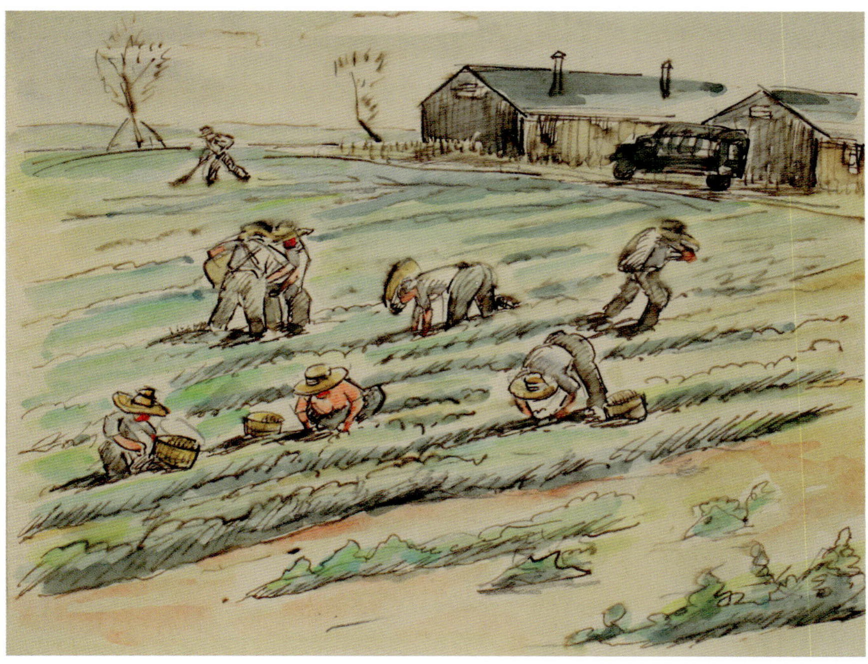

3.36
Truck Farm, May 1943
Watercolor (and oil?) on paper, 12 × 16 in.
Tacoma Art Museum, George and Betty Nomura Collection, 2013.7.14

3.37
Picking Peas, ca. 1943–1945
Ink and watercolor on paper, 5 × 6 in.
Tacoma Art Museum, George and Betty Nomura Collection, 2013.7.19

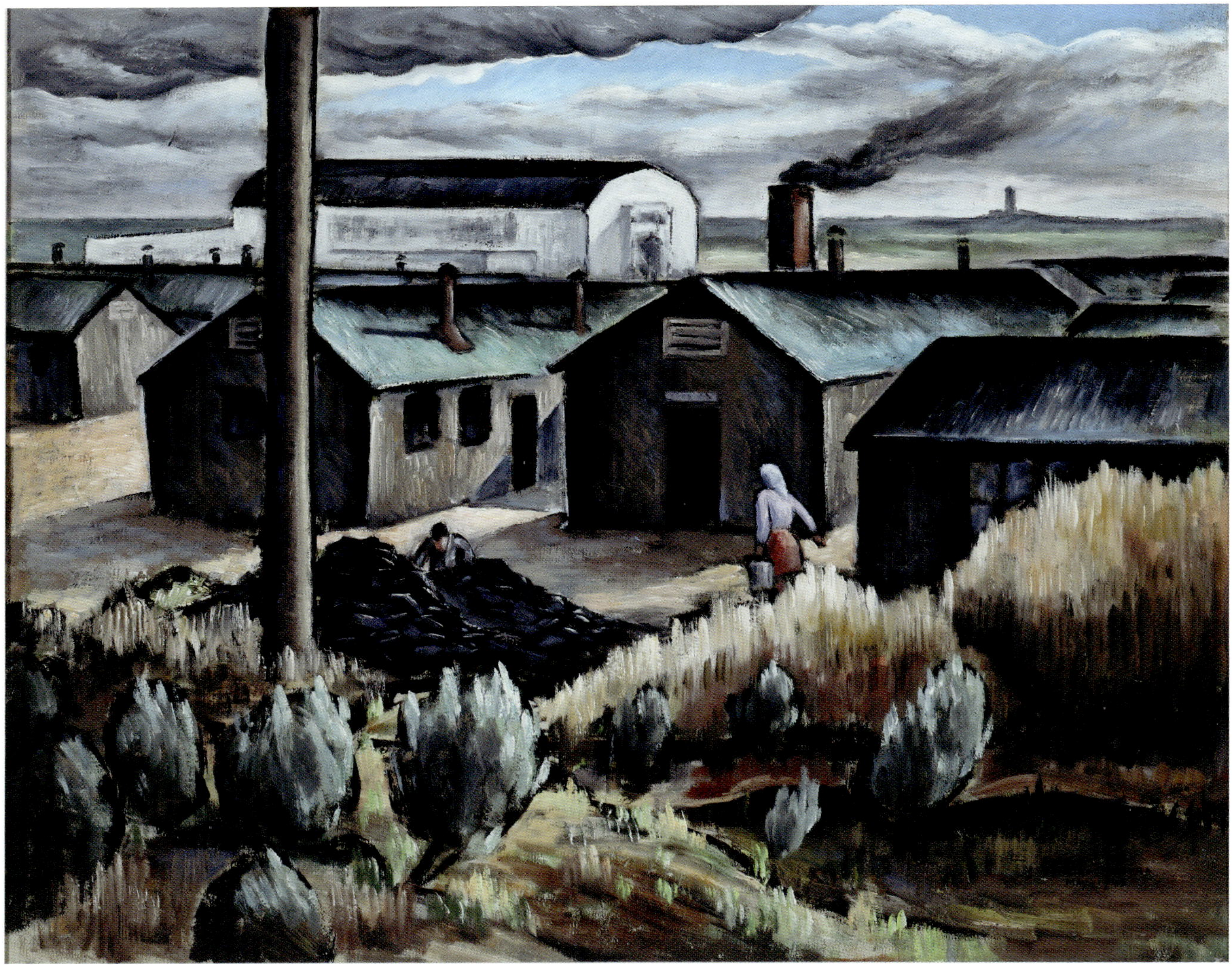

3.38
Gymnasium, 1945
Oil on canvas, 24 × 30 in.
Tacoma Art Museum, museum purchase, 2013.6

time, the need for soldiers had opened military service to Nisei, first volunteer, and then by draft. The departures of young adults meant an increasing shortage of labor and professionals such as doctors and nurses. By the time the gymnasium was declared occupiable, WRA administrators were pushing Minidoka toward closure and progressively shutting down services. In Fujii's view, it had "now become worse than useless."[56] But while the painting portrays the new gymnasium, it also tells of coal, which is piled in the near mid-ground. Stretching across the center of the composition is a barracks block, where the coal-fired laundry and sanitation building is identified by its smoking chimney. Coal had been an issue at Minidoka since the first cold weather in September 1942 and in such acute shortage throughout the fall that the local WRA director, Harry L. Stafford, had wired WRA headquarters, "Give us some coal or face a public scandal."[57] Moreover the job of hauling was one of the least liked—"Nobody wants to carry coal for $16 a month," Tokita remarked. Tension mounted over the frequent use of "volunteer" labor; at times inmates hauled their own coal or gleaned leftovers.[58] Nomura pictures a man leaning over the coal pile and a woman with her arm extended as

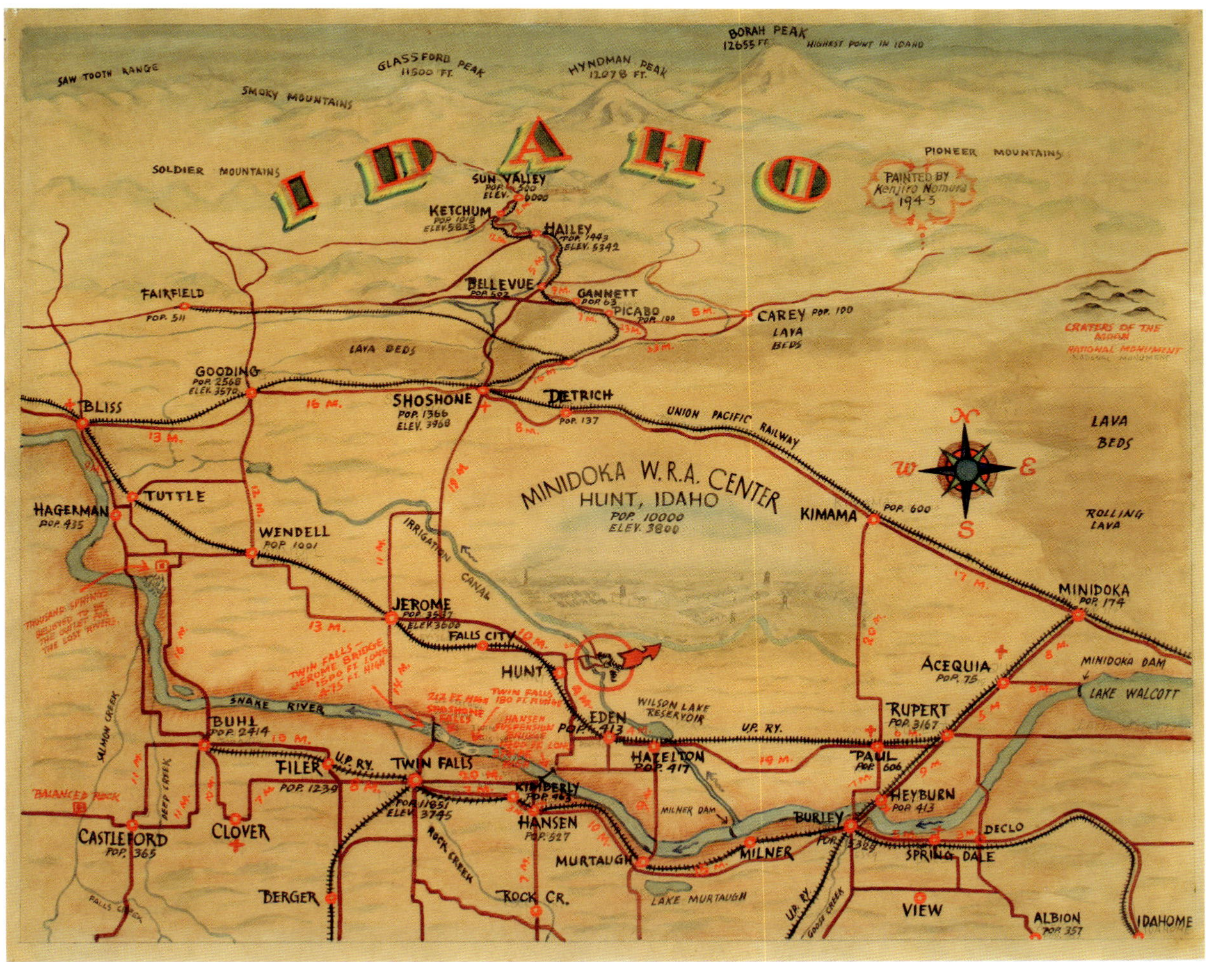

3.39
Map of Idaho, 1943
Ink, color pencil, and watercolor, 19 × 24 in.
Tacoma Art Museum, George and Betty Nomura Collection, 2013.7.16

she balances a heavy bucket. While it is a celebratory painting by its size and finish, *Gymnasium* carries within it deeper stories of the reality of incarcerees' experience.

One painting, a map of south-central Idaho (fig. 3.39), stands apart from the others. Rendered in watercolor, ink, and color pencil on the same nineteen-by-twenty-four-inch paper he used at Puyallup, the painting is an intricately detailed map of the Minidoka vicinity: towns and their populations, highways with section mileage, railroad tracks, landmarks such as bridges and springs, mountain ranges and peaks to the north with elevations noted, and, in the center, a delicately enlarged drawing of the camp. Beside the title "Idaho" is the inscription "Painted by Kenjiro Nomura, 1943." Incarcerees would not normally have access to such maps (earlier in the war, the possession of maps made a Nikkei suspect), leaving the purpose of this one a matter of speculation. The specific navigational information could have been useful to WRA staff members or Nisei truck drivers whose job was to deliver coal and supplies.[59] Possibly the watercolor, which remained in the artist's possession, was a study for a larger official sign. No record provides an answer.

Nomura exhibited paintings in at least three, and surely more if not all, of the art and crafts exhibitions at Minidoka. Exhibitions of arts such as ikebana, as well as the painting exhibitions in which Nomura first gained recognition, had been well-established community occasions in Nihonmachi. These expanded in the WRA camps, where they became widely popular events. The first exhibition at Minidoka in December 1942 drew five thousand visitors, the high attendance hinting of the large number of Nikkei who turned to craft activities in confinement.[60] The largest exhibition by the number of objects was presented at the Twin Falls Public Library in June 1943, where town visitors enthusiastically viewed three hundred pieces ranging from walking sticks and furniture to oil paintings.[61] Promoting an exhibition in the camp the following November, the weekly *Minidoka Irrigator* called special attention to Nomura and his fellow Seattle painters: "The exhibition promises to be an interesting and attractive one with notable and highly acclaimed artists participating. From among the ten best artists in the state of Washington, Messrs. Fujii, Tokita, and Nomura have their masterpieces on display."[62] The three had earned the honor in better times by their inclusion in New York City's *First National Exhibition of American Art*. Nomura submitted a painting of the newly completed root cellar, which was placed at the center of the art section and flanked by paintings by Tokita and Fujii (see fig. 3.35).

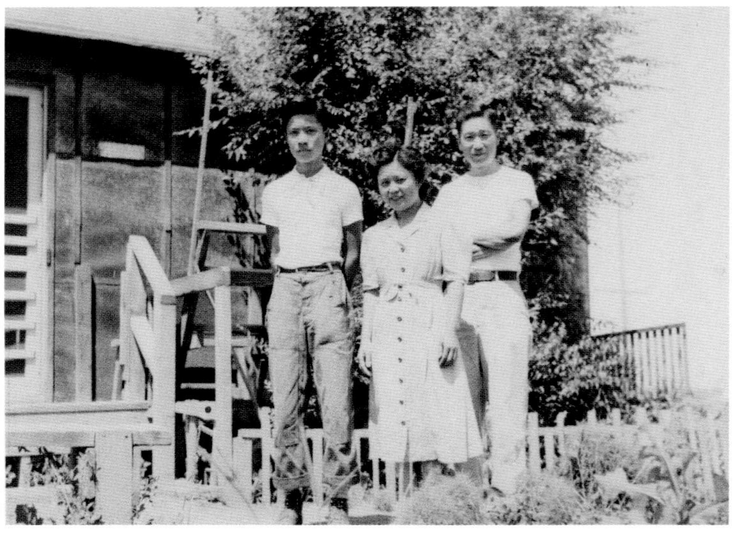

3.40
George, Fumiko, and Kenjiro Nomura, ca. 1945
Nomura Estate

"Camp Culture": Resistance and Resilience

Nomura's images of Minidoka tell of the Nikkei's construction of their own environment.[63] In addition to their labor on WRA-mandated construction and agriculture, they built facilities such as the root cellar and the pickling plant; they built baseball fields, playfields, Japanese-style baths, a swimming hole, and the gymnasium featured in his painting. Nomura's viewpoint is also personal. Gardens flourish outside family barracks. Drawings of his barrack show the process of making a home. Outside, a laundry tub hangs by the door and a bench sits in the beginnings of a garden (fig. 3.42); in another drawing, the garden has matured. A small oil painting of the interior depicts shelves with a hot plate, a rice pot, and a jug of soy sauce, markers of cultural identity (fig. 3.43). In an unusually personal image and the only one he labeled, a sketch portrays "Mrs. Saito's 49-day ceremony" as a Buddhist priest marks the end of the mourning period for a resident of Nomura's block, a centuries-old ritual of grief enacted in an American WRA camp (fig. 3.44).[64]

Moreover, Minidoka provides the only example among Nomura's extant work of his painting in a traditional Japanese style. Two slim wood panels in the shape of *tanzaku*, holders for the display of poetry, depict time-honored motifs and are signed in Japanese (fig. 3.45). On one is the ancient motif of plum blossoms, which bloom when the ground is still cold from winter and are emblematic of the strength and perseverance needed to overcome winter. The other pictures a full moon and geese, a symbol of autumn when birds migrate. Both themes connote perseverance during hardship, but it is one of the signatures, which identifies the maker as a "recluse" or "mountain man," that secures the images in their

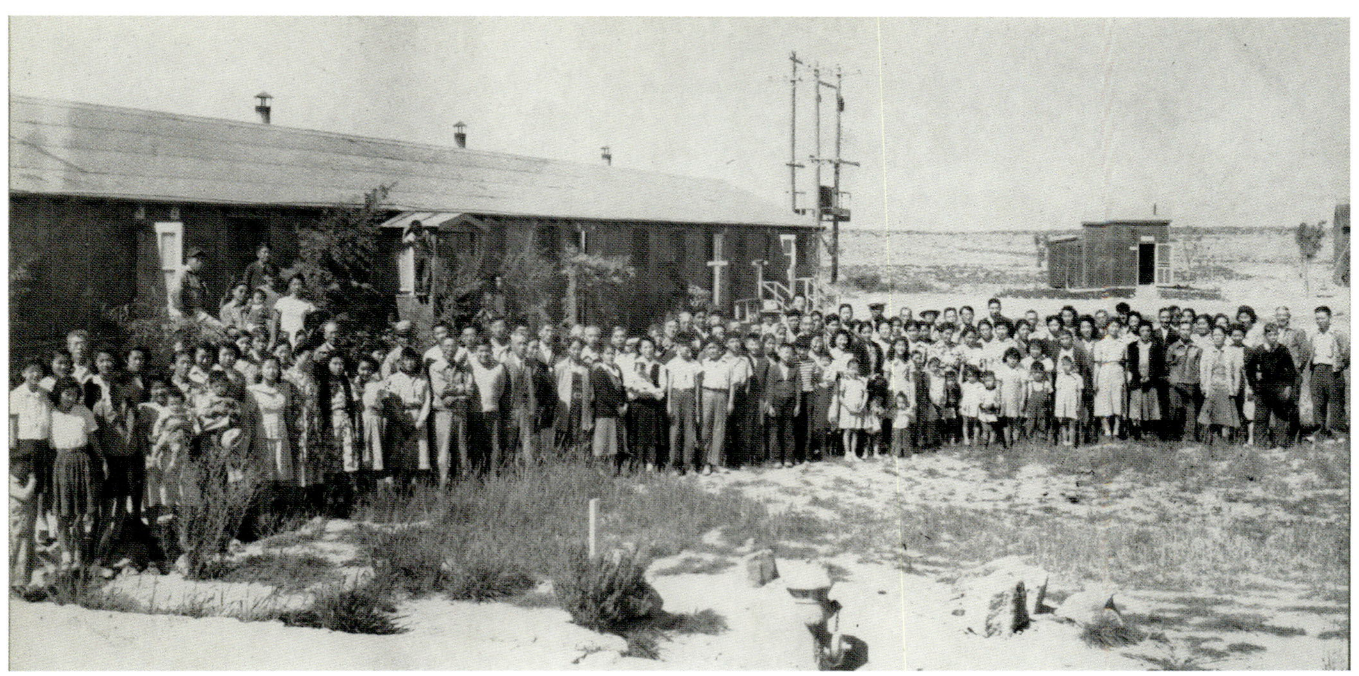

3.41
Block 28, group portrait for the *Minidoka Interlude*, 1943
Photo: R. Ochi
Courtesy of Wing Luke Museum, gift of June Mukai McKivor

The block served as an extended family unit.

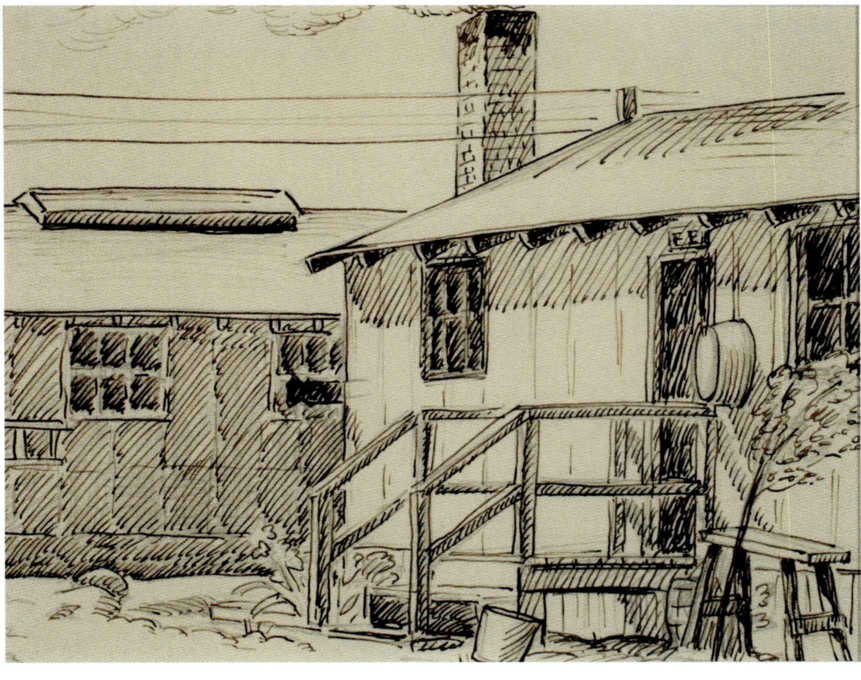

3.42
Minidoka 28-7-F, ca. 1943–1945
Ink on paper, 5 × 6 in.
Tacoma Art Museum, George and Betty Nomura Collection, 2013.7.24

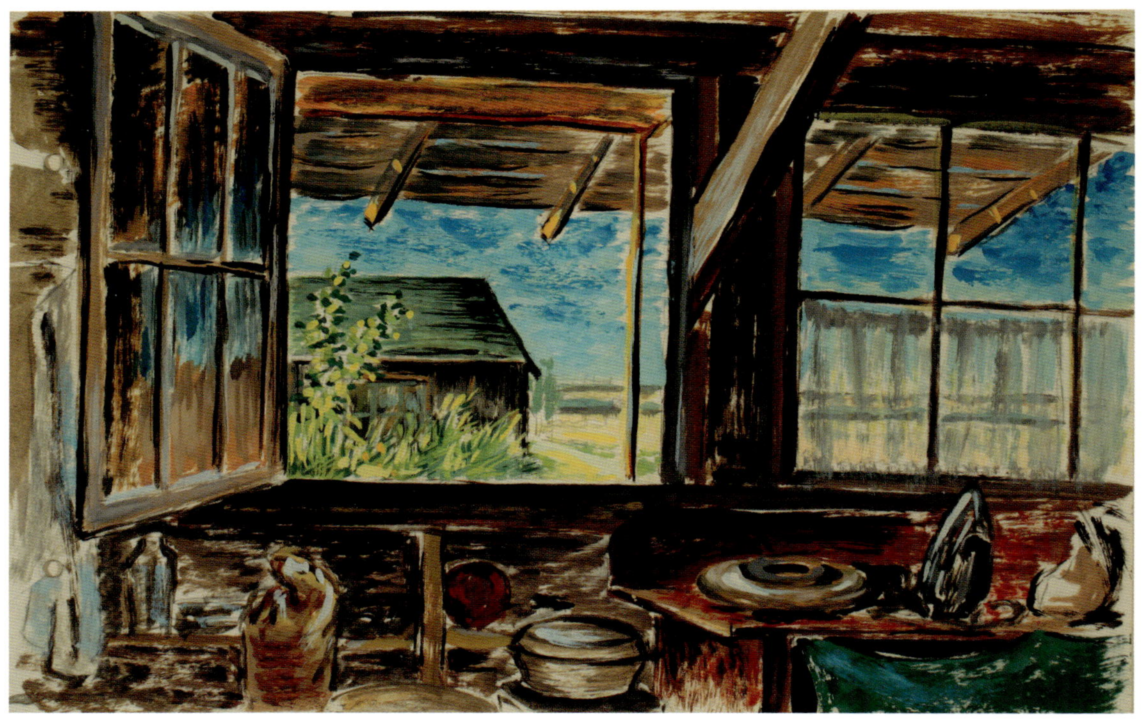

3.43
From Barrack Window, ca. 1943–1945
Oil on paper, 5 × 8 in.
Tacoma Art Museum, George and Betty Nomura Collection, 2013.7.17

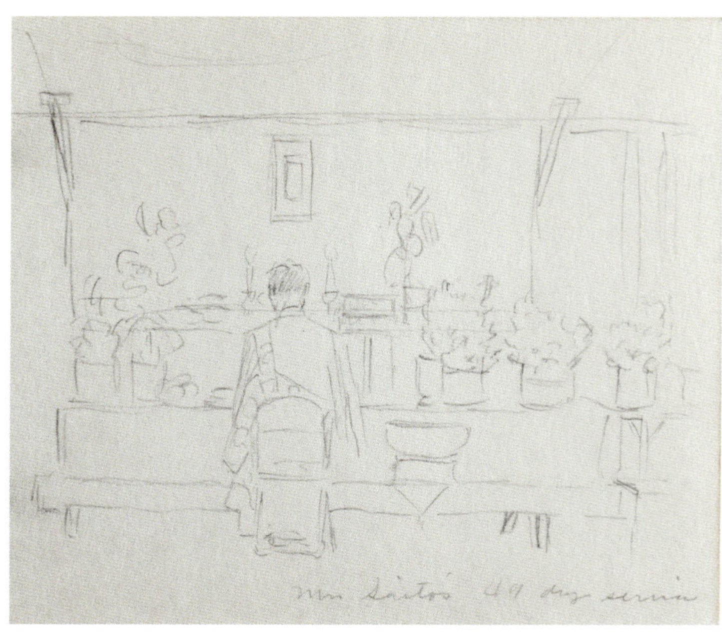

3.44
Artist-made sketchbook, "Mrs. Saito's 49-day ceremony," ca. 1942–1945
Graphite on paper, 4 × 5 in.
Tacoma Art Museum, George and Betty Nomura Collection, 2013.24.1.A-K

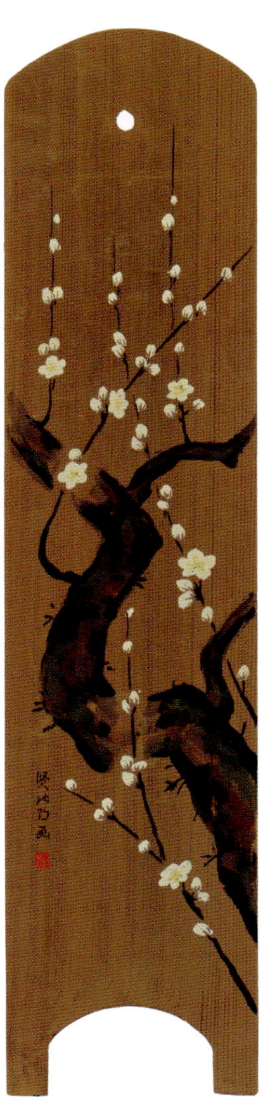

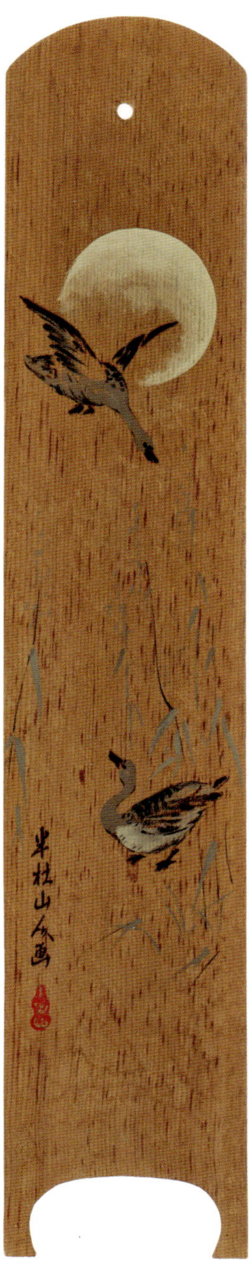

3.45
Untitled (plum blossoms, and geese and moon), ca. 1942–1945
Oil on wood, 19 × 4½ × ¼ in. (*left*) and 24½ × 4⅝ × ⅛ in. (*right*)
Nomura Estate

historically specific time and place at Minidoka.[65] Similarly, Tokita inscribed "Minidoka mountain-man" on his paintings of Daruma, the legendary founder of Zen Buddhism who represents extraordinary self-discipline and persistence.[66] Nomura's painted *tanzaku*, like *haiku*, serve as visual poetry that distills human emotion in imagery from nature.

Cultural practices that had bound together the prewar Nikkei community continued, and in some cases intensified, under the conditions of ethnic segregation and confinement.[67] Incarcerated solely on the basis of their ethnicity, the Nikkei demonstrated by their actions the cultural pluralism ever present in American experience. The creation of gardens, the popularity of arts and crafts of many kinds, the formation of poetry groups, and such community-wide, intergenerational celebrations as New Year's and Bon Odori were among the ways that inmates at all the camps embraced their shared heritage and resisted the WRA's policy of assimilation and "Americanization."[68] Landscaped gardens, flower arrangements, and bonsai were created from the plants and rocks of the desert, while the gnarled wood of the greasewood bush became a prized material for walking sticks and carved objects. Poetry in its several forms reflected the conditions of camp life. The formally organized activities also provided opportunity to demonstrate Issei knowledge and leadership, which had been undermined by the government's elevation of Nisei leadership in the camps.[69] Other activities, like the individualized nameplates outside each barrack door or the wearing of *getas*, raised wooden clogs, began as practical matters and became aesthetic objects. All became part of Japanese American "camp culture," a collective expression of ethnic identity and, in the context of the Nikkei's imprisonment, acts of resistance.[70] But while they echo forms and practices in Japan, they are distinctively American, made of the materials of the American desert and in response to wartime confinement. In recording these "Japanese" practices in an American incarceration camp, Nomura quietly celebrates these statements of Nikkei agency and resilience.

The Honor Roll, designed and painted by Nomura and Tokita, may be *the* outstanding

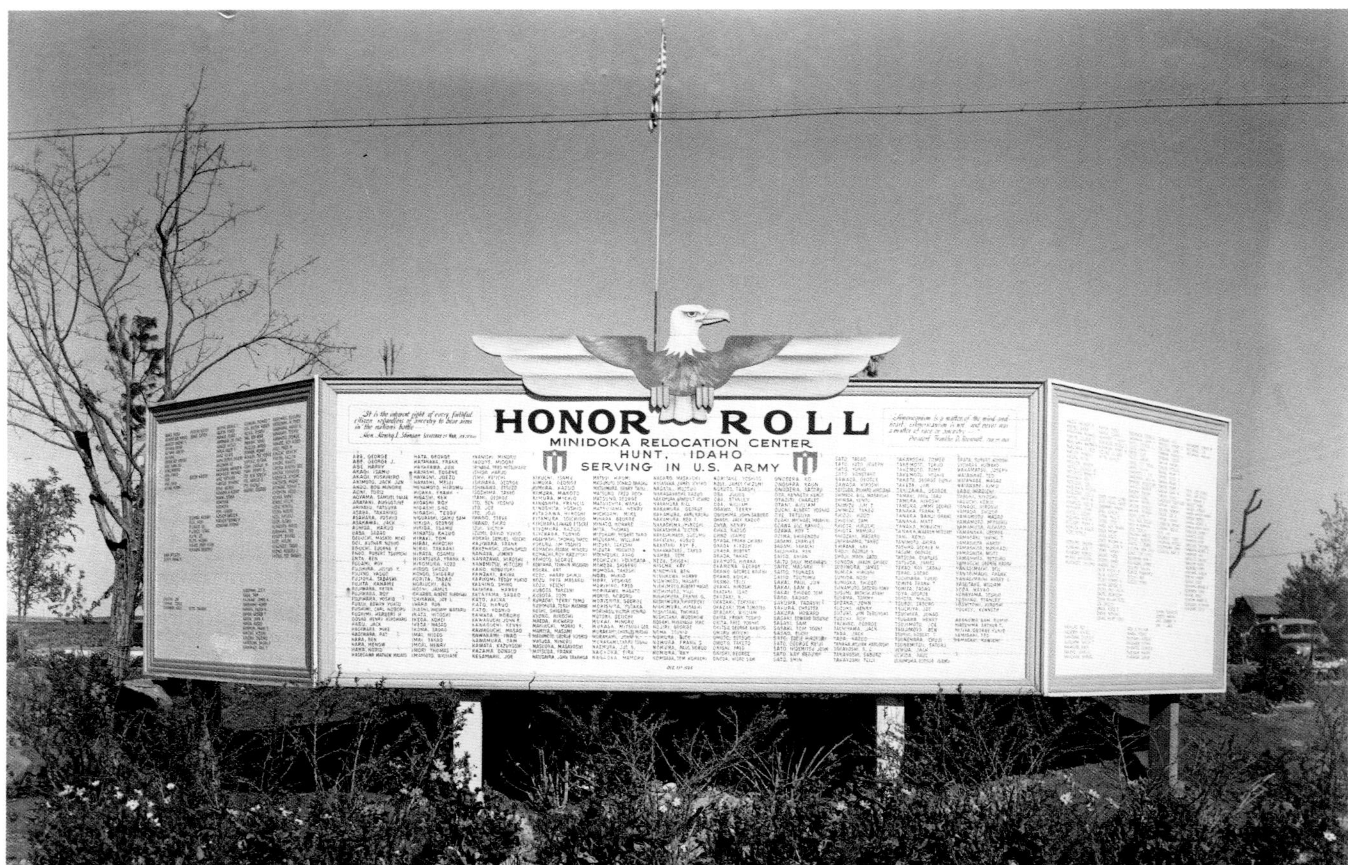

3.46
The Honor Roll at Minidoka, 1943
Minidoka National Historic Site, National Parks Service, courtesy of National Archives and Records Administration, Photograph No. 210-CMB-12-1348.

example of culturally pluralist expression at Minidoka (fig. 3.46). When Nisei began to be recruited from Minidoka for military service and, soon, drafted from the camp, Nomura and Tokita created an honor roll sign that bore the names of those serving.[71] Standing symbolically inside the main gate, the sign was erected in autumn 1943 to recognize the Nisei from Minidoka who had volunteered for military service and was expanded in 1944 when others were drafted.[72] At center top was an iconic American eagle with outstretched wings, an emblem of the United States since the nation's beginning. At the sign's base was a Japanese-style ceremonial garden composed of desert rocks and plants, designed by the Issei Fujitaro Kubota, a well-known Seattle nurseryman and the chief gardener of Minidoka. The sign stood as a powerful testament to two-generational Japanese American loyalty, as well as a tragically ironic statement of the injustice of the incarceration.[73]

Closure

On December 18, 1944, the adult Nikkei remaining at Minidoka—those who had not left for military service or school or work elsewhere in the country—were called to an assembly addressed by Project Director Harry L. Stafford. Effective January 2, 1945, he announced, the West Coast would be open for all who wished to return, and as of year-end, all the WRA camps were ordered closed. The closure had been discussed between the Departments of War and Interior for more than a year, and the decision made in September 1944, but the announcement was delayed until after the presidential election, when Roosevelt won an unprecedented fourth term. When it finally came, the news was met with anxiety rather than relief. Those remaining, including Nomura, Tokita, and Fujii, were mostly the older Issei and families with young children. They had lost homes, livelihoods, and possessions and had nowhere to go; rumors of resistance and violence on the West Coast were widespread. Camp at least provided security.

Having urged resettlement since 1943, now, in early 1945, the WRA stepped up its campaign to move the remaining seven thousand Nikkei out of Minidoka. In coming months administrators increased the pressure to leave and successively shut down facilities and services. By the first of August, with the end of war imminent, more than four thousand people remained in camp, and a similar proportion remained at other WRA centers. The national WRA office resorted to eviction. The practice was conducted particularly harshly at Minidoka, where evictions were issued with only the minimum-required three-day notice.[74] Nomura left no record to reveal his emotion at this time, but Fujii's diary pictures the prevalent dark anxiety.[75] On September 5, three years after their arrival, Nomura, his wife, Fumiko, and their fifteen-year-old son, George, boarded a train to begin the return journey to Seattle.

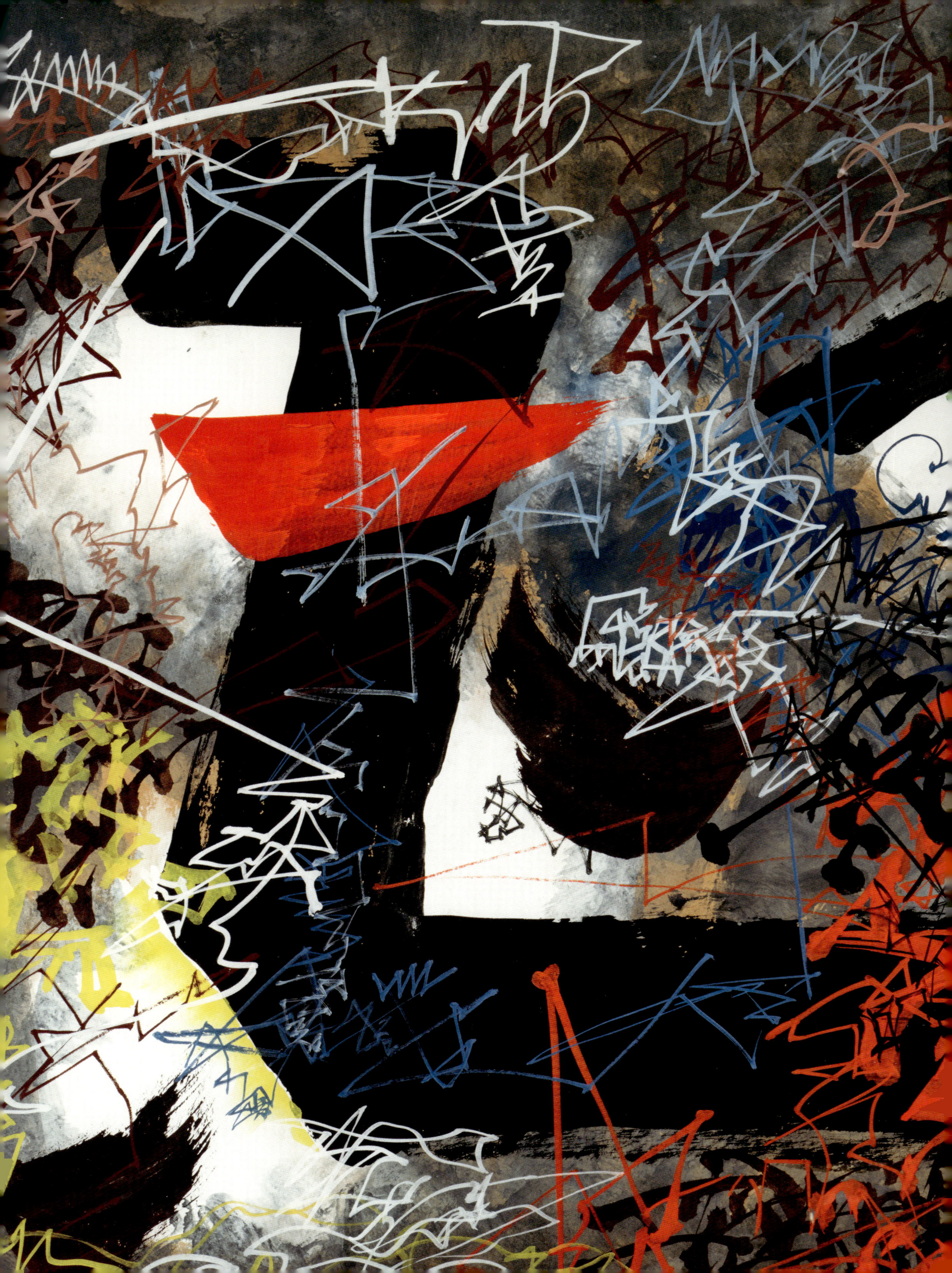

4.

THE NEW CITIZEN

Nomura returned to a city transformed by World War II. Seattle's population had grown by more than a quarter during his absence and in 1945 approached a half million people. Even before the United States' entry into World War II, the Seattle area had become the focus of war industry buildup, with the result that by August 1941 the region held several times the number of military contracts as Los Angeles or the San Francisco Bay Area.[1] Workers were recruited nationwide for the shipbuilding and aircraft industries, with most coming from the Midwest and South. For the first time, women and African Americans entered the workforce in numbers, although without seniority, they would be the first to lose their jobs when the war ended. In Nihonmachi, African American and Chinese American entrepreneurs moved into spaces vacated by the Nikkei.

As the end of the war drew within sight, government, labor, and industrial leaders were determined to mitigate a recurrence of the sudden economic contraction that had wreaked damage and unrest after World War I. The newly industrialized West was especially vulnerable; the Seattle area was said to have experienced the impact of the war more than any other region in the country.[2] Planning for the transition began early in 1944, and around Seattle was a coordinated federal, state, and local effort. Substantial federal investment eased the impact of postwar plant closures and layoffs, helping industries shift to a domestic economy, and, through GI loans, spurred new home construction. The federal partnership with industry would shape the region's future in aircraft, military contracts, and cheap electrical power. Programs gave priority access to jobs and home ownership to white veterans returning, but not to those of color.

At Minidoka, rumors abounded about resistance to the Nikkei's return to the West Coast. Nomura was one of many who feared the white reaction at home and remained in camp. Mr. and Mrs. Nomura, a WRA official wrote, "want to return to Seattle" but "are handicapped by their fear of discrimination and they have only a minor son upon whom they could rely upon for help."[3] Indeed, the opposition, always present, had become more strident after the WRA issued a "loyalty questionnaire" in spring 1943 and declared nearly all incarcerated Japanese Americans free of suspicion.[4] In the Seattle area that year, public figures such as Washington congressmen Henry Jackson and Warren Magnuson

International Carnival, 1950
Detail of Fig. 4.12

and governor Arthur Langlie, along with organizations ranging from the Seattle Chamber of Commerce to the Japanese Exclusion League, campaigned for their continued, and some hoped permanent, exclusion. As the movement grew, and the closure of camps was announced, the U.S. senator and incoming Washington governor Monrad Wallgren declared his adamant opposition to resettlement.[5]

Faced with the possibility of violence, Seattle mayor William Devin enlisted the Seattle Civic Unity Committee, which had been formed of business, labor, and education leaders to address racist practices during the war, and met with leaders of the opposition groups. Their joint leadership helped turn the momentum and quell the most outspoken resistance. At the same time, public sentiment nationwide began to turn as citizens learned of the battlefield heroism of the all-Nisei 442nd Regimental Combat Team.[6] Signs of "No Japs wanted" and cases of property destruction were jarring evidence of opposition, but, in general, the return to Seattle was orderly. In contrast, opposition to resettlement remained vehement in the White River valley, where Nikkei had dominated agricultural production, and few returned. In Tacoma, Nomura's first American home, a small fraction returned as the community dispersed.

Housing and employment in Seattle were immediate challenges. Returning Nikkei like Nomura faced the prospect of starting all over with what savings, if any, they had. For the Issei, who had labored and sacrificed so that their children might prosper, the prospect was especially daunting. While some families were able to return to homes and businesses that had been protected by white neighbors, most could not. Many of those who returned found their homes vandalized, their possessions stolen, and their businesses mismanaged or sold. Moreover, racially restrictive housing covenants and redlining limited many parts of the city to whites only, leaving the

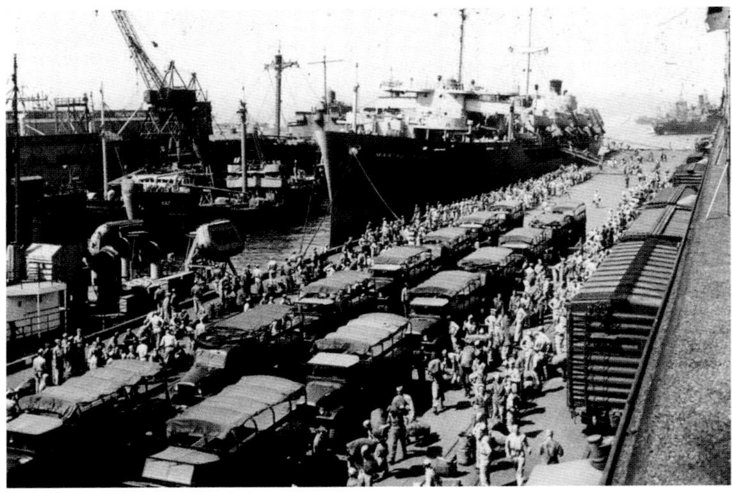

4.1
Soldiers disembarking the *Marine Phoenix* at Pier 39, Seattle, ca. 1946
Department of Parks and Recreation, Discovery Park Photograph Collection, Seattle Municipal Archives, 170365

Nikkei and others of color in the Nihonmachi-Chinatown area, the Central District, and Beacon Hill, where families often lived in shared and substandard housing. Discrimination in employment as well as housing was persistent. Many employers refused to hire the new returnees; others were employed well below their qualifications. Limited assistance in securing housing and employment was available through the WRA resettlement office in downtown Seattle, which could leverage its federal connections. Religious groups including the Church Council, American Friends Service Committee, and the Maryknoll Mission provided substantial support. Some provided jobs directly in mission-related industries, such as St. Vincent de Paul, where Tokita gained employment.

Nomura and his family returned to Seattle in early September 1945 and moved into the Amelia Apartments at Seventeenth and Yesler Way, a neighborhood east of the old Nihonmachi that in prewar years had been predominately Japanese American and Jewish. They unpacked stored belongings, thirty boxes and bundles including the paintings he had saved. Nomura appealed to the Seattle WRA office in a search to

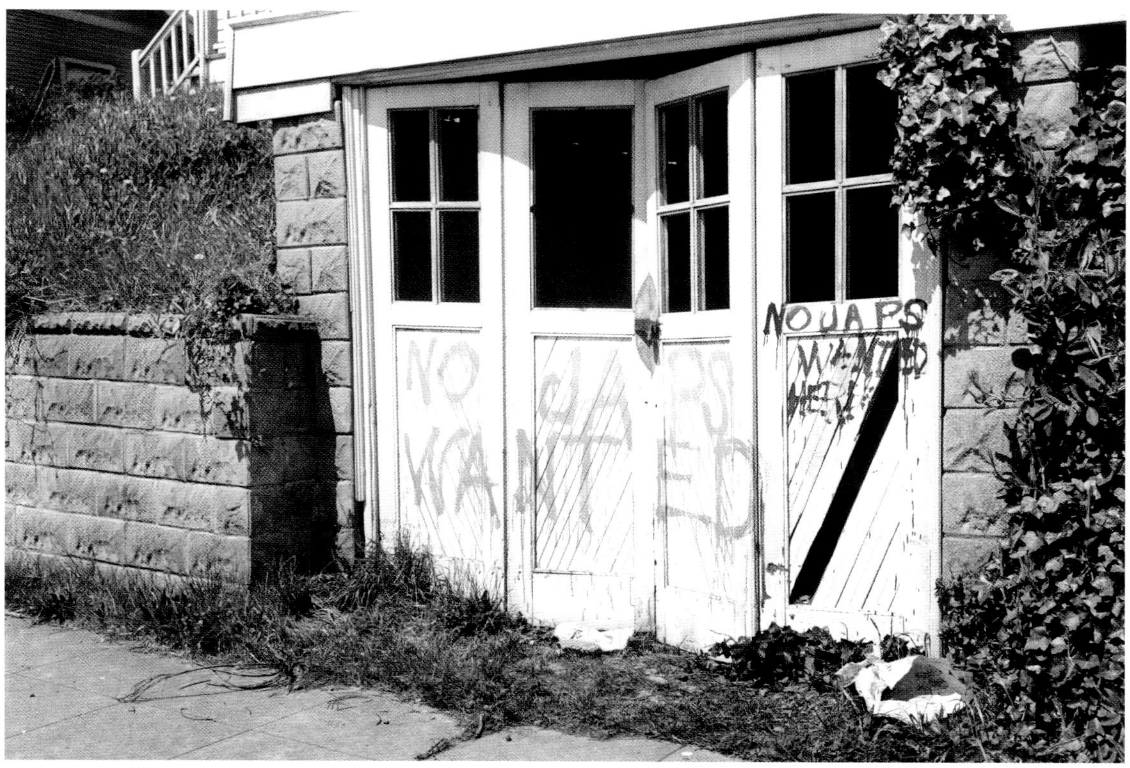

4.2
"No Japs wanted," Seattle, 1945. The Nagashi family returns home.
Seattle Post-Intelligencer Collection, Museum of History and Industry, Seattle, PI-28084

find art-related work, naming Richard E. Fuller, director of the Seattle Art Museum, as a reference. His desire to work as a creative craftsman is evident in the message written by the acting director of Minidoka on his behalf: "Mr. Kenjiro Nomura would like to know if there are any possibilities of his getting work in a store making show cards and assisting at window display or with toy or novelties manufacturers or art work painting lamp shades, glass ware, or knitting bags." The search was not successful, nor did Fuller, who after "highly recommend[ing] applicant in every respect," offer him work at the museum, as he had for several artists during the Depression. Unions blocked sign painters and retail stores from hiring him.[7] Two months after their return, Nomura again wrote the WRA office asking about their delayed paychecks and clothing allowance from Minidoka.[8] Eventually, he and Fumiko found work in a women's clothing manufacturing company, Doreme, at Eleventh and Pine, where he pressed clothes and she sewed. Their son, by then fifteen, enrolled at Garfield High School.

Around them, Jackson Street again drew the Nikkei as former shop owners reestablished their businesses. The Higo Ten-Cent Store, whose boarded-up windows had been pictured in the *Seattle Post-Intelligencer* in May 1942, reopened as a place of welcome familiarity.[9] Their efforts, however, represented a small fraction of prewar businesses. Most, like Nomura, had lost their shops, equipment, and inventory during the mass removal. The great majority of Issei were elders, worn by years of hard work, the loss of hard-won gains, and the deprivations of incarceration. The homes and shops they had vacated in haste in spring 1942 were quickly occupied by others. While Nihonmachi and the surrounding areas grew by a third during the decade, African Americans replaced Japanese Americans as the city's largest ethnic minority. Nihonmachi itself was a shadow of its former vibrancy. "Everybody had to find their own survival way, anywhere they could find homes and jobs," recalled Tokita's son Shokichi. "So it was a real big dispersal."[10] George Tsutakawa described trying to find friends such as Nomura and Tokita: "Everything was all torn up; it was not like the old days anymore. We had a heck of a time trying to locate them because they had lost their . . . homes, business, everything was really dislocated. It took some time before we got together again."[11]

For Nomura, any sense of stability was short-lived. Fumiko became ill and depressed, and in November 1946, little more than a year after their return from Minidoka, she took her own life.

Deeply disillusioned by the toll of the war Nomura had stopped painting. Only with the encouragement of the younger Issei artist Paul Horiuchi did he begin again. As Nomura's first biographer, June Mukai McKivor, recounts, "In spite of Nomura's refusals, Horiuchi came to the house and insisted that Nomura go with him on sketching excursions around Seattle. They painted together, encouraged each other, and teamed up to submit their work to art exhibitions."[12] Some forty sketches and paintings, many dated 1947, mark this time. The number of works he saved from this short period highlights the significance of Horiuchi's support.

He also took a deeply symbolic step to fulfill a long-held wish. In October 1947, two years after his release from Minidoka, Nomura signed a Declaration of Intention with the Immigration and Naturalization Service: "It is my intention in good faith," the document read, "to become a citizen of the United States and to reside permanently therein."[13] It would be another five years before the federal law was changed to allow his naturalization, and another two years before he realized his goal.

As Nomura recovered emotionally, he found new hope in marrying Chiyo (Alice) Fukasaki (1897–1956) in 1949. He continued, however, to struggle economically. Chiyo, a widow, had experience in hotel management and together the new couple bought the management business of the Crystal Hotel in the Belltown neighborhood.[14] They lost their investment when the hotel failed six months later. Nomura then worked as a presser in a garment factory until the physical strain became too much. He at last found satisfying work as a frame maker at the Pacific Picture Frame Company, "Mfrs in Seattle since 1893."[15]

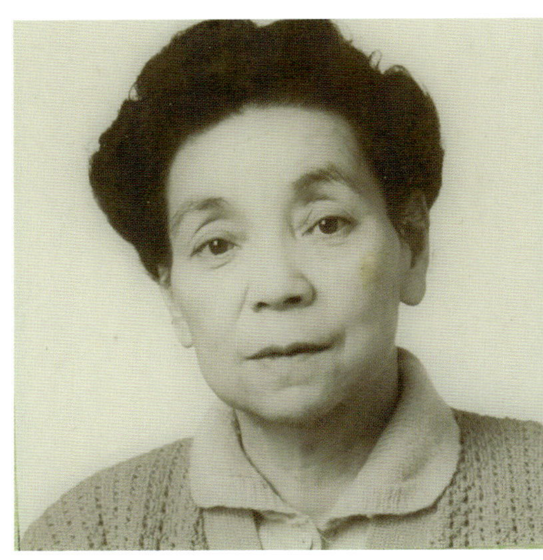

4.3
Alice Chiyo Nomura, U.S. Citizen Identification Card photo, 1953
Nomura Estate

The passage of the McCarran-Walter Act in 1952 ended the exclusion of Asian immigrants and the laws prohibiting their naturalized citizenship.[16] In December 1953 Chiyo became a naturalized citizen. On the following Veterans Day, 1954, Nomura became a citizen with the Americanized name Ken Kenjiro Nomura.[17] George Nomura described his father as a proud American who had long considered the United States his home. He and Chiyo bought a house of their own at 1830 Weller Street, not far from the apartment building where he had first lived after the war. Again, however, contentment was to be short-lived. Chiyo died during an illness in early 1956. Only four months later Nomura, who had been ill for some time, died on June 30, 1956, of complications after surgery.[18]

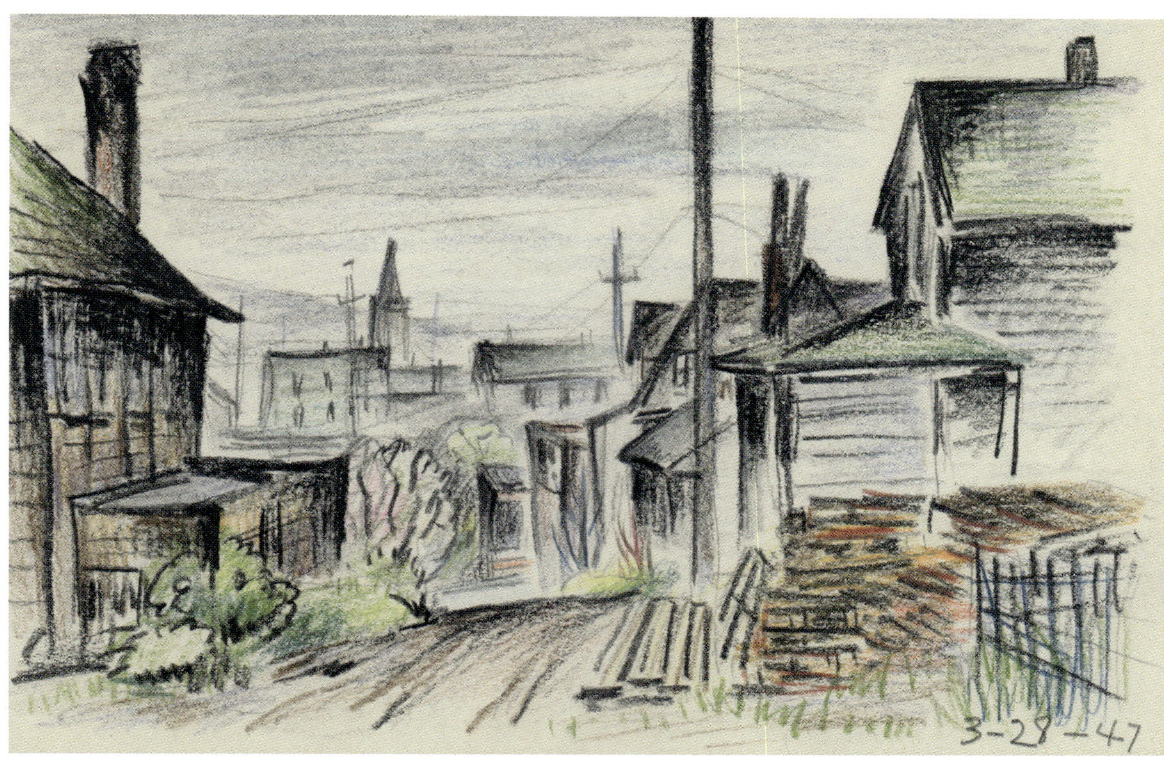

4.4
Untitled (houses on First Hill), March 28, 1947
Color pencil on paper, 5 × 8 in.
Nomura Estate

A Return to Painting

With his resumption of painting, Nomura began by returning to some of the Issei artists' favorite sites of the 1930s. He explored the streets of his old neighborhood, the city's waterways, and shoreline sites along Puget Sound. The numerous paintings and sketches from 1947 trace his artistic explorations as he began to turn from realism to abstraction. Lucid watercolors open vistas onto buildings and docks, water, and skies (figs. 4.5–4.8). Pencil drawings trace compositional development and note colors. A few of these drawings transform structures into linear vectors, hints of his abstract work to come. In an early composition, houses rendered in the wet and dry brush of watercolor rise on the hill above Lake Union, where tender springtime hues display Nomura's color sensibility; the sun-struck sides of buildings are left white, allowing the blocky structures to merge into geometry where sunlight and shadow meet. Several paintings picture the brick-red and rust-brown buildings of an industrial area, possibly along Salmon Bay, in variously considered compositions of the same view (fig. 4.9). In the more finished versions, the edges of buildings are outlined in black and others dissolve without definition; opaque white accentuates the black, isolating building elements as geometric forms and flattening the perspective in semi-abstract resolution. Similarly, a series of paintings in watercolor or oil transform old pilings along the shoreline of Puget Sound, where Nomura reassembles the seascape into blocks of color with the pilings as patterned black accents. In one, tendrils of giant kelp encircle the scene, an evocative mix of art and nature (fig. 4.10). The pace of invention within several months makes palpable Nomura's renewed energy for painting.

In September 1947 Nomura exhibited his new work at the Western Washington State Fair, the same fairgrounds where he and his family had been incarcerated in 1942. The fair was the first since wartime and met by an enthusiastic crowd. Supervising the ambitious, multiple-part

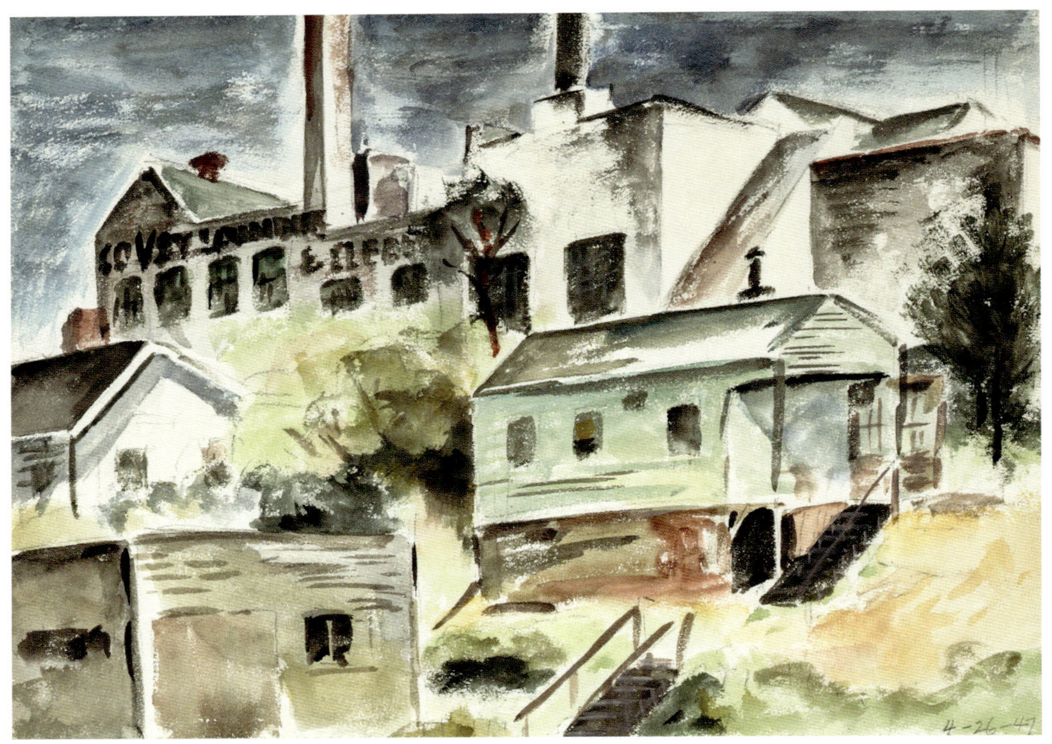

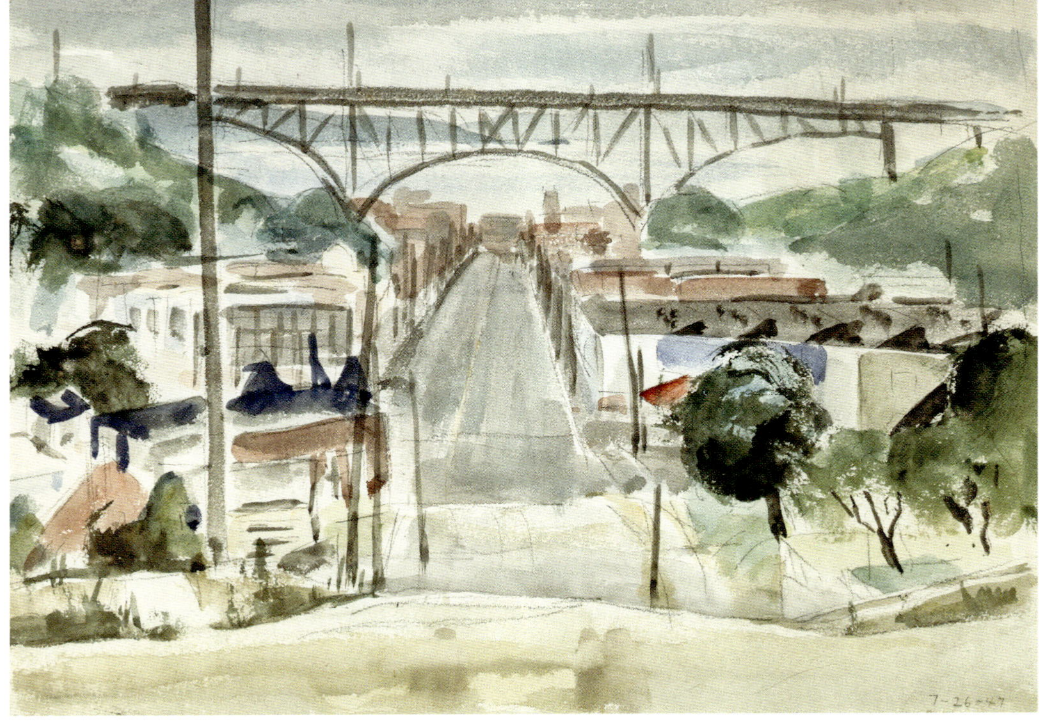

4.5
Untitled (Eastlake), April 26, 1947
Watercolor on paper, 9½ × 13½ in.
Nomura Estate

4.6
Untitled (Dearborn Avenue), July 26, 1947
Watercolor on paper, 9¾ × 10¾ in.
Nomura Estate

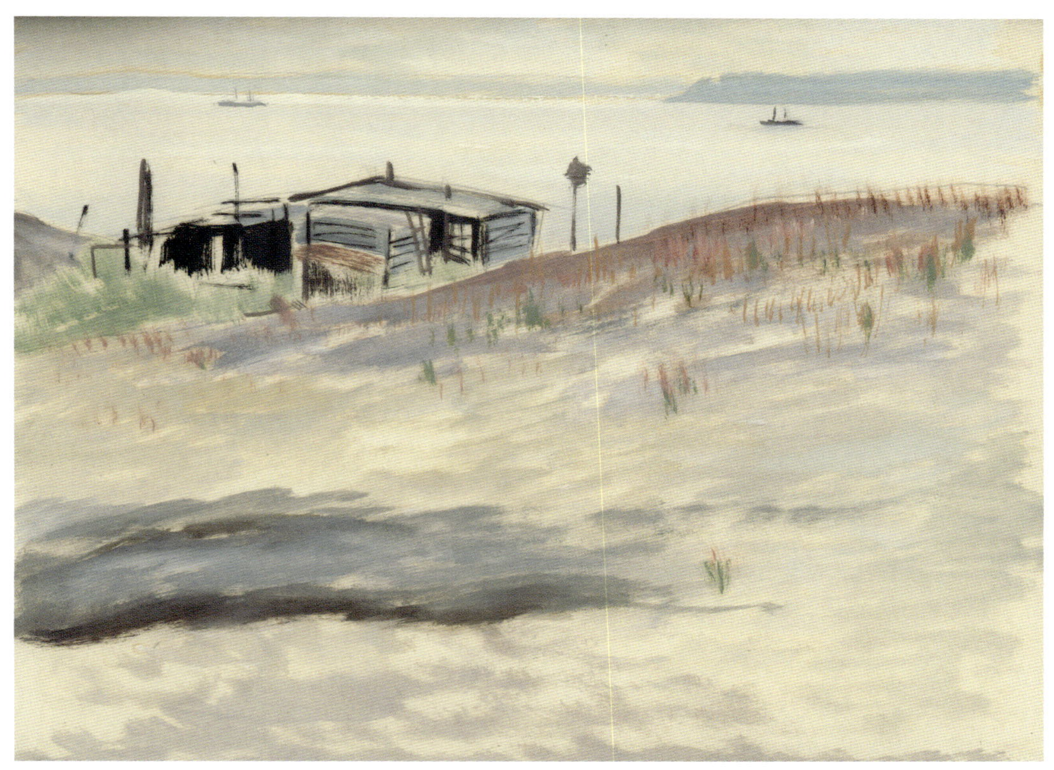

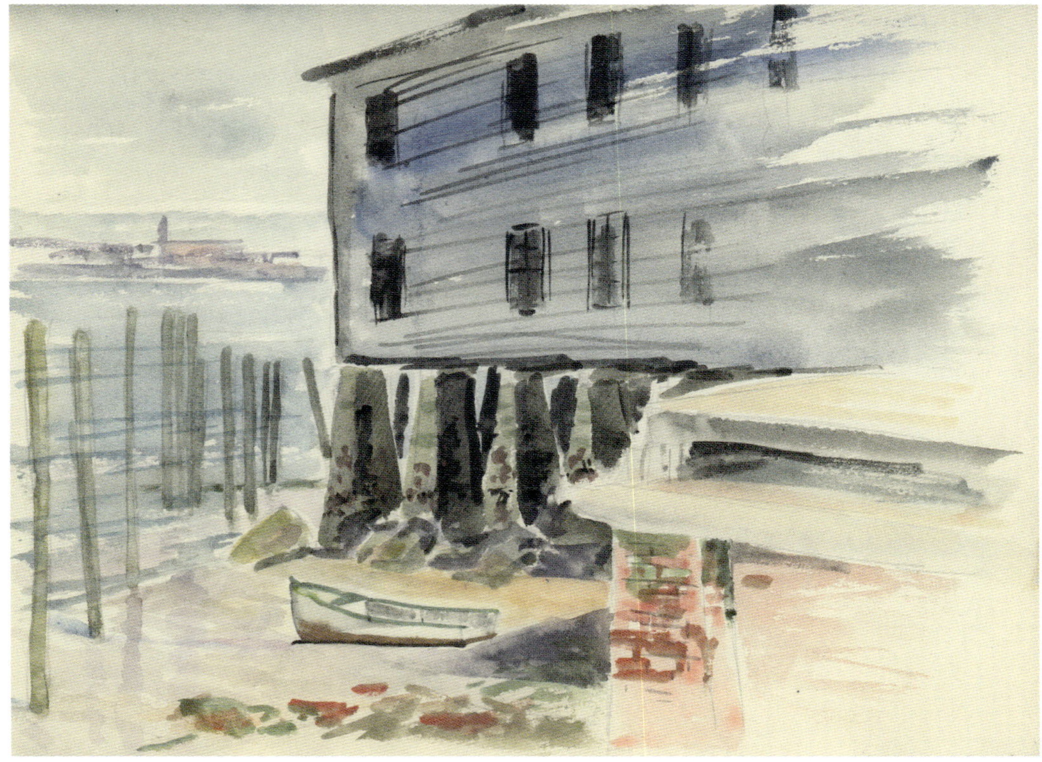

4.7
Untitled (Puget Sound), ca. 1947
Watercolor on paper, 8½ × 11 in.
Nomura Estate

4.8
Untitled (Alki shore, West Seattle), ca. 1947
Watercolor on paper, 8¾ × 11¾ in.
Nomura Estate

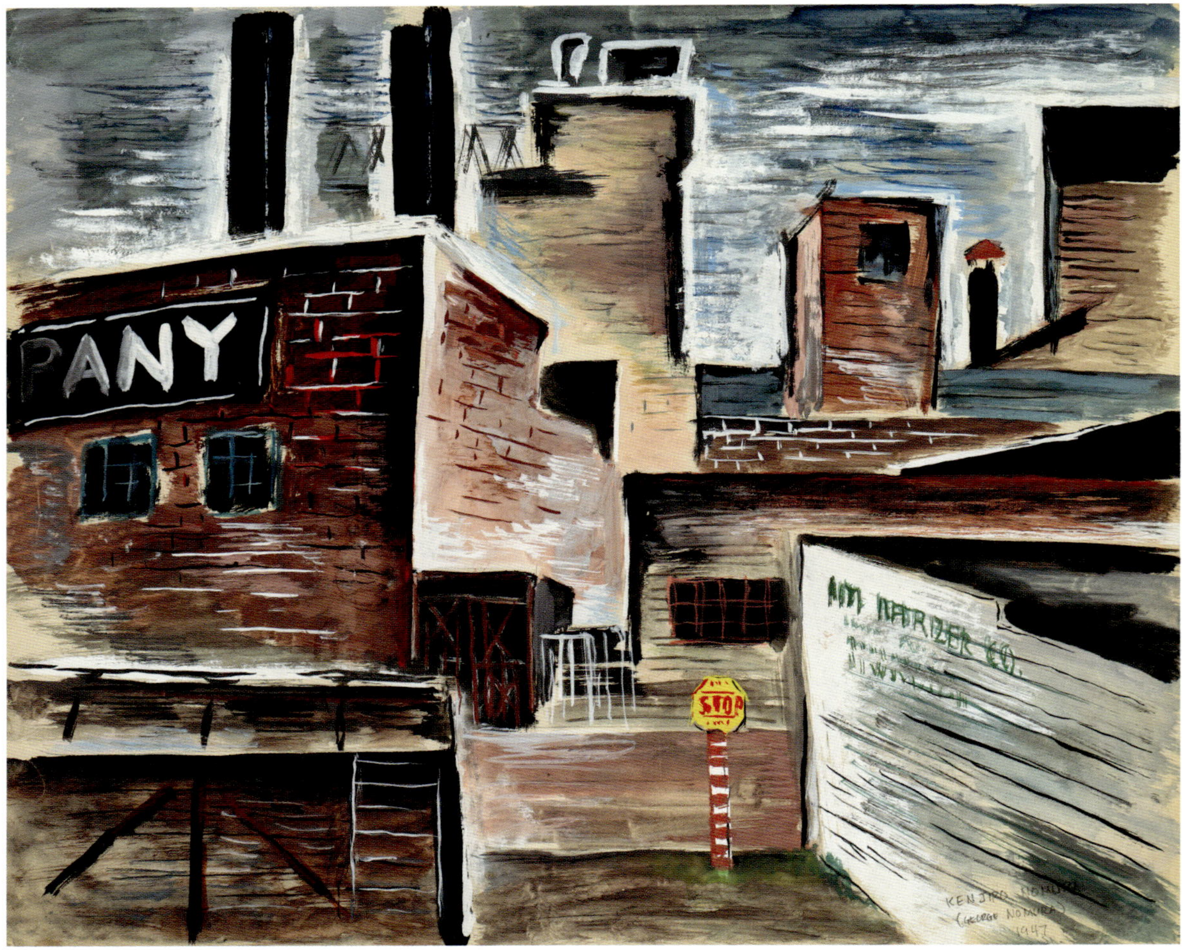

4.9
Untitled ([Com]pany), 1947
Gouache on cardboard, 19 × 24 in.
Nomura Estate

art exhibition, *Contemporary Arts for Today's Living*, was Melvin Kohler, associate director of the University of Washington's Henry Gallery. In successive years Kohler would build strong representations of regional art by inviting nationally known art professionals to serve as jurors in the fair's statewide competitive exhibition. Nomura's recognition in his first postwar exhibitions was immediate. A month after the fair, his painting *An Old Brewery* won honorable mention at the Seattle Art Museum's Northwest Annual (see fig. M.31).

Despite his renewed recognition, Nomura did not exhibit paintings again for two years. Fumiko's recent death, his remarriage, and continued economic insecurity surely preoccupied him. He sometimes asked his son to bring art books from the library and in this interim seems to have developed the steps toward abstraction he had begun in 1947. His absence from public life is reminiscent of his withdrawal from exhibiting in the late 1920s, when he emerged with a solidly developed, modernist-inflected style. He reentered the Western Washington Fair in 1949, and by 1950 he presented an entirely abstract body of work. For the next five years he enjoyed multiple opportunities and honors.

Nomura's subjects of the 1950s are urban, but unlike his paintings of the 1930s, it is the human activity in urban spaces that draws him. Calligraphic-like brushstrokes denote structure, space, and energy. His skill in Japanese brushwork is apparent in the fluid gestures and the rhythms of pressure and release. Some are gouache, an opaque water-based paint and a new medium for him.

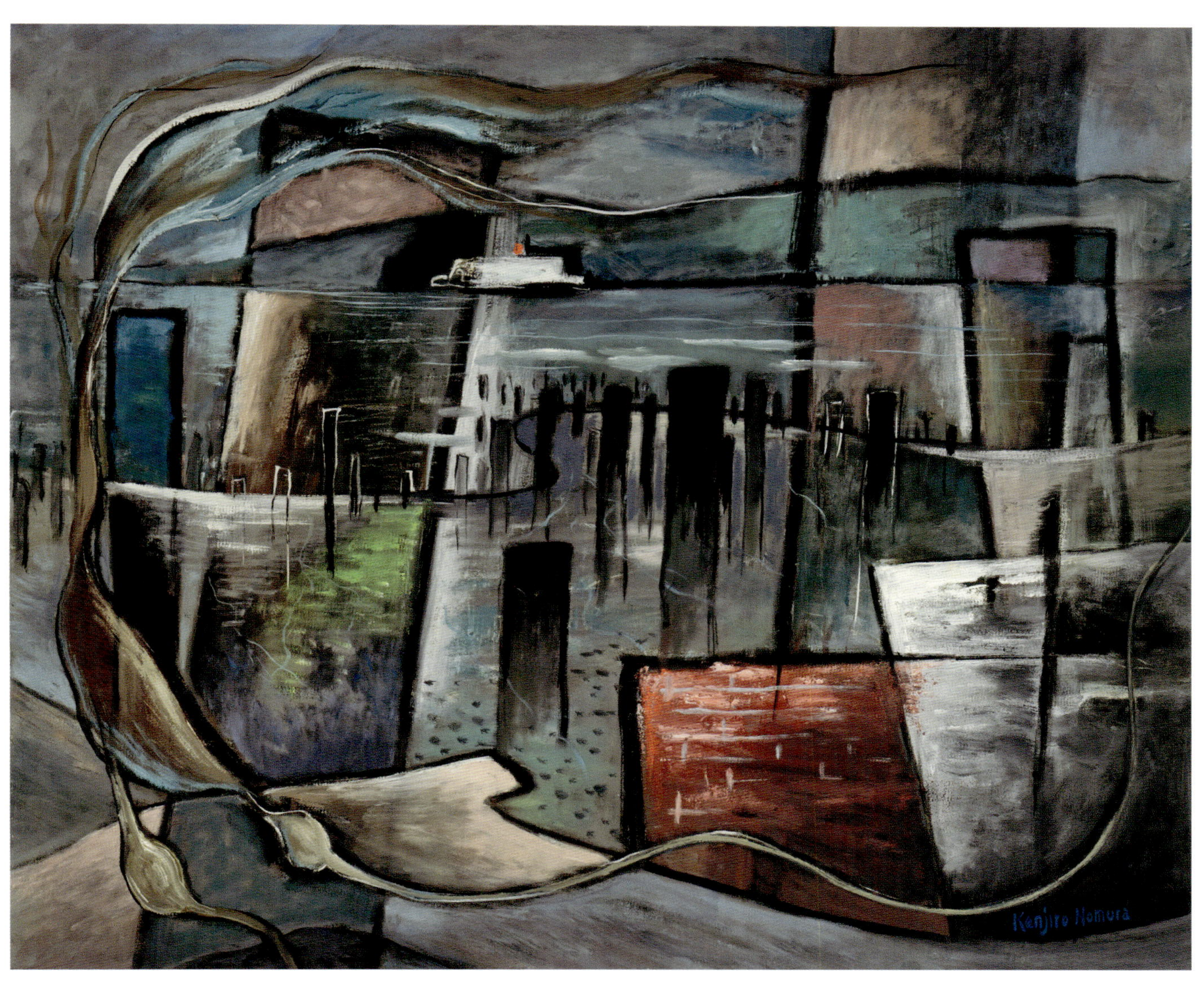

4.10
Puget Sound, 1947
Oil on canvas, 23½ × 29½ in.
Nomura Estate

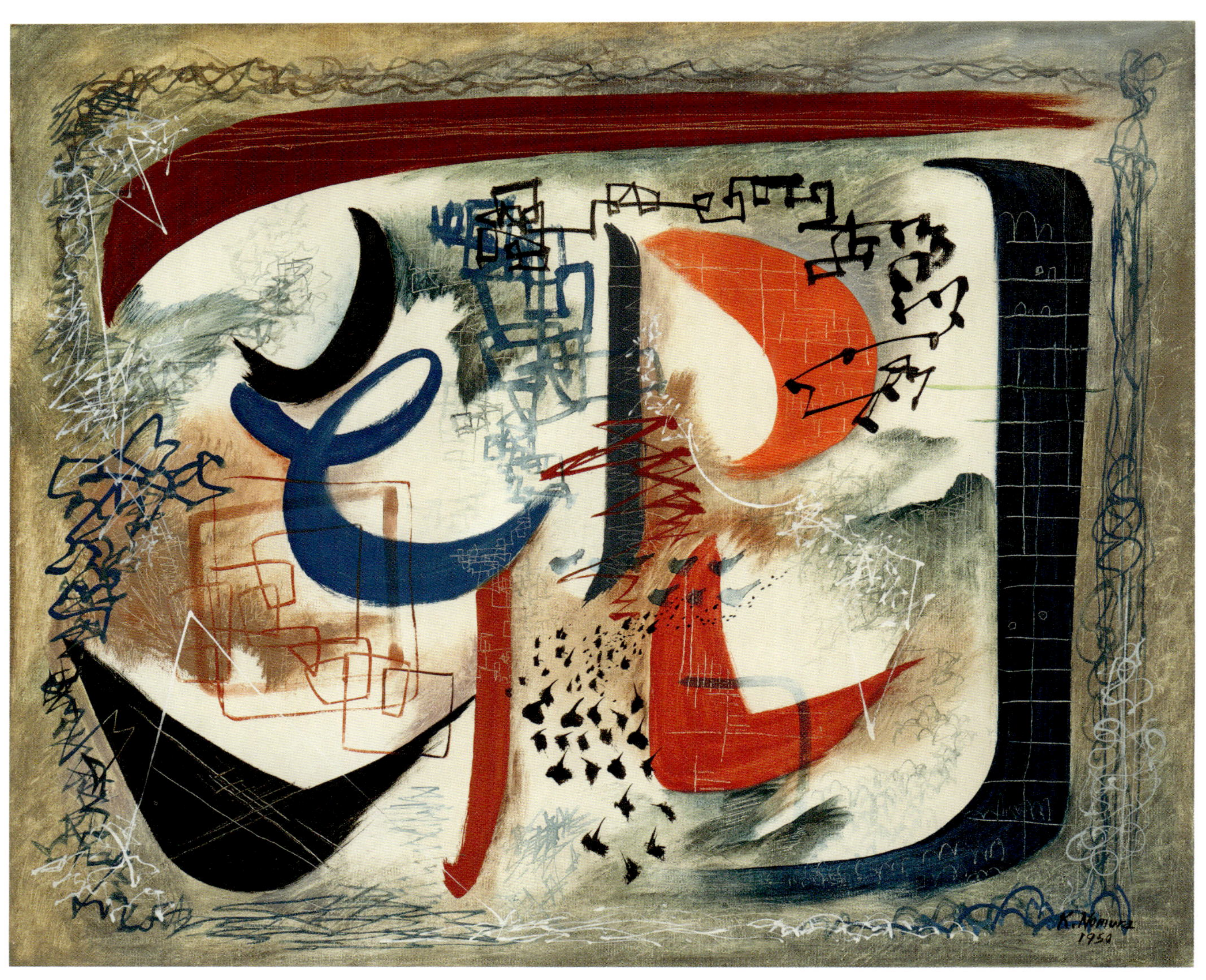

4.11
Shopping Center, 1950
Oil on canvas, 24 × 30 in.
Collection of Lindsey and Carolyn Echelbarger, promised gift to Cascadia Art Museum

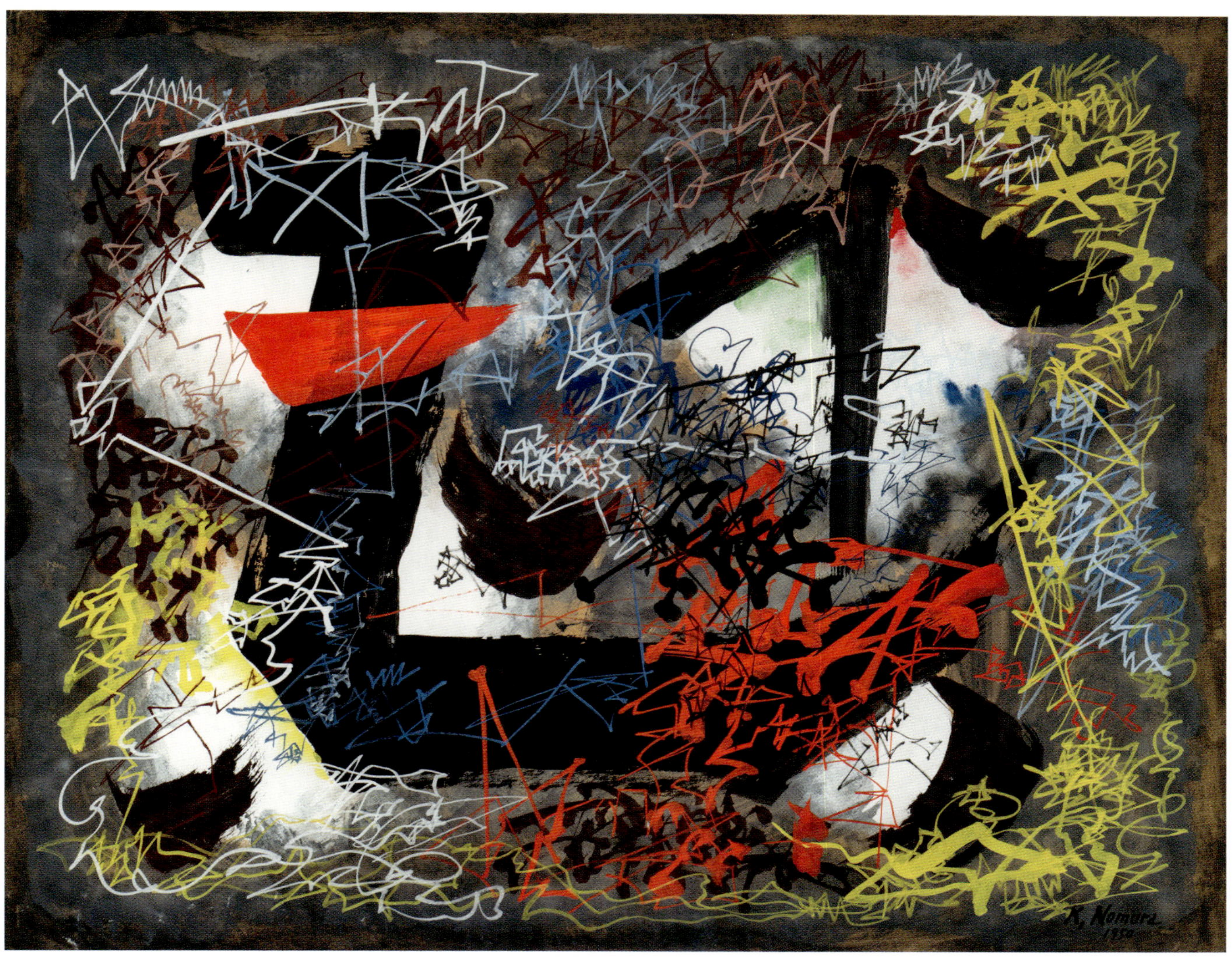

4.12
International Carnival, 1950
Gouache on kraft paper, 22¾ × 29½ in.
Nomura Estate

Shopping Center is a celebration of midcentury geometry: boomerang shapes in orange, blue-green, black, and brown; bundles of interlocking rectangles; and rambling linear chains in black and blue, all overlaid by delicate white lines in paint and incised pattern (fig. 4.11). In *International Carnival*, the primary forms are replaced by broad black brushstrokes, unconstrained by geometric precision, and highlighted by patches of white that seem to radiate from behind (fig. 4.12). Energetic lines in primary colors of red, blue, and yellow animate the entire composition. The same elements create dynamic circular compositions in paintings such as *Folk Dance*.

In August 1950 Nomura participated in the International Art Exhibition, where *International Carnival* was among his paintings on display. The exhibition was part of the International Carnival held in the Nihonmachi-Chinatown neighborhood; the artists represented were Asian American and African American. It was sponsored by the Jackson Street Community Council and the International Improvement Association and held in conjunction with the new Seattle Seafair, the first citywide celebration since the war.[19] Japanese, Filipino, and Chinese performances filled a stage on King Street; a Japanese folk dance was held Saturday night, and a dragon dance paraded down Yesler and Jackson—all

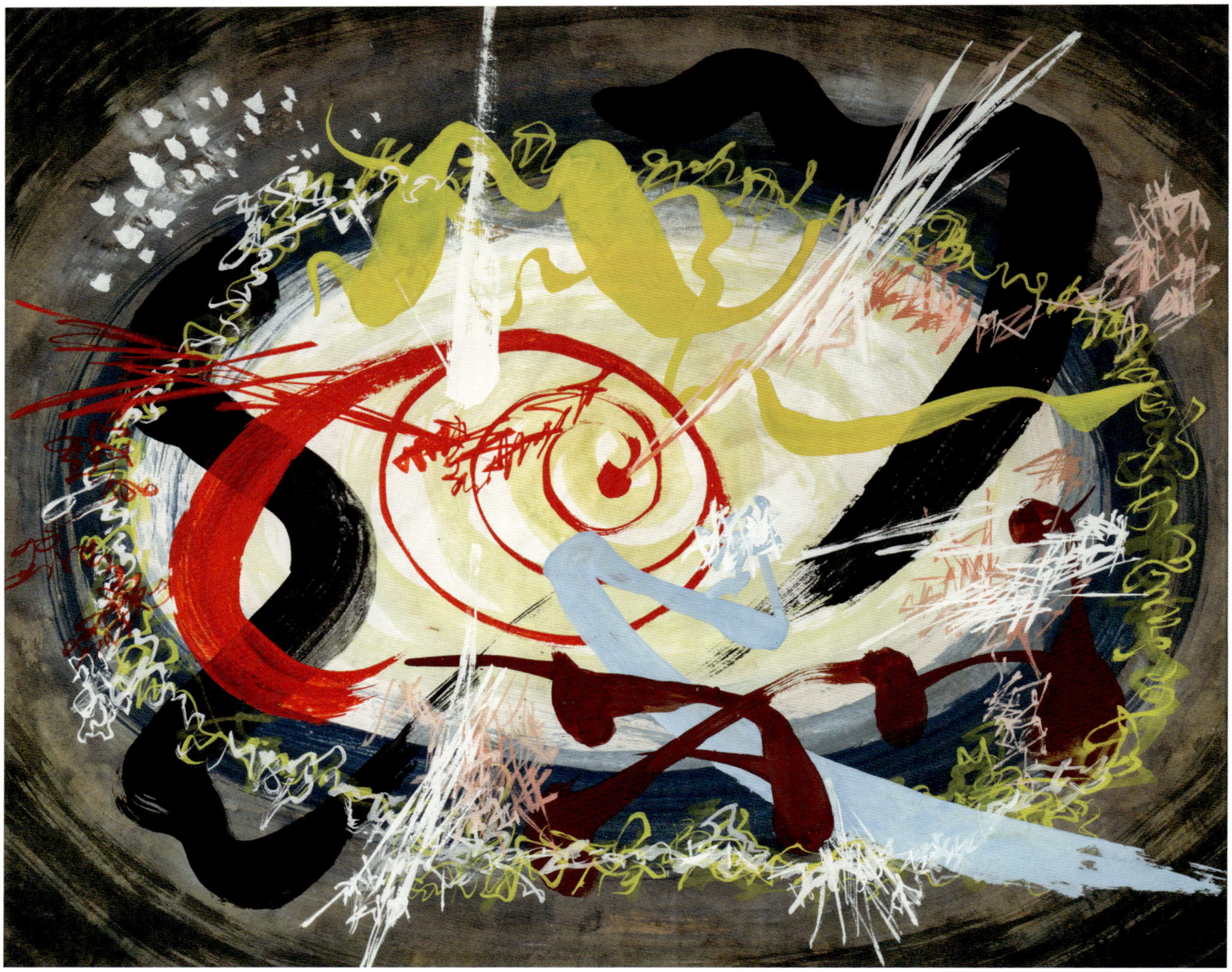

4.13
Folk Dance, 1950
Gouache on kraft paper, 12 × 24 in.
Collection of Michael and Danielle Mroczek

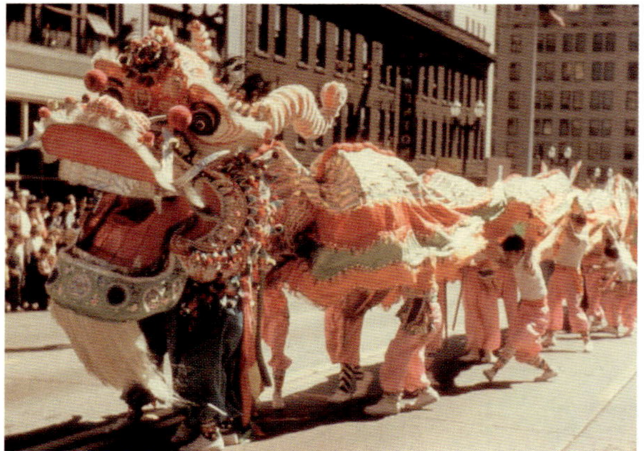

4.14
Chinese dragon during the Seafair Parade, ca. 1951–1954
Photo: William Ward Miller
Special Collections, University of Washington Libraries, UW 40975

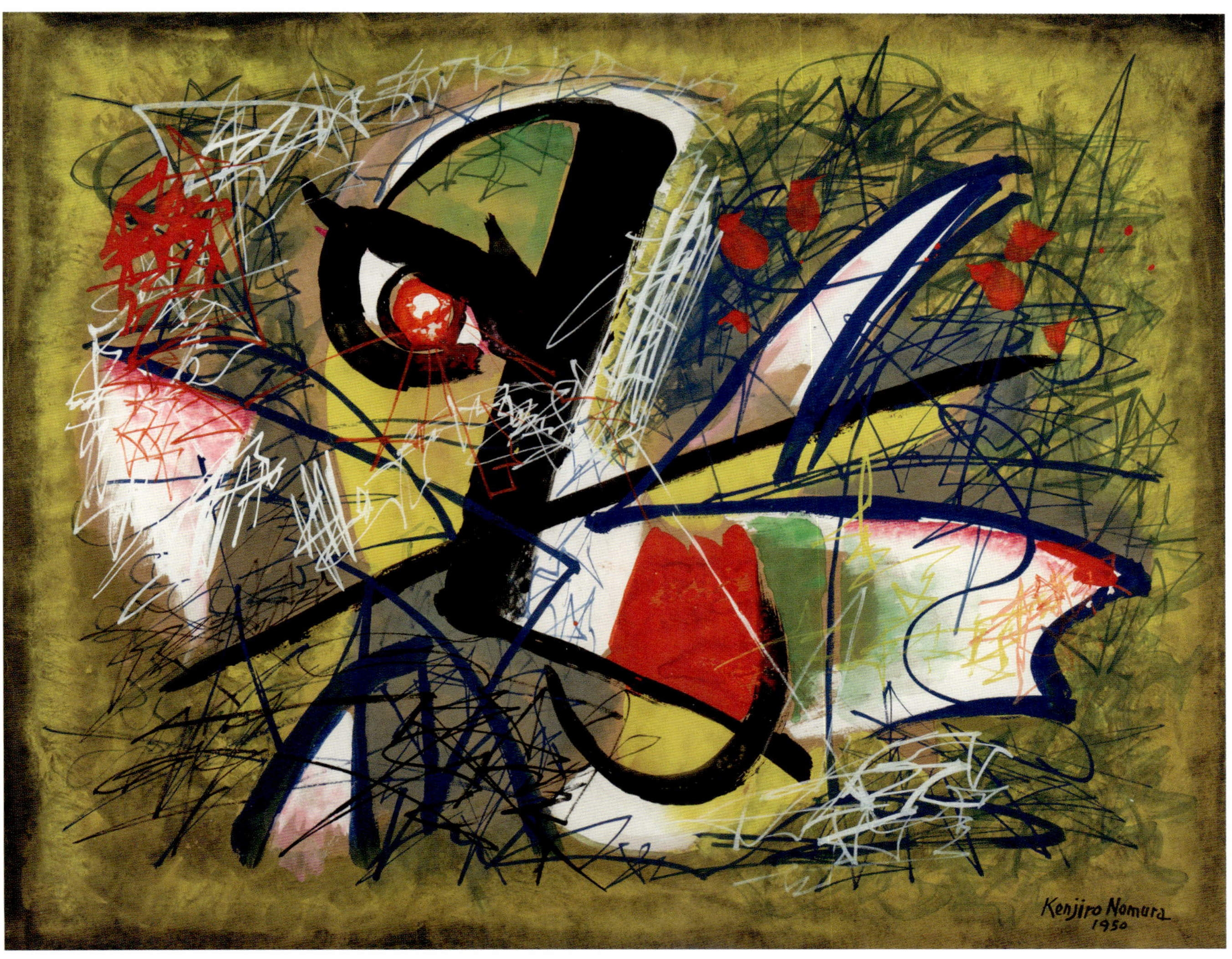

4.15
Dragon Dance, 1950
Gouache on kraft paper, 22⅝ × 29⅝ in.
Nomura Estate

subjects for Nomura's paintings (figs. 4.13–4.15). He participated in the popularly received exhibitions for the next two years.

A month later Nomura's *Chinese Lion Dance* won honorable mention at the Western Washington Fair.[20] The sole juror, Andrew Carnduff Ritchie, director of painting and sculpture at the Museum of Modern Art in New York, declared that he was "extremely impressed with the level of quality of the works submitted" and found "an imaginative and a freshness of expression and execution to many of the paintings."[21] In 1951 Nomura again won honorable mention. He was one of four Japanese Americans to win such recognition at the fair, an occasion highlighted by the press. Joining him were Horiuchi, who had won first prize at the 1947 fair, and the Nisei artists George Tsutakawa and John Matsudaira. Exhibition organizer Melvin Kohler pointed out to visitors that the four artists' paintings hung in a building used for grain storage when Japanese Americans were confined at Puyallup.[22]

The early 1950s gave rise to several new exhibition venues that offered Nomura opportunity. The Henry Gallery joined the older Music and Art Foundation in co-sponsoring an annual invitational exhibition, in which Nomura was regularly included. *Rush Hour* was his entry in 1952 (fig. 4.16). Art Week on Pine Street was organized by the Seattle chapter of the Artists Equity Association and became a popular annual

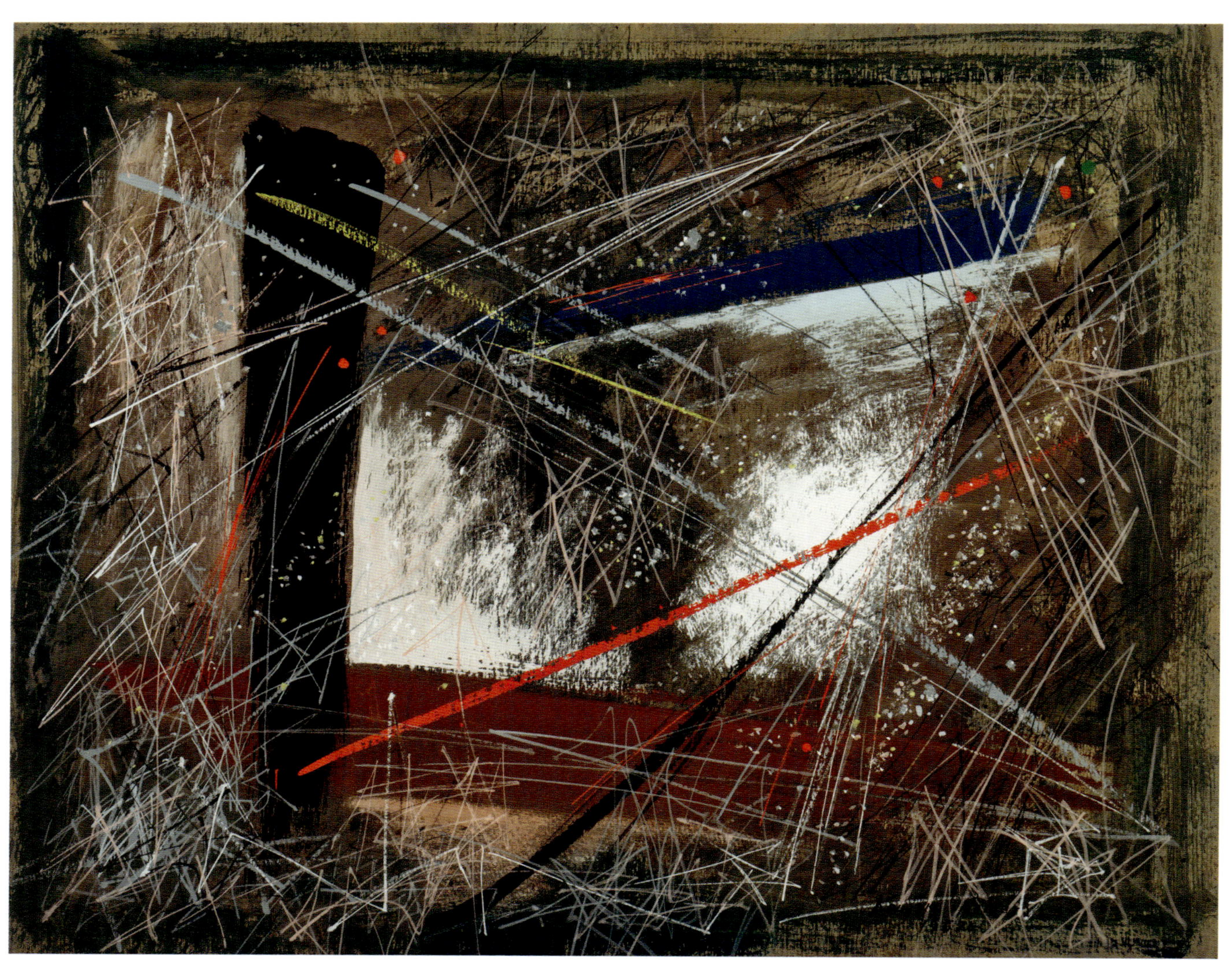

4.16
Rush Hour, 1952
Gouache on paper, $17\frac{5}{8} \times 22\frac{3}{4}$ in.
Nomura Estate

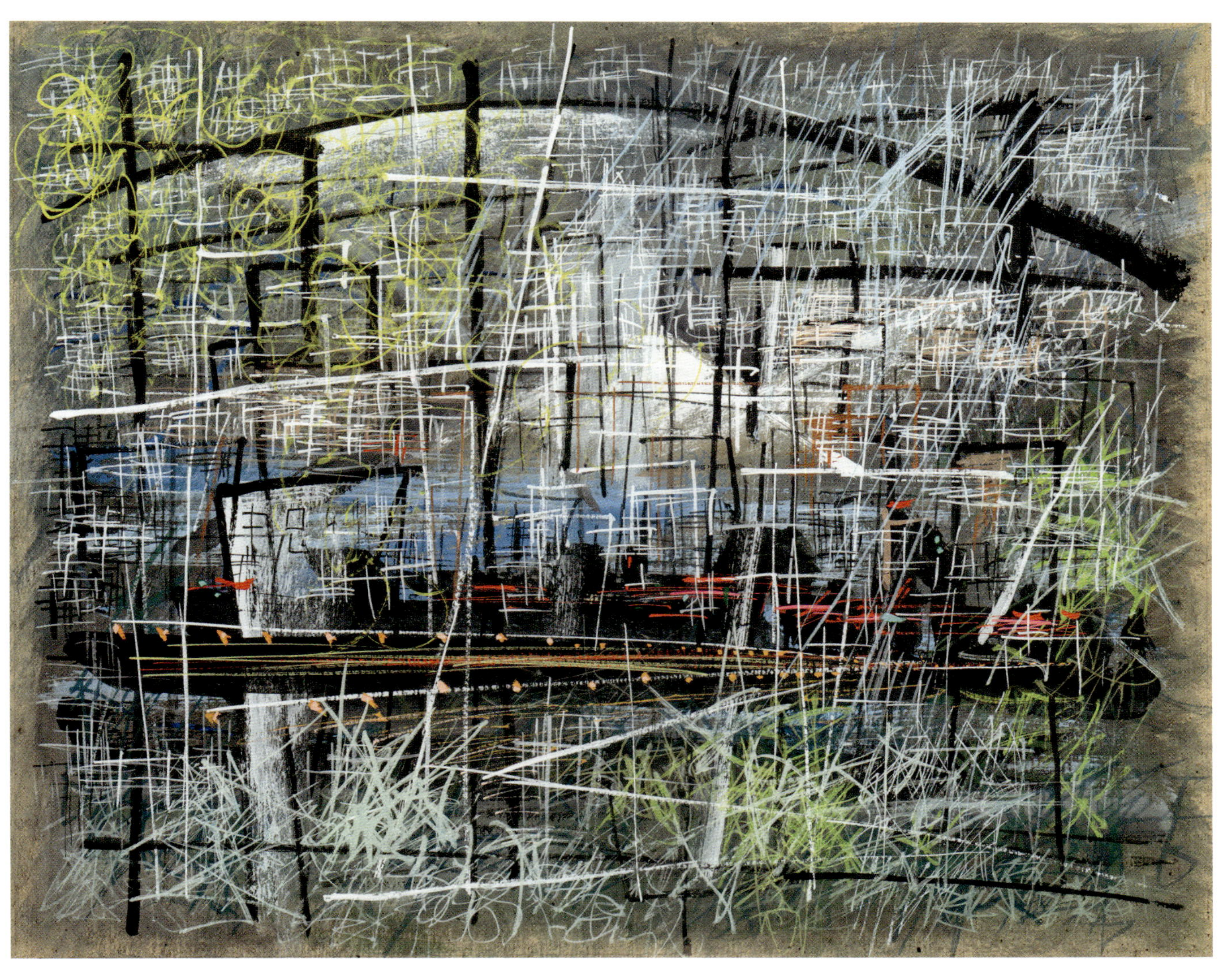

4.17
City Lights, ca. 1952
Gouache on cardboard, 19 × 24 in.
Collection of Michael and Danielle Mroczek

event displaying local artists' work in downtown department store windows. Nomura was among the artists selected for the first exhibition in 1952, where his painting *City* was an award winner. An annual Art Collectors' Tea, intended to promote art's accessibility to middle-class households, drew professional artists as jurors and some of the best-known artists in the region as exhibitors, Nomura among them. In 1953 he showed once again in the Northwest Annual.

Overriding all in impact was Nomura's affiliation with the gallerist Zoe Dusanne. Dusanne took note of the recognition given the Japanese American artists at the 1951 state fair and invited them to show at her gallery. Dusanne had one of the first private galleries in Seattle, where she presented contemporary European and American art. Of modest midwestern origins, she had lived in Seattle as a young woman before moving to New York's Greenwich Village in the late 1920s, where she befriended artists such as Marcel Duchamp and Stuart Davis and gradually assembled a collection of art by outstanding European and American modernists. At the outbreak of war, she returned to Seattle, and at the war's end commissioned the young architect Roland Terry to design a small house overlooking Lake Union to serve as a home and a gallery. There, beginning in 1950, she exhibited work by Paul Klee, Wassily Kandinsky, Pablo Picasso, and others in her collection alongside that of local artists such as Mark Tobey, Guy Anderson, and Viola and Ambrose Patterson, and introduced young artists whose work she believed promising. She worked tirelessly for the artists she represented, promoting not only the sale of their work but also its publication and exhibition elsewhere in the United States and abroad. "Perhaps more than any other person here," wrote *Seattle Times* columnist Louis R. Guzzo, "she broke down provincial resistance to modern art and introduced bold contemporaries to persons who hadn't dared to endorse artists who hadn't been dead at least 50 years."[23]

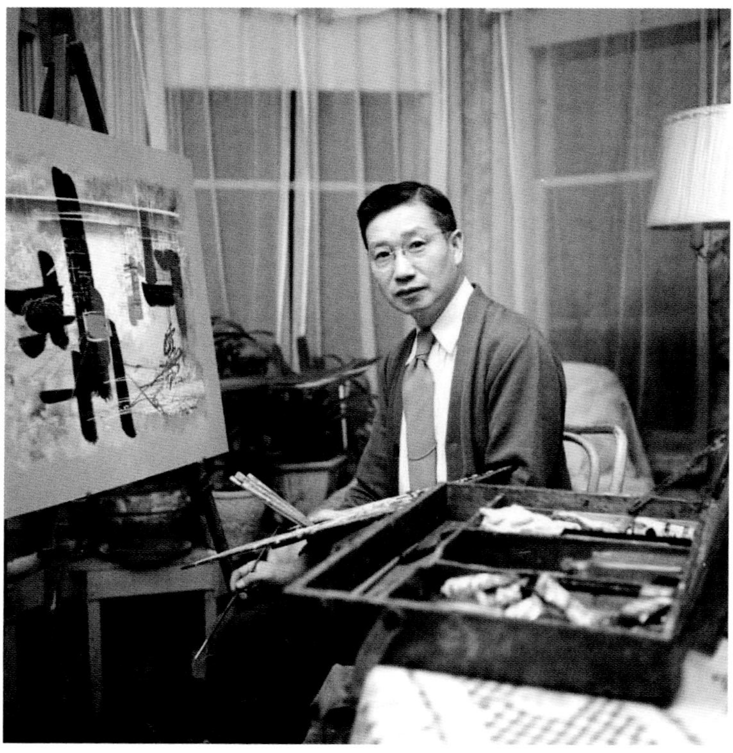

4.18
Kenjiro Nomura at easel, 1952
Photo: Charles Pearson
University of Washington Libraries, Special Collections, Pearson 5210-64A

Dusanne presented the four Japanese Americans' work in February 1952 and, given the positive response, extended the closing date into March. Writing for the weekly *Argus*, David B. Pennell cited the exhibition "of particular significance for Seattle" that featured "the work of Japanese-American artists who have been active here as nowhere else in this country."[24] Elmer Ogawa photographed the artists in the gallery in images that have become emblematic of their and Dusanne's relationship. One pictures Nomura standing proudly next to his *International Carnival* (figs. 4.19 and 4.30). Nomura, Pennell continued, had "evolved an extremely personal new style which is perhaps the most interesting in the show. To subjects like Japanese traditional dancing . . . , the International Carnival, and a shopping center, he imparts the authentic feeling by means of colors, shapes, and brush techniques

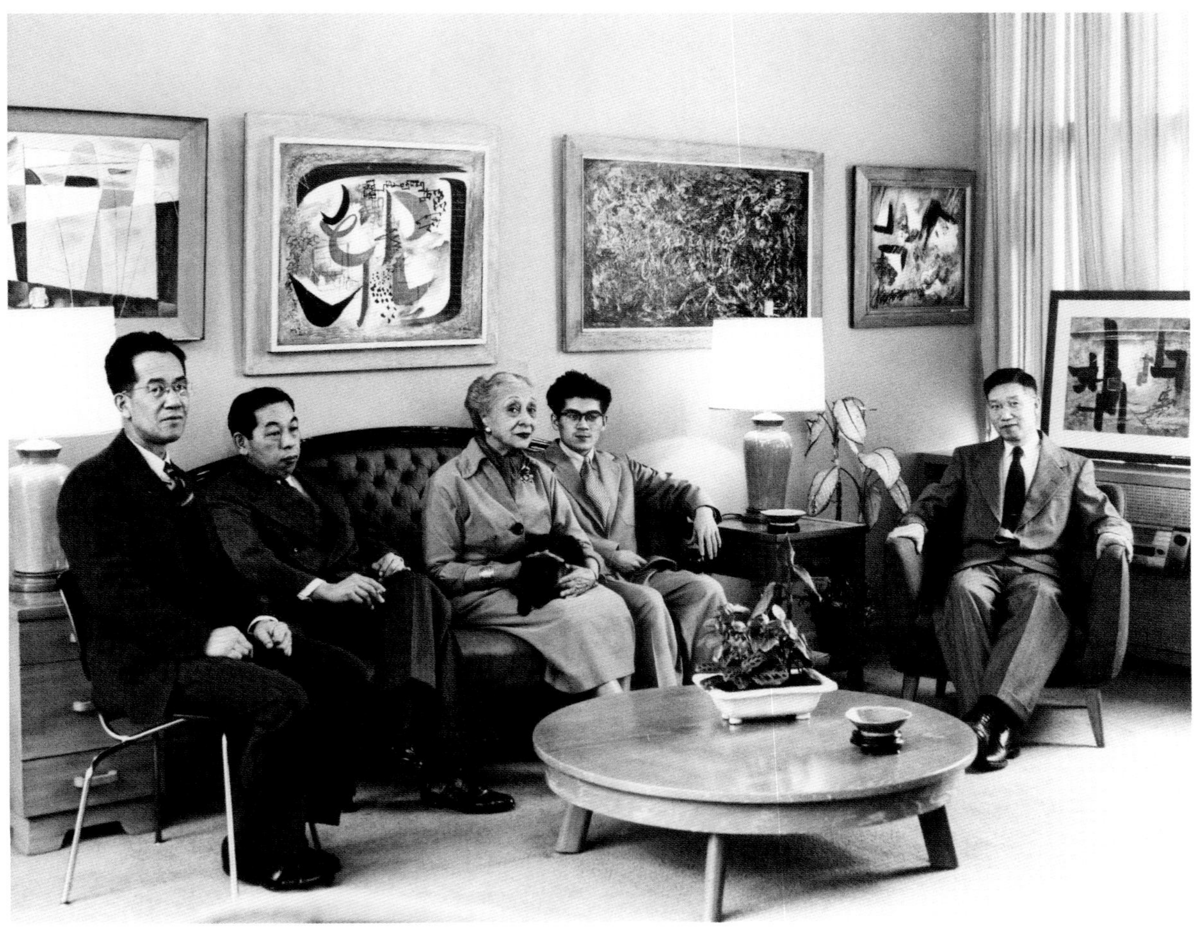

4.19
Paul Horiuchi, George Tsutakawa, Zoe Dusanne, John Matsudaira, and Kenjiro Nomura at the home of Zoe Dusanne, 1952
Photo: Elmer Ogawa
Special Collections, University of Washington Libraries, UW 23046z

that are ultimately Japanese and yet have a special abstract splendor that is all his own. . . All four artists represent a very high standard of Pacific Northwest painting, as their success in the more selective exhibitions and competitions hereabouts has shown, and they represent a combination of cultural resources." The four exhibited together at Dusanne's gallery again the next year. Arts critic Maxine Cushing Gray applauded their work: "These are four Seattle individuals who know what to do with paint and are going their own absorbing ways."[25] Amid the artists' collective recognition, Margaret Callahan wrote a feature article for the *Seattle Times*, framing their individual stories by a brief history of the achievements of Issei artists in Seattle and noting that the earlier group had been "dispersed" during the war. "The loss was felt keenly," she declared, "and it was with a warmly welcoming feeling that art viewers saw the return of Kenjiro Nomura and the rise of some promising new talent."[26] Here and elsewhere, Nomura was respectfully identified as senior among the city's Japanese American artists.

In 1955 Nomura was selected as one of eight Washington artists to exhibit in the *Third São Paulo Biennial*, where his painting *Harbor* was displayed in the city's Museum of Modern Art (fig. 4.22). Once again, Richard E. Fuller was instrumental in his inclusion. The São Paulo Biennial was the first international modern art biennial to be founded since the original one in Venice, which dated to 1895, and in São Paulo reached its full realization in 1955. Nomura's

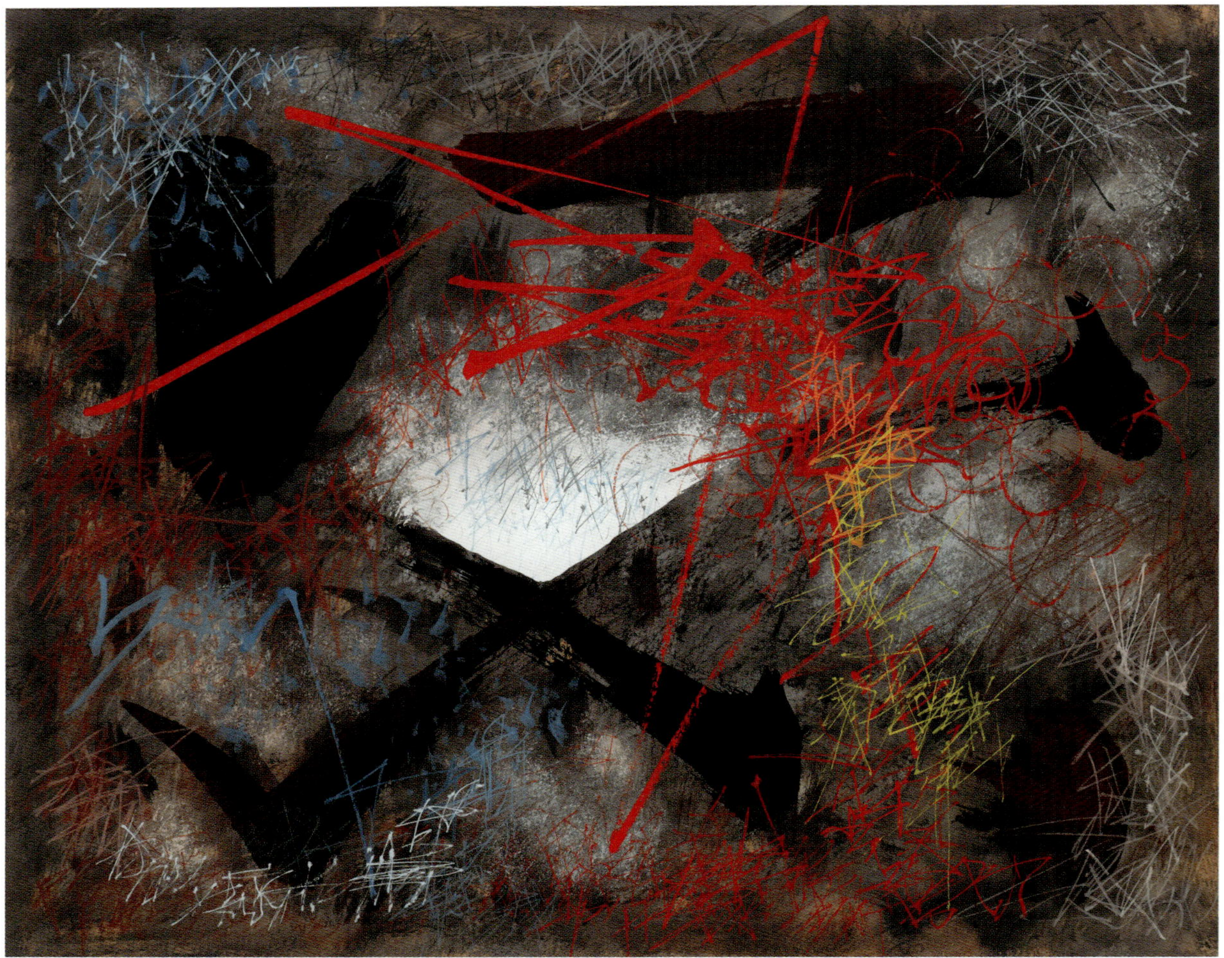

painting was on view in the United States section, which featured West Coast artists that year, subsequently was shown in Rio de Janeiro, and then traveled to Cincinnati, Colorado Springs, Minneapolis, and San Francisco.[27] It was Nomura's final honor during his lifetime.

4.20
Untitled, 1952
Gouache on paper, 17¼ × 22¼ in.
Seattle Art Museum, gift of the Estate of Mr. Nomura, 60.87

Affinities

Nomura's paintings of the 1950s abandon Western perspective to explore variations of the gestural stroke and linear networks of color. He worked in oil, which he had used throughout the 1930s, and his newer medium of gouache. Several paintings in 1952 refine the compositional format developed in *International Carnival* (see fig. 4.12). Two untitled abstractions in gouache employ broad, black, foundational brushstrokes, backlit in white and overlaid by fine linear networks in white, red, yellow, and blue (figs. 4.20 and 4.26). Like calligraphy, the energy of each stroke is sustained to the end and stopped with intention. Brushstrokes "breathe" as the paint diminishes. The networking lines are at once delicate and firm; some draw precise angles, most are a free-running style. Energy radiates throughout the compositions.[28]

Nomura further explored this brushwork in paintings in oil on Masonite. The support provides a warm brown ground, negating the need for a dark base color, and the fatness of oil paint glides on the surface. One untitled painting, which Nomura's son identified in later years as expressive of Hiroshima, is an explosive abstract composition dominated by orange against blues and black and the brown of Masonite, a singular

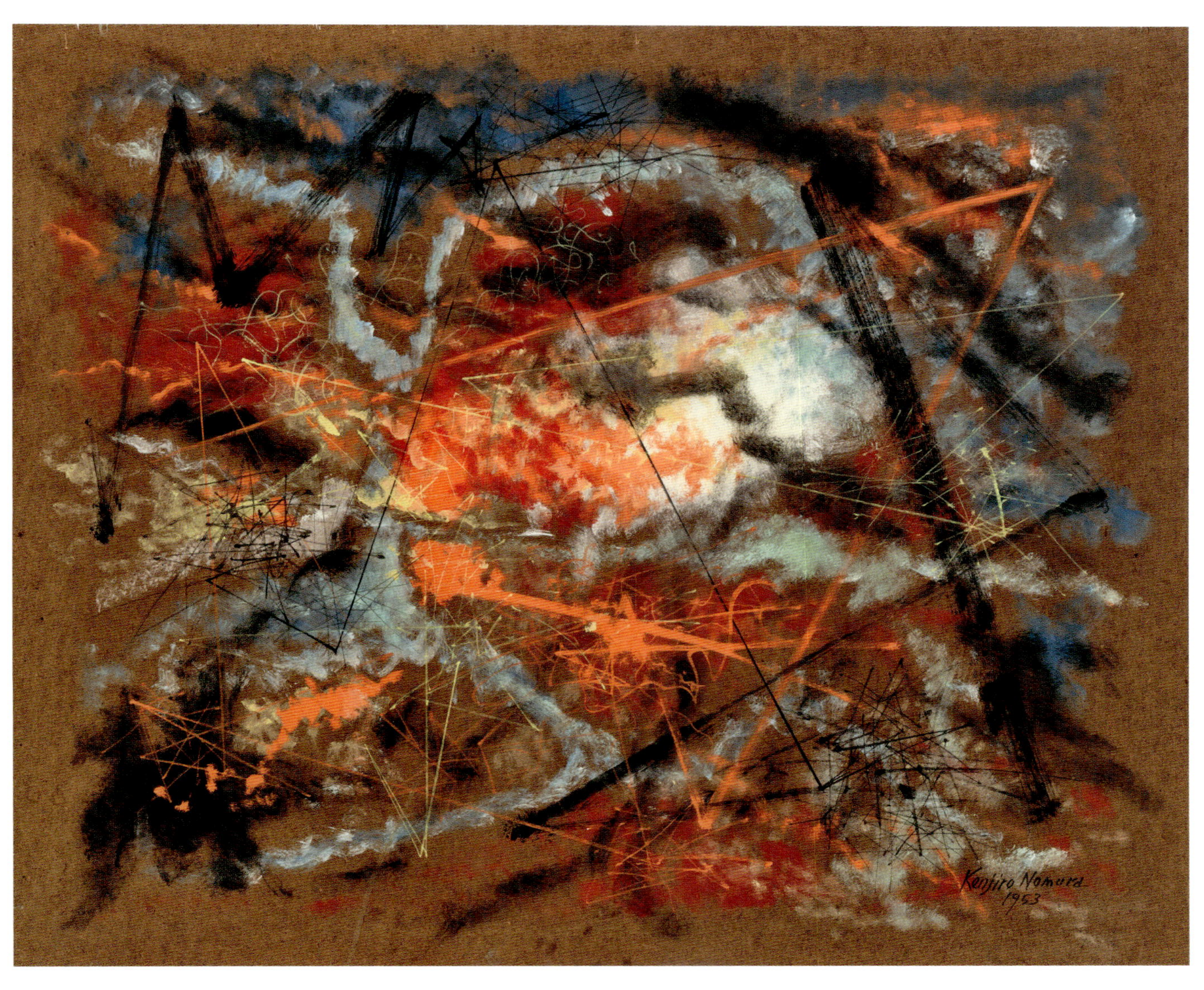

4.21
Untitled, 1953
Oil on Masonite, 24 × 29¾ in.
Private collection

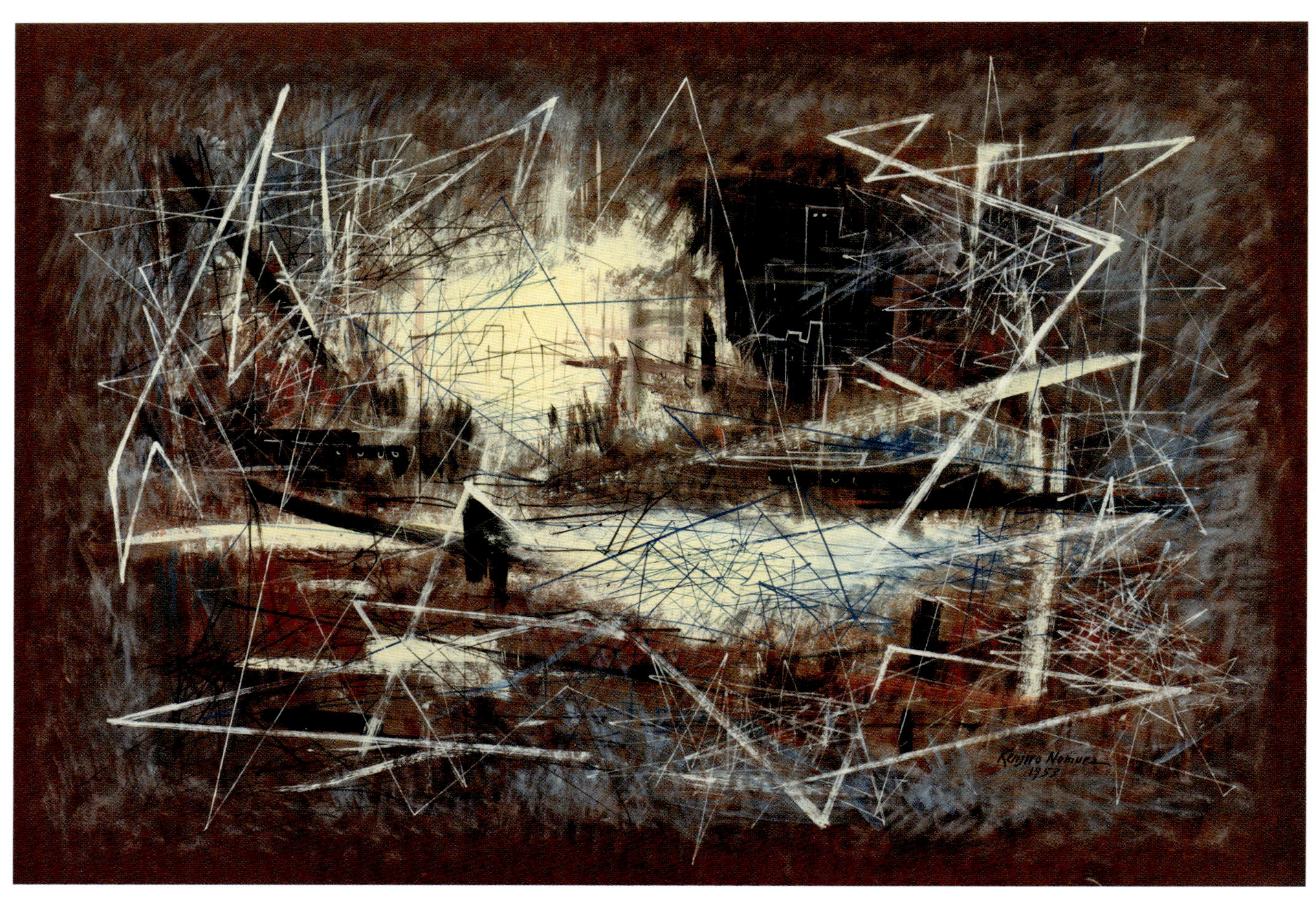

4.22
Harbor, 1953
Oil on Masonite, 24¼ × 36 in.
Nomura Estate

4.23
Fish Market, 1952
Oil on Masonite, 24 × 30 in.
Collection of Michael and Danielle Mroczek

4.24
Ball Game, 1955
Oil on Masonite, 23 × 29 in.
Nomura Estate

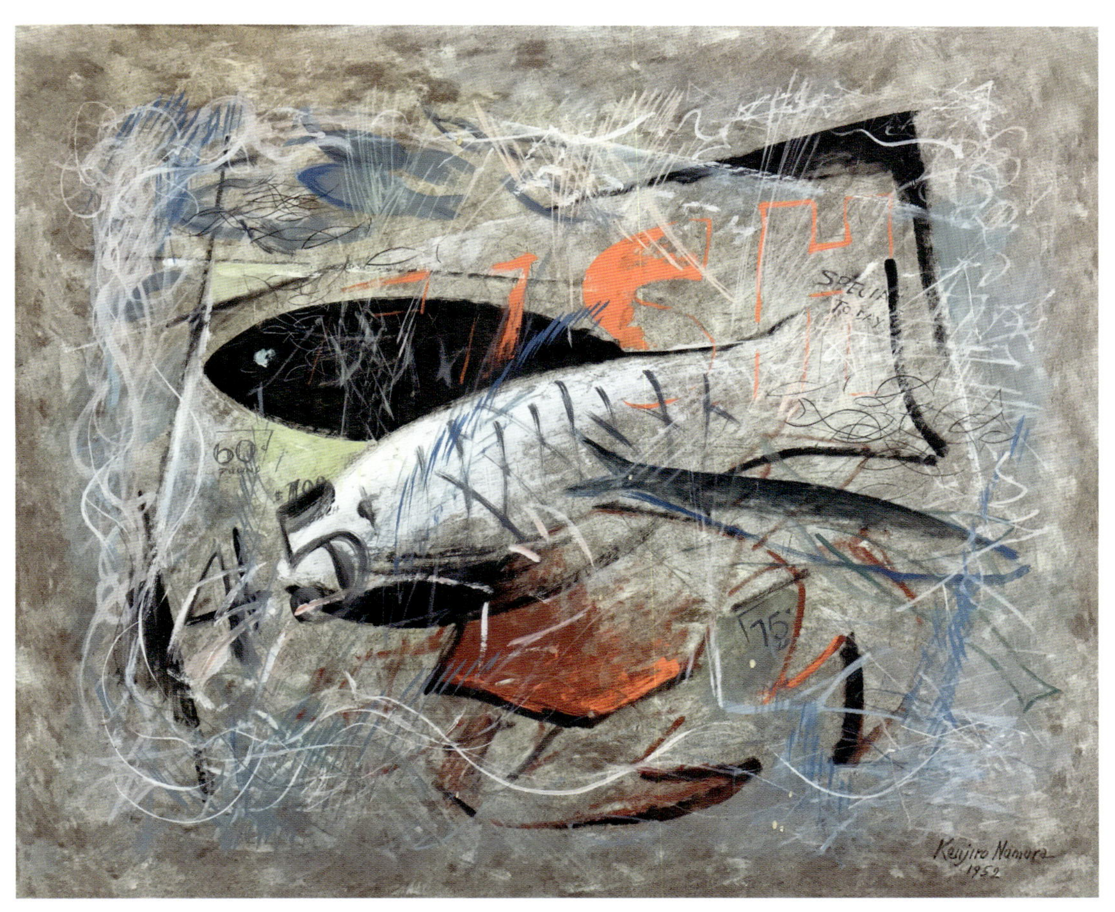
Kenjiro Nomura
1952

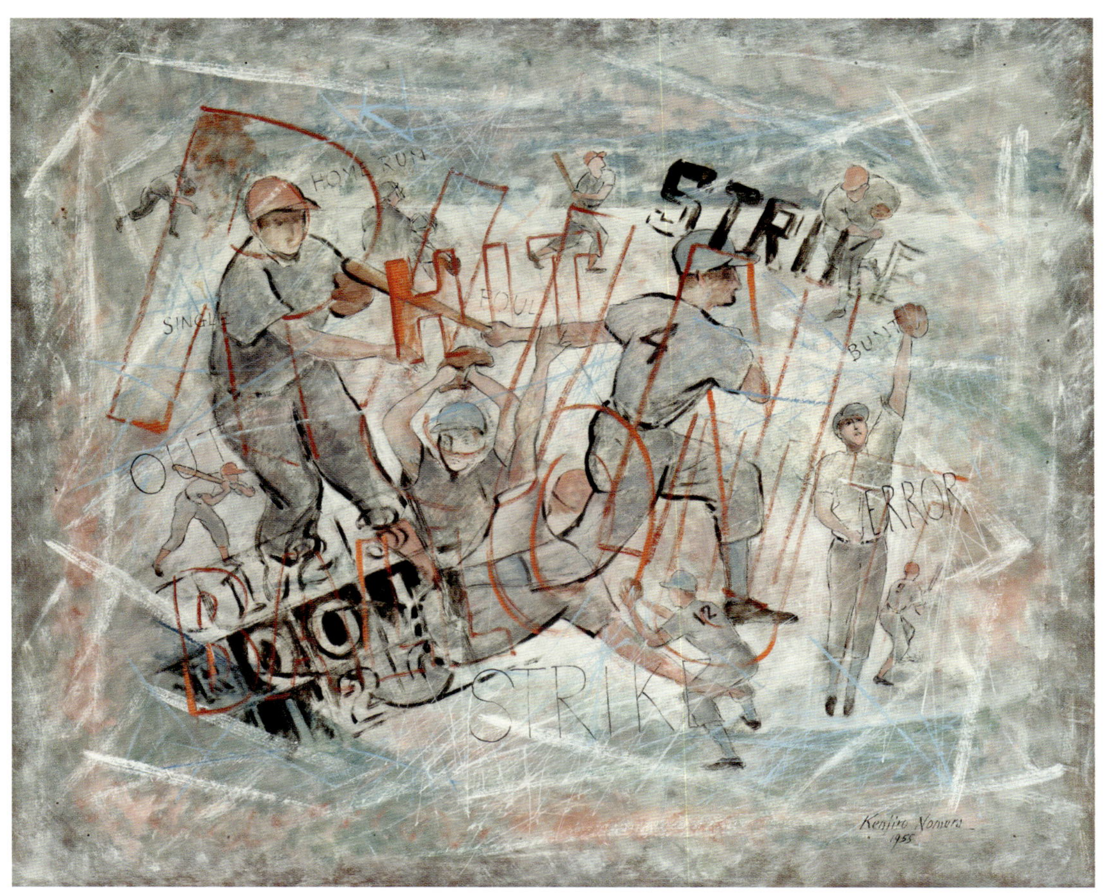
HOME RUN
STRIKE
SINGLE
FOUL
BUNT
ERROR
STRIKE
Kenjiro Nomura
1955

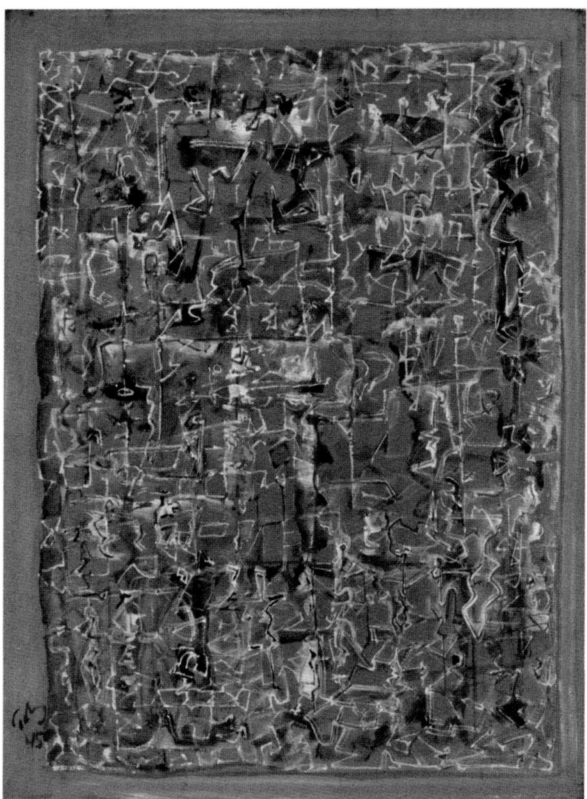

4.25
Mark Tobey, *Agate World*, 1945
Opaque watercolor on composite board, 14⅞ × 11 in.
Seattle Art Museum, Eunice P. Clise Fund, Seattle Foundation, 50.110

example of the subject (fig. 4.21).[29] In *Harbor*, a few minimal, representational details emerge from the angles and networks to recognizably link image and title (fig. 4.22). The color is representational, limited to blue, black, and white.

Two paintings, *Fish Market* (1952) and *Ball Game* (1955), feature representation figures amid an overall gestural ground (figs. 4.22 and 4.23). Both were painted for national art competitions sponsored by the Tupperware company, whose stated aim was to support contemporary American art and encourage other businesses to follow suit.[30] It is tempting to think that Nomura intended the recognizable images of his competition entries to be more broadly appealing than the abstractions. Both paintings feature his lettering skills as a sign painter, and in *Ball Game,* his skill in representing the human figure. Reviewing Dusanne's 1953 exhibition, Kenneth Callahan thought Nomura's and Horiuchi's paintings the "bolder and more imaginative" of the group and noted especially *Fish Market* and *Harbor*.[31]

Any painting in Seattle of the 1940s and 1950s that employs a calligraphic-like line was, then and now, compared to the contemporary production of Mark Tobey. Regarded as the honored elder in Seattle's art community, Tobey developed a gossamer, gesturally based abstract style that he termed "white writing" as a means to deconstruct solid form and signify spatial movement (fig. 4.25). Tobey's study had begun as early as the 1920s, with lessons in brushwork from the Chinese artist Teng Baiye, and in 1934 he spent a month's residency in a monastery near Kyoto; he would later publish articles about the importance of these experiences.[32] In the 1950s in Seattle, he maintained close relationships to artists Paul Horiuchi and George Tsutakawa and the Zen master and Japanese art connoisseur Tamotsu Takizaki. He was singularly important to Horiuchi in encouraging him to look to his Japanese heritage and to "let the nature out," which was, in Tobey's interpretation, the nature in oneself.[33]

Nomura surely received similar encouragement, although no record tells whether it came from Tobey personally or through Horiuchi. That Tobey and Nomura knew one another's work is certain. Tobey had wanted to talk with Nomura and Tokita, Tsutakawa recounted, but the Issei artists deferred. From youth they had been taught such deference to superiors and elders as part of the Japanese code of conduct. "Because he was regarded as so superior, they were modest. . . . They were immigrants. . . . There was a very strong feeling about this. . . . They have to contain themselves."[34] Whatever encouragement Nomura received, his artistic resolution was his own, then, as it had been in earlier years. His masterfully varied use of brushwork, love of color, and evocation of light produce paintings of radiant energy and lyricism.

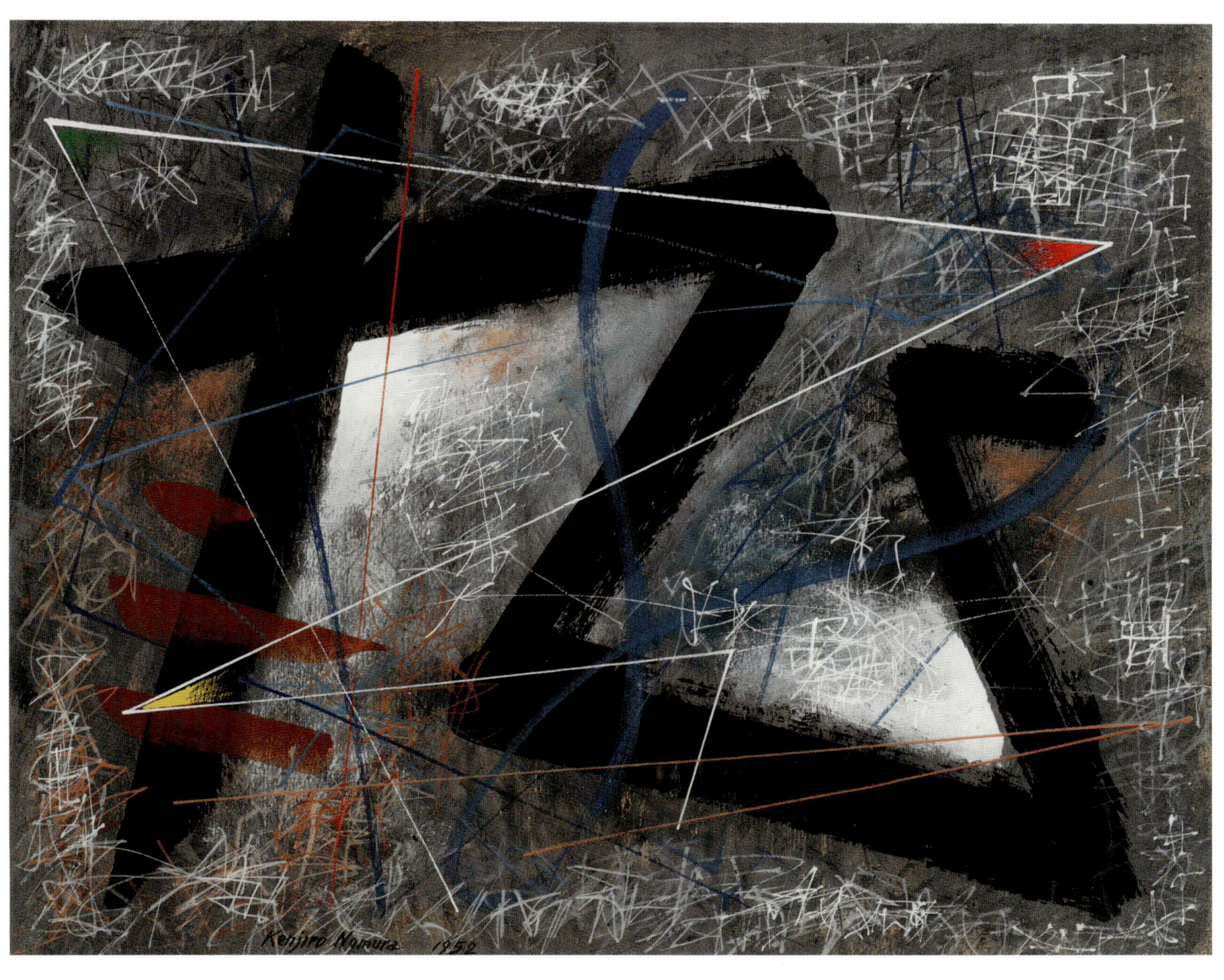

4.26
Untitled, 1952
Gouache on paper, 17¼ × 22¼ in.
Seattle Art Museum, gift of the Estate of Mr. Nomura, 60.88

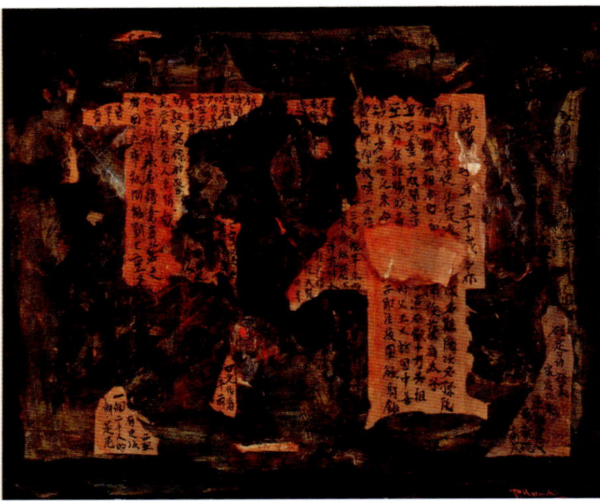

4.27
Paul Horiuchi, *Weathered*, 1956
Collage on board, 28⅛ × 34¼ in.
Tacoma Art Museum, gift of Paul and Bernadette Horiuchi in honor of Dr. Leonard Baskin, 1988.11

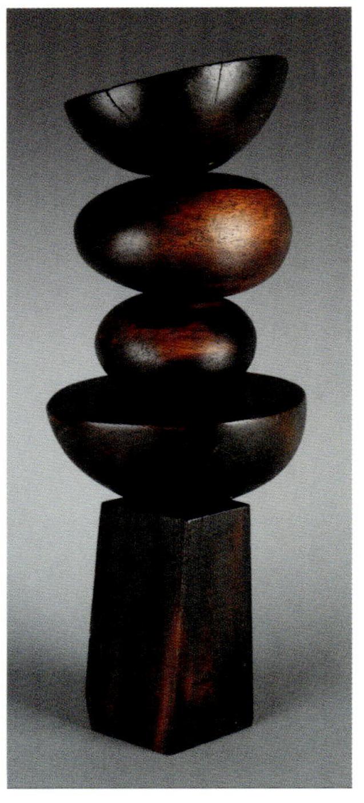

4.28
George Tsutakawa, *Obos #1*, 1956
Teak, 23¼ × 9¾ in.
Seattle Art Museum, gift of Seattle Art Museum Guild, 79.7

Nomura's abstract style emerged amid a broad postwar interest in Japanese culture in the United States. The interest was encouraged initially by cultural exchange programs and the increased interaction between the two nations during American occupation and spread from the intelligentsia to popular embrace. It peaked in the mid-1950s with D. T. Suzuki's lectures about Zen Buddhism in New York, the artist Saburō Hasegawa's demonstrations of calligraphy as an expressive art, and discussions by artists and critics of the gestural impulse of abstract expressionism that rose out of the war.[35] In New York–centered art circles, the relationship of abstract painting to Asian practices was generally dismissed, as New York was proclaimed to be the home of an original American style and replaced Paris as the world's art capital.[36]

In Seattle, however, the interest in Japanese, and more broadly Asian, culture had taken root earlier. The context was set by the proximate relationships of ethnic Japanese and white artists before and after the war, the institutional prominence of the Seattle Art Museum and its Asian collection, and Tobey's return to Seattle in 1939 as the elder among a circle of progressive artists.[37] In 1946 Kenneth Callahan defined a regional artistic identity that he declared arose from the artists' shared query of universalist themes, Asian art and philosophy, and "man's" place in nature.[38] Nomura was not part of these discussions, limited by social boundaries before the war, excluded by his wartime incarceration, and burdened by the struggle to resettle afterward. Nor was his or his colleagues' contribution acknowledged as the concept of a "Northwest school" took hold.

Still driven by creativity with ideas yet to express, Nomura died before he could pursue the potential of his abstract style.[39] Coincidentally the year of his death, both Horiuchi and Tsutakawa introduced new work that established their signature styles, Horiuchi in torn-paper collage, and Tsutakawa in lyrically stacked sculpture (figs. 4.27 and 4.28). As they became identified with a second-generation Northwest school, their Japanese ancestry reinforced its reputed Asian influence. It would be yet another generation that Nomura's work once again was brought to full light.

Legacy

In 1960, four years after his death, the Seattle Art Museum presented a memorial exhibition for Nomura. Proposed by George Nomura to honor his father, the exhibition surveyed Nomura's artistic production with a sampling of student work, several paintings of the 1930s at the height of his reputation, and a number of the postwar paintings.[40] The wartime works with their dark memories remained stored away, carefully bundled and tied as the artist had left them. Thirty years later when George brought them out of storage, much had happened to change the understanding of the Japanese American experience. The newly defined field of Asian American studies had taken root amid the political activism and assertion of ethnic identity in the 1960s. Research about the Japanese in America and especially the wartime years began to be published at an increasing pace, making the incarceration the most extensively documented subject in the panethnic field. Amid growing community advocacy in the 1970s and 1980s, Nisei members of Congress pressed for a governmental apology and redress. The case was strengthened during two years of investigative hearings by the Commission on Wartime Relocation and Internment of Civilians, in which many survivors talked of their experience for the first time.[41] In 1988 President Ronald Reagan signed the Civil Liberties Act. The legislation acknowledged the "fundamental injustice" of the forced removal and incarceration, issued a formal apology on behalf of the United States, and authorized redress payment to survivors.

In this context, Nomura's paintings of the Puyallup and Minidoka confinement camps found a receptive and appreciative audience when they were first shown in 1991 at Seattle's Wing Luke Museum. For nearly twenty years afterward, the collection traveled to small and large venues throughout the Northwest and beyond, including the rotunda of the U.S. House of Representatives office building in Washington, DC, and the then

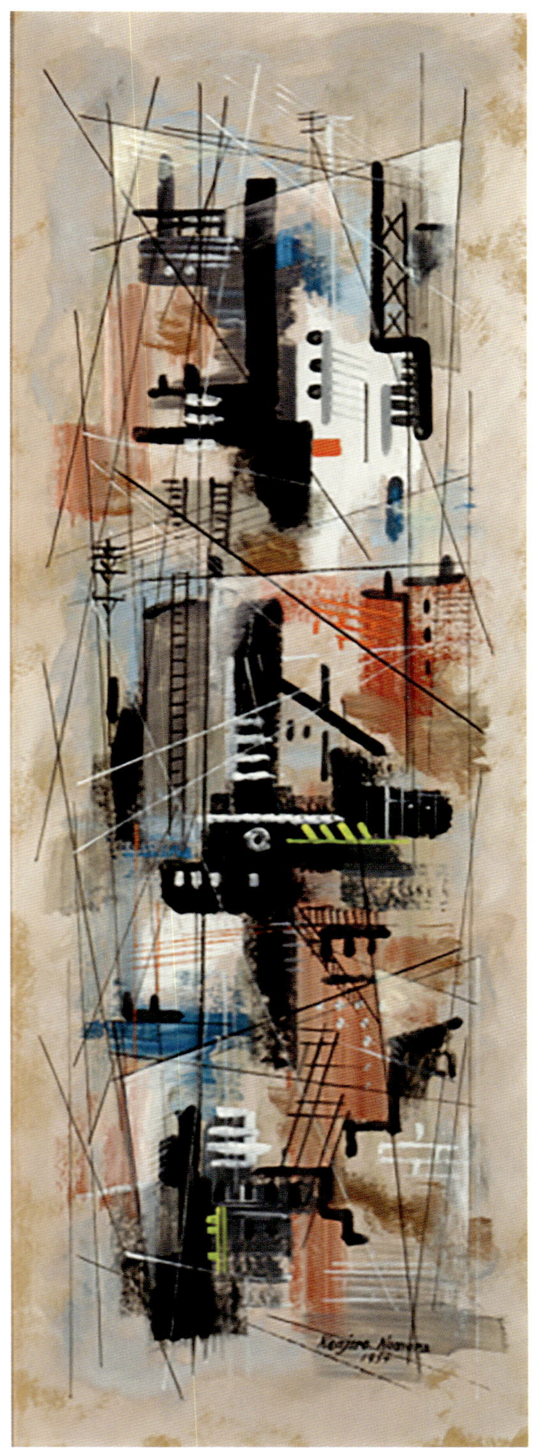

4.29
Structures #2, 1954
Tempera on board, 25 × 9¼ in.
Museum of Northwest Art, gift of Cyril and Jean Spinola, 1999

new Japanese American National Museum in Los Angeles. Four paintings were shown in a major survey of Japanese American art in Japan, which was, for many, an introduction to the American incarceration camps.[42] More recently, Nomura's distinctive clarity of form and cadenced composition have made his paintings a choice for covers of books about the incarceration.[43]

Another thirty years later, this study presents the full trajectory of Nomura's accomplishment, a legacy of paintings that tell of an immigrant–Japanese American experience. He was a careful observer who represented the places he knew. He depicted the intimate character of an urban neighborhood: the relationship of its walkways and buildings, its particular vistas, and the atmospheric qualities that lit them. Nature was in the sky overhead and the vegetation sprouting alongside concrete, at the waterfront where nature and industry meet, the bridges that span the city's waterways, and the valley farms he occasionally visited. Unjustly forced to leave his home, he maintained his aesthetic sensibility in the direst times, turning his attention to the way places are inhabited and finding beauty in a new landscape. In later years he gained renewed inspiration in the activity of the city, which he represented with painterly fluency and originality.

Nomura's legacy is that of an immigrant who made his home in the United States and contributed substantially to its cultural life. It is an immigrant experience enriched by his Japanese and American understanding and yet constricted by laws, language, and custom. It is an ethnic minority experience, constrained by mainstream assumptions, biases, and social norms. It is an American experience in seeking opportunity, making a home, and testing and expanding one's abilities. It is that of a careful observer of the places he knew and their habitation. It is that of an artist who continued to inquire about and expand his expressive means. His paintings add meaningfully to an expanded, inclusive view of American art and experience. They are eloquent, present objects through which we interpret and reflect upon not only his time but also our own.

4.30
Kenjiro Nomura with *International Carnival* in Zoe Dusanne's gallery, 1952
Photo: Elmer Ogawa
Nomura Estate

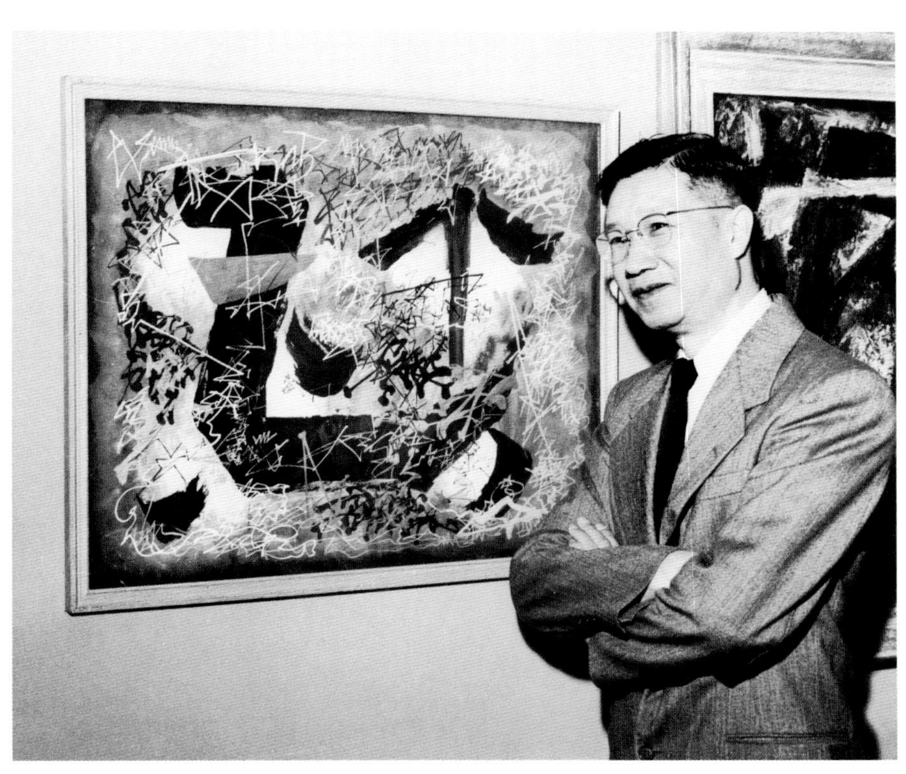

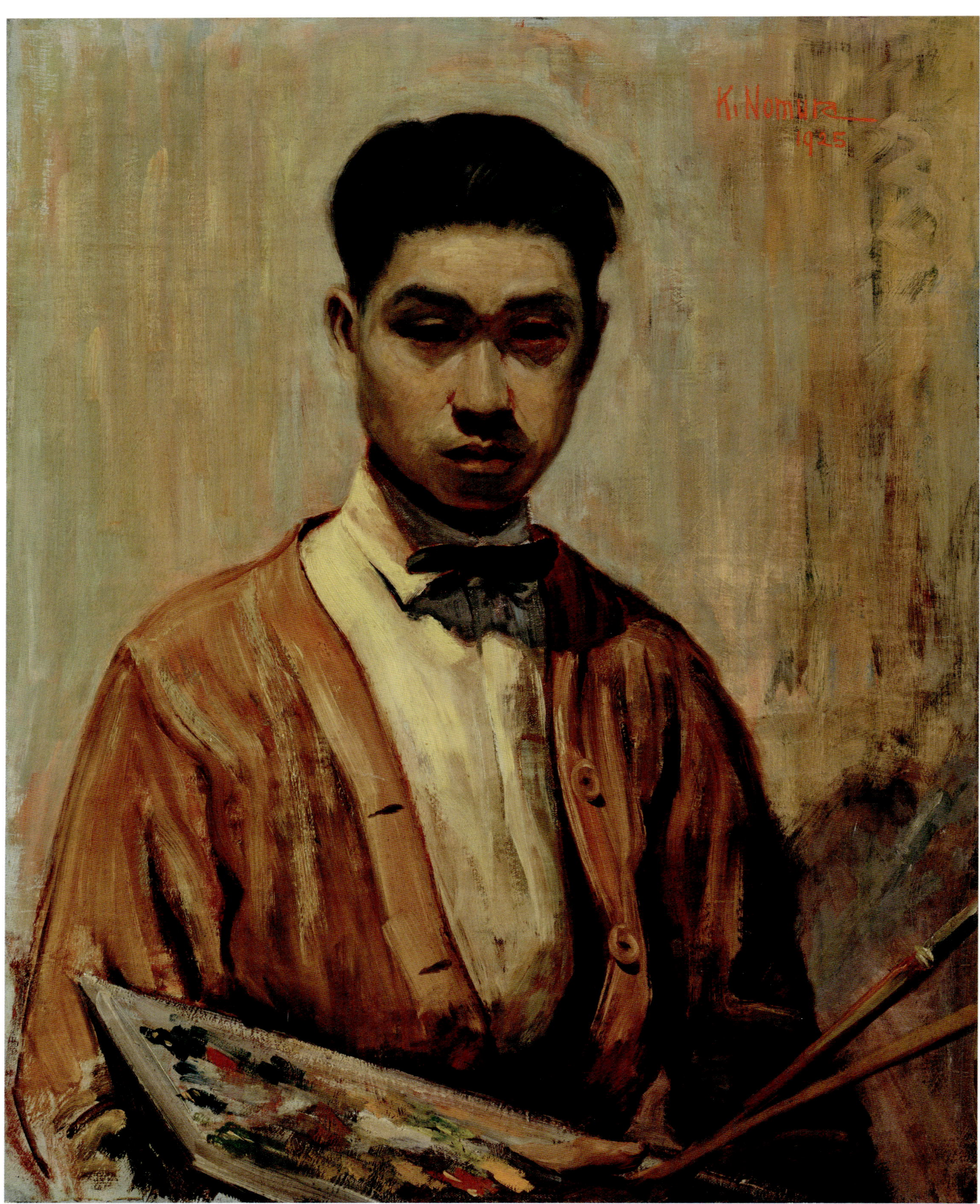
K. Nomura
1925

BRIDGES TO MODERNISM: THE ART OF KENJIRO NOMURA

DAVID F. MARTIN

Most studies of the fine arts in Washington State usually begin with the activities surrounding the cultural growth that resulted from the 1909 Alaska-Yukon-Pacific Exposition (AYPE), an important world's fair that provided Seattle with early international attention. Although there was an exhibition of regional visual artists in the Women's Building, there is no extant catalogue to identify the artists or what they exhibited. The few records that are known were derived from individual artists' scrapbooks and archives. At the time of the exposition, there were a significant number of Japanese immigrants in Washington State to celebrate "Japan Day" on Saturday, September 4, 1909, which included various cultural events and culminated in a spectacular fireworks display at night.[1] Just two years earlier, in 1907, several young Japanese men arrived in Washington State who would soon play important roles in the region's cultural history: painter/photographer Soichi Sunami (1885–1971), photographer Yukio Morinaga (1888–1968), and painters Toshi Shimizu (1887–1945) and the young Kenjiro Nomura (1896–1956). Yasushi Tanaka (1886–1941), who would become a leading figure in the development of modern art in the Northwest, arrived in 1904.

M.1
Kenjiro Nomura
Self-portrait, 1925
Oil on canvas (trimmed), 32 × 26½ in.
Nomura Estate

Perhaps drawn by the publicity surrounding the AYPE, Dutch artist Fokko Tadama (1871–1937) arrived in New York in 1909 and soon relocated to Seattle by 1910. Having established a successful reputation in Europe, Tadama brought with him the techniques and aesthetic practiced at the art colony at Egmond-Binnen in Holland, along the North Sea. The colony included local artists as well as American painters George Hitchcock (1850–1913) and Gari Melchers (1860–1932). Hitchcock gave up his career as a Harvard-educated attorney to pursue the study of art in Europe and remained in the Netherlands until his death. Although Tadama was exposed to the modern impressionist techniques promulgated at the colony, he preferred a more limited palette and rarely used high-key values in his work. Tadama's aesthetic was much more aligned with the nineteenth-century Italian Macchiaioli group, whose technique of subdued, quick brushwork to capture the fleeting play of light was compatible with his approach to landscape and portraiture.

Tadama had created a school of art in Seattle around 1913. Kenjiro Nomura became one of his students shortly after the school was founded. In

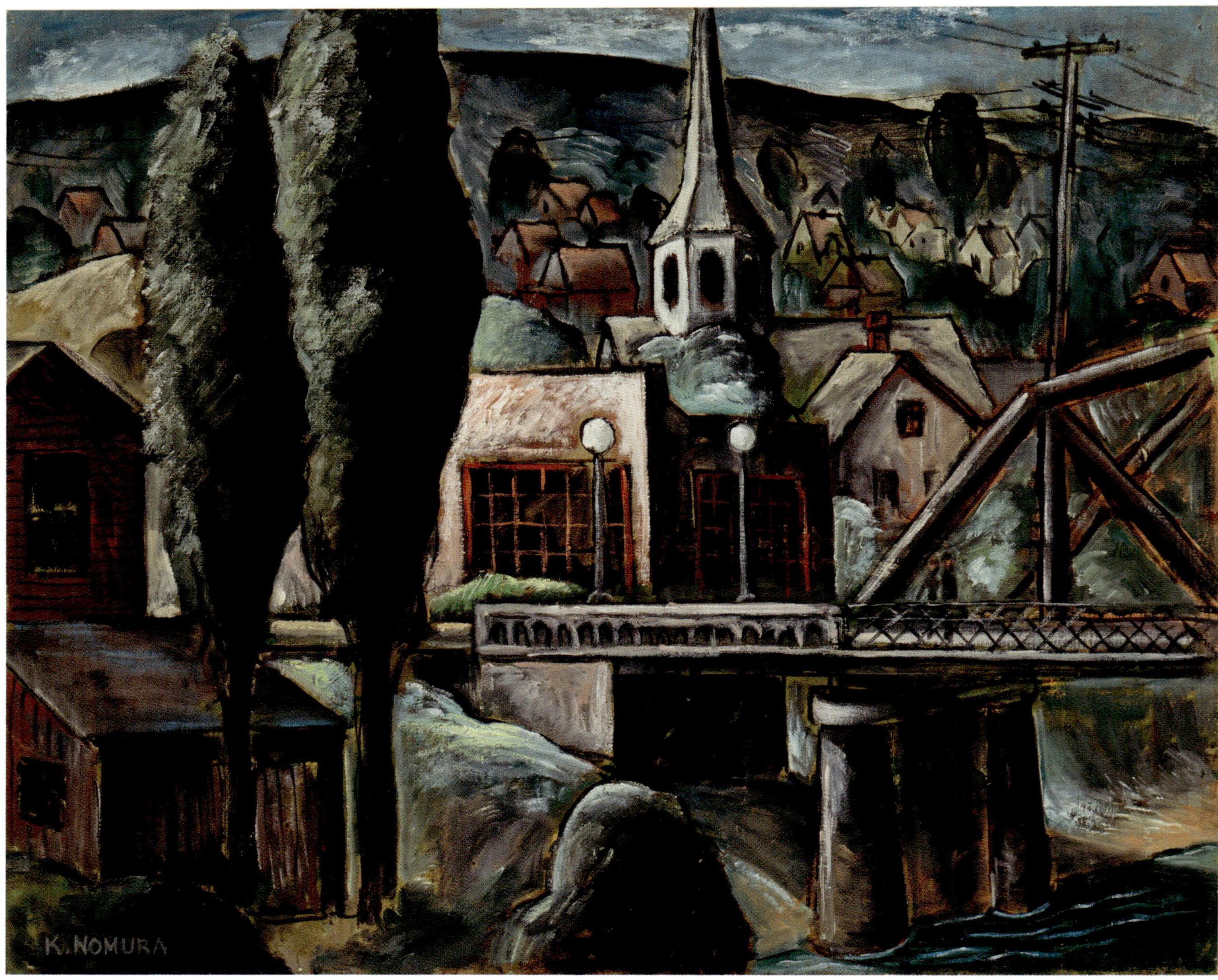

M.2
Kenjiro Nomura
Renton Bridge, 1938
Oil on canvas, 23¼ × 29½ in.
Nomura Estate

1914 American artist William Merritt Chase (1849–1916) gave an important summer class in Carmel, California, the only time that he was to teach on the West Coast. Two Seattle artists, John Davidson Butler (1890–1976) and Louise Crow (1891–1968), won the top awards at the Chase class.[2] Butler, who had been an exhibitor at the AYPE, and photographer Imogen Cunningham (1883–1976) along with her husband, etcher Roi Partridge (1888–1984), were among the major forces in modern art in Seattle in the early twentieth century.

Recently discovered paintings by Nomura dated 1915 and 1916 indicate that he was progressing steadily in Tadama's class beyond the numerous academic drawings that he created from the human figure (fig. M.7). These oil paintings display a promising talent utilizing the techniques developed and promoted by New York artist Robert Henri (1865–1929), a key figure in the Ashcan School movement who depicted scenes of everyday life in New York. Nomura's urban scenes are certainly an outgrowth of this movement looking within his own community for inspiration. Henri was also among the leading art instructors of that era and was especially known for his facile technique in portraiture. Several early Seattle artists studied with Henri in New

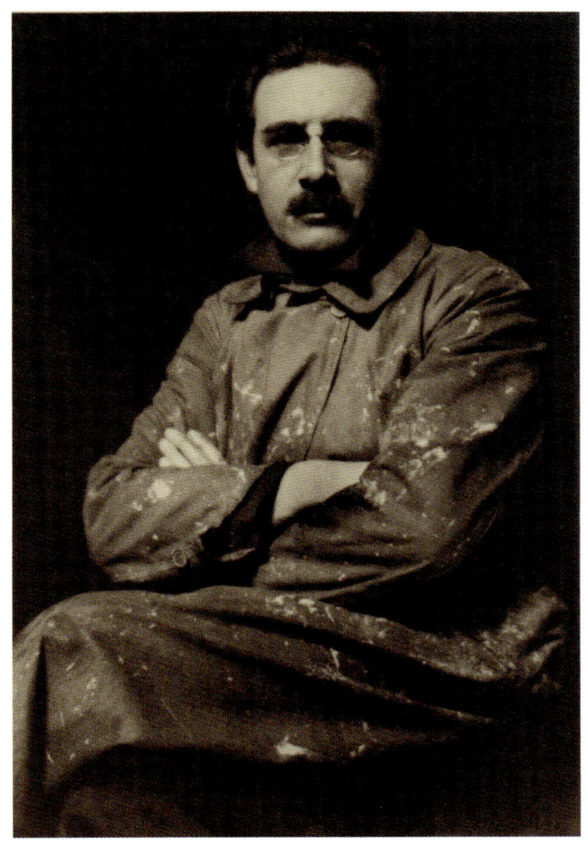

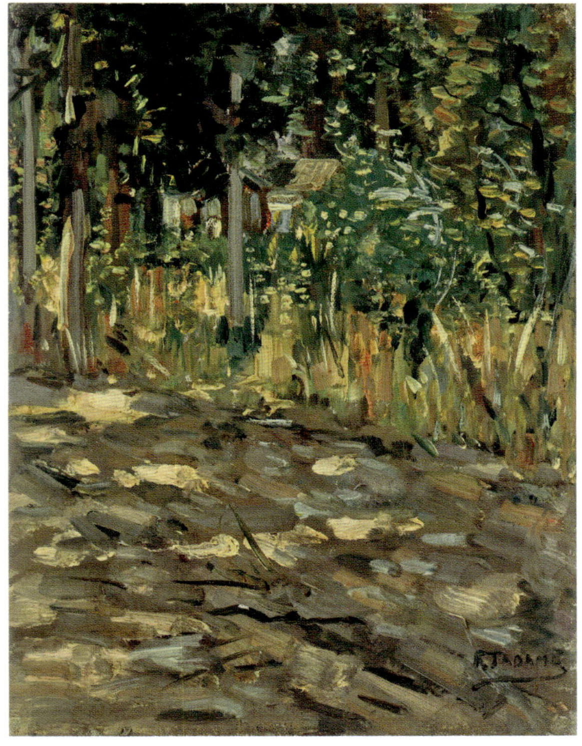

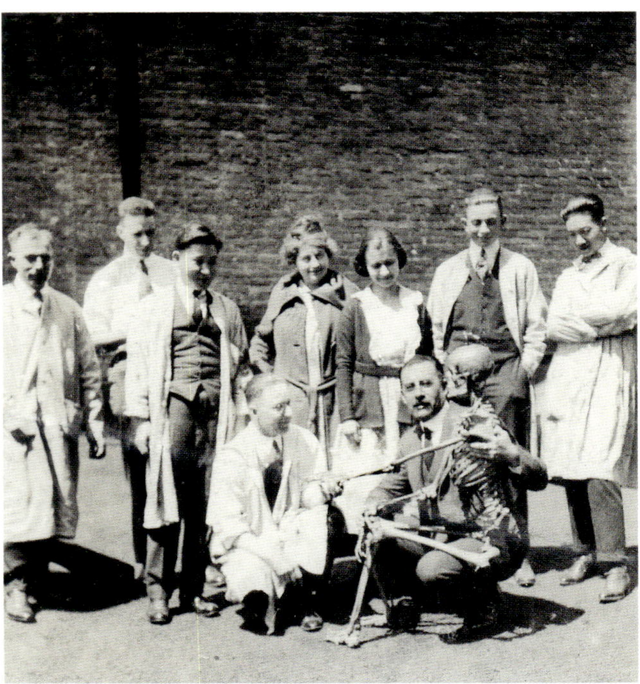

M.3
Soichi Sunami
Portrait of Fokko Tadama, ca. 1921
Bromide print
Private collection
Courtesy of the Sunami Family

M.4
Fokko Tadama
Untitled, ca. 1918
Oil on canvas, 15½ × 12 in.
Private collection

M.5
Soichi Sunami
Fokko Tadama and students, ca. 1918–1921
Courtesy of the Sunami Family

Tadama is seen holding a skeleton used for anatomy instruction. Sunami is standing third from left; Nomura is standing far right.

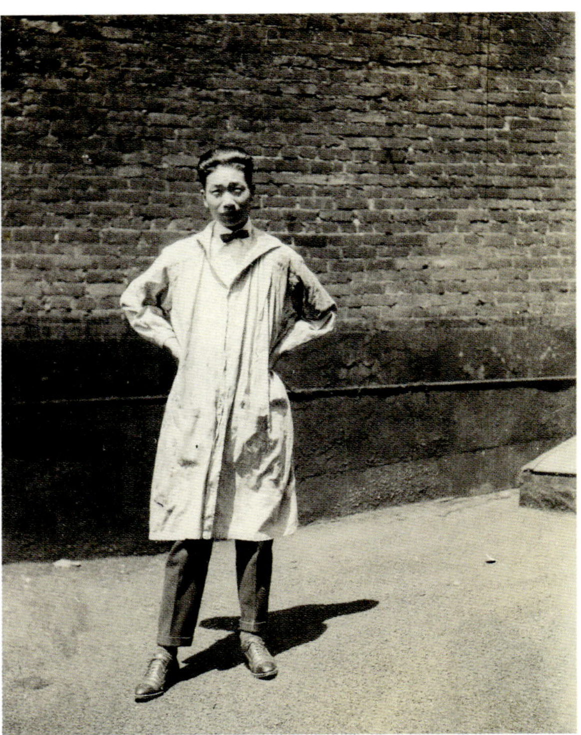

M.6
Soichi Sunami
Kenjiro Nomura, ca. 1918–1921
Courtesy of the Sunami Family

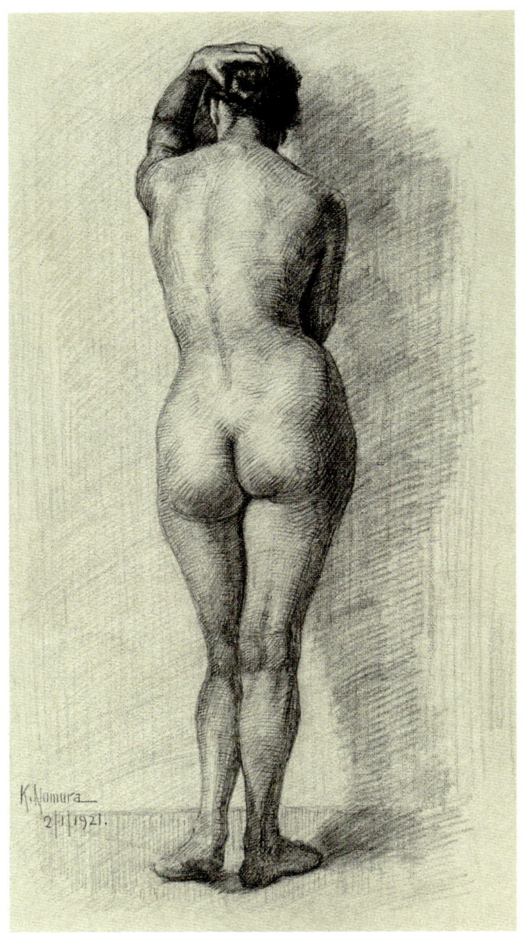

M.7
Kenjiro Nomura
Figure study, dated 2/1/1921, one of numerous academic drawings created during his study with Tadama
Graphite on paper, 25 × 20 in.
Nomura Estate

York, including Ella Shepard Bush (1861–1948) and Kathleen Houlahan (1884–1964), who not only studied with Henri but lived with him and his wife, painter Marjorie Organ (1886–1931), while a student in Manhattan. Another Henri student, Margaret Gove Camfferman (1881–1964), arrived in Washington State from Minnesota in 1915 with her painter husband, Peter Camfferman (1890–1957), settling at Langley, Whidbey Island, where they painted and initiated an arts colony for other regional artists.

Henri's influence is evident in Nomura's November 8, 1915, portrait of an unidentified woman (fig. M.8). The figure is modeled with rapidly applied wide brushstrokes while eliminating realistic detail. Earlier that year, one of Henri's oil portraits, *Little Irish Girl* (1913), was displayed at the Seattle Fine Arts Society's gallery as part of an exhibition of twenty-five American paintings circulated by the American Federation of Fine Arts.[3] The exhibition allowed Nomura access to study Henri's technique firsthand. A 1916 landscape (see fig. 1.14) also illustrates his fluid technique in building form with large, quickly applied brushwork, a subdued palette, and the clever depiction of atmospheric, glaring light that demonstrates his command of values.

Besides Nomura, Tadama's other students from this time included Issei artists Soichi Sunami, Yasushi Tanaka, and Toshi Shimizu, as well as Caucasian artists Mabel Lisle Ducasse (1895–1976) and Leon Derbyshire (1896–1981). Like Nomura, Shimizu worked in the Henri manner for portraiture, as indicated in his figure study of an elderly male model (fig. M.9).

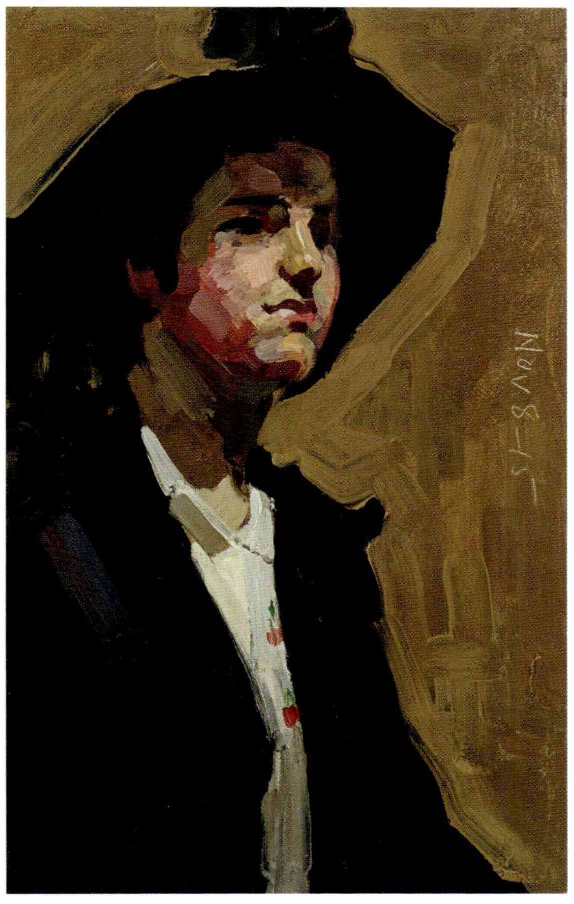

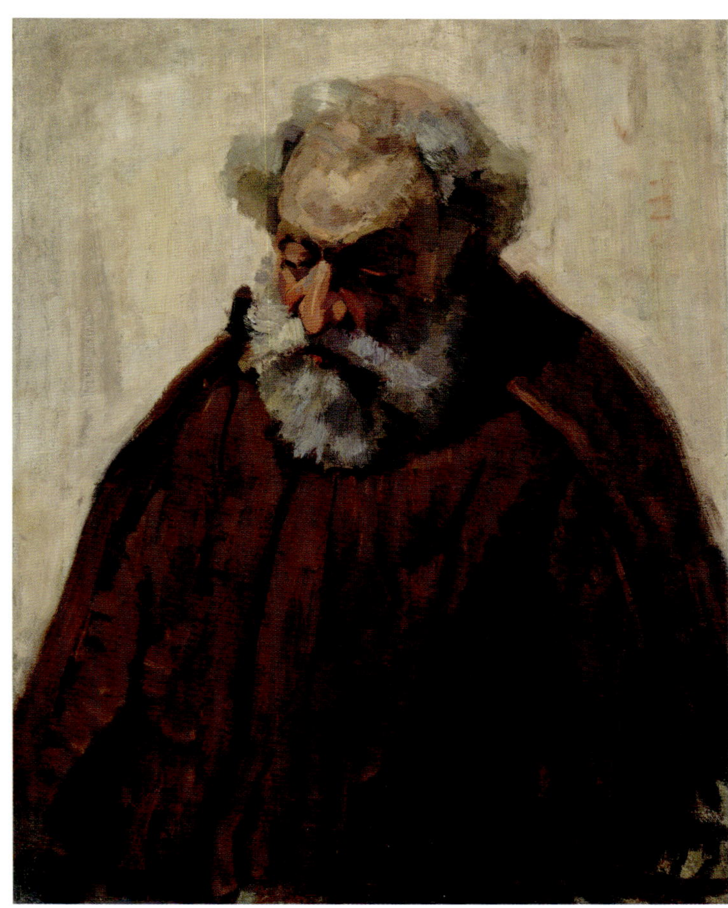

M.8
Kenjiro Nomura
Untitled, dated November 8, 1915
Oil on canvas, 20⅝ × 13⅛ in.
Nomura Estate

M.9
Toshi Shimizu
Untitled, ca. 1915
Oil on canvas, 25 × 20¼ in.
Nomura Estate

But unlike Shimizu and especially Tanaka, Nomura maintained a more reserved approach. His colleagues would later use vibrant colors and experimented with more modernist techniques, which Nomura seemed to disdain, at least until after WWII. Tanaka and Shimizu had reached an initial level of success when they were included in the Washington State Commission Exhibit of Fine Arts in 1914. Sponsored by the Society of Fine Arts in Seattle, it was the first of what would later be referred to as the Northwest Annual, which showcased the region's top talents in the visual arts. It became the most important regional venue until it ceased in 1977. The 1914 exhibition was created to assemble the works of the more advanced artists of the region to compete for inclusion in an exhibit in the Washington State Building at the Panama-Pacific International Exposition in San Francisco in 1915. Among the thirty-five works selected were two by Shimizu and two by Tanaka. Their instructor, Fokko Tadama, won an award at the fair for his painting *Public Market, Seattle*. In 1916 Nomura would join Tanaka and Shimizu in an exhibition of local Japanese artists at the Japanese Art Association, on Main Street, in Seattle's Nihonmachi, or Japantown.[4] Tanaka by that time was receiving praise and sometimes stirring controversy for his use of cubist techniques, inspired by *Nude Descending a Staircase, No. 2* (1912), by cubist/

futurist Marcel Duchamp (French; 1887–1968), which was exhibited in Seattle the previous year after creating a sensation at the New York Armory Show in 1913.[5]

By 1917 Shimizu had gone to New York to pursue further studies, and in 1920 Tanaka moved permanently to Paris. Shimizu would join him in the French capital in 1924, remaining there until 1927 when he returned to Japan, where he had an illustrious career in the arts.[6] Soichi Sunami, who had a parallel interest in photography, left Seattle in 1922 to study in New York. He eventually became one of the country's finest dance photographers and had an important career at New York's Museum of Modern Art, where he served as chief photographer for nearly forty years.[7] By now, Kenjiro Nomura was the remaining significant Issei from this circle, and he initiated his career by being accepted in the Annual Exhibition of the Work of the Artists of the Pacific Northwest (Northwest Annual) in 1922 in its seventh exhibition. His painting was singled out by art critic Madge Bailey as "one of the best pieces in the exhibit. No matter where it is hung, the cool movement of the water beneath the old hull attracts the attention. It will be interesting to follow the development of the talent of this young artist."[8] This auspicious beginning provided Nomura recognition and encouragement by being included in this annual, the most important local venue for regional artists.

That same year, Nomura opened a commercial sign-painting business called Noto with his friend and fellow artist Show Toda. Toda's creative output was relatively short-lived and he ended his business partnership with Nomura within a few years. Nomura continued the company with painter friend Kamekichi Tokita (1897–1948) in 1924, providing both men with an income to pursue their artistic aspirations.

After 1926, there are no extant exhibition records for Toda and it is presumed that he returned to Japan before World War II.

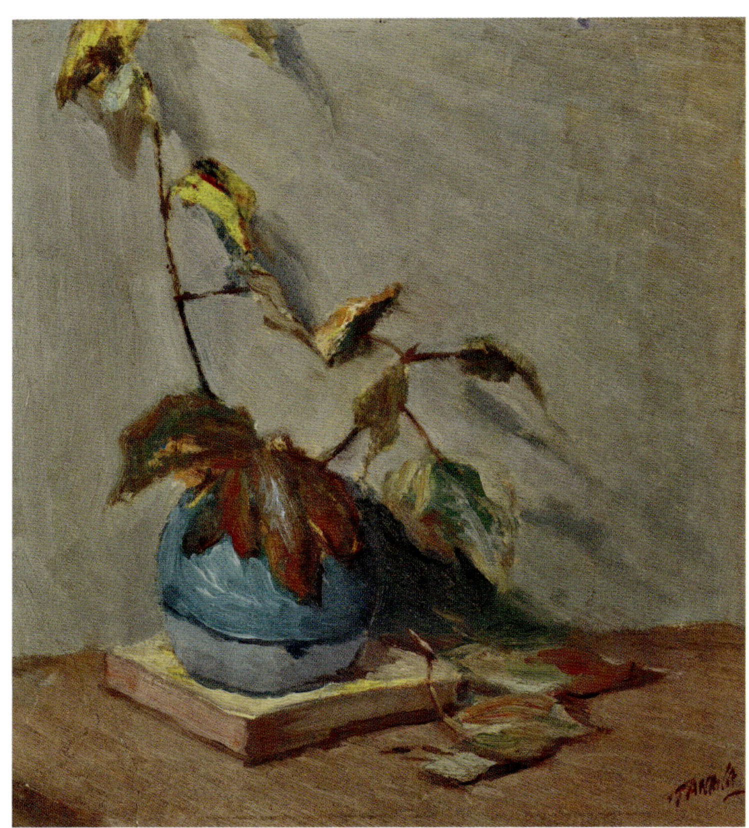

M.10
Yasushi Tanaka
Le bouquet Japonais, ca. 1918
Oil on board, 12½ × 13½ in.
Private collection

For the remaining decade, Nomura's work would appear in the Northwest Annuals, concentrating primarily on still lifes, landscapes, marine scenes, and portraiture. His subjects reflected the local natural environment and industries, painted en plein air when time allowed. Although most of Nomura's earlier works are lost, enough have survived to discern his stylistic approaches. His 1925 *Mountain Peaks* (see fig. 1.19), exhibited in that year's Northwest Annual, beautifully illustrates the subdued impressionism he learned under Tadama's tutelage, using a horizontal light source to add dramatic illumination to the trees and mountains. That same year, he produced a self-portrait, a fragment of which has survived. Outstanding portraiture was produced in the region at that time by exceptional talents such as Louise Crow, Lance Wood Hart (1891–1941),

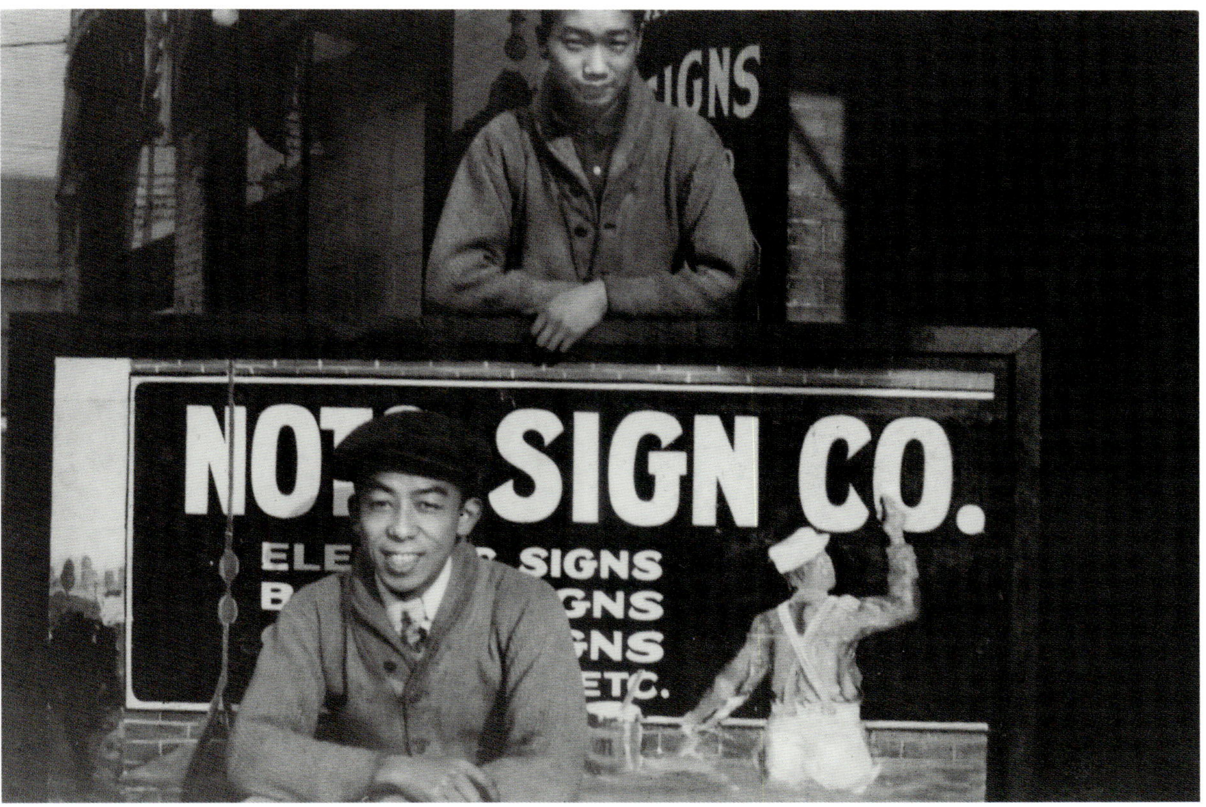

M.11
Nomura (top) and Show Toda, ca. 1922
Nomura Estate

M.12
Noto Sign Company invoice, ca. 1930
Private collection

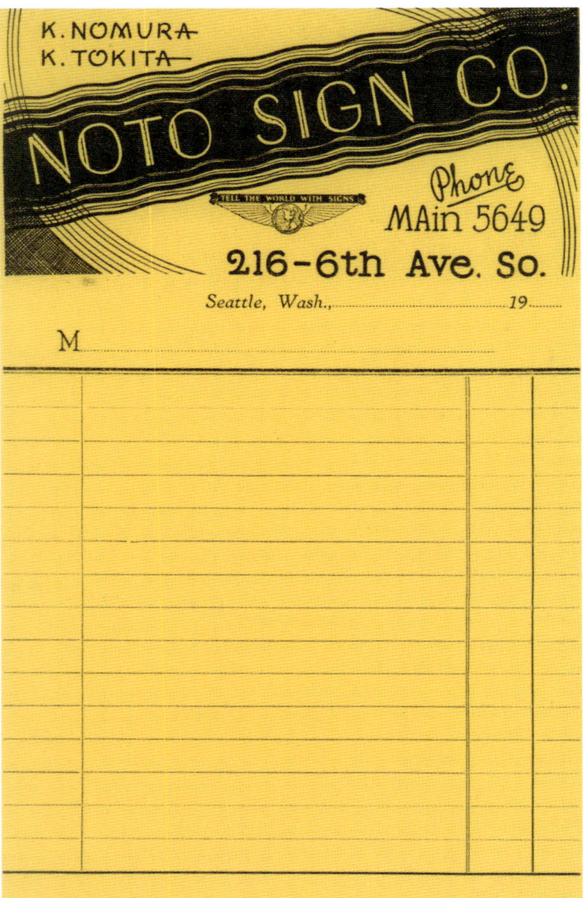

Walter Isaacs (1886–1964), Ambrose Patterson (1877–1967), and another Henri student, Jeannie Walter Walkinshaw (1885–1976), among others. Nomura's portraiture sometimes reflected a different technical approach that was not common in the region. Undoubtedly, Tadama was immersed in the painting manner of the Dutch masters, and it was among the techniques he imparted to his students. This influence is evident in Nomura's self-portrait (see fig. M.1) with the use of an orange/red imprimatura, or underpainting, commonly used in Rembrandt's portraits. Imprimatura is an initial stain of color painted on a ground that provides the unifying element in structuring the dimensional modeling of the figure. The term itself stems from the

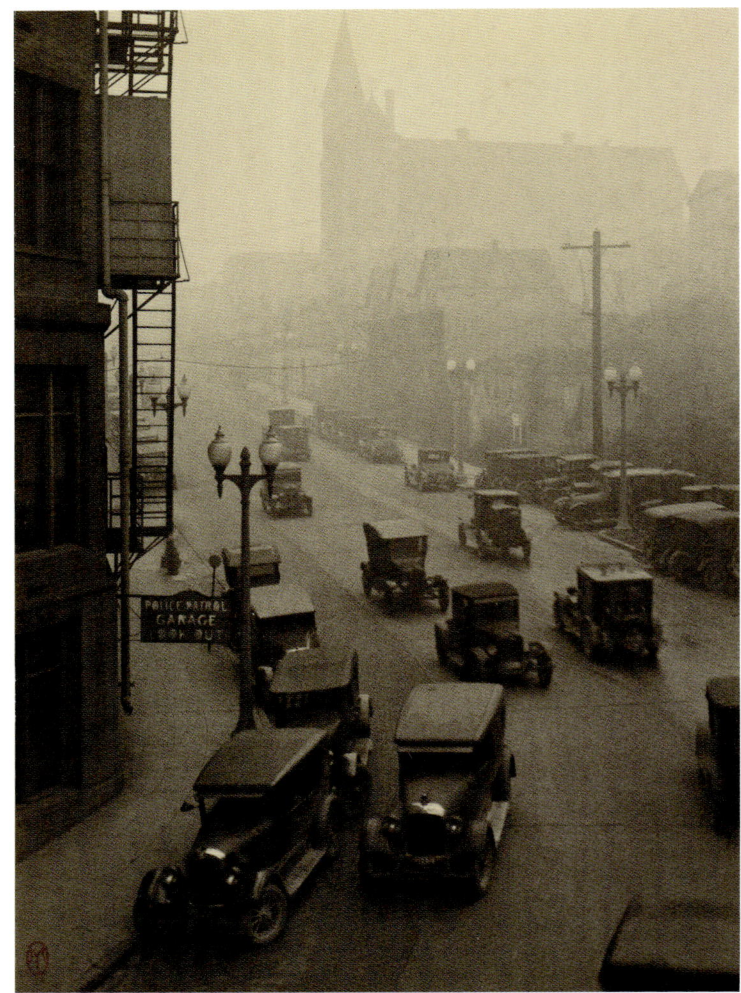

M.13
Yukio Morinaga
Untitled, ca. 1925
Bromide print, $13\frac{5}{8}$ × 10 in.
Collection of Norman and Susan Randall

Italian and literally means "first paint layer." The underpainting can be seen in the facial features of the self-portrait as well as the right section that falls into shadow, where the composition needed to appear denser. Nomura added a veil of scumbled, opalescent layers to the background that creates a crepuscular effect. The entire composition is illuminated to give the appearance of a natural light source from twilight, similar to the effect he used in his mountain landscape discussed earlier.

With the ascension of art production in Seattle during the 1920s, Nomura was certainly aware of the mostly Issei Seattle Camera Club (SCC), the first internationally acclaimed art group in the region. Like many of the Issei painters, the SCC's members often stayed within the parameters of the Nihonmachi, making studies of the bustling neighborhoods that were within walking distance of where they lived and worked. This mutual interest can be seen in the circa 1925 photograph by Yukio Morinaga and in Nomura's oil sketch of roughly the same period (figs. M.13 and M.14). Morinaga, eight years Nomura's senior, distinguished himself from his fellow Issei photographers by concentrating on the city's urban environment, as opposed to the poetic landscapes of his colleagues.[9] Nomura's oil painting of the same scene, looking north from Seattle's Fourth Avenue, utilizes the same vantage point as Morinaga's photograph. Nomura was also a friend of another internationally acclaimed photographer in the SCC, Frank Asakichi Kunishige (1878–1960), whose fate would interact with Nomura in the near future.

Since Nomura did not date most of his work, and gave such simple titles to his paintings, it is difficult to trace the exact transition of his stylistic development. It is assumed that he remained working in the Tadama impressionist style through the 1920s, but there is a gap in his exhibitions from 1927 through 1930. Several factors may have contributed to this break, including his marriage to Fumiko Mukai in 1928, the busy schedule from his sign-painting business, and the birth of his son, George, in 1930. An extant photograph of the lost painting *Fishing Boats*, exhibited at the Oakland Art Gallery in 1930, shows the beginning of a transition in his painting style (see fig. 2.1). Nomura's friend and colleague Tokita was also regularly producing work at this time, and some of his paintings from 1929/1930 show the beginnings of an interest in urban dwellings and city scenes as well (fig. M.15). Although this type of subject matter was common in the United States at that time through the work of, among others, John Sloan (1871–1951) and Charles Burchfield (1893–1967), it was not in

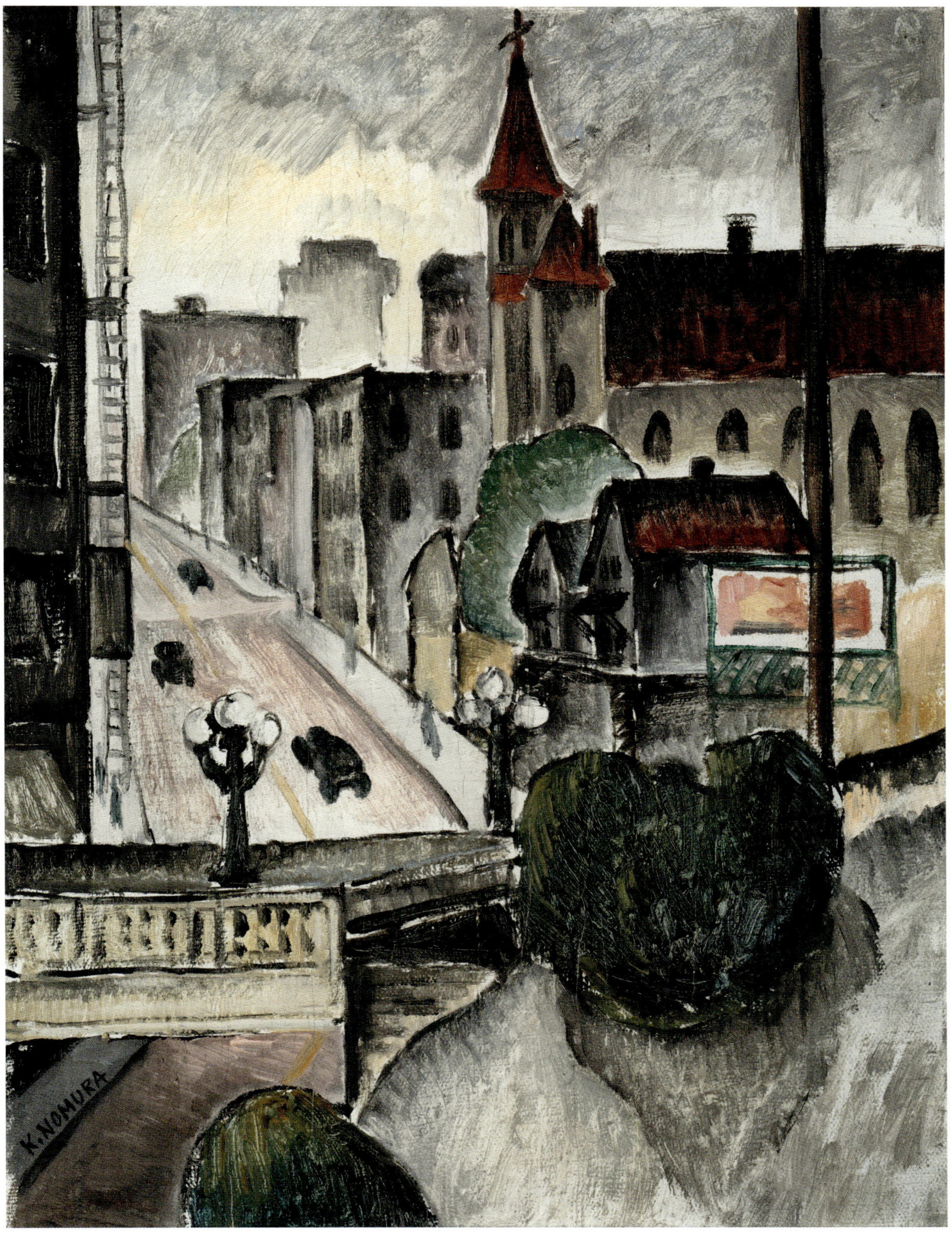

M.14
Kenjiro Nomura
Untitled (Our Lady of Good Help from Fourth Avenue),
ca. 1920s
Oil on canvas, 16 × 12 in.
Nomura Estate

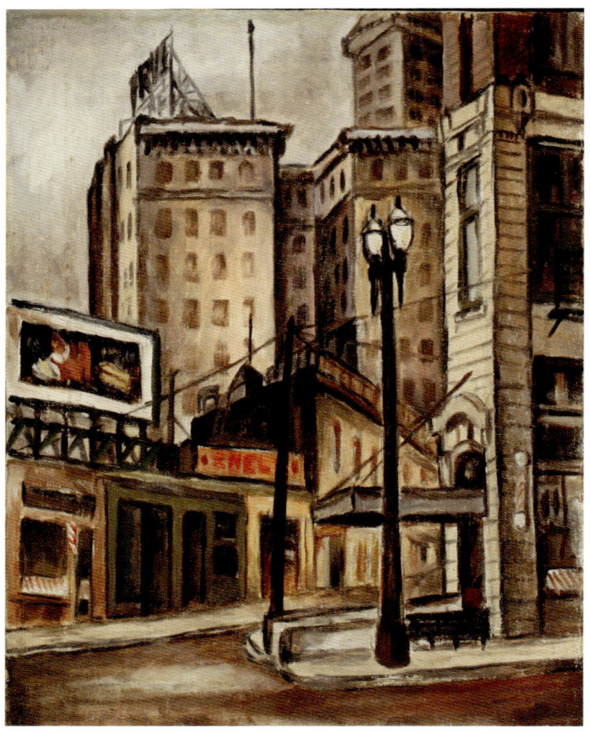

M.15
Kamekichi Tokita
Untitled (Prefontaine Street), 1930
Oil on canvas, 21 x 17 in.
Collection of Yoshiko Tokita-Schroder and Jerry Schroder

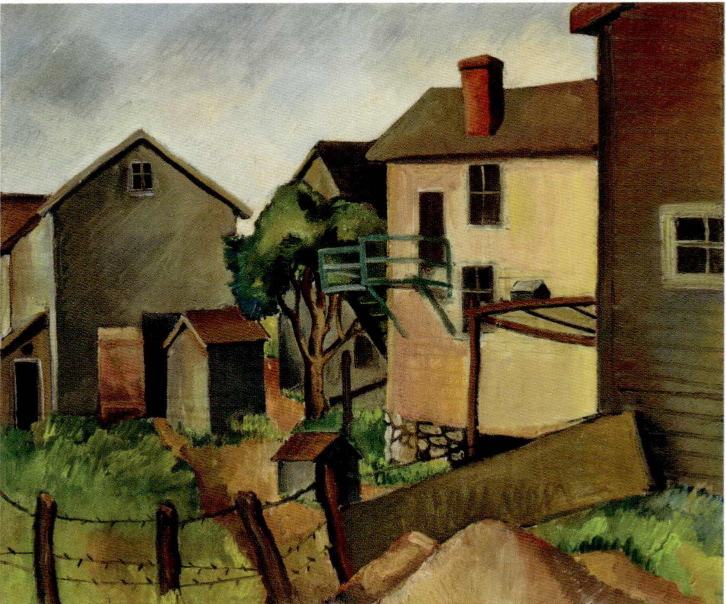

M.16
Lauretta Sondag
Untitled, ca. 1928
Oil on canvas, 20 × 24 in.
Private collection

Seattle.[10] Very few urban scenes by regional artists were created outside of Tokita's and Nomura's in the 1930s. These artists would soon be joined by Takuichi Fujii (1891–1964), who would become the third Issei associated with their style.

Two somewhat obscure local artists might be a key to understanding this transition for both Tokita and especially Nomura. Lauretta Sondag (1897–1930) and fellow Tadama student Leon Derbyshire were both successful in their lifetimes but became forgotten through unfortunate circumstances. Both of them were gay and both had their works distributed after their deaths by relatives who had no concern for the preservation of their artistic reputations. With no children to carry on their legacy, their bodies of work and archival materials have been lost and indiscriminately scattered. In Sondag's case, the few extant oil paintings by her are remarkably compatible with Nomura's paintings of the 1930s.

Since she died prematurely in 1930, due to a fatal anesthetic reaction from tooth surgery at the age of thirty-two, it is safe to assume that her style predates Nomura's.[11] Sondag and another gay Seattle artist, Guy Anderson (1906–1998), both received Tiffany Foundation grants in 1929 and spent that summer painting on the Louis Comfort Tiffany estate at Oyster Bay, Long Island. A Sondag oil in the collection of the Seattle Art Museum, as well as the few paintings that have been located in private collections, shows the same stylistic approaches that Nomura utilized. These would include the grouping of middle-class urban and rural structures (fig. M.16) and the use of modernist compositional elements in the arrangements of the architectural forms. The most telling technical similarity is the use of constructive brushstrokes placed side by side to create geometric structure. This technique was inspired by the French artist Paul Cézanne (1839–1906), whose revolutionary work formed the basis for modern art in Europe.

Leon Derbyshire's trajectory is very similar to Nomura's. Both were born in 1896 and arrived

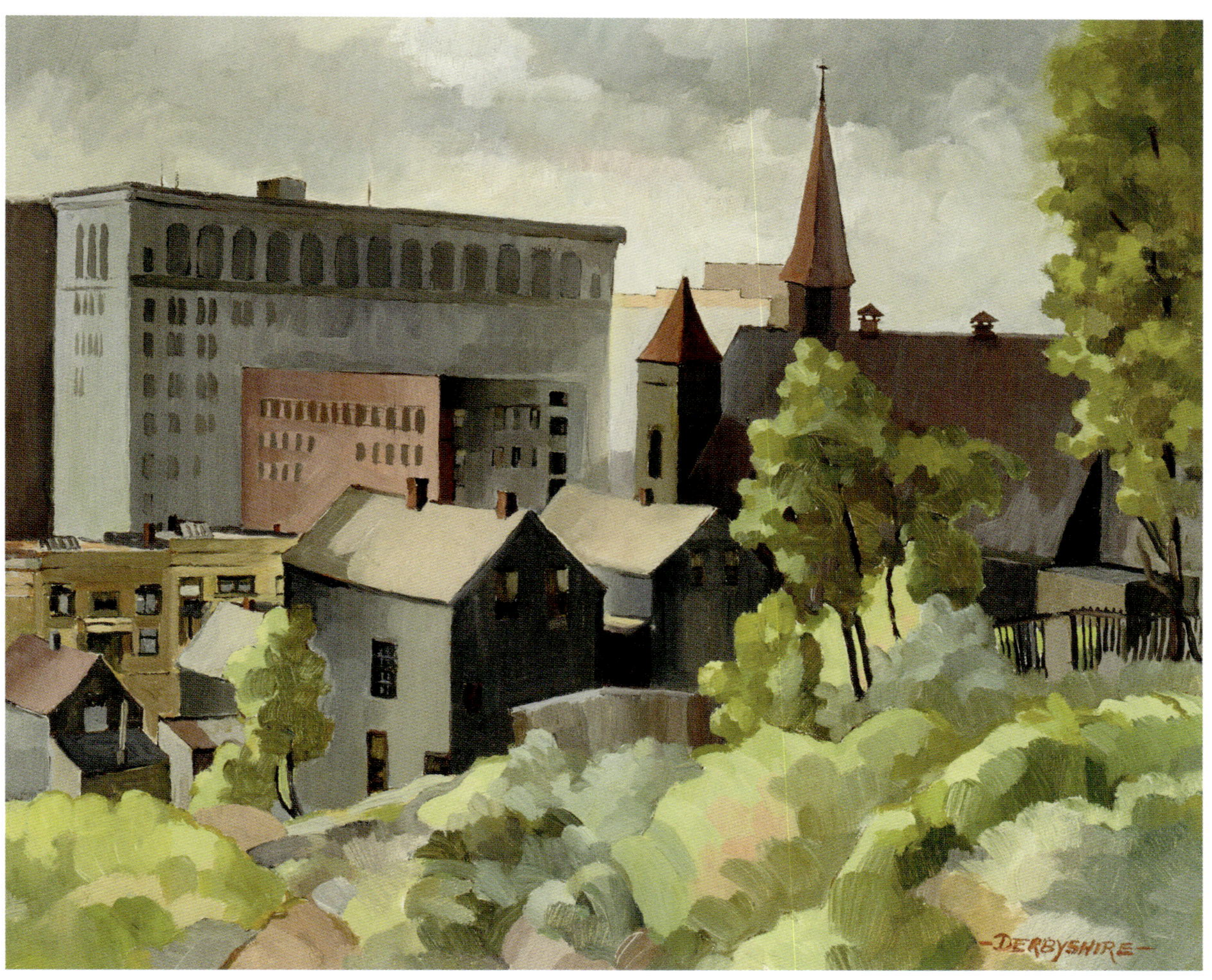

M.17
Leon Derbyshire
Untitled, ca. 1936
Oil on canvas, 16 × 20 in.
Collection of Lindsey and Carolyn Echelbarger

in Washington State in 1907, both studied with Tadama during the same period, and both produced landscapes and urban scenes of Seattle. However, after studying with Tadama, Derbyshire left Seattle to attend the Pennsylvania Academy of Fine Art, where he studied with Daniel Garber (1880–1958) and Hugh Breckenridge (1870–1937), noted American impressionists. Afterward he studied in Europe, and particularly with the cubist master Andre L'Hote (1885–1962) in 1929. L'Hote was clearly a disciple of Cézanne and his methods, and Derbyshire's work reflected it thereafter. When he returned to Seattle, he undoubtedly shared what he learned with colleagues such as Nomura, who, unlike his friends, never left Seattle to study nationally or abroad. This shared modernist approach can be seen in Derbyshire's untitled oil depicting downtown Seattle, bearing the same hallmarks of the subdued palette and implied, non-realistic details and Cézanne-inspired constructive brushwork that appear in many of Nomura's paintings. Derbyshire's oil even includes subject matter and landmarks that appear in Nomura's and Tokita's works, such as the King County Courthouse and the Our Lady of Good Help Catholic church (fig. M.17, and see also fig. 2.7).

When the Seattle Art Museum opened in Volunteer Park in 1933, it relied heavily on the work of regional artists for exhibitions since it had a small permanent collection and few local resources for loans. As an indication of his stature in the community, Nomura had the first solo exhibition at the museum from June 28 to

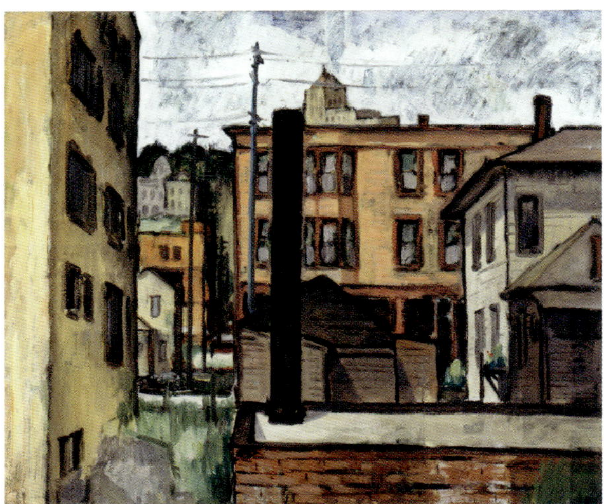

M.18
Sumio Arima
Untitled, ca. 1935
Oil on canvas, 18 × 22 in.
Collection of the Arima Family

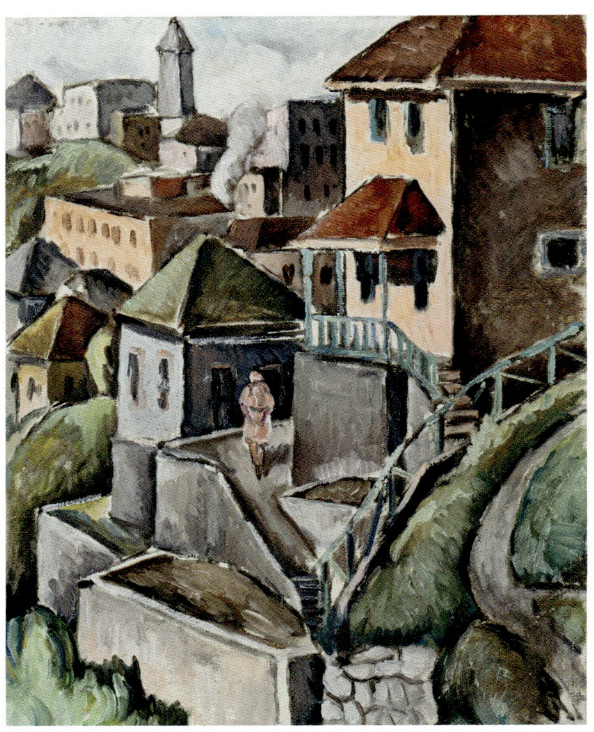

M.19
Paul Horiuchi
Untitled, ca. 1935
Oil on canvas, 19¼ × 15¾ in.
Collection of Sharon Archer and Don Eklund

July 31, followed the next month by a memorial exhibition of paintings by Sondag from August 3 to September 3. Tokita's solo exhibition occurred from December 11, 1935, to January 5, 1936, and Derbyshire's from June 8 to July 3, 1938. From this point on, Derbyshire never exhibited with the Northwest Annuals again at the Seattle Art Museum, although he would later exhibit at the Henry Art Gallery and the Frye Art Museum, which sponsored a retrospective exhibition for him in 1953. Rather than compete, Derbyshire chose to dedicate his life to teaching in his Seattle studio for the remainder of his life.[12]

In December 1933, just five months after Nomura's Seattle Art Museum exhibition ended, the relatively new Museum of Modern Art in New York held an exhibition titled *Painting and Sculpture from 16 American Cities*. Among the Seattle artists included were Nomura, represented with his painting *Puget Sound* (see fig. 2.5), along with four other Seattle painters, Kenneth Callahan (1905–1986), Peter Camfferman, Walter Isaacs, and Ambrose Patterson, and sculptor Halford Lembke (1889–1962).

Just as an economic depression was taking hold during this time, Seattle artist Sumio Arima's (1901–1987) brief, promising career in the arts was coming to an end. After some initial art studies in Seattle and Portland, Oregon, Arima followed the lead of his friend Soichi Sunami by moving to New York in 1922 to study at the Art Students League with John Sloan. Before Arima returned to Seattle in 1925, his paintings were accepted in prominent New York venues such as the Salons of America and the Society of Independent Artists. After initial success in New York, he planned to continue his art studies in Paris but reluctantly put his art career on hold to join the family publishing business in Seattle. He became manager and editor of the *North American Times*, Seattle's leading Japanese-language newspaper. Unable to paint full-time as he desired, he only produced a few works in the 1930s, one of which shows the influence of Nomura and Tokita, whom he likely painted with on occasion.[13]

Painter Chikamasa Paul Horiuchi (1906–1999) arrived in Seattle in 1920 but soon moved

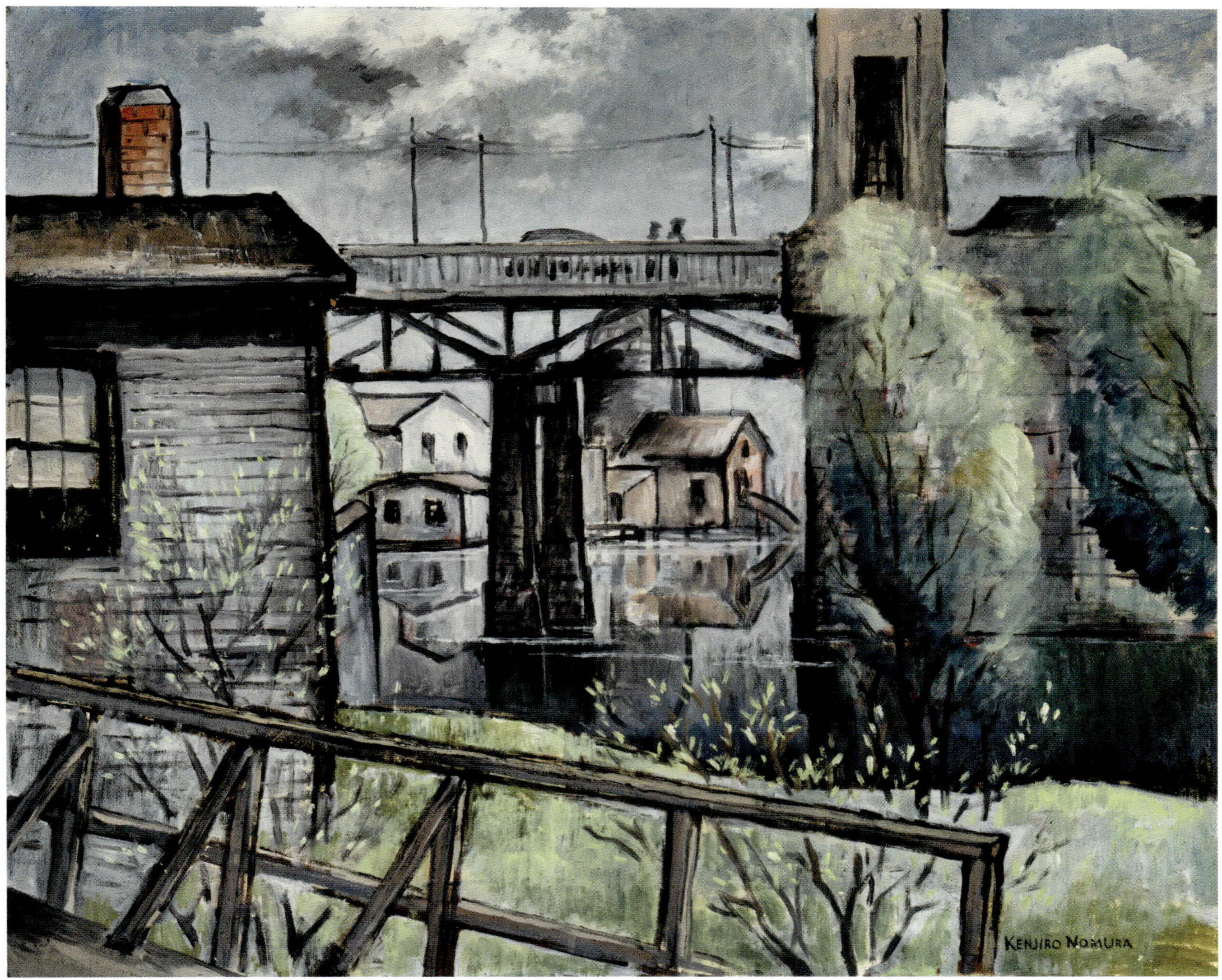

M.20
Kenjiro Nomura
Spring, 1932
Oil on canvas laid down on Masonite, 24 × 30 in.
Nomura Estate

to Rock Springs, Wyoming, to join his family and begin working for the Union Pacific Railroad. It was during his family visits to Seattle that he met Nomura and Tokita and fell under their influence (fig. M.19). In 1934 Horiuchi met Seattle resident Bernadette Suda, fell in love, and converted to her religious affiliation, Roman Catholicism. At the time, in order to be baptized, Catholics were required to use the name of a saint for their given name, and Horiuchi selected "Paul" as an homage to painter Paul Cézanne, who was such an important influence on many regional artists of that period. Horiuchi and his wife relocated to Wyoming and began to raise a family, before returning to Seattle after World War II.[14]

Throughout the 1930s, Nomura was consistently included in most of the region's important exhibitions. In 1933–1934 he became part of the short-lived Public Works of Art Project (PWAP), one of President Franklin D. Roosevelt's New Deal programs of the Depression. During this period, when the artists were provided free paint and materials, Nomura produced some of his finest works, including *Houseboat* (see fig. 2.17) and *Yesler Way* (see fig. 2.6). His painting *The Farm* was included in the National Exhibition of Art by the PWAP at the Corcoran Gallery in

Washington, DC, in the spring of 1934, before traveling to the Museum of Modern Art in New York later that year (see fig. 2.13). The following year, 1935, he became part of Seattle's Group of Twelve, which also included Tokita and other leading modernists in the region. In 1936 he and some of the group were included in the *First Annual Exhibition of American Art*, with New York's Rockefeller Center as the impressive venue. Nomura would be included in the second exhibition the following year as well. The group appears to have lasted only for a few years, culminating with an exhibition at Mills College in Oakland, California, in September 1937, the same year that a small booklet titled *Some Work of the Group of Twelve* was published (by Dogwood Press in Seattle), documenting the members of the group. During the organization process, the Mills exhibition, now titled *Pacific Northwest Painters*, consisted of forty paintings including artists from Oregon and other non-members of the Group of Twelve from Washington State. Nomura's *Canal* and *Spring*, painted five years earlier, were his entries (fig. M.20).

Roi Partridge, the internationally acclaimed etcher from Centralia, Washington, was an old friend of several of the members of the Group of Twelve, having exhibited with some of them in the nascent Seattle Fine Arts Society shows in the 1910s and 1920s. Partridge along with his wife, photographer Imogen Cunningham, had moved to California by 1917. He began teaching at Mills College in 1920, where he also served as its gallery's first director from 1925 to 1936.[15] He was likely the connection for the group's exhibition at Mills.

Unfortunately, along with Nomura's continuing success, 1937 was also marred by a great personal loss when his mentor and friend Fokko Tadama committed suicide, shocking the local arts community and illustrating just how devastating the effects of the economic depression could be on an artist.

George Tsutakawa, who would eventually become one of the region's leading artists, had just received his bachelor of fine arts from the University of Washington that same year. Like Horiuchi, Tsutakawa had considered the elder Nomura, Tokita, and Takuichi Fujii as mentors who helped shape his talents in the early years of his career.

By 1938, Nomura would exhibit his last painting, simply titled *Landscape*, at the Seattle Art Museum's Northwest Annual, until after the war. As the decade was coming to an end, two major world's fairs were produced in 1939 on the West and East Coasts: San Francisco's Golden Gate International Exposition and the New York World's Fair. Nomura was included in the San Francisco exhibition but not the more high-profile New York fair's *American Art Today*. This exhibition was supposed to represent the finest regional artists from across the country. Three painters were to be selected to represent each state. In Washington State, the finalists were selected by a local jury, or "committee of selections," at the University of Washington's Henry Art Gallery and then were to be sent to New York for the national jury to make the final decision. No local Issei artists were included. Initially, the three artists selected to represent the state were Mark Tobey (1890–1976), Morris Graves (1910–2001) (both Tobey and Graves were heavily promoted by the Seattle Art Museum at this time), and Elizabeth Warhanik (1880–1968). When the paintings went to New York for the final cut, Warhanik's work had mysteriously disappeared and was replaced by paintings made by three of the jurors—Walter Isaacs, R. Bruce Inverarity (1909–1999), and Kenneth Callahan. Inverarity (who was also head of the state's Works Progress Administration [WPA] program) was the final artist to be included and replaced Warhanik, the only female.[16] Viewing these works today in the exhibition catalogue, one can see that nepotism, rather than a fair assessment of artistic

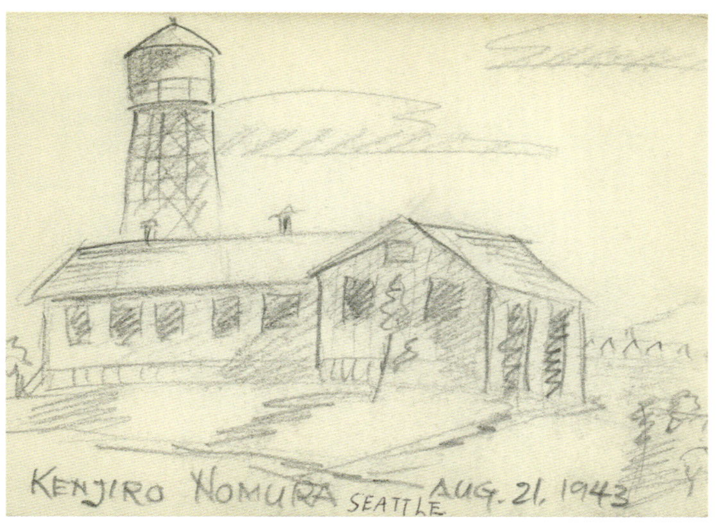

M.21
Kenjiro Nomura
Sketch of the Minidoka fire station, August 21, 1943
Graphite on paper, 4 x 5⅞ in.
From the sketchbook of George Tsutakawa
Collection of the Tsutakawa Family

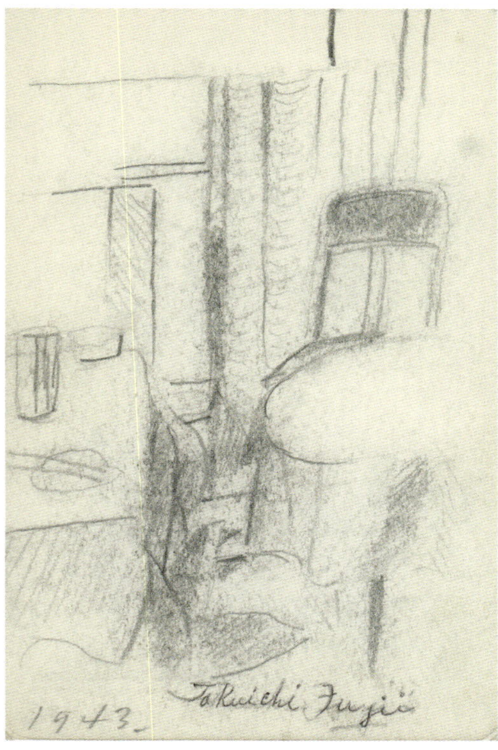

M.22
Takuichi Fujii
Sketch of Fujii's Minidoka room interior, 1943
Graphite on paper, 5⅞ x 4 in.
From the sketchbook of George Tsutakawa
Collection of the Tsutakawa Family

achievement, was the guiding force behind these selections.

As the new decade began with the lingering economic depression appearing to have no end in sight, the future did not look optimistic. Nomura's painting output began to dwindle, as for most artists, survival became top priority. Unlike many of his contemporaries, Nomura could not rely on an income from the WPA art programs. In fact, the government put an incomprehensible burden on all local residents of Japanese heritage when the same president who initiated the successful WPA viciously turned his back on them. Roosevelt signed Executive Order 9066 on February 19, 1942, forcefully removing anyone of Japanese heritage on the West Coast to incarceration camps. This devastating assault on democracy remains a blight on this president's otherwise admirable achievements. Nomura, his family, and most of his friends and artistic contemporaries in the Japanese community were forcibly removed in 1942 to the ironically named "Camp Harmony" (see fig. 3.14), a holding center at the Washington State Fairgrounds in Puyallup, before being transferred to Minidoka in Hunt, Idaho.

George Tsutakawa escaped incarceration, having been drafted into the U.S. Army after Pearl Harbor was attacked on December 7, 1941. In the summer of 1943, while still in the army, Tsutakawa visited his friends Nomura and Fujii in their confinement at Minidoka. He brought a small sketchbook with him and had Nomura make a drawing of Minidoka's fire station and then had Fujii create a small, sensitive sketch of the interior of his room (figs. M.21 and M.22). Fujii never returned to Seattle, resettling first in Ogden, Utah, and then in Chicago by 1947, where he lived until his death in 1964.[17]

The February 1945 issue of *Fortune* magazine featured a tribute to the industrial and cultural activities in the western United States (fig. M.23). It was published just seven months before the Nomuras would return to Seattle from Minidoka. One of the main articles was titled "Northwest

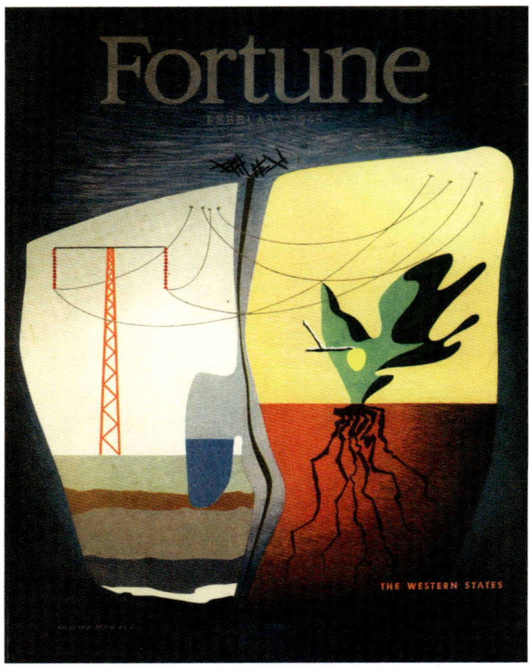

M.23
Cover of *Fortune* magazine, February 1945 issue
Private collection

Painting" and was likely written by artist Kenneth Callahan, who was curator at the Seattle Art Museum. He and his wife, Margaret Callahan, were also the two main newspaper art critics and wielded great influence in the art community during that time. The article focused, as usual, on the Asian-influenced work of Morris Graves and Mark Tobey but also featured the now obscure artist Darrel Austin (1907–1994), whose kitschy portrayal of animals was a questionable choice considering the large pool of local talent to choose from. Austin's work predates the big-eyed paintings of Margaret Keane that would become part of popular culture in the following decade. Why this artist was selected remains a mystery, and the exclusion of any of the regional Asian American artists reflects the lingering racism toward the end of the war. The *Fortune* cover featured a striking illustration by the talented California artist Charles Howard (1899–1978), whose biomorphic, surrealistic style would certainly have caught the attention of younger regional painters and possibly Nomura himself.

With Nomura, Tokita, and Fujii being such important members of the Seattle art community, it is somewhat disheartening that their non-Japanese colleagues appeared to display no reaction, support, or condemnation of the incarceration in their artwork. A few exceptions exist in the work of two artists of the period. Yvonne Twining Humber's (1907–2004) cryptic *Spoiled Carnival* of 1946 is one example (fig. M.24). The artist had moved to Seattle in 1943 from Massachusetts, after an arranged marriage to Seattle resident Irving Humber, a Jewish refugee who escaped persecution in his native Austria by posing as a Christian.[18] Most of Irving Humber's family members who remained in Europe were killed in the Holocaust. After the war his mother, a survivor of the Terenzenstadt death camp, came to Seattle to live with her son and daughter-in-law in 1946, the year *Spoiled Carnival* was painted. Because of her personal experiences with her husband's family, Yvonne Humber was sensitive to the plight of people in detention centers and concentration camps. She was particularly offended by Camp Harmony, which detained Japanese Americans in 1942 on the site of the Western Washington Fairgrounds at Puyallup. When the fair resumed in 1946, Humber attended with her husband and created multiple sketches from different vantage points. The original composition was intended to show the fair as a joyful regional celebration on a sunny, late summer day. When she learned of the fairground's incarceration history, she decided to change the appearance of the painting by making it gloomy, with a rain-soaked and ominous intrusion on the figures and a dramatic foreboding sky looming above. For her, the experience was ruined by the memories of the incarcerees' unjust confinement.

The work of photographer Virna Haffer (1899–1974) also took a dark turn following the incarceration of her close friend and fellow SCC member Yukio Morinaga. Haffer and her son frequently visited Morinaga not only in Puyallup

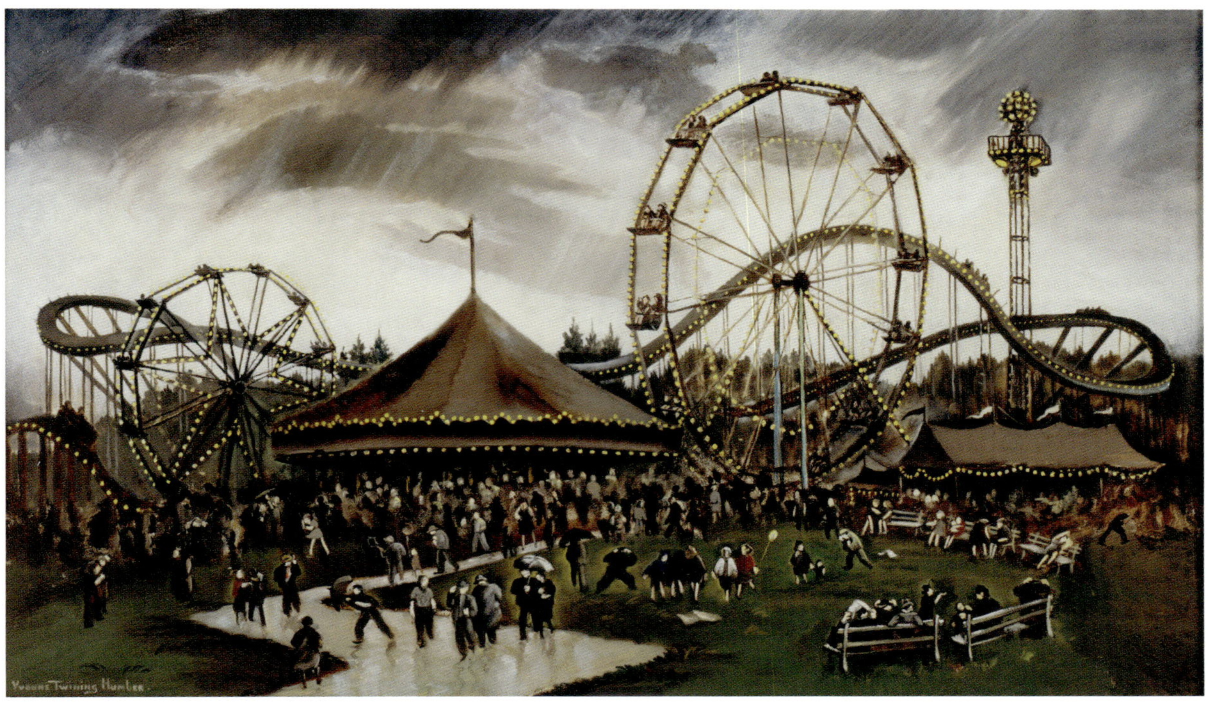

M.24
Yvonne Twining Humber
Spoiled Carnival, 1946
Oil on canvas, 22 × 38 in.
Seattle Art Museum, Eugene Fuller Memorial Collection, 47.154

but after he was sent to Minidoka. Her son, Jean Paul (named after the French journalist and politician Jean-Paul Marat of the French Revolution), recalled holding his "Uncle Mori's" hand through barbed-wire fencing while they all cried in frustration. When Morinaga was finally released, Haffer purchased a house for him in Tacoma and provided him with work in her photography studio, until he ended his own life in 1968. Following his death, Haffer's work in the field of photograms concentrated on the dark side of life, including human annihilation and environmental ruin.[19]

The incarceration also took a devastating personal toll on Kenjiro Nomura. His wife Fumiko's suicide in 1946 followed their release from Minidoka the previous year. Initially, he fell into a deep depression and lost the passion to paint. However, his younger friends, Horiuchi, Tsutakawa, and others, helped to pull him out of his sadness by bringing him along on painting expeditions and engaging him with new ideas and techniques in painting. When Nomura reluctantly resumed painting with his young friends in 1947, he began experimenting with abstraction. An old, covered bridge in nearby Renton, Washington, was painted by Fujii, likely in the mid-1930s, and then by Nomura and Tsutakawa in 1947 (figs. M.25, M.26, M.27).

That same year saw the beginning of Jackson Pollock's "drip paintings" that would soon initiate sharp critical debate in the art world. Some historians place Pollock's drip paintings within the same rubric as Tobey's "white writing" technique (see fig. 4.25). However, Tobey's paintings can also be considered as the antithesis of Pollock's, with his use of carefully placed and meticulously arranged lines and curves derived from a wide range of influences including Japanese sumi paintings. They are mostly smaller and introspective images created using tempera and gouache on paper. Pollock's work, in contrast, utilized large canvases with oil and enamel paints to convey a larger-than-life expressionistic bravado. Several Northwest artists experimented with Pollock's

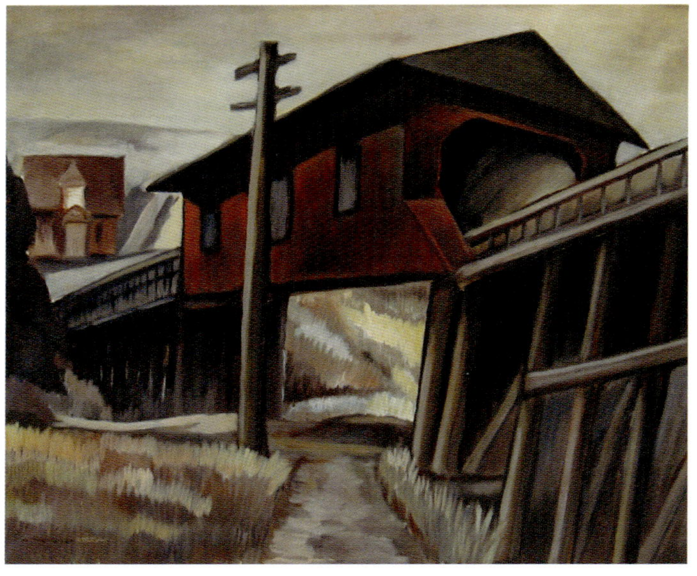

M.25
Takuichi Fujii
Untitled, ca. 1930s
Oil on canvas, 25 × 31 in.
Private collection

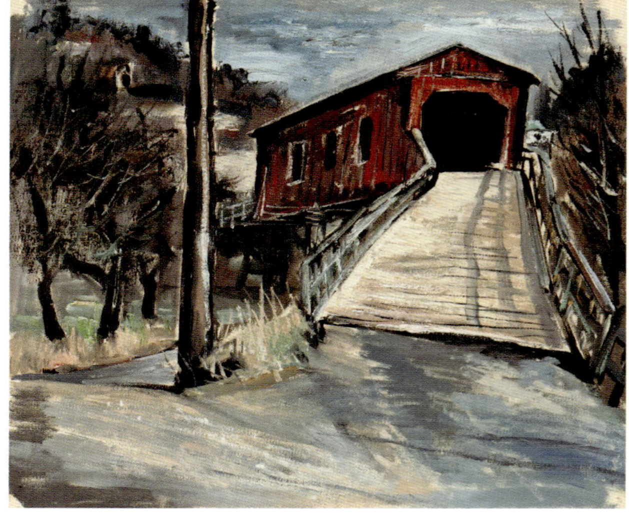

M.26
Kenjiro Nomura
Untitled, ca. 1947
Oil on canvas, 12⅞ × 15½ in.
Collection of Tom and Dorothy Sheehan

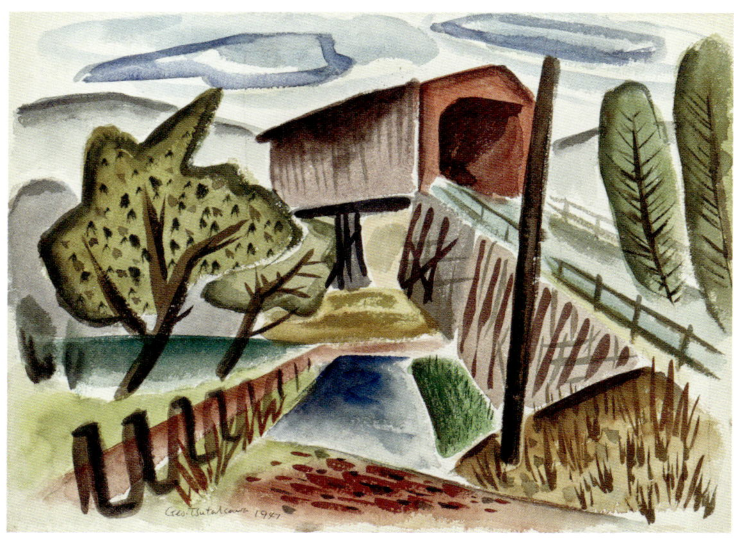

M.27
George Tsutakawa
Untitled, 1947
Watercolor, 15 × 21 in.
Collection of the Tsutakawa Family

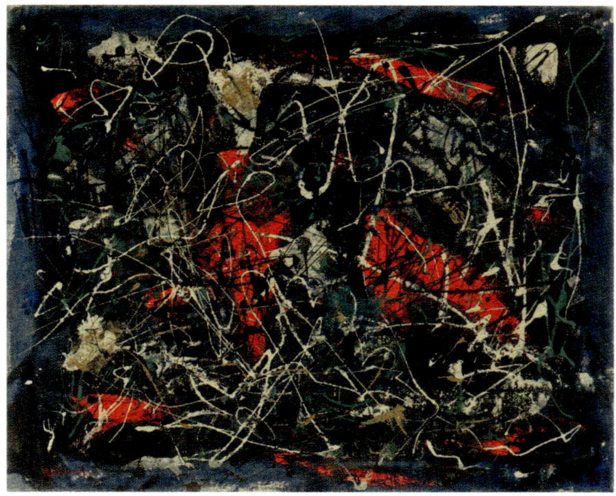

M.28
Paul Horiuchi
Untitled, ca. 1948–1950
Oil on canvas, 16¼ × 20¼ in.
Private collection

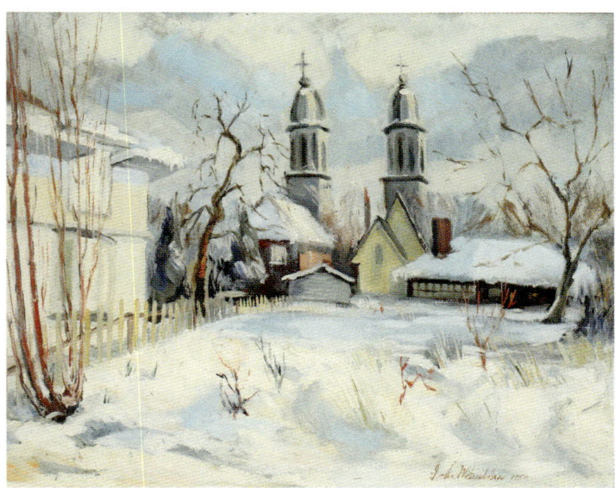

M.29
John Matsudaira
Untitled (winter landscape with Immaculate Conception Church), 1950
Oil on canvas, 20 × 26 in.
Collection of the Matsudaira Family

drip technique including Horiuchi, although most followed Tobey's Asian-inspired aesthetic (fig. M.28). Nomura's abstract work is an amalgamation, using the biomorphic shapes of surrealism with a series of frenetic lines derived from Tobey's white writing.

John Matsudaira (1922–2007), like most of Seattle's Japanese American community, was incarcerated along with his large family at Minidoka, but in spite of this he volunteered to serve in the U.S. Army and became part of the legendary 442nd Regimental Combat Team, the most decorated military unit of its size in U.S. history. He began his journey as an artist after returning from World War II with a nearly fatal injury sustained during combat in Italy. Against the odds, he overcame his physical challenges and attended the Burnley Art School in Seattle with funds provided by the GI Bill. Matsudaira vacillated between a somewhat realistic style, including portraiture, and abstraction simultaneously. One of his earliest successful works in this genre is the energetic *Port at Night* of 1948, the first of his paintings accepted in the Northwest Annual at the Seattle Art Museum.[20] His carefully arranged plein air paintings of familiar neighborhoods gave way to a type of lyrical abstraction that allowed him to create some of the region's finest works at midcentury (figs. M.29 and M.30).

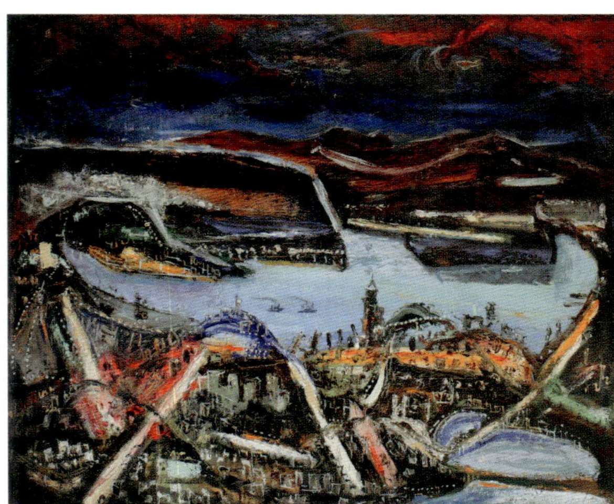

M.30
John Matsudaira
Port at Night, 1948
Oil on canvas, 24 × 30 in.
Private collection

Nomura remained a regular exhibitor at the Seattle Art Museum in the 1930s, and as the new decade began, he was included in several of the museum's exhibitions: *Paintings by Northwest Artists*, which ran from May 8 through June 1, 1940, and then two consecutive exhibitions,

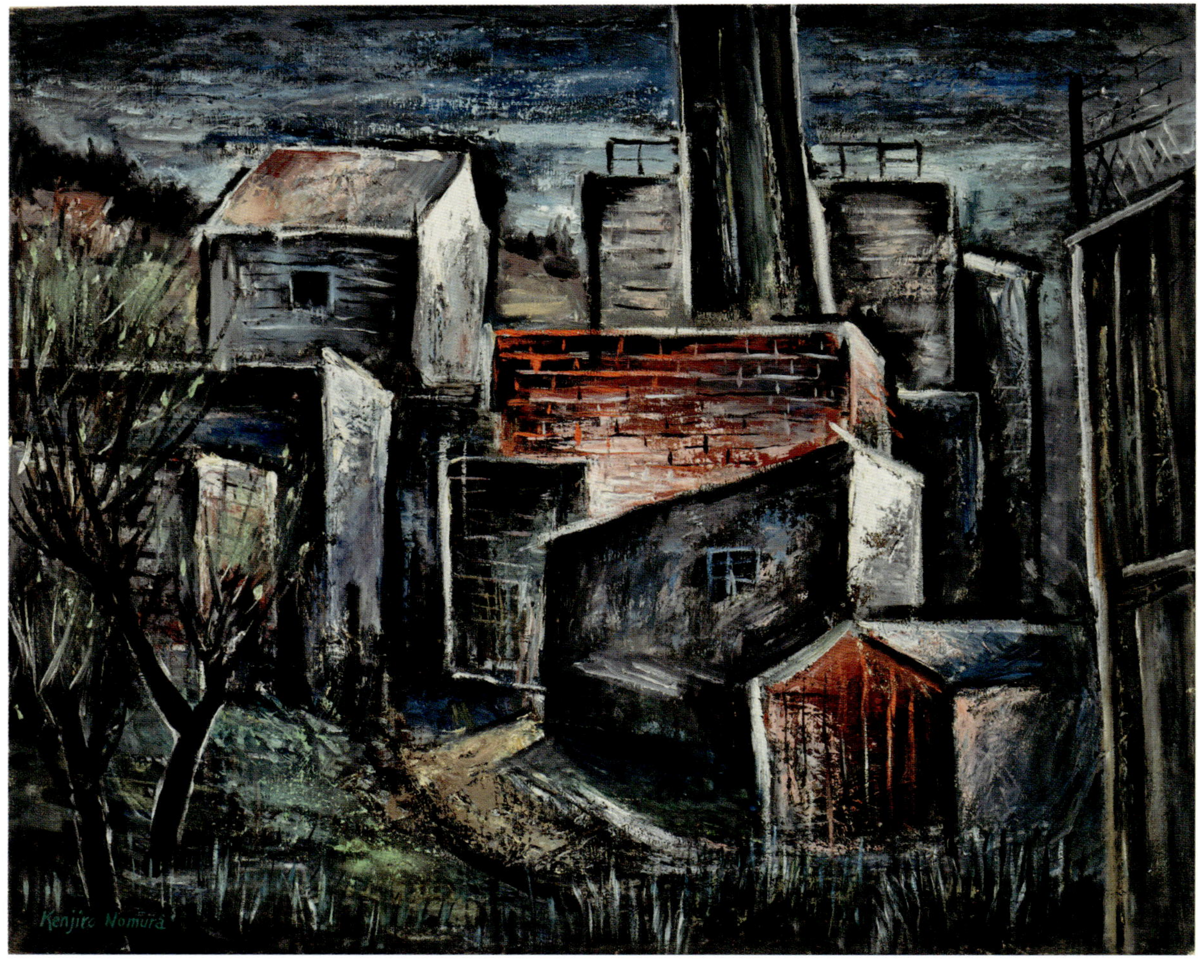

M.31
An Old Brewery, 1947
Oil on canvas, 23½ × 29½ in.
Private collection

Development of Landscape Painting, November 6–24, 1940, followed by *Paintings by the Group of Twelve*, from November 25 to December 1, 1940. In 1947 Nomura returned to the Northwest Annual, exhibiting a gouache painting titled *Brewery* (also titled *An Old Brewery*), but it would be his last painting accepted in the annual. In an ironic twist of fate, Nomura's work was accepted into another prominent regional venue in 1949. The Western Washington Fair at Puyallup had a long history of art exhibitions, sometimes featuring national traveling shows of major American painters along with celebrated Washington State artists in their own separate show. His oil *Aurora Avenue Bridge* (lost) hung on the site where he and his family were detained just seven years earlier. That same year, Nomura entered a new beginning by marrying Chiyo Fukasaki. The couple along with Nomura's son, George, rented a duplex that they shared with the ailing photographer Frank Asakichi Kunishige and his wife, Gin, who returned to Seattle in 1950 after living briefly in Twin Falls, Idaho, following their release from Minidoka.[21]

The new decade of the 1950s brought increasing possibilities and opportunities for exhibition to Nomura, who was poised to have renewed success as an abstractionist. Although his days of exhibiting in the Seattle Art Museum's Northwest Annuals had ended, he participated in the International Art Exhibitions sponsored by the International Improvement Association in Seattle's Chinatown (fig. M.31). This new artistic venue featured the work of ethnic minorities including

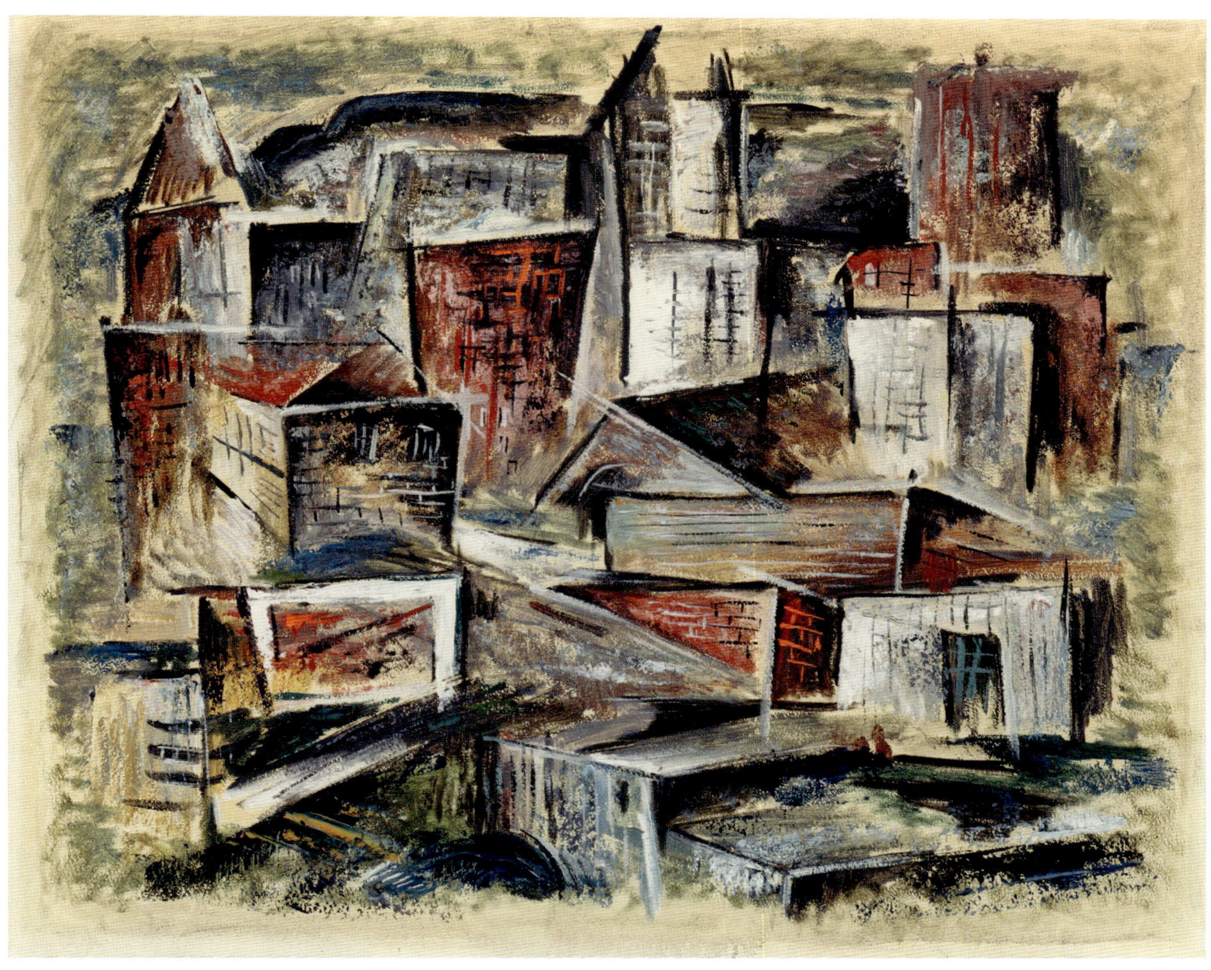

M.32
Untitled, circa 1952
Oil on board, 19 × 24 in.
Private collection

Asian American and black artists. Because of the racial diversity, these exhibitions were referred to as "international" even though they only included regional artists. Around this same time, other venues appeared in which Nomura participated, including the International Art Exhibitions sponsored by Mount Zion Baptist Church, a black congregation with artistic cultural leanings. One of the congregants and the organizer of the exhibitions was James W. Washington Jr. (1909–2000), a local painter and sculptor whose arrival in Seattle in 1944 had attracted attention in the community. Washington and Milt Simons (1923–1973) were the only exhibiting black artists in the region during this time. Washington promoted his own work and that of his contemporaries by creating a welcoming feeling of inclusion among the minority artists he was exhibiting with. Nomura also exhibited in the extremely popular Art Week on Pine Street, an invitational sponsored by the Seattle chapter of the Artists Equity Association. This ingenious concept brought together the region's top artists to hang their works in the high-traffic windows of the city's prominent businesses. In 1952 Nomura won an eighty-dollar prize for his work titled *City*, which was displayed in the window of downtown Seattle's most exclusive department store, Frederick & Nelson. Two years later, his oil titled *On the Rooftops* was displayed in the window of another prominent department store, Best's Apparel.

Most poignantly, Nomura's work was included once again in the 1951 Western Washington State Fair at Puyallup, where he won an

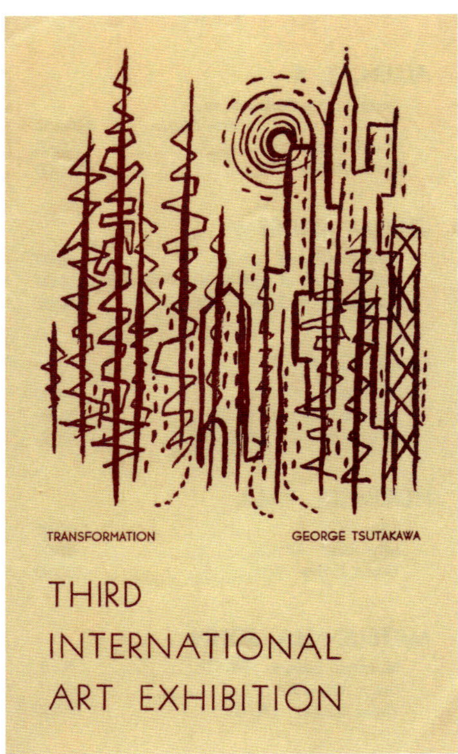

M.33
Catalogue of the Third International Art Exhibition
Sponsored by the International Improvement Association, 616 King Street, Seattle, WA, August 6–9, 1952
Courtesy of the Matsudaira Family

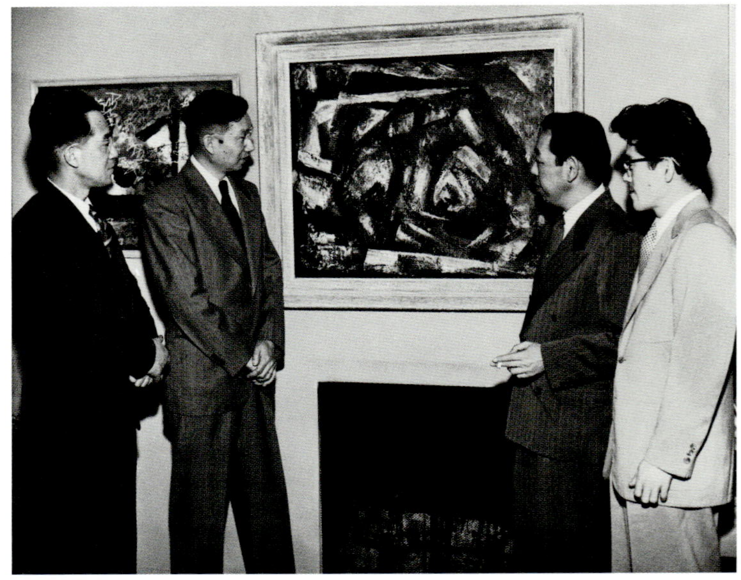

M.34
From left, Paul Horiuchi, Kenjiro Nomura, George Tsutakawa, and John Matsudaira admiring a painting by Paul Horiuchi at the Zoe Dusanne Gallery, 1952. Photo: Elmer Ogawa
Nomura Estate

Nomura's painting *Shopping Center*, 1950, can be seen behind the artist.

honorable mention for his oil *Shopping Center* (see fig. 4.11). One extremely popular local organization was the Northwest Watercolor Society, which began in 1940. Even though Nomura was a capable watercolorist and produced excellent works in water-based mediums, he never joined the organization, thus eliminating significant exhibition opportunities. However, his son, George, became a member and won an honorable mention in 1960 for *Seascape #2*. It is also significant to note that Nomura, Tokita, and Fujii never created any prints, an unusual omission from their oeuvre considering the popularity of printmaking in Seattle, exemplified by the internationally renowned Northwest Printmakers Society, which had been active since 1929.

In the Sunday, August 1, 1954, edition of the *Seattle Times*, Margaret Callahan wrote an article titled "Seattle's Japanese Artists." The sub-headline listed the artists' occupations as "auto painter, aircraft worker, professor, and a picture-frame maker." Perhaps unintentionally, the heading insinuates an amateur categorization that diminished their individual success by grouping them together by race. Callahan even managed to cloud the devastating effects on the artists who were incarcerated, stating, "The second World War dispersed the group and for a period, shows here were lacking in pictures from Japanese painters. The loss was felt keenly, and it was with a warmly welcoming feeling that art viewers saw the return of Kenjiro Nomura and the rise of some promising new talent."[22] The article was accompanied by a photograph of Horiuchi, Nomura, Tsutakawa, and Matsudaira admiring one of Horiuchi's abstract paintings hanging on the wall of the gallery that represented them, owned by Zoe Dusanne (see fig. M.34). Dusanne, a fascinating figure in Seattle's art history, was a black woman whose gallery was among the first to show internationally acclaimed, museum-quality artists in Seattle. She rounded

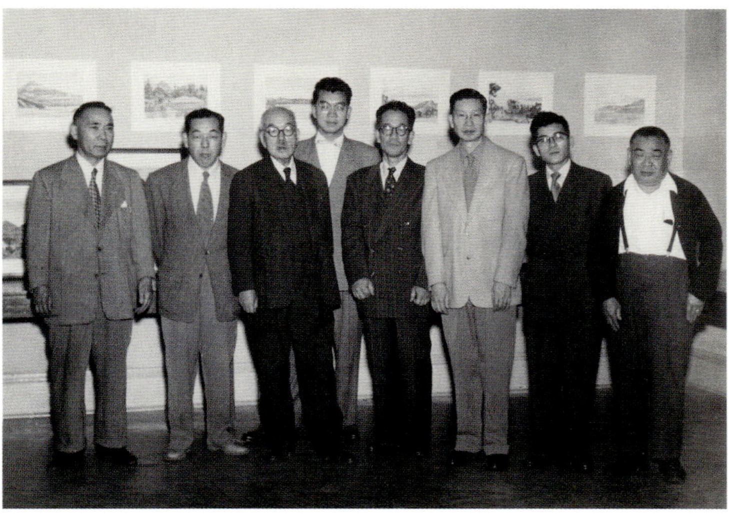

M.35
Artists at the Seattle Art Museum exhibition of watercolors by the Japanese artist Hakutei Ishii, 1954
Courtesy of the Matsudaira Family

From left: Genji Mihara, president of the Seattle Japanese American Community Service, George Tsutakawa, Hakutei Ishii, photographer Johsel Namkung, Paul Horiuchi, Kenjiro Nomura, John Matsudaira, and local businessman Fujimatsu Moriguchi, Tsutakawa's brother-in-law

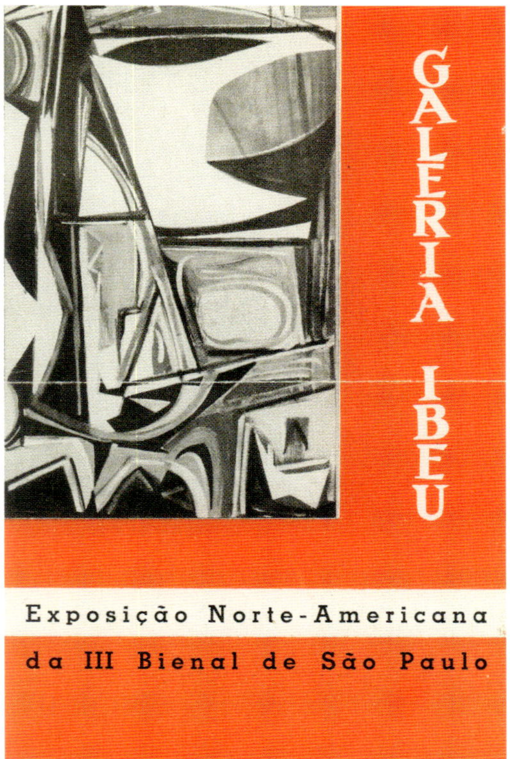

M.36
Exhibition pamphlet for the Third Biennial of the Museum of Modern Art in São Paulo, Brazil, 1955
Nomura Estate

out her stable by representing the local Japanese American artists and gave the first American exhibition to the young Yayoi Kusama (b. 1929), who came from Japan to Seattle for her opening in 1953, forming friendships with some of the artists including Matsudaira and Tsutakawa.

The apotheosis of Nomura's career came in 1955 when he was included in an exhibition at the Third Biennial of the São Paulo Museum of Modern Art in Brazil. Nomura was one of the thirteen Northwest artists represented in this important international exhibition, which also included Tsutakawa.[23] That same year, his work was included in *Eight Washington Painters* at the Portland Art Museum, illustrating his importance and stature in the artistic community of the Northwest. His final honor came with his inclusion in the 1956 traveling group exhibition titled *Pacific Coast Art* displayed at several high-profile national art museums. At the height of this second phase of his career, Nomura died on June 30, 1956, at the age of fifty-nine, following complications from surgery. In 1960, he was posthumously honored at the Seattle Art Museum with a solo exhibition of eighteen works displaying the representative phases of his career.

Kenjiro Nomura, whether by intent or coincidence, seemed to have an interest in bridges. They appear frequently in his paintings from all phases of his art production. In retrospect, a bridge could present a metaphor for his life and career. He was an immigrant who bridged the ancient cultural history of his native Japan to his adopted home in Washington State, then in the early stages of creating its own individual cultural identity, which he helped to shape. He was an artist who never left the Northwest for study or subject matter, yet he managed to connect with teachers like Tadama and some of his fellow artists who traveled and absorbed techniques

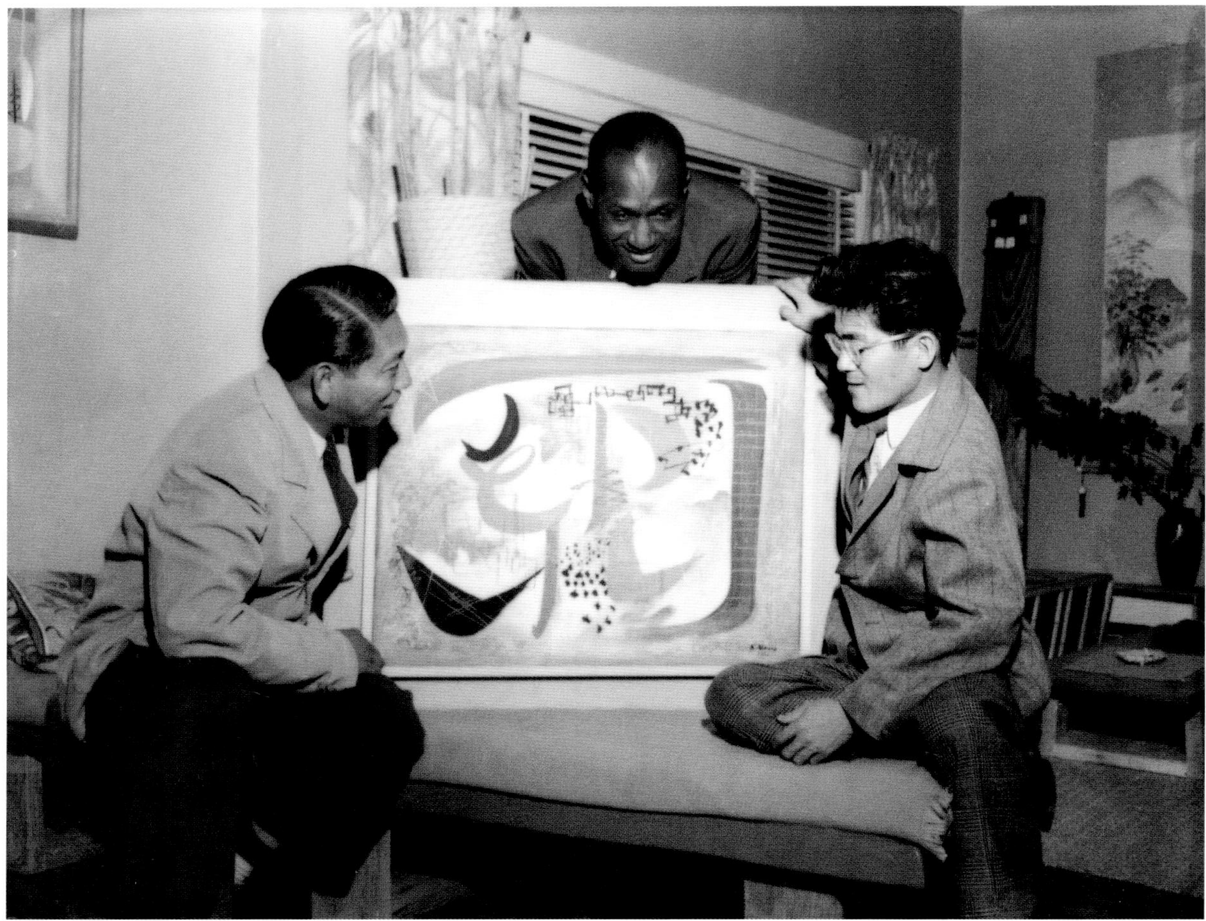

M.37
Elmer Ogawa
Artists admiring Nomura's painting *Shopping Center*, December 25, 1951
From left: Fay Chong, James W. Washington Jr., and John Matsudaira
Special Collections, University of Washington Libraries, Elmer Ogawa Collection, PH Coll 178, UW374

from firsthand international sources. He painted in Seattle, but his work was exhibited nationally and internationally. His stylistic techniques began with impressionism followed by a type of formalist realism and ended with abstractions derived from his imagination and personal spiritual awareness. And finally, because of his talent, tenacity, and spirit, he bridged a gap between his generation and the younger Issei and Nisei artists who viewed him as a mentor and guide for success. Nomura now bridges time itself, because although he passed away sixty-five years ago, his work is still fresh and relevant, and provides ongoing inspiration to artists into the future.

Kenjiro Nomura, 1930s
Nomura Estate

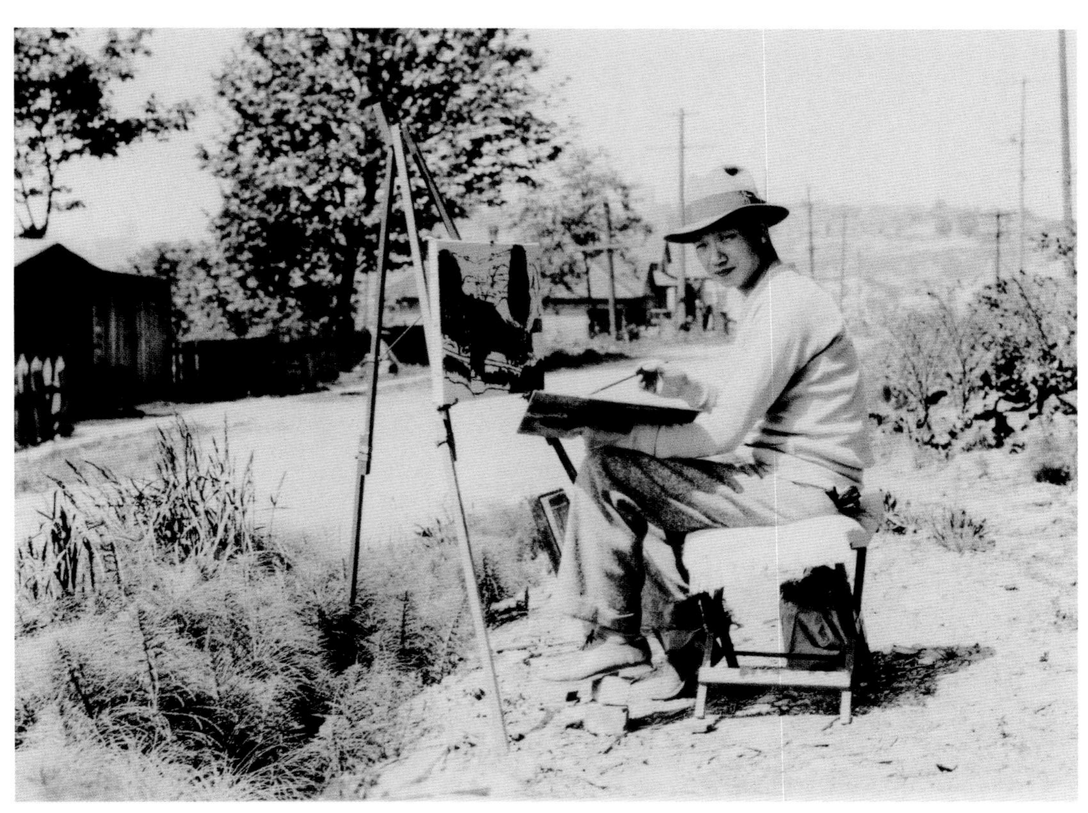

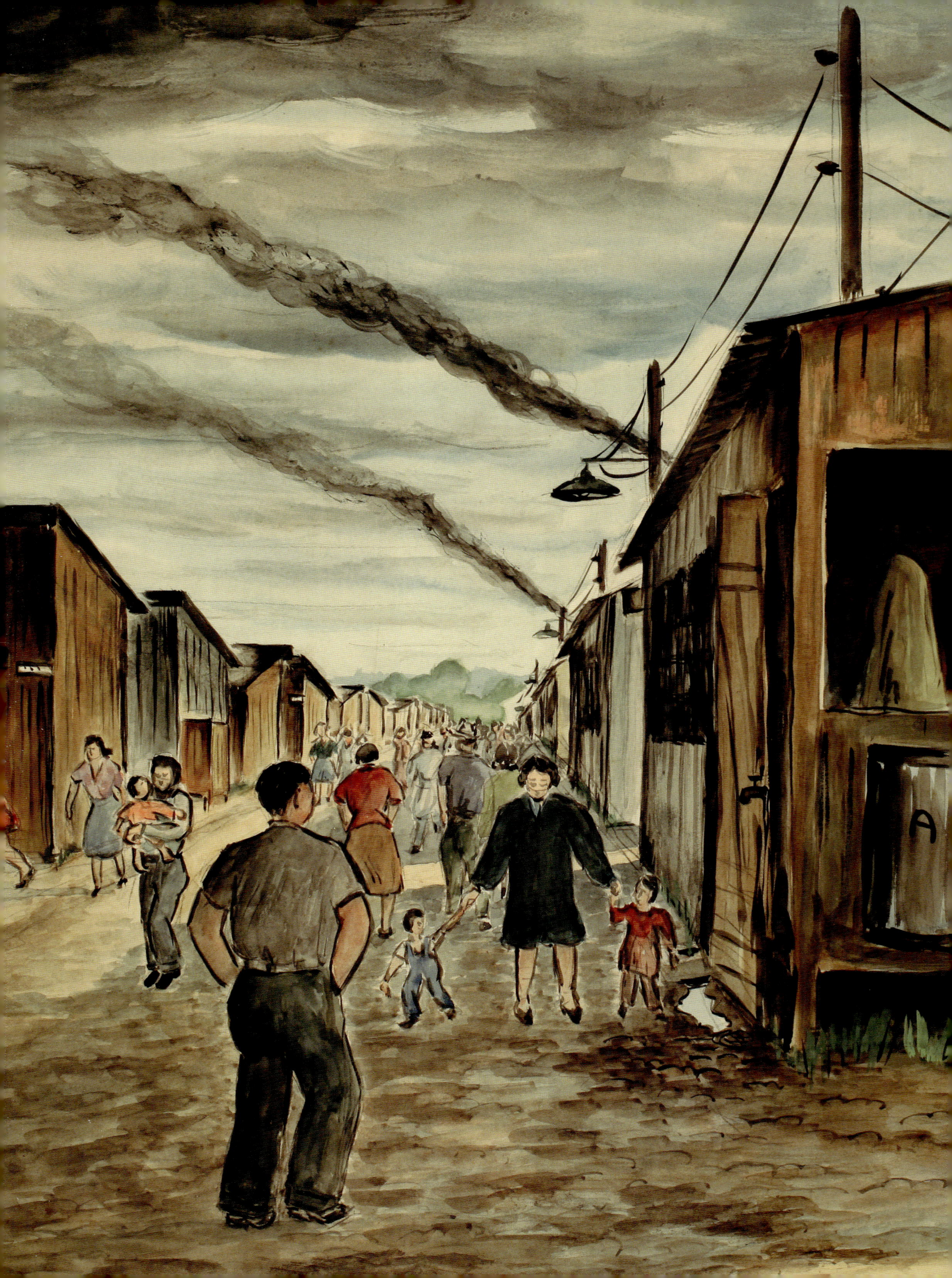

ACKNOWLEDGMENTS

Producing a book requires the expertise and generosity of many people. David Martin and I are grateful to have known George and Betty Nomura, who opened their home and shared memories and the artwork and personal papers in their possession. Without their contributions, this account of Kenjiro Nomura would be greatly diminished. Their daughter, Lisa Nomura-Kidwell, has become heir and caretaker, and we thank her warmly for her help with the loan of paintings and papers.

This account is deeply indebted to the scholars who have constructed and interpreted the history of Japanese America and, in doing so, have contributed to a more inclusive and representative American history and American art history. Several scholars contributed specifically to my text. To the historian Gail M. Nomura (no relation to the subject of this study), associate professor emerita of American ethnic studies at the University of Washington, I extend my appreciation for the thoughtful foreword that frames Kenjiro Nomura's story. Stephen H. Sumida, professor emeritus of American ethnic studies at the University of Washington and a specialist in American literature, read early and late drafts of the manuscript and enriched my reading of Nomura's artwork. Greg Robinson, professor of history at l'Université du Québec à Montréal, shared documents I hadn't found and added precision to my account. My thanks to Sandy Kita and Terry Kita for Japanese language translation, and to Michiyo Morioka for the translation and interpretation of Nomura's *tanzaku* imagery. It was with the urging of the distinguished historian Roger Daniels that my own engagement with Japanese American studies became part of the narrative. I am grateful to each of them for their support.

Thanks to the archivists and librarians who helped with access to primary source material at the National Archives, University of Washington Libraries Special Collections, Seattle Public Library, Tacoma Public Library, Washington State Historical Society, Seattle Art Museum, Museum of History and Industry, and San Juan Historical Museum. The White River Valley Museum, site of an active prewar Japanese American community, provided an opportunity to present work in progress. For agreeing to the loan and reproduction of artwork, thank you to Margaret Bullock and Ellen Ito at the Tacoma Art Museum, Bob Fisher at the Wing Luke Museum, Theresa Papanikolas at the Seattle Art Museum, Chris Skaugset at the Longview Public Library, Gregg Schlanger at Central Washington University, the Smithsonian American Art Museum, the Japanese American National Museum, several private collectors, and Lisa Nomura-Kidwell.

The cultural funding agency of King County, 4Culture, provided early support for this book

Mess Hall, 1942
Detail of Fig. 3.6

through both its Arts and Heritage divisions, and I thank Brian J. Carter, executive director of 4Culture, for encouraging the dual application, and Chieko Phillips, Heritage Program Director, and Heather Dwyer, Arts Program Manager, for help along the way. To Ellen Ferguson, trustee of the Hugh and Jane Ferguson Foundation, heartfelt thanks for generous and sustained commitment to the Issei artists' legacies. As the book neared completion, the Edmonds Arts Commission provided funds toward design and printing. Additional contributions from many supporters of the Cascadia Art Museum's mission and the telling of Nomura's story (listed elsewhere) helped make this publication possible.

The release of this book accompanies an exhibition of Nomura's artwork at the Cascadia Art Museum. Thank you to Lindsey Echelbarger and the board of trustees; the former executive director, Leigh Ann Gilmer; and especially David Martin, the museum's curator, for supporting the book and exhibition from the beginning. David has been a partner in all phases of the project and organized the exhibition.

Because we had access to nearly all known artworks by Nomura, David and I committed to having as many as possible photographed. Thanks to Tod Gangler and Rob Fraser for new photography, and the conservator Patty West, who brought damaged paintings back to life. We extend our thanks to Jane Lichty for her careful editing of the text, to Carrie Wicks for her precise proofreading, and to Susan Stone for compiling the index. For this book, as often the case, it seems as if the designer should share credit on the title page; we thank Phil Kovacevich for his skill, patience, and good humor in working with us to bring elegant visual clarity to the story. Nicole Mitchell, the director of the University of Washington Press, committed to distributing the book at its inception. The press has been a valued partner in the Cascadia Art Museum's publications and in my previous studies of Seattle Issei artists, now brought full cycle with this one of Nomura. David adds appreciation to the families of artists addressed in his essay: Ann Matsudaira Otani; Soichi Sunami's daughter, Reiko Kopelson; Gerry Tsutakawa and the Tsutakawa family; John Arima and the Arima family; and to George and Betty Nomura's son-in-law, Kevin Kidwell, for help handling materials from the estate.

All have contributed meaningfully to this reaffirmation of Kenjiro Nomura's achievement and legacy.

NOTES

Foreword

1 Gail M. Nomura, "*Tsugiki*, a Grafting: A History of a Japanese Pioneer Woman in Washington State," in *Women in Pacific Northwest History: An Anthology*, ed. Karen J. Blair (Seattle: University of Washington Press, 1988), 207–229. Versions of the essay have been published in numerous other books and journals.

2 I am not, to my knowledge, related to Kenjiro Nomura, but when I first came to know about him through my research in Japanese American history in the Pacific Northwest, I was, of course, quite interested in learning more about this possible Nomura relative.

3 James A. Wood, "Aspirations of Early Settlers Have Persisted and Blossomed into Well-Based Achievements," *Seattle Times*, July 28, 1935.

4 Kenjiro Nomura became a naturalized U.S. citizen in 1954, after racial restrictions to naturalization were removed in 1952.

5 Similarly, Teiko Tomita burned all her prewar poetry before being taken to the camps, but she continued to write poetry in the camps, depicting the harsh life there, and later was able to reconstruct much of her prewar poetry, which she had committed to memory.

6 Barbara Johns's three previous books are *Paul Horiuchi: East and West* (Seattle: University of Washington Press in association with Museum of Northwest Art, La Conner, WA, 2008); *Signs of Home: The Paintings and Wartime Diary of Kamekichi Tokita* (Seattle: University of Washington Press, 2011); and *The Hope of Another Spring: Takuichi Fujii, Artist and Wartime Witness* (Seattle: University of Washington Press, 2017).

Introduction

1 Martha Kingsbury included Nomura and Tokita in two early exhibitions that considered the region's art history. Kingsbury, *Art of the Thirties: The Pacific Northwest* (Seattle: University of Washington Press for the Henry Art Gallery, 1972); and her essay "Seattle and the Puget Sound," in *Art of the Pacific Northwest: From the 1930s to the Present* (Washington, DC: Smithsonian Institution Press for the National Collection of Fine Arts, 1974), 39–92. She credits George Tsutakawa, then a fellow professor at the University of Washington School of Art, for encouraging the Issei artists' inclusion. Kingsbury, communication with the author, February 29, 2012.

2 At the time I was the manager of the Northwest Asian American Artists Project, a special project of the Archives of American Art. I thank Paul J. Karlstrom, then the director of the West Coast Region of the archives, for the opportunities this and the preceding Northwest Oral History Project provided.

3 See n3.11 on the varying number of incarcerees.

4 Barbara Johns, *Paul Horiuchi: East and West* (Seattle: University of Washington Press in association with Museum of Northwest Art, La Conner, WA, 2008).

5 Barbara Johns, *Signs of Home: The Paintings and Wartime Diary of Kamekichi Tokita* (Seattle: University of Washington Press, 2011). The book led to several related projects: the exhibition *Painting Seattle: Kamekichi Tokita and Kenjiro Nomura,* which I organized for the Seattle Art Museum (2011–2012); "Community Stories: I Put Down My Pen; The Wartime Reflections of an Issei Artist," Seattle Channel (2014), https://www.seattlechannel.org/CommunityStories/episodes?videoid=x20595; and *Gaman*, a multimedia musical work commissioned by Music of Remembrance and composed by Christophe Chagnard (2018).

6 Barbara Johns, "Knowing Your Place: Issei Artists in Seattle; Kenjiro Nomura, Kamekichi Tokita, and Takuichi Fujii" (PhD diss., University of Washington, 2014).

7 Roger Daniels, foreword to *The Hope of Another Spring: Takuichi Fujii, Artist and Wartime Witness*, by Barbara Johns (Seattle: University of Washington Press, 2017), viii. The exhibition *Witness to Wartime: The Painted Diary of Takuichi Fujii*, which I organized, opened at the Washington State History Museum in 2017 and is touring nationally through 2025.

8 Johns, *The Hope of Another Spring*.

9 See also Johns, *Signs of Home*, 11; Johns, *The Hope of Another Spring*, 15–16. Tokita studied classical Chinese painting before emigrating at age twenty-two and was known as a superb calligrapher. Fujii studied brushwork and watercolor as a youth.

10 The regional characterization is from Nancy Wilson Ross, *Farthest Reach: Oregon and Washington* (New York: Alfred A. Knopf, 1941), in The American Scene series.

11 Kenneth Callahan, "Pacific Northwest," *ArtNews* 45 (July 1946), 22–27ff. Callahan's premise was reinforced in a traveling exhibition and catalogue by Harris K. Proctor, *Ten Painters of the Pacific Northwest* (Utica, NY: Munson-Williams-Proctor Institute, ca. 1947).

12 June Mukai McKivor, "Kenjiro Nomura (1896–1956)," in *Kenjiro Nomura: An Artist's View of the Japanese American Internment* (Seattle: Wing Luke Asian Museum, 1991); Kenjiro Nomura papers, Nomura estate. McKivor organized the exhibition for the Wing Luke Museum and initiated the tour.

13 Three-quarters of Tokita's diary and examples of his poetry in translation appear in Johns, *Signs of Home*. Half of Fujii's diary is reproduced in Johns, *The Hope of Another Spring*. Fujii's diary in its entirety is planned for publication by the University of Washington Press.

14 Shokichi Tokita, communication with the author, October 2, 2019.

15 The major sources besides McKivor's essay are George Tsutakawa, "A Conversation on Life and Fountains," *Journal of Ethnic Studies* 4 (Spring 1976): 4–36; George Tsutakawa, oral history interview, 1983, Archives of American Art, Smithsonian Institution, https://www.aaa.si.edu/collections/interviews/oral-history-interview-george-tsutakawa-11913; Kingsbury, *Art of the Thirties*; Kingsbury, "Seattle and Puget Sound"; Mayumi Tsutakawa, "A Canvas Diary: Painters before the War," in *Turning Shadows into Light: Art and Culture of the Northwest's Early Asian/Pacific Community*, ed. Mayumi Tsutakawa and Alan Chong Lau (Seattle: Young Pine Press, 1982),72–81; Mayumi Tsutakawa, ed., *They Painted from Their Hearts: Pioneer Asian American Artists* (Seattle: Wing Luke Asian Museum, 1994); and Kazuko Nakane, "Facing the Pacific: Asian American Artists in Seattle, 1900–1970," in *Asian American Art: A History, 1850–1970*, ed. Gordon H. Chang, Mark Dean Johnson, and Paul J. Karlstrom (Stanford, CA: Stanford University Press, 2008), 55–81. See also Johns, "Knowing Your Place."

16 Roger Daniels, "Words Do Matter: A Note on Inappropriate Terminology and the Incarceration of the Japanese Americans," in *Nikkei in the Pacific Northwest: Japanese Americans and Japanese Canadians in the Twentieth Century*, ed. Louis Fiset and Gail M. Nomura (Seattle: University of Washington Press, 2005), 183–207; essay reissued online by Discover Nikkei, February 1, 2008, http://www.discovernikkei.org/en/journal/2008/2/1/words-do-matter. See also Denshō: The Japanese American Legacy Project, "Terminology," https://densho.org/terminology (accessed November 20, 2020).

Chapter 1

1 The Sino-Japanese War of 1894–1895 and the Russo-Japanese War of 1904–1905 established Japan not only as a world power but also as an imperialist power. The United States established imperialist claims at the same time with its victory in the Spanish-American War and annexation of the sovereign kingdom of Hawai'i in 1898.

2 List or Manifest of Alien Passengers for the U.S. Immigration Officer at Port of Arrival, Seattle, June 13, 1907, Ancestry.com, https://www.ancestrylibrary.com/.

3 George Nomura, communication with the author, November 12, 2012; confirmed by Betty Nomura, December 30, 2018. My interviews with George Nomura took place on several dates in 2012 and are hereafter cited as George Nomura. The family account appears earlier in McKivor, *Kenjiro Nomura*, 8–9. A possible scenario to reconcile the different accounts is that he established a tailoring business in Tacoma that catered to miners heading to Alaska. As I describe later in the chapter, Tacoma vied with Seattle as a supplier to Klondike prospectors in coming years.

4 George Nomura.

5 Kenjiro Nomura, Box 4621, 8/20/1, Washington Office Records Evacuee Case Files, E.22, War Relocation Authority (WRA), Record Group (RG) 210, National Archives and Records Administration, Washington, DC (hereafter cited as WRA case file).

6 Shunichi Otsuka, *History of the Japanese of Tacoma*, trans. James Watanabe (Seattle: Pacific Northwest District Council, Japanese American Citizens League, 1986), 2; originally published as *Tacoma nihonjin hattenshi*, 1917.

7 Otsuka, *History*, 5–6. Otsuka attributes a subsequent rise in anti-Japanese agitation to the arrival on the mainland

of Japanese laborers from Hawai'i. (Japanese workers had gone to Hawai'i, then a sovereign kingdom, as contract laborers. Contract labor was banned under U.S. law. When the United States took possession of Hawai'i, the Japanese contracts no longer held and freed workers could go to the mainland, where pay was higher and conditions were generally less severe.)

8 Otsuka, *History*, 6.

9 *Tacoma Daily Ledger*, January 7, 1898.

10 World Population Review, "Tacoma, Washington," https://worldpopulationreview.com/us-cities/tacoma-wa-population (accessed September 20, 2020).

11 On the Gentlemen's Agreement, Roger Daniels, *Asian America: Chinese and Japanese in the United States since 1850* (Seattle: University of Washington Press, 1988), 125–126. See also Yuji Ichioka, *The Issei: The World of the First Generation Japanese Immigrants, 1885–1924* (New York: Free Press, 1988), 4. Ichioka emphasizes that Japan never intended that labor emigrants settle permanently.

12 Harukichi Nomura came under the sponsorship of S. Okada, Tacoma's only Japanese tailor at the time, and in coming years its most prominent. List or Manifest of Alien Passengers, June 13, 1907.

13 Otsuka, *History*, 1–2.

14 Ronald E. Magden, *Furusato: Tacoma–Pierce County Japanese, 1888–1977* (Tacoma, WA: Nikkeijinkai, Tacoma Japanese Community Service, 1998), 26–27. Magden notes that eighty-seven merchants applied for citizenship. See also Lisa M. Hoffman and Mary L. Hanneman, *Becoming Nisei: Japanese American Lives in Prewar Tacoma* (Seattle: University of Washington Press, 2021), chapter 2, on Nikkei businesses in Tacoma.

15 On the directives for adaptation and "assimilation," Ichioka, *The Issei*, 185–189.

16 Magden, *Furusato*, 26.

17 Seattle's efforts are the subject of Shelley Sang-Hee Lee, *Claiming the Oriental Gateway: Prewar Seattle and Japanese America* (Philadelphia: Temple University Press, 2011).

18 The photo album appears to have been assembled in the 1920s and offers rich clues to an otherwise scant record of Nomura's early life.

19 McKivor, *Kenjiro Nomura*, 9; attendance reports, Tacoma School District, Puget Sound Regional Branch, Washington State Archives; on night school, WRA case file. Accounts of Nomura's education in Tacoma vary. Records of the Tacoma School District, which begin in 1909, list him only for the 1910–1912 school years, although his WRA case file and McKivor state otherwise.

20 On the Japanese Language School and Nomura's attendance, Otsuka, *History*, 54–59; Magden, *Furusato*, 69–72; Lisa Hoffman, "Tacoma's Japanese Language School: An Alternative Path to Citizenship and Belonging in Pre-WWII Urban America," Conflux 6 (Urban Studies Program, University of Washington Tacoma, 2014), https://digitalcommons.tacoma.uw.edu/conflux/6. On the characterization of the Yamasakis and the nonsectarian school, Hoffman and Hanneman, *Becoming Nisei*, especially 143–172. Magden states that Nomura attended until 1915; Nomura more likely quit when he was left to live on his own in 1913.

21 Family accounts date his move to 1916, but a painting, a portrait dated November 1915 (see fig. M.8), supports the earlier date.

22 Census numbers in S. Frank Miyamoto, *Social Solidarity among the Japanese in Seattle* (1939; repr., Seattle: University of Washington Press in cooperation with the Asian American Studies Program, University of Washington, 1984), 14. The Nikkei population grew from 6,127 in 1910 to 7,874 in 1920. Seattle grew explosively in the first decade of the century, nearly tripling to 237,000 by 1910. Rapid city growth continued to 1930. The federal Immigration Act in 1924 had a severe impact on the Nikkei community, which increased by only about 600 during the 1920s, most of them newly born Americans. In the intensifying nativism of the early 1920s, Seattle city directories declared the city's population to be 73 percent native-born. *Seattle City Directory*, vols. 1900–1930 (Seattle: R. L. Polk & Company).

23 On labor contractors and cannery workers, Doug Chin, *Seattle's International District: The Making of a Pan-Asian American Community* (Seattle: International Examiner Press, 2001), 31.

24 "War Increases the Fish Business," *Friday Harbor (WA) Journal*, May 20, 1915; "Many to Work in Salmon Canneries," *Friday Harbor (WA) Journal*, May 24, 1917.

25 Jesse Frederick Steiner, *The Japanese Invasion* (Chicago: A. C. McClurg & Company, 1917), 130, cited in Miyamoto, *Social Solidarity*, 3.

26 Kazuo Ito, *Issei: A History of Japanese Immigrants in North America*, trans. Shinichiro Nakamura and Jean S. Gerard (Seattle: Executive Committee for Publication of Issei, Japanese Community Service, 1973), 729–730.

27 See David F. Martin and Nicolette Bromberg, *Shadows of a Fleeting World: Pictorial Photography and the Seattle Camera Club* (Seattle: University of Washington Press in association with University of Washington Libraries and the Henry Art Gallery, 2011).

28 Miyamoto, *Social Solidarity*, 14, 71. On the high number of small businesses in Seattle relative to population, see also Edna Bonacich and John Model, *The Economic Basis of Ethnic*

Solidarity: Small Business in the Japanese American Community (Berkeley and Los Angeles: University of California Press, 1980), 38–39.

29 See, for example, Brian Masaru Hayashi, *Democratizing the Enemy: The Japanese American Internment* (Princeton, NJ: Princeton University Press, 2004), 8–10.

30 "Situation Wanted, Male," *Seattle Times*, July 19, 1916.

31 WRA case file; *Seattle City Directory*, 1921–1937. Nomura later dated his start in sign painting to 1921. Hirayama moved to California in 1931, a result of the Depression.

32 George Tsutakawa, oral history interview.

33 Tooru Kanazawa, "Seattle's Artists of Palette and Brush," *Japanese American Courier*, October 7, 1933. Within a few years Shimizu and Tanaka would leave for New York and Paris.

34 "Japanese Artists to Exhibit Art Drawings," *Seattle Times*, October 1, 1916; "Many See Exhibit of Japanese Art," [source and date NA], Nomura papers.

35 Adele M. Ballard, "With the Fine Arts Folk," *Town Crier*, October 7, 1916, 12–13. The *Town Crier* was published in Seattle from 1910 to 1937. In 1916 the Seattle Fine Arts Society, an early predecessor to the Seattle Art Museum, began using the magazine as its vehicle to publish art news.

36 "Many See Exhibit of Japanese Art." Nomura signed and dated his work in English.

37 WRA case file.

38 Seattle Art Museum, Accession No. 2636-1, Box 34/12, Special Collections, University of Washington Libraries (hereafter cited as Seattle Art Museum records). The five were Yasushi Tanaka, Toshi Shimizu, Azo Nakagawa, S. Haigiuda, and S. Oishi.

39 Madge Bailey, "In Art Circles," *Seattle Post-Intelligencer*, [ca. February 1922], Nomura papers.

40 Kanazawa, "Seattle's Artists of Palette and Brush." See also Margaret B. Callahan, "Seattle's Japanese Artists," *Seattle Times*, August 1, 1954.

41 A reviewer in the *Seattle Post-Intelligencer* praised the painting while calling the subject "unusual." Whether the subject's apparent ethnicity or another characteristic makes it "unusual" is unstated. "Artists Show Many Fine Paintings," *Seattle Post-Intelligencer*, [date NA, ca. March 22, 1926], Nomura papers.

42 Kanazawa, "Seattle's Artists of Palette and Brush."

43 Earlier laws rescinded a woman's citizenship if she married a foreign man, based on the premise that she assumed her husband's citizenship. The Cable Act of 1922 reversed these laws, but the reversal applied only to women marrying those eligible for naturalization. Since Asian-born immigrants were legally barred from citizenship, the 1922 act did not apply to Nisei women. The Cable Act was amended in 1931 to correct this omission, and the legislation was repealed altogether in 1936.

Mukai's parents were originally from Yamaguchi Prefecture and moved to Washington after having worked on a plantation in Hawai'i. I am indebted to George Nomura for the information about his mother.

Chapter 2

1 His *Fishing Boats* showed at the Oakland Art Gallery's annual in 1926 and was among twenty-five paintings selected for a special extension of the exhibition at the Haviland Hall art gallery, University of California, Berkeley; the next year he was cited among "well-known names" to exhibit again in Oakland. H. L. Dungan, "Artists and Their Work," *Oakland (CA) Tribune*, March 14, 1926; "145 Canvases Representing All Schools on Exhibition," *San Francisco Chronicle*, February 13, 1927, reporting on the "fifth annual" exhibition at the Oakland Art Gallery. I thank Greg Robinson for these sources.

2 Nomura's 1930 *Fishing Boats* would have differed from the 1926 version. Annual exhibitions typically required work done within the year. The Oakland Art Gallery also reformulated its annual exhibition in 1930 to focus on western artists.

3 "Art in the Northwest," *Town Crier*, April 9, 1930, 12.

4 Gobind Behari Lal, "Annual Exhibition at Oakland Gallery: Tolerance in Selection Shown," *San Francisco Examiner*, April 6, 1930, Nomura papers. Alongside Nomura's work, Lal highlighted Stanton MacDonald-Wright's *The Fisherman* (*Old Fisherman Synchromy*) as an "extraordinarily challenging" painting that was said to show the influence of Japanese prints and Persian paintings. Lal's attention to MacDonald-Wright was not coincidental. MacDonald-Wright, an influential early American modernist, had established his reputation in Paris and upon returning to Los Angeles, was a charismatic teacher whose students included a number of Japanese Americans, among them Hideo Date. On his and Date's shared interest in Asian and European art, see Karin Higa, *Living in Color: The Art of Hideo Date* (Los Angeles: Japanese American National Museum, 2001).

5 Lal, "Annual Exhibition at Oakland Gallery"; "Gobind Behari Lal, Reporter; Shared Pulitzer Prize in 1937," *New York Times*, April 3, 1982, http://www.nytimes.com/1982/04/03/obituaries/gobind-behari-lal-reporter-shared-pulitzer-prize-in-1937.html. Born in India, Lal would win a Pulitzer Prize as a science reporter for the Hearst papers and became a prominent advocate for Indian independence.

6 WRA case file. Nomura's citation of the prize appears in several wartime documents.

7 Floyd Spencer, radio script, July 27, 1933, Box 23/ Publicity Materials for Exhibitions Already Shown, 1935–1936, Seattle Art Museum records.

8 "Seattle Artist's Work on Display at New Museum," *Japanese American Courier*, July 1, 1933; "The Seattle Museum That Selected Our Artist," *Taihoku Nippō*, [ca. June 1933], translated from the Japanese by Sandy Kita, Nomura papers.

9 "Artistic Recognition," *Japanese American Courier*, October 7, 1933.

10 Kenneth Callahan, "Seattle Art Museum Fete Is Announced," *Seattle Times*, June 25, 1933.

11 Kenneth Callahan, "The Art Situation—Nomura Exhibition," *Town Crier*, July 15, 1933, 9–10.

12 Line as an outstanding formal element of Japanese art was espoused by the American educator and curator, Ernst F. Fennollosa (1853–1908) together with the Japanese art critic Okakura Tenshin (1863–1913). Hired to teach at Tokyo University in 1878, Fennollosa became an ardent student of and advocate for the historic arts of Japan, which he found neglected during the drive for modernization. He codified a history of Japanese art, drawing a distinction between Meiji and pre-Meiji, and urged artists to incorporate "traditional" practices. Following his work in Japan, he and Okakura brought such teaching to the United States as the successive heads of the Oriental Department of the Boston Museum of Fine Arts. Callahan displays his knowledge of this particularized history in naming line as a key element in Nomura's paintings.

13 James A. Wood, "Aspirations of Early Settlers Have Persisted and Blossomed into Well-Based Achievements," *Seattle Times*, July 28, 1935. The others named are painters Mark Tobey, Ambrose Patterson, Peter Camfferman, Walter Isaacs, and Kenneth Callahan and printmakers Richard Bennett and, from earlier years, Roi Partridge. Nomura is notable as the only person of color.

14 Clarence Bagley, *History of King County* (Chicago: S. J. Clarke Publishing Company, 1929), 678, 681, 684. Recounting conversations in the major cities, Bagley writes, "It is the concensus [*sic*] of opinion that not one of them has moved as many yards of earth . . . as has Seattle since the year 1900." He estimates the total volume to be fifty million cubic yards and describes it as equivalent to a pyramid a half-mile long at the base of each side and ninety feet taller than the Smith Tower. He writes that the methods employed continually changed with innovation, implying that Seattle was unsurpassed in engineering imagination and new technology.

15 Masakazu Iwata, *Planted in Good Soil: A History of the Issei in United States Agriculture*, 2 vols. (New York: Peter Lang, 1992), 2:541.

16 Stan Flewelling, *Shirakawa: Stories from a Pacific Northwest Japanese American Community* (Auburn, WA: White River Valley Museum, 2002), 57–61, 66–68; Iwata, *Planted in Good Soil*, 2:588. In entering the dairy industry, Northwest Issei farmers were distinguished from Issei farmers elsewhere. Flewelling (59) states that of the eighty-three Issei dairy farms in Washington in 1920, over 95 percent were in the White River valley, and in 1922 they supplied 50 percent of Seattle's milk.

17 [Carl F. Gould], President's Report, Art Institute of Seattle, 1927, Box 33/23, Seattle Art Museum records. Gould, an architect and president of the board at the time of its name change, would design the new Seattle Art Museum.

18 Frank Asakichi Kunishige's photographs of the galleries at the Henry home appear in "The New Home of the Seattle Fine Arts Society," *Town Crier*, December 25, 1928, 17–24.

19 For a discussion of Hatch's leadership, see Johns, "Knowing Your Place," 115–120.

20 The Indian and Indonesian (called "Indonese") sequel was the concluding exhibition before the Art Institute closed its doors in advance of the new museum. "Quarterly Bulletin of the Art Institute of Seattle," March 1932, unpaginated. The fourth of the series, never achieved, was to have been Middle Eastern art. Art Institute of Seattle reports, Dorothy Stimson Bullitt Library, Seattle Art Museum.

21 Margaret Bundy, "Art in the Northwest," *Town Crier*, March 26, 1930, 12. The statement is credited to Hatch, but the "authorities" are not named.

22 "Japanese Art Exhibit," Seattle Art Institute, 1930, Dorothy Stimson Bullitt Library, Seattle Art Museum. Foremost among Issei lenders was Shigetoshi Horiuchi, an importer and collector, the manager of *Taihoku Nippō*, and the older cousin of the artist Paul Horiuchi. See Johns, *Paul Horiuchi*, 4, 8–9.

23 Hatch to Chiura Obata, February 12, 1931, Box 32/61, Seattle Art Museum records.

24 Hatch to Noboru Foujioka, November 12, 1929, Box 32/53, Seattle Art Museum records.

25 Hatch to Spencer Macky, San Francisco Art Association, May 8, 1931, Box 32/65, Seattle Art Museum records.

26 Fuller occupied the joint position of president of the board and director of the museum, as well as its primary donor, until his resignation in 1973. He described himself as a benevolent dictator, adding that he had called the acquisitions committee once in 1933 and never again. His position was strikingly different from that of Hatch, who was answerable to the board and left a record of reports, some implicitly eliciting support of the board. See Richard E. Fuller, *A Gift to the City: A History of the Seattle Art Museum and the Fuller Family* (Seattle: Seattle Art Museum, 1993).

27 Fuller, typescript, June 28, 1933, Box 23/Writings re: Museum Opening 1933, Seattle Art Museum records.

28 Fuller to Tokita, November 13, 1932, Kamekichi Tokita papers, Archives of American Art, Smithsonian Institution; Nomura and Fuller correspondence, November 17 and 18, 1932, Box 31/64, Seattle Art Museum records; "The Seattle Museum That Selected Our Artist," *Taihoku Nippō*. Tokita donated his 1929 prizewinning painting, *Alley*, as the first of five of his "best" paintings. Fuller's letter to Nomura thanks him for the gift of *Street*, although museum records list the painting as a purchase prize, the Katherine B. Baker Award, sponsored by the West Seattle Art Club.

Fuller appointed four Life-Members. The third of three Artist Life-Members was George Fischer, whose work is not represented in the museum collection. The fourth was the art collector and general manager of *Taihoku Nippō*, Shigetoshi Horiuchi.

29 Fuller, typescript.

30 Brian T. Callahan, comp. and ed., *Margaret Callahan: Mother of Northwest Art* (Victoria, BC, Canada: Trafford Publishing, 2009), 110; see also Kenneth Callahan to Kamekichi Tokita, October 12, 1935, Tokita papers.

31 Hatch to F. H. Varley, January 20, 1930, Box 32/31, Seattle Art Museum records.

32 Catalogue online, https://www.moma.org/documents/moma_catalogue_2063_300061867.pdf. The others were Kenneth Callahan, Peter Camfferman, Walter Isaacs, Ambrose Patterson, and sculptor Halford Lembke. Grant Wood, discussed earlier in this chapter, and Charles Burchfield were also represented in the exhibition.

33 "Canvas of Nisei Art Accepted in Display," *New World Daily News* (San Francisco), English edition, January 9, 1934. The paper misidentifies Nomura as Nisei rather than Issei. Thanks to Greg Robinson for the source.

34 "Will Rotate along West Coast Beginning with Seattle," [source NA], ca. July 1934, Tokita papers; Japanese-language news clippings translated by Terry Kita. Nomura papers.

35 "Art and Artists: To Show Work of Japanese Artists," *Berkeley (CA) Daily Gazette*, September 7, 1934.

36 *First National Exhibition of American Art* (New York: Municipal Art Committee, 1936); Kenneth Callahan, "10 Seattle Art Works at Show," *Seattle Times*, May 15, 1936; "Mayor Opens Show of American Art," *New York Times*, May 19, 1936. The fourth Issei artist in 1936 was sculptor Yoshimatsu Onaga from Pennsylvania. Initiated by Mayor Fiorello La Guardia, the exhibition was organized by the Municipal Art Committee of New York, and the selection made by locally appointed juries. A second exhibition was held in 1937, but the third was postponed by the 1939 New York World's Fair and canceled by World War II. Correspondence, Boxes 3/4, 3/20, 4/2, Seattle Art Museum records.

37 Nomura to Richard E. Fuller, January 26, 1939, Box 4/3, Seattle Art Museum records.

38 Industrial production calculations from Randall Parker, "An Overview of the Great Depression," EH.net (Economic History Association), http://eh.net/encyclopedia/an-overview-of-the-great-depression/ (accessed February 20, 2020).

39 Miyamoto, *Social Solidarity*, 9.

40 Figures for 1930 population from Miyamoto, *Social Solidarity*, 14; for 1940, Roger Daniels, "The Exile and Return of Seattle's Japanese," *Pacific Northwest Quarterly* 88, no. 4 (1997): 166, http://www.jstor.org/stable/40492331. Miyamoto notes of the 1930 number that slightly over half were foreign-born.

41 U.S. Bureau of Labor Statistics, *100 Years of Consumer Spending* (2006), https://www.bls.gov/opub/100-years-of-u-s-consumer-spending.pdf. The average annual family income of $1,524 in 1934 had remained nearly flat since World War I.

42 Works Progress Administration (WPA), Federal Art Project scrapbook, Seattle Public Library.

Tokita wrote PWAP director Edmund Bruce urging the program's continuation, but the Federal Art Project of the WPA that followed was limited to citizens only and thus excluded Nomura and Tokita. Edmund Bruce to Tokita, April 11, 1934, Tokita papers; Living New Deal, "Asian Americans and the New Deal—and the Second World War," https://livingnewdeal.org/what-was-the-new-deal/new-deal-inclusion/asian-americans-and-the-new-deal-and-the-second-world-war/ (accessed April 7, 2019).

43 *National Exhibition of Art by the Public Works of Art Project*, April 24, 1934–May 20, 1934, Corcoran Gallery of Art, Washington, DC, Forbes Watson papers, Archives of American Art, Smithsonian Institution. *The Farm* was transferred to the Smithsonian American Art Museum in 1964.

44 "Visitors Linger Longest before P.W.A. Paintings," *Seattle Times*, May 10, 1934.

45 Nomura appears to have established Stadium Cleaners, 616 East Forty-Fifth Street, as a new business rather than acquiring an existing business as he had done with the grocery. *Seattle City Directory*, vols. 1935–1938.

46 *The Green Lake Japanese American Community, 1900–1942* (Seattle: Green Lake Japanese American Community Booklet Committee, 2005).

47 On Nomura's activities, WRA case file; on charitable contribution, Miyamoto, *Social Solidarity*, 61. By 1941 Nomura had accumulated $900 in an account at the Yokohama Specie

Bank, about $16,000 in today's currency. Miyamoto notes the Nikkei community's pride in donating more than it received from the Community Chest (forerunner of today's United Way) and being among the first to exceed its annual goal.

48 Washington's Alien Land Law of 1921 reinforced and expanded provisions in the state constitution. Washington was among a number of states, mostly in the West, that passed restrictive legislation designed to discourage permanent settlement of "aliens ineligible for citizenship." The U.S. Supreme Court ruled alien land laws unconstitutional in 1952. Washington State's were repealed by popular vote only in 1966, having twice failed to win a plurality.

49 Ito, *Issei*, 729–730.

50 *American Artists' Congress, Inc., National Membership Exhibition, Portland Branch* (Portland, OR: Portland Branch of the American Artists' Congress, Inc., 1937). The exhibition was presented at the Portland and Seattle art museums.

51 Among landmark developments, the American wing of the Metropolitan Museum of Art opened in 1924. In 1927 University of Washington professor of English Vernon Louis Parrington published the first two volumes of *Main Currents in American Thought*, an intellectual history combining literary criticism and history, which won the Pulitzer Prize in history in 1928 and is credited with launching the field of American studies. Harvard University established a doctoral program in the history of American civilization in 1937, and in 1942 Princeton University established the Program in American Studies.

52 Kenneth Callahan, "The Art Situation," *Town Crier*, October 21, 1933, 10.

53 Charles Burchfield, "On the Middle Border," *Creative Art* 3, no. 3 (September 1928): xxxi; Kenneth Callahan, "Pacific Northwest," 26; see also Callahan on behalf of the Group of Twelve, in letter to the editor, *Life*, June 20, 1938.

54 Jan Gordon, *Modern French Painters* (New York: Dodd, Mead and Company, 1923), 36; copy in Tokita papers.

55 George Tsutakawa, oral history interview. Tsutakawa (1910–1997) was born in Seattle, educated in Japan, and returned to Seattle in 1927—in generational terms, a Kibei.

56 "Penthouse Art Gallery Plans to Show Work," *Seattle Times*, October 20, 1935.

57 *Some Work of the Group of Twelve* (Seattle: Dogwood Press, 1937). The foreign-born painters, in addition to the three Japanese, were Peter Camfferman, the Netherlands; Elizabeth Cooper, England; Earl Fields, Finland; and Ambrose Patterson, Australia.

58 *Paintings by the Group of Twelve* showed at the Seattle Art Museum in 1936 and traveled to Mills College in 1937 under the title *The Pacific Northwest Painters*.

59 Nomura, in *Some Work of the Group of Twelve*, unpaginated.

60 The literature about Western artists' interest in a synthesis of Western and Japanese art is well documented, from the stylist innovations of such artists as Édouard Manet, Edgar Degas, Vincent van Gogh, and James McNeill Whistler, to the more philosophical inquiries of Wassily Kandinsky, Mark Tobey, and others. More recent studies examine the perspective of modernist Japanese artists. See, for example, Alicia Volk, *In Pursuit of Universalism: Yorozu Tetsugō and Japanese Modern Art* (Berkeley and Los Angeles: University of California Press, 2010).

61 Kenneth Callahan, "The Art Situation—Nomura Exhibition," 9–10.

62 [Kenneth Callahan], "Artists Scored by Critics Here for Exhibition," *Seattle Times*, October 4, 1933.

Chapter 3

1 Brian T. Callahan, *Margaret Callahan*, 56–57, 134.

2 "Northwest Artists Display Works at Seattle Art Museum," *New World-Sun Daily News* (San Francisco), May 17, 1940. Besides Nomura were Tokita, Fujii, and Genzo (Frank) Tomita. Kenneth Callahan showed Nomura's *Bridge*, 1930, from his personal collection.

3 Kamekichi Tokita, December 7, 1941, in Johns, *Signs of Home*, 110.

4 Tetsuden Kashima traces the progression of surveillance in *Judgment without Trial: Japanese American Imprisonment during World War II* (Seattle: University of Washington Press, 2003), 15–49.

5 Tokita, December 27, 1941, in Johns, *Signs of Home*, 125.

6 George Nomura remembered feeling fortunate as a child that his father had not been subject to FBI arrest and imprisoned separately from the family.

7 Roger Daniels, *Concentration Camps: North America; Japanese in the United States and Canada during World War II*, rev. ed. (Malabar, FL: Robert E. Krieger Publishing Company, 1981), 42–71; updated in 1989; original edition published as *Concentration Camps USA* (New York: Holt, Rinehart and Winston, 1971). More recent studies add to this account, among them, Brian Masaru Hayashi's on military assessments of intelligence, *Democratizing the Enemy*, 76–84.

8 Tokita, March 31 and April 22, 1942, in Johns, *Signs of Home*, 174, 176.

9 Nancy Langdon to Betty Nomura, April 16, 2008, Nomura papers. Langdon recounts the story of her grandmother, who had a shop next to Nomura's, witnessed the fire, and spoke to Nomura, who gave her a painting.

10 George Nomura.

11 The approximate number of Nikkei initially removed under Executive Order 9066 was 110,000. Births and transfers from other types of detention sites brought the total in War Relocation Authority (WRA) camps to some 120,000. B. B. Cozzens, WRA, San Francisco, Information on Statistics of the War Relocation Authority, [n.d.], Press Release Vol. 1, File 000.7, Box 1, Record Group 210.3.1, National Archives, Washington, DC.

12 *Engineering News-Record*, 128, no. 24 (June 11, 1942): 952–953; on construction per capita cost, File 323.7, Box 58, Record Group 499, National Archives, College Park, MD. The cost of construction was $600,000, or $81 per capita, somewhat less than $1,300 today. Thanks to Louis Fiset's *Camp Harmony: Seattle's Japanese Americans and the Puyallup Assembly Center* (Urbana: University of Illinois Press, 2009) for the reference to *Engineering News-Record*. The book provides a valuable study of the center.

13 The Puyallup camp was not large enough to hold all ethnic Japanese in western Washington. Nikkei within Seattle city limits went to Puyallup, while those from surrounding communities were sent to confinement sites in California.

14 Monica Sone, *Nisei Daughter* (Seattle: University of Washington Press, 1979), 177; originally published by Little, Brown and Company, 1953.

15 "Questions and Answers for Evacuees," War Relocation Authority Regional Office, San Francisco, [1942], Denshō, Bigelow Family Collection, https://ddr.densho.org/ddr-densho-156-165.

16 Sone, *Nisei Daughter*, 173; Fujii, in Johns, *The Hope of Another Spring*, 154.

17 Hannah Lai, interview, March 14, 2011, Denshō, https://ddr.densho.org/ddr-densho-1000-324-13.

18 See James M. Sakoda, "Minidoka: An Analysis of Changing Patterns of Social Interaction" (PhD diss., University of California, Berkeley, 1949), 89–90. In Sakoda's words, once the decision for mass removal was made, army and civil authorities "demanded the cooperation of the JACL," which "immediately capitulated." Sakoda, a Nisei, was a researcher for the Japanese Evacuation and Resettlement Study (JERS) under the direction of University of California, Berkeley, sociologist Dorothy Swaine Thomas. Incarcerated graduate students such as Sakoda were embedded on-site researchers.

19 Administrators from the WPA on loan to the WCCA held civil service staff positions overseeing the Service, Works, Finance, and Mess and Lodging Divisions. Fiset, *Camp Harmony*, 107.

20 The army and many in the WRA adhered to a simple three-way division of Issei, Nisei, and Kibei (Nisei who had been educated in Japan and were often assumed to be loyal to Japan). See, for example, Sakoda, "Minidoka," 93; Eiichiro Azuma, *Between Two Empires: Race, History, and Transnationalism in Japanese America* (New York: Oxford University Press, 2005), 158–159. On the conflation of race and culture among army and navy officers, see Hayashi, *Democratizing the Enemy*, 34–36.

21 In these depictions, Nomura differs notably from Tokita and Fujii, whose diaries tell of generational differences and tensions.

22 On Nomura's employment, typescript of text panel for the exhibition of Nomura's wartime work, ca. 1991, prepared by or based upon George Nomura's account, Nomura papers; unsigned memo, July 15, 1942, General Correspondence, 1942–1946, Box 58, Puyallup Assembly Center, File 323.3, Record Group 499, National Archives, College Park, MD. The typescript states only that Nomura worked as a sign painter at the "camps." His job at Minidoka is well documented, but there is little to confirm his employment at Puyallup.

23 See Ed Tsutakawa's remarks in the chapter's next section. Restrictions on going from one area to another relaxed as weeks passed, enabling inmates to visit friends and family in other areas. Guards continued to monitor the process.

24 Cameras were eventually allowed at most, but not all, of the WRA camps.

25 On the artists' diaries, see Introduction n12. Fujii also produced dozens of watercolors, drawings, oil paintings, and wood carvings from Puyallup and Minidoka.

26 Along with Obata, Hibi helped establish the curriculum at Tanforan and co-founded the art school at Topaz, where he assumed leadership after Obata's release. On Obata, see Kodani Hill, ed., *Topaz Moon: Chiura Obata's Art of the Internment* (Berkeley, CA: Heyday Books, 2000). Miné Okubo, who held a graduate art degree from the University of California, Berkeley, taught at Tanforan and Topaz and became the best known of the incarcerated artists for her 1946 book *Citizen 13660* (University of Washington Press, 2014; originally published by Columbia University Press). *Miné Okubo: Following Her Own Road* examines the roles of gender, generation, agency, and resistance in her work (Greg Robinson and Elena Tajima Creff, eds., University of Washington Press, 2008). Among numerous others, the acclaimed artist Henry Sugimoto, who had exhibited with Nomura (see chapter 2, page 42), taught classes at the Jerome WRA center, Arkansas. At the Heart Mountain, Wyoming, camp, Hideo Date and Benji Okubo established the Art Students League, naming it after the school in Los Angeles where Benji Okubo had studied and later led.

For overviews of the artists and camp schools, see Gordon H. Chang, "Deployments, Engagements, Obliterations: Asian American Artists and World War II," in Chang, Johnson, and Karlstrom, *Asian American Art*, 127–131; and Karin M. Higa, *The View from Within: Japanese American Art from the Internment Camps, 1942–1945*, rev. ed. (Los Angeles: Japanese American National Museum, UCLA Wight Art Gallery, and UCLA Asian American Studies Center, 1992). Higa's publication and the accompanying exhibition were among the first to present artwork from the camps as a subject of study rather than as supporting historical evidence. The earliest effort to document art and craft production in the camps, a project begun during the war, is Allen H. Eaton, *Beauty behind Barbed Wire: The Arts of Japanese in Our War Relocation Camps* (New York: Harper and Brothers, 1952). More about individual artists is published in the online encyclopedia by Denshō, https://encyclopedia.densho.org.

27 Ed Tsutakawa to Bill and Margaret Gamble, July 8, 1942, George Tsutakawa papers, estate of George Tsutakawa; Ed Tsutakawa, oral history interview, 2006, Denshō, Visual History Collection, https://ddr.densho.org/ddr-densho-1000-196. Tsutakawa credited their leader, Keith Oka, for the pay and respect the team held. The other two team members were Shozo Koneko and Hisashi Hirai.

28 Masako Fujii to George Tsutakawa, June 28, 1942, George Tsutakawa papers; Ed Tsutakawa, oral history interview, 2003–2004, Denshō, Visual History Collection, https://ddr.densho.org/ddr-densho-1016-5. Ed Tsutakawa's own drawings of Puyallup were published in the *Seattle Times* and Portland's *Oregonian*. Altogether he produced about fifty paintings and drawings of Puyallup and Minidoka; fourteen remain and are in the family's possession.

29 I thank Stephen H. Sumida for the insight about Nomura's shift from ahistorical to historical representation in his wartime artwork. Communication with the author, March 13, 2020.

30 Masako Fujii to George Tsutakawa, May 15, 1942, George Tsutakawa papers.

31 Masako Fujii to George Tsutakawa, June 29, 1942, George Tsutakawa papers.

32 The indexed and searchable interviews in the online resource Denshō include numerous accounts. https://densho.org/.

33 Sone, *Nisei Daughter*, 179.

34 Fujii, diary entries, 1942, in Johns, *The Hope of Another Spring*, 165, 173, 183.

35 Sone, *Nisei Daughter*, 177.

36 Fiset, *Camp Harmony*, 167. See, for example, S. Frank Miyamoto, oral history interview, 1998, Denshō, Visual History Collection, https://ddr.densho.org/ddr-densho-1000-52.

37 I have found nothing in the WCCA records at the National Archives or in personal papers. George Nomura maintained that his father's wartime artistic production was personal, as described by Ron Chew in McKivor, *Kenjiro Nomura*, 5, and reiterated to me. With respect for his important role in preserving his father's story, I raise the question about intent on the evidence of the paintings at Puyallup, particularly the composite image.—BJ

George assigned descriptive titles to the Minidoka images when they were first exhibited in 1991; the Puyallup images are framed and whether or not they are formally titled has not been verified. Betty Nomura, communication with the author, July 8, 2019.

38 "Camp Harmony News-Letter," August 14, 1942.

39 Minayo Kimura to George Tsutakawa, August 28, 1942, George Tsutakawa papers.

40 WRA case file.

41 Information Division, WRA Minidoka Project, MWRP #1 [press release], [ca. September 1942], WRA, Japanese American Evacuation and Resettlement Records, BANC MSS 67/14c, Bancroft Library, University of California, Berkeley (hereafter cited as Bancroft), https://oac.cdlib.org/ark:/13030/k6377gwv/?brand=oac4.

42 Information Division, WRA Minidoka Project, MWRP #1. The blocks were numbered 1–44 but skipped several numbers where the terrain restricted the layout.

43 The WRA was first within the Executive Office and in February 1944 transferred to the Department of the Interior. Daniels, *Concentration Camps*, 151; see also Greg Robinson, *By Order of the President: FDR and the Internment of Japanese Americans* (Cambridge, MA: Harvard University Press, 2001), 129–130, 204–205.

44 Lon Kurashige, *Two Faces of Exclusion: The Untold History of Anti-Asian Racism in the United States* (Chapel Hill: University of North Carolina Press, 2016), 184–187; see also Kashima, *Judgment without Trial*, 7. Kurashige argues that the WRA was in general egalitarian. Kashima, however, states of the controlling authorities of all types of Japanese American confinement centers: "These government units had virtually unlimited power over the internees and inmates. They administered the entire imprisonment process as well as legitimated it socially and politically" (7). Administrators' personal views did not necessarily match agency policy but they influenced implementation.

45 Tokita, September 25, 1942, in Johns, *Signs of Home*, 184. For a Minidoka staff debate about Issei and Nisei relations in community government, following strife at the Manzanar

WRA center in California, see Report of Division Heads Meeting, December 24, 1942, File 17.200, Entry 48, Record Group 210, National Archives, Washington, DC.

46 On orders, Assistant Adjunct General to Division Engineer, South Pacific Division, September 12 and October 16, 1942, File 654, Box 93, Record Group 499, National Archives, College Park, MD; on Minidoka, [John E. deYoung], "The Fence at Minidoka," Community Analysis Series No. 4, April 1943, File 61.317, Entry 16, Record Group 210, National Archives, Washington, DC; see also John Bigelow, Minidoka Report No. 14, December 2, 1942, WRA, Bancroft, https://oac.cdlib.org/ark:/13030/k6p84k2t/?brand=oac4. The Western Defense Command ordered fences built at all WRA camps.

47 Daniels, *Concentration Camps*, 92–96.

48 On the Nomuras' employment, WRA case file; for examples of sanitation work, Tokita, November 8 and 10, 1942, in Johns, *Signs of Home*, 194. The WRA file is in Kenjiro's name as head of household and does not give the dates of Fumiko's employment.

49 John Bigelow, Special Industry Report, Minidoka Report No. 60, stamped April 15, 1943, WRA, Bancroft, https://oac.cdlib.org/ark:/13030/k6dv1s2j/?brand=oac4. Minidoka opened with so little equipment, Bigelow reports, that the WRA director used his car as an office for three weeks.

50 Memoranda dated August 18–October 10, 1942, Signage, File 415, 323.7, Record Group 499, National Archives, College Park, MD.

51 Tokita, October 15, 1942, in Johns, *Signs of Home*, 190.

52 Bigelow, Minidoka Report No. 60.

53 Bigelow, Minidoka Report No. 60.

54 On original projection, Minidoka Report No. 1, September 19, 1942, WRA, Bancroft, https://oac.cdlib.org/ark:/13030/k6p84k2t/?brand=oac4; on results, Karl Lillquist, "Minidoka," chap. 5 in *Imprisoned in the Desert: The Geography of World War II–Era, Japanese American Relocation Centers in the Western United States* (Ellensburg: Central Washington University, 2007), 167, https://www.cwu.edu/geography/geography-japanese-american-relocation-centers. By the end of 1944, 1,166 acres were cleared, and 440 were in production. All agricultural activity was stopped at the end of 1944 when the intention to close camps in 1945 was announced.

55 James M. Sakoda, "The 'Residue': The Unresettled Minidokans, 1943–1945," in *Views from Within: The Japanese American Evacuation and Resettlement Study*, ed. Yuji Ichioka (Los Angeles: Asian American Studies Center, University of California at Los Angeles, 1989), 262–263; on construction issues, Sakoda, "Minidoka," 284–297.

56 Fujii, unpublished diary entry, ca. December 1944–early 1945, copy in author's possession.

57 Harry L. Stafford to Dillon S. Myer, Project Director's Report, September 26, 1945, WRA, Bancroft, https://oac.cdlib.org/ark:/28722/bk000404p8d/?brand=oac4.

58 Tokita, October 8, 1942, in Johns, *Signs of Home*, 188; see also Tokita's entries, 194, 195, 197–198, 201, and *Minidoka Irrigator*, December 23, 1944, photo caption: "While community leaders argue . . . the 'little people' take what they can get."

59 See, for example, John Bigelow, Minidoka Report No. 10, stamped November 2, 1942, WRA, Bancroft, https://oac.cdlib.org/ark:/13030/k6p84k2t/?brand=oac4.

60 On attendance, John Bigelow, Report for the Quarter Ended December 31, 1942, WRA, Bancroft, https://oac.cdlib.org/ark:/13030/k69311cz/?brand=oac4.

61 "Hunt Residents Display Work at Library Exhibit," *Twin Falls (ID) Times-News*, June 25, 1943; *Minidoka Interlude: September 1942–October 1943* (Hunt, ID: Minidoka Relocation Center, 1943), "Art & Handicraft Exhibit," unpaginated; John Bigelow, Minidoka Report No. 70, stamped July 10, 1943, WRA, Bancroft, https://oac.cdlib.org/ark:/13030/k6dv1s2j/?brand=oac4.

62 "Project Artistic Talent on Display Next Week," *Minidoka Irrigator*, November 20, 1943, Denshō, https://ddr.densho.org/ddr-densho-119-64. The first exhibition was in January 1943; "Art Exhibit Scheduled in January," *Minidoka Irrigator*, December 19, 1942, Denshō, https://ddr.densho.org/ddr-densho-119-20.

63 Architectural historian Lynne Horiuchi views many of the camp facilities built by the inmates as signs of resistance, in which they worked nominally within WRA strictures but determined their own course of action. Lynne Horiuchi, "Dislocations: The Built Environments of Japanese American Internment," in *Guilt by Association: Essays on Japanese Settlement, Internment, and Relocation in the Rocky Mountain West*, edited by Mike Mackey (Powell, WY: Western History Publications, ca. 2001), 255–275.

64 "Mrs. Saito" presumably refers to Kimiko Saito, who lived with her family in Block 28, as pictured and named in *Minidoka Interlude* (unpaginated) (see fig. 3.41). The block came to serve as an extended family unit. See Gary Y. Okihiro, "Religion and Resistance in America's Concentration Camps," *Phylon* 45, no. 3 (1984): 227–228, https://www.jstor.org/stable/274406.

65 The panel picturing a full moon and geese is signed "Hanto a recluse [literally, 'mountain man'] painted." "Hanto" is an assumed artistic name; the seal could read "Nomura" but is unclear. A third *tanzaku* among the wartime work saved by Nomura holds a poem in running script that was written

by someone other than Nomura. I am indebted to Michiyo Morioka for her translation of the signatures and explanation of *tanzaku* and the symbolism.

Tanzaku originated as wall-hanging holders for poetry, written on paper and attached to the panel by cords. Nomura's differ from the customary practice in being painted. George Nomura identified both panels as his father's; personal communication.

66 See Johns, *Signs of Home*, 90–92.

67 For a discussion of Meiji-era sources that underlay prewar Japanese American immigrant communities, see Okihiro, "Religion and Resistance." Okihiro describes the syncretic mix of Buddhist, Confucian, and Shintō sources that influenced the Meiji era.

68 The WRA "Americanization" policy was premised upon establishing the camps as model democracies. It privileged the Nisei on the basis of their citizenship and included English and citizenship classes for the Issei, even though federal law prohibited their naturalization.

69 The Activities Division, administered by Nisei under the supervision of a WRA officer, organized programs and events. The Nisei head of the division at Minidoka designated a committee of Issei to manage "Japanese" programs, which, a Nisei reporter wrote, were "enjoyed so much by Issei and [had been] curtailed by WCCA authorities in assembly centers." The inversion of authority, as well as the acknowledgment of experience, is evident. Japanese-language literary production was mainly by Issei and Kibei. Robert Hosokawa, Minidoka Report No. 9, stamped October 29, 1942, WRA, Bancroft, https://oac.cdlib.org/ark:/13030/k6p84k2t/?brand=oac4; John Bigelow, Minidoka Report No. 58, stamped April 10, 1943, WRA, Bancroft, https://oac.cdlib.org/ark:/13030/k6p84k2t/?brand=oac4; on Japanese-language literary production, Junko Kobayashi, "'Bitter Sweet Home': Celebration of Biculturalism in Japanese Language Japanese American Literature, 1936–1952" (PhD diss., University of Iowa, 2005), 90, https://ir.uiowa.edu/etd/97.

70 On "camp culture," Kobayashi, "'Bitter Sweet Home,'" 95–96. Kobayashi quotes Masao Yamashiro, incarcerated at Tule Lake in California, who describes handmade nameplates as an example of bicultural camp culture.

71 "Minidoka's Honor Roll," Minidoka National Historic Site, National Parks Service, U.S. Department of the Interior, September 3, 2019, https://www.nps.gov/miin/learn/historyculture/minidokas-honor-roll.htm.

72 More Nisei volunteered from Minidoka than from any other WRA camp. Their families remained incarcerated.

73 "Minidoka's Honor Roll." On the role of Fujitaro Kubota, who created Kubota Garden in Seattle, see Anna Tamura, "Minidoka's Chief Gardener," in *Spirited Stone: Lessons from Kubota's Garden* (Seattle: Chin Music Press, 2020), 134–145.

74 Sakoda, "Minidoka," 229–332.

75 Fujii, in Johns, *The Hope of Another Spring*, 260–263, 276–282.

Chapter 4

1 Richard C. Berner, *Seattle Transformed: World War II to Cold War*, vol. 3 of *Seattle in the 20th Century* (Seattle: Charles Press, 1999), 45. Berner states twice the number of military contracts as Los Angeles and four times those of the Bay Area.

2 Clark Kerr, cited in Berner, *Seattle Transformed*, 45; on the transition, see Berner, 171–173. Kerr, best known as the president of the University of California during its major period of expansion, 1958–1967, taught labor economics at the University of Washington, 1940–1945.

3 Newell, interview, June 30, 1944, WRA case file.

4 To justify to the public the War Department's plan to recruit Nisei and the WRA's efforts to resettle inmates, the WRA issued a hastily conceived "loyalty questionnaire" to all incarcerated Nikkei aged eighteen and over. Despite bitter controversy over two questions that appeared to compromise citizenship, 83 percent of all respondents replied positively; at Minidoka, 88 percent of the Issei did so. Daniels, *Concentration Camps*, 112–114; on Minidoka, J. H. Nichols, Final Report of the Statistics Section, January 31, 1942, Bancroft, https://oac.cdlib.org/ark:/13030/k68s4x49/?brand=oac4. Nomura's questionnaire, labeled "Application for Leave Clearance," is part of his WRA case file.

5 For an overview of the return to the West Coast, see Greg Robinson, foreword to *Making Home from War: Stories of Japanese American Exile and Resettlement*, ed. Brian Komei Dempster, viii–xiii (Berkeley, CA: Heyday Books, 2011).

6 Berner, *Seattle Transformed*, 120–123, on Seattle Civic Unity Committee, 124–128, on reaction to Japanese Americans' resettlement. The 442nd Regimental Combat Team, which comprised mainland Nisei and the 100th Infantry Battalion from Hawaiʻi, was the most highly decorated unit in American military service for its size and length of service.

7 W. A. Dougherty to W. E. Rawlings, September 14, 1945; Rawlings to Dougherty, September 20, 1945, WRA case file.

8 Nomura to WRA, Seattle, November 5, 1945, WRA case file.

9 Ken Mochizuki, *Meet Me at Higo: An Enduring Story of a Japanese American Family* (Seattle: Wing Luke Museum, 2011), 91–93.

10 Shokichi Tokita, in Mochizuki, *Meet Me at Higo*, 91.

11 George Tsutakawa, oral history interview.

12 McKivor, *Kenjiro Nomura*, 13.

13 Declaration of Intention, U.S. Department of Justice, Immigration and Nationalization Service, October 31, 1947, Nomura papers. See also Index to Declarations of Intention and Petitions for Naturalization, District Court, Washington, October 19, 1946, National Archives, NARA microfilm publication M1232, online Ancestry.com.

14 George Nomura. Having been widowed, Chiyo Fukasaki managed the downtown Lincoln Hotel in partnership with Mr. Inada.

15 *Seattle City Directory*, 1951.

16 The McCarran-Walter Act, formally the Immigration Act of 1952, enabled naturalized citizenship but reinforced the controversial national origins quota system. The Immigration Act of 1965 abolished the national origins restriction and established a uniform cap on the annual number of immigrants.

17 Chiyo became a citizen in the name of Alice Chiyo Nomura; U.S. Citizen Identification Card, U.S. Department of Justice, December 28, 1953. For Kenjiro Nomura's naturalization, Certificate of Naturalization, U.S. Department of Justice, November 11, 1954; both in Nomura papers.

18 Nomura's surgery was to alleviate "acute atrophy of the liver." Certified copy of death certificate, Seattle-King County Department of Public Health, Vital Statistics Division, courtesy of David Martin.

19 The Jackson Street Community Council was a community-led interethnic organization established in 1946 to address a wide range of social services such as housing, employment, family support, and individual rights. Lee, *Claiming the Oriental Gateway*, 206–211, describes the council's role in promoting the diversity and advocating for the welfare of what would be named the International District; see also Quintard Taylor, *The Forging of a Black Community: Seattle's Central District from 1870 through the Civil Rights Era* (Seattle: University of Washington Press, 1994), 174–175.

20 Nomura made a second painting very similar to *Dragon Dance*. Both paintings are untitled, signed, and dated 1950. It is not clear if the titles refer to the same painting or different versions of the same theme.

21 Andrew Carnduff Ritchie, juror's statement, "Washington Artists" (exhibition brochure), Western Washington Fair, Puyallup, 1950.

22 Maxine Cushing Gray, "Cows and Culture Vie at Fair in Puyallup," *Seattle Post-Intelligencer*, September 22, 1951.

23 Louis R. Guzzo, "Mrs. Dusanne, Pioneer in Arts, Retiring," *Seattle Times*, July 5, 1964.

24 David B. Pennell, "Four Japanese-Americans," *Argus* (Seattle), March 1, 1952.

25 Maxine Cushing Gray, "Two Exhibits Attract N.W. Art Students," [source and date NA], Zoe Dusanne papers, Accession No. 2430-4, Box 12, Special Collections, University of Washington Libraries.

26 Margaret B. Callahan, "Seattle's Japanese Artists," *Seattle Times*, August 1, 1954.

27 *Exposição Norte-Americana, da III Bienal de São Paulo* (São Paulo, 1955), Nomura papers; for the U.S. tour, *Pacific Coast Art: United States' Representation at the Third Biennial of São Paulo* (San Francisco: San Francisco Museum of Art, 1956); see also Isobel Whitelegg, "The Bienal Internacional de São Paulo: A Concise History, 1951–2014," *Perspective* 2 (2013), http://journals.openedition.org/perspective/3902. The U.S. portion of the exhibition was organized by the San Francisco Museum of Art, under the leadership of Grace McCann Morley, in cooperation with the Los Angeles County Museum of History, Science, and Art.

28 I thank Fumiko Kimura, an accomplished sumi artist, for discussing the paintings with me, October 10, 2019.

29 George Nomura, communication to David F. Martin, July 2, 2013.

30 Kenneth Callahan, "Show Has Foreign Ceramics, Local Art," *Seattle Times*, June 12, 1955.

31 [Kenneth Callahan], "With the Artists," *Seattle Times*, May 31, 1953.

32 Mark Tobey, "Japanese Traditions in Modern Art," *College Art Journal* 18, no. 1 (Fall 1958): 24; Tobey to Paul Horiuchi, [1961], retyped letter, Paul Horiuchi papers, Accession No. 5443-1, Special Collections, University of Washington Libraries.

33 See Tobey, "Japanese Traditions in Modern Art," 24. Tobey credited the lesson to Takizaki.

34 George Tsutakawa, quoted in Martha Kingsbury, *George Tsutakawa* (Seattle: University of Washington Press; Bellevue Art Museum, Bellevue, WA, 1990), 36.

35 On Hasegawa, see Bert Winther-Tamaki, *Art in the Encounter of Nations: Japanese and American Artists in the Early Postwar Years* (Honolulu: University of Hawai'i Press, 2001), 32–43, 63; for a recent study, see Dakin Hart and Mark Dean Johnson, eds., *Changing and Unchanging Things: Noguchi and Hasegawa in Postwar Japan* (New York: Isamu Noguchi Foundation and Garden Museum in association with University of California Press, Oakland, 2019). Hasegawa wrote in 1937 about calligraphy as "a huge gold mine, particularly in abstract painting"; quoted in Koichi Kawasaki, "Regretting the Future: Noguchi and Hasegawa Consider

the Direction of Postwar Japanese Art," in Hart and Johnson, *Changing and Unchanging Things*, 70.

36 On the influence and contested role of Asian forms, see Winther-Tamaki, *Art in the Encounter of Nations*; and Jeffrey Wechsler, ed., *Asian Traditions / Modern Expressions: Asian American Artists and Abstraction, 1945–1970* (New York: Harry N. Abrams in association with the Jane Voorhees Zimmerli Art Museum, Rutgers, the State University of New Jersey, 1997).

37 Fuller, *A Gift to the City*, 26–27. The Seattle Art Museum acquired major works of Japanese art during the tenure of the art historian Sherman E. Lee from 1948 to 1952. Lee served in Japan during the war and from 1946 to 1948 was adviser on art and monuments at General Douglas MacArthur's Tokyo headquarters. Subsequently hired as deputy director of the Seattle Art Museum, he acquired renowned works such as the *Poem Scroll with Deer* by the painter Tarawaya Sōtatsu and the calligrapher Hon'ami Kōetsu.

38 Kenneth Callahan, "Pacific Northwest."

39 George Nomura.

40 George Nomura to Richard E. Fuller, June 27, 1959; Millard Rogers to George Nomura, July 7 and 9, 1959, Box 12, Seattle Art Museum records.

41 U.S. House of Representatives, Committee on Interior and Insular Affairs, *Personal Justice Denied: Report of the Commission on Wartime Relocation and Internment of Civilians* (Washington, DC: Civil Liberties Public Education Fund; Seattle: University of Washington Press, 1997); originally published in two volumes by the U.S. Government Printing Office, 1982–1983. For a study of the redress movement, see Alice Yang Murray, *Historical Memories of the Japanese American Internment and the Struggle for Redress* (Stanford, CA: Stanford University Press, 2007).

42 *Japanese and Japanese American Painters in the United States: A Half Century of Hope and Suffering, 1896–1945* (Tokyo: Tokyo Metropolitan Teien Art Museum and Nippon Television Network Corporation, 1995). The exhibition opened in Tokyo and traveled to Oita Prefectural Art Hall and the Hiroshima Museum of Art. Records of the venues are in the Nomura papers.

43 These include Kashima, *Judgment without Trial*; Fiset, *Camp Harmony*; and Neil Nakadate, *Looking After Minidoka: An American Memoir* (Bloomington: Indiana University Press, 2013).

Bridges to Modernism

1 "Four Thousand Sons of Japan to Celebrate," *Seattle Times*, September 1, 1909.

2 Eunice T. Gray, "The Chase School of Art at Carmel-by-the-Sea, California," *Art and Progress* 6, no. 4 (February 1915): 120. In the article, Crow's last name was misspelled as Crowe.

3 "Canvases Shown by Local Society," *Seattle Times*, January 4, 1915.

4 Nomura's paintings were titled *The Corner of Main Street*, *From Capitol Hill*, and *Sunset on Lake Union*, but possibly more were exhibited as suggested by the inclusion of "and so forth" following the titles listed. "Many See Exhibit of Japanese Art," [source and date NA], in scrapbook dated 1916, Nomura papers.

5 Adele M. Ballard, "With the Fine Arts Folk," *Town Crier*, June 12, 1915.

6 For further information on Shimizu, see *Japanese and Japanese American Painters in the United States: A Half Century of Hope and Suffering, 1896–1945* (Tokyo: Tokyo Metropolitan Teien Art Museum and Nippon Television Network Corporation, 1995). Toshi Shimizu's brother Kiyoshi Shimizu (1900–1969), also a talented artist, had a noteworthy career in New York. He was associated with New York's Japanese Artists Society, which included Soichi Sunami.

7 For further information about Sunami, see David F. Martin, *Invocation of Beauty: The Life and Photography of Soichi Sunami* (Edmonds, WA: Cascadia Art Museum in association with University of Washington Press, 2018).

8 Madge Bailey, "In Art Circles," *Seattle Post-Intelligencer*, March 5, 1922.

9 For further information on the SCC, see David F. Martin and Nicolette Bromberg, *Shadows of a Fleeting World: Pictorial Photography and the Seattle Camera Club* (Seattle: University of Washington Press in association with University of Washington Libraries and the Henry Art Gallery, 2011).

10 John Sloan had a profound influence on his students Shimizu and Sunami; Sunami developed such a close friendship with Sloan that he named his son John in his honor.

11 Sondag researcher Lori Robbins, e-mail message to David F. Martin, January 4, 2019.

12 Derbyshire's art was inherited by a niece, who sold off his work through classified ads and yard sales after his death. She also disposed of his archival materials.

13 Information about Sumio Arima was provided by his son, John Arima.

14 For further information on Horiuchi, see Barbara Johns, *Paul Horiuchi: East and West* (Seattle: University of Washington Press in association with Museum of Northwest Art, La Conner, WA, 2008).

15 Jennifer Kate Ward, "The Etchings of Roi Partridge," in *The Graphic Art of Roi Partridge: A Catalogue Raisonné,* ed. Anthony R. White, American Prints and Printmakers, No. 2 (Los Angeles: Hennessy and Ingalls, 1988), 10.

16 Spencer Moseley and Gervais Reed, *Walter F. Isaacs, an Artist in America, 1886–1964* (Seattle: University of Washington Press, 1982), 116.

Elizabeth Warhanik's daughter, Winifred Clifton, stated to me that her mother's painting selected for the 1939 New York World's Fair was apparently lost by the Henry Art Gallery before it was supposed to be sent to New York and was never returned to her mother. Warhanik had been informed that her painting was selected, but she was never told that it would not be sent to New York. Thinking that it was going to be exhibited at the New York World's Fair, Warhanik went with her family by train to New York to see the painting on display and was devastated to learn it was not included. The painting was never recovered. Winifred Clifton, personal communication with David F. Martin.

17 For further information on Fujii, see Barbara Johns, *The Hope of Another Spring: Takuichi Fujii, Artist and Wartime Witness* (Seattle: University of Washington Press, 2017).

18 Changing his name from Hamber, Irving Humber came to the United States in 1939 under the sponsorship of the American Committee for Christian Refugees through the Episcopal Church. By 1940, he had relocated to Seattle and started a wholesale business. *Seattle Times,* August 17, 1940. For further information on Humber, see David F. Martin, "Yvonne Twining Humber: A Washington Painter of Renown and Obscurity," *Columbia: The Magazine of Northwest History* 23, no. 4 (Winter 2009–2010): 19–25.

Yvonne Humber was a great admirer of Nomura's work and included images of his paintings in lectures that she gave at the Seattle Art Museum, where she served as a docent for nearly forty years. Humber personally explained the symbolism behind her painting *Spoiled Carnival* to me during our close friendship.

19 Virna Haffer's relationship with Yukio Morinaga was conveyed to me on numerous occasions by her son, Jean Paul, who later changed his name to Gene Randall. Randall referred to Morinaga as "Uncle Mori," indicating the stature he held within Haffer's family. Randall felt that Morinaga was gay and that had he been heterosexual, he and his mother would likely have married, referring to them as "soul mates." I found no evidence of Morinaga's sexual orientation, either hetero or homo, in my extensive research on the artist.

20 David F. Martin, curator, Cascadia Art Museum, *Against the Moon: The Art of John Matsudaira,* May 13–August 28, 2016, original biographical wall text for the exhibition.

21 George and Betty Nomura, telephone interview with David F. Martin, March 22, 2008.

22 In the article, Callahan was referring to the following artists with their respective jobs outside of painting: auto painter (Horiuchi), aircraft worker (Matsudaira), professor (Tsutakawa), and picture-frame maker (Nomura).

23 The Northwest artists included at the São Paulo Biennial were Louis Bunce (OR), Kenneth Callahan (WA), Jacob Elshin (WA), Morris Graves (WA), Tom Hardy (OR), Charles Heaney (OR), Carl Morris (OR), Hilda Morris (OR), Kenjiro Nomura (WA), Danny Pierce (WA), Ernest C. Schwidder (WA), Mark Tobey (WA), and George Tsutakawa (WA).

BIBLIOGRAPHY

*Denotes reference to Nomura

*American Abstract Artists, ed. *The World of Abstract Art.* New York: George Wittenborn, 1957.

**American Artists' Congress, Inc., National Membership Exhibition, Portland Branch.* Portland, OR: Portland Branch of the American Artists' Congress, Inc., 1937.

Andersen, Irene Poon, Mark Dean Johnson, Dawn Nakanishi, and Diane Tani. *With New Eyes: Toward an Asian American Art History in the West.* San Francisco: San Francisco State University Art Department Gallery, 1995.

**Art of the Pacific Northwest: From the 1930s to the Present.* Washington, DC: Smithsonian Institution Press for the National Collection of Fine Arts, 1974.

Azuma, Eiichiro. *Between Two Empires: Race, History, and Transnationalism in Japanese America.* New York: Oxford University Press, 2005.

Bagley, Clarence. *History of King County.* Chicago: S. J. Clarke Publishing Company, 1929.

Berner, Richard C. *Seattle, 1921–1940: From Boom to Bust.* Vol. 2 of *Seattle in the 20th Century.* Seattle: Charles Press, 1992.

———. *Seattle Transformed: World War II to Cold War.* Vol. 3 of *Seattle in the 20th Century.* Seattle: Charles Press, 1999.

Bonadich, Edna, and John Modell. *The Economic Basis of Ethnic Solidarity: Small Business in the Japanese American Community.* Berkeley and Los Angeles: University of California Press, 1980.

*Bullock, Margaret E. *New Deal Art in the Northwest: The WPA and Beyond.* Tacoma, WA: Tacoma Art Museum, 2020.

*Callahan, Brian T., comp. and ed. *Margaret Callahan: Mother of Northwest Art.* Victoria, BC, Canada: Trafford Publishing, 2009.

Callahan, Kenneth. "Pacific Northwest." *ArtNews* 45 (July 1946): 22–27, 53–56.

*———. "Pacific Northwest Painters." *Art and Artists of Today* 1 (September–October 1937): 6–7, 17.

*Chang, Gordon H. "Deployments, Engagements, Obliterations: Asian American Artists and World War II." In Chang, Johnson, and Karlstrom, *Asian American Art,* 110–139.

*Chang, Gordon H., Mark Dean Johnson, and Paul J. Karlstrom, eds. *Asian American Art: A History, 1850–1970.* Stanford, CA: Stanford University Press, 2008.

*Chew, Ron. Foreword to McKivor, *Kenjiro Nomura,* 5–6.

Chin, Doug. *Seattle's International District: The Making of a Pan-Asian American Community.* Seattle: International Examiner Press, 2001.

*Conkleton, Sheryl. *What It Meant to Be Modern: Seattle Art at Mid-century.* Seattle: Henry Art Gallery, University of Washington, 1999.

Conroy, Hilary, and T. Scott Miyakawa, eds. *East across the Pacific: Historical and Sociological Studies of Japanese Immigration and Assimilation.* Santa Barbara, CA: American Bibliographical Center–Clio Press, 1972.

*Cornell, Daniell, and Mark Dean Johnson, eds. *Asian/American/Modern Art: Shifting Currents, 1900–1970.* Essays by Gordon H. Chang, Karin M. Higa, Sharon Spain, and ShiPu Wang. San Francisco: Fine Arts Museums of San Francisco; Berkeley: University of California Press, 2008.

Daniels, Roger. *Asian America: Chinese and Japanese in the United States since 1850.* Seattle: University of Washington Press, 1988.

———. *Concentration Camps: North America; Japanese in the United States and Canada during World War II.* Rev. ed. Malabar, FL: Robert E. Krieger Publishing Company, 1981. Updated in 1989. Original 1971 ed. published by Holt, Rinehart and Winston, New York, under title *Concentration Camps USA.*

———. "The Exile and Return of Seattle's Japanese." *Pacific Northwest Quarterly* 88, no. 4 (1997): 166–173. http://www.jstor.org/stable/40492331.

———. Foreword to Johns, *The Hope of Another Spring*, vii–viii.

———. "Words Do Matter: A Note on Inappropriate Terminology and the Incarceration of the Japanese Americans." In Fiset and Nomura, *Nikkei in the Pacific Northwest*, 183–207. Essay reissued online by Discover Nikkei, February 1, 2008. http://www.discovernikkei.org/en/journal/2008/2/1/words-do-matter.

Daniels, Roger, Sandra C. Taylor, and Harry H. L. Kitano, eds. *Japanese Americans: From Relocation to Redress.* Seattle: University of Washington Press, 1991.

Dempster, Brian Komei, ed. *Making Home from War: Stories of Japanese American Exile and Resettlement.* Berkeley, CA: Heyday Books, 2011.

*Denshō. Digital Repository, https://ddr.densho.org/.

Dorpat, Paul, and J. R. Sherrard. *Seattle Now and Then* (blog). https://pauldorpat.com.

Fiset, Louis. *Camp Harmony: Seattle's Japanese Americans and the Puyallup Assembly Center.* Urbana: University of Illinois Press, 2009.

*———. *Imprisoned Apart: The World War II Correspondence of an Issei Couple.* Seattle: University of Washington Press, 1997.

Fiset, Louis, and Gail M. Nomura, eds. *Nikkei in the Pacific Northwest: Japanese Americans and Japanese Canadians in the Twentieth Century.* Seattle: University of Washington Press, 2005.

Flewelling, Stan. *Shirakawa: Stories from a Pacific Northwest Japanese American Community.* Auburn, WA: White River Valley Museum, 2002.

Fuller, Richard E. *A Gift to the City: A History of the Seattle Art Museum and the Fuller Family.* Seattle: Seattle Art Museum, 1993.

Gordon, Jan. *Modern French Painters.* New York: Dodd, Mead and Company, 1923.

**The Green Lake Japanese American Community, 1900–1942.* Seattle: Green Lake Japanese American Community Booklet Committee, 2005.

Hart, Dakin, and Mark Dean Johnson, eds. *Changing and Unchanging Things: Noguchi and Hasegawa in Postwar Japan.* New York: Isamu Noguchi Foundation and Garden Museum in association with University of California Press, Oakland, 2019.

Hayashi, Brian Masaru. *Democratizing the Enemy: The Japanese American Internment.* Princeton, NJ: Princeton University Press, 2004.

Higa, Karin M. Introduction to *Henry Sugimoto: Painting an American Experience*, by Kristine Kim, ix–xiv. Berkeley, CA: Heyday Books, 2000.

———. *Living in Color: The Art of Hideo Date.* Los Angeles: Japanese American National Museum in association with Heyday Books, Berkeley, CA, 2001.

———. "Some Notes on an Asian American Art History." In Andersen et al., *With New Eyes*, 11–14.

*———. *The View from Within: Japanese American Art from the Internment Camps, 1942–1945.* Rev. ed. Los Angeles: Japanese American National Museum, UCLA Wight Art Gallery, and UCLA Asian American Studies Center, 1992.

Hoffman, Lisa. "Tacoma's Japanese Language School: An Alternative Path to Citizenship and Belonging in Pre-WWII Urban America." Conflux 6. Urban Studies Program, University of Washington Tacoma, 2014. https://digitalcommons.tacoma.uw.edu/conflux/6.

Hoffman, Lisa M., and Mary L. Hanneman. *Becoming Nisei: Japanese American Lives in Prewar Tacoma*, Seattle: University of Washington Press, 2021.

Horiuchi, Lynne. "Dislocations: The Built Environments of Japanese American Internment." In Mackey, *Guilt by Association*, 255–275.

*Horiuchi, Paul. Papers. Accession No. 5443-1. Special Collections, University of Washington Libraries.

Ichioka, Yuji. *Before Internment: Essays in Prewar Japanese American History.* Edited by Gordon H. Chang and Eiichiro Azuma. Stanford, CA: Stanford University Press, 2006.

———. *The Issei: The World of the First Generation Japanese Immigrants, 1885–1924.* New York: Free Press, 1988.

———. "JERS Revisited: Introduction." In Ichioka, *Views from Within*, 3–27.

———, ed. *Views from Within: The Japanese American Evacuation and Resettlement Study.* Los Angeles: Asian American Studies Center, University of California at Los Angeles, 1989.

Ito, Kazuo. *Issei: A History of Japanese Immigrants in North America.* Translated by Shinichiro Nakamura and Jean S. Gerard. Seattle: Executive Committee for Publication of Issei, Japanese Community Service, 1973.

Iwata, Masakazu. *Planted in Good Soil: A History of the Issei in United States Agriculture.* 2 vols. New York: Peter Lang, 1992.

**Japanese and Japanese American Painters in the United States: A Half Century of Hope and Suffering, 1896–1945.*

Tokyo: Tokyo Metropolitan Teien Art Museum and Nippon Television Network Corporation, 1995.

*Johns, Barbara. *The Hope of Another Spring: Takuichi Fujii, Artist and Wartime Witness*. Seattle: University of Washington Press, 2017.

*———. "Knowing Your Place: Issei Artists in Seattle; Kenjiro Nomura, Kamekichi Tokita, and Takuichi Fujii." PhD diss., University of Washington, 2014.

*———. *Paul Horiuchi: East and West*. Seattle: University of Washington Press in association with Museum of Northwest Art, La Conner, WA, 2008.

*———. *Signs of Home: The Paintings and Wartime Diary of Kamekichi Tokita*. Seattle: University of Washington Press, 2011.

*Kangas, Matthew. "Merchants, Mavens, and Money: A History of Art Dealers in Seattle." *Arts Line* (Seattle), October 1986.

Kanzaki, Kiichi. *California and the Japanese*. Reprint ed. San Francisco: R and E Research Associates, 1971. Originally published 1921.

Kashima, Tetsuden. Foreword to U.S. House of Representatives, *Personal Justice Denied*, xv–xxv.

———. *Judgment without Trial: Japanese American Imprisonment during World War II*. Seattle: University of Washington Press, 2003.

Kawasaki, Koichi. "Regretting the Future: Noguchi and Hasegawa Consider the Direction of Postwar Japanese Art." In Hart and Johnson, *Changing and Unchanging Things*, 62–75.

*"Kenjiro Nomura: An Artist's-Eye View of the Japanese Internment." *Columbia: The Magazine of Northwest History* 6, no. 4 (Winter 1992–1993): 22–25.

Kingsbury, Martha. *Art of the Thirties: The Pacific Northwest*. Seattle: University of Washington Press for the Henry Art Gallery, 1972.

———. *George Tsutakawa*. Seattle: University of Washington Press; Bellevue Art Museum, Bellevue, WA, 1990.

———. "Seattle and the Puget Sound." In *Art of the Pacific Northwest*, 39–92.

Kobayashi, Junko. "'Bitter Sweet Home': Celebration of Biculturalism in Japanese Language Japanese American Literature, 1936–1952." PhD diss., University of Iowa, 2005. https://ir.uiowa.edu/etd/97.

Kurashige, Lon. *Two Faces of Exclusion: The Untold History of Anti-Asian Racism in the United States*. Chapel Hill: University of North Carolina Press, 2016.

Lee, Shelley Sang-Hee. *Claiming the Oriental Gateway: Prewar Seattle and Japanese America*. Philadelphia: Temple University Press, 2011.

Lillquist, Karl. "Minidoka." Chap. 5 in *Imprisoned in the Desert: The Geography of World War II–Era, Japanese American Relocation Centers in the Western United States*. Ellensburg: Central Washington University, 2007. https://www.cwu.edu/geography/geography-japanese-american-relocation-centers.

Mackey, Mike, ed. *Guilt by Association: Essays on Japanese Settlement, Internment, and Relocation in the Rocky Mountain West*. Powell, WY: Western History Publications, ca. 2001.

*Magden, Ronald E. *Furusato: Tacoma–Pierce County Japanese, 1888–1977*. Tacoma, WA: Nikkeijinkai, Tacoma Japanese Community Service, 1998.

*———. Papers. Accession No. 33-112. Northwest Room, Tacoma Public Library, Tacoma, WA.

*Martin, David F. *Invocation of Beauty: The Life and Photography of Soichi Sunami*. Edmonds, WA: Cascadia Art Museum in association with University of Washington Press, 2018.

———. "Yvonne Twining Humber: A Washington Painter of Renown and Obscurity." *Columbia: The Magazine of Northwest History* 23, no. 4 (Winter 2009–2010): 19–25.

*Martin, David F., and Nicolette Bromberg. *Shadows of a Fleeting World: Pictorial Photography and the Seattle Camera Club*. Seattle: University of Washington Press in association with University of Washington Libraries and the Henry Art Gallery, 2011.

*McKivor, June Mukai. *Kenjiro Nomura: An Artist's View of the Japanese American Internment*. Seattle: Wing Luke Asian Museum, 1991.

Minidoka Interlude: September 1942–October 1943. Hunt, ID: Minidoka Relocation Center, 1943. Reissued with an introduction by Tom Takeuchi. Gresham, OR: privately published [ca. 1990].

*Minidoka National Historic Site, National Parks Service, U.S. Department of the Interior. https://www.nps.gov/miin/index.htm.

Miyamoto, S. Frank. "An Immigrant Community in America." In Conroy and Miyakawa, *East across the Pacific*, 217–243.

———. Oral history interview, 1998. Denshō, Visual History Collection, https://ddr.densho.org/ddr-densho-1000-52.

———. *Social Solidarity among the Japanese in Seattle*. Seattle: University of Washington Press in cooperation with the Asian American Studies Program, University of Washington, 1984. First published 1939.

Mochizuki, Ken. *Meet Me at Higo: An Enduring Story of a Japanese American Family*. Seattle: Wing Luke Museum, 2011.

*Morley, Grace L. McCann. "Abstract Art on the Pacific Coast." In American Abstract Artists, *The World of Abstract Art*, 123–129.

Moseley, Spencer, and Gervais Reed. *Walter F. Isaacs, an Artist in America, 1886–1964*. Seattle: University of Washington Press, 1982.

Munroe, Alexandra. *The Third Mind: American Artists Contemplate Asia, 1860–1989*. New York: Solomon R. Guggenheim Foundation, 2009.

———. "The Third Mind: An Introduction." In Munroe, *The Third Mind*, 20–33.

*Nakane, Kazuko. "Facing the Pacific: Asian American Artists in Seattle, 1900–1970." In Chang, Johnson, and Karlstrom, *Asian American Art*, 55–81.

*———. "Personalizing the Abstract: Asian American Artists in Seattle." In Wechsler, *Asian Traditions / Modern Expressions*, 186–189.

*Nomura, Kenjiro. Artist file, Seattle Public Library.

*———. Papers. Nomura Estate.

Okihiro, Gary Y. "Religion and Resistance in America's Concentration Camps." *Phylon* 45, no. 3 (1984): 220–233. https://www.jstor.org/stable/274406.

*Otsuka, Shunichi. *History of the Japanese of Tacoma*. Translated by James Watanabe. Seattle: Pacific Northwest District Council, Japanese American Citizens League, 1986. Originally published as *Tacoma nihonjin hattenshi*, 1917.

**Pacific Coast Art: United States' Representation at the Third Biennial of São Paulo*. San Francisco: San Francisco Museum of Art, 1956.

*Prelinger, Elizabeth. *Scenes of American Life: Treasures from the Smithsonian American Art Museum*. New York: Watson-Guptill Publications; [Washington, DC]: Smithsonian American Art Museum, 2001.

*Ridley, Jo Ann. *Zoë Dusanne: An Art Dealer Who Made a Difference*. McKinleyville, CA: Fithian Press, 2011.

Robinson, Greg. *After Camp: Portraits in Midcentury Japanese American Life and Politics*. Berkeley: University of California Press, 2012.

———. *By Order of the President: FDR and the Internment of Japanese Americans*. Cambridge, MA: Harvard University Press, 2001.

———. Foreword to Dempster, *Making Home from War*, viii–xiii.

———. *A Tragedy of Democracy: Japanese Confinement in North America*. New York: Columbia University Press, 2009.

Sakoda, James M. "Minidoka: An Analysis of Changing Patterns of Social Interaction." PhD diss., University of California, Berkeley, 1949.

———. "The 'Residue': The Unresettled Minidokans, 1943–1945." In Ichioka, *Views from Within*, 247–281.

*Seattle Art Museum. Records. Accession No. 2636-1. Special Collections, University of Washington Libraries.

**Seattle City Directory*. Seattle: R. L. Polk & Company, various years.

Sims, Robert C. "The Japanese American Return to the Pacific Northwest." In Stacey, *An Eye for Injustice*, 143–152.

**Some Work of the Group of Twelve*. Seattle: Dogwood Press, 1937.

Sone, Monica. *Nisei Daughter*. Seattle: University of Washington Press, 1979. Originally published 1953 by Little, Brown and Company.

Speidel, Jennifer. "After Internment: Seattle's Debate over Japanese Americans' Right to Return Home." Seattle Civil Rights and Labor History Project, 2005. http://depts.washington.edu/civilr/after_internment.htm.

Spirited Stone: Lessons from Kubota's Garden. Seattle: Chin Music Press, 2020.

Stacey, Susan M., ed. *An Eye for Injustice: Robert C. Sims and Minidoka*. Pullman: Washington State University Press, 2020.

Sullivan, Michael Sean. *Tacoma History* (blog). https://tacomahistory.live/.

**Tacoma City Directory*. Tacoma, WA: R. L. Polk & Company, various years.

*Tacoma School District, Puget Sound Municipal Branch. Washington State Archives.

Takahashi, Jere. *Nisei/Sansei: Shifting Japanese American Identities and Politics*. Philadelphia: Temple University Press, 1997.

Takami, David A. *Divided Destiny: A History of Japanese Americans in Seattle*. Seattle: Wing Luke Museum in association with University of Washington Press, 1998.

———. *Executive Order 9066: 50 Years Before and 50 Years After; A History of Japanese Americans in Seattle.* Seattle: Wing Luke Asian Museum, 1992.

———. "Japanese Farming." HistoryLink, October 29, 1998. http://www.historylink.org/File/298.

Tamura, Anna. "Minidoka's Chief Gardener." In *Spirited Stone,* 134–145.

Tate, E. Mowbray. *Transpacific Steam: The Story of Steam Navigation from the Pacific Coast of North America to the Far East and the Antipodes.* New York: Cornwall Books, 1986.

Taylor, Quintard. *The Forging of a Black Community: Seattle's Central District from 1870 through the Civil Rights Era.* Seattle: University of Washington Press, 1994.

Tobey, Mark. "Japanese Traditions in Modern Art." *College Art Journal* 18, no. 1 (Fall 1958): 20–24.

Tokita, Kamekichi. Papers. Archives of American Art, Smithsonian Institution.

Tsutakawa, Ed. Oral history interviews, 2003–2004, 2006. Denshō, Visual History Collection. https://ddr.densho.org/ddr-densho-1016-5; https://ddr.densho.org/ddr-densho-1000-196.

*Tsutakawa, George. "A Conversation on Life and Fountains." *Journal of Ethnic Studies* 4 (Spring 1976): 4–36.

*———. Oral history interview, 1983. Archives of American Art, Smithsonian Institution. https://www.aaa.si.edu/collections/interviews/oral-history-interview-george-tsutakawa-11913.

*———. Papers. Estate of George Tsutakawa.

*Tsutakawa, Mayumi. "A Canvas Diary: Painters before the War." In Tsutakawa and Lau, *Turning Shadows into Light,* 72–81.

*———, ed. *They Painted from Their Hearts: Pioneer Asian American Artists.* Seattle: Wing Luke Asian Museum, 1994.

*Tsutakawa, Mayumi, and Alan Chong Lau, eds. *Turning Shadows into Light: Art and Culture of the Northwest's Early Asian/Pacific Community.* Seattle: Young Pine Press, 1982.

U.S. House of Representatives. Committee on Interior and Insular Affairs. *Personal Justice Denied: Report of the Commission on Wartime Relocation and Internment of Civilians.* Washington, DC: Civil Liberties Public Education Fund; Seattle: University of Washington Press, 1997. Originally published in two volumes by the U.S. Government Printing Office, 1982–1983.

U.S. War Agency Liquidation Unit (formerly U.S. War Relocation Authority). *People in Motion: The Postwar Adjustment of the Evacuated Japanese Americans.* Washington, DC: Government Printing Office, 1947. https://archive.org/details/peopleinmotionpooounit.

U.S. War Relocation Authority (WRA). Files, Record Group 210, National Archives, Washington, DC.

———. *Community Government in War Relocation Centers.* Washington, DC: Government Printing Office, 1946. https://www.ibiblio.org/hyperwar/ATO/Admin/WRA/WRA-CommGov/index.html.

———. Japanese American Evacuation and Resettlement Records. BANC MSS 67/14c, Bancroft Library, University of California, Berkeley, https://oac.cdlib.org/ark:/13030/.

———. *The Relocation Program: A Guidebook for the Residents of Relocation Centers.* Washington, DC: Government Printing Office, 1943. https://ia600407.us.archive.org/22/items/TheRelocationProgram/.

U.S. Wartime Civil Control Administration (WCCA). Files, Record Group 499, National Archives, College Park, MD.

Volk, Alicia. *In Pursuit of Universalism: Yorozu Tetsugō and Japanese Modern Art.* Berkeley and Los Angeles: University of California Press, 2010.

Warren, James R. "World War II Home Front on Puget Sound." HistoryLink, September 13, 1999. https://historylink.org/File/1664.

Watson, Forbes. Papers. Archives of American Art, Smithsonian Institution.

Weber-Roochvarg, Lynn. "Japanese Community in the San Juan Islands, 1880–1942." HistoryLink, March 7, 2016, http://www.historylink.org/File/11198.

*Wechsler, Jeffrey, ed. *Asian Traditions / Modern Expressions: Asian American Artists and Abstraction, 1945–1970.* New York: Harry N. Abrams in association with the Jane Voorhees Zimmerli Art Museum, Rutgers, the State University of New Jersey, 1997.

White, Anthony R., ed. *The Graphic Art of Roi Partridge: A Catalogue Raisonné.* American Prints and Printmakers, No. 2. Los Angeles: Hennessy and Ingalls, 1988.

Whitelegg, Isobel. "The Bienal Internacional de São Paulo: A Concise History, 1951–2014." *Perspective* 2 (2013). http://journals.openedition.org/perspective/3902.

Winther-Tamaki, Bert. *Art in the Encounter of Nations: Japanese and American Artists in the Early Postwar Years.* Honolulu: University of Hawaiʻi Press, 2001.

———. "The Asian Dimensions of Postwar Abstract Art: Calligraphy and Metaphysics." In Munroe, *The Third Mind,* 144–197.

INDEX

Works by Nomura are listed under their titles.

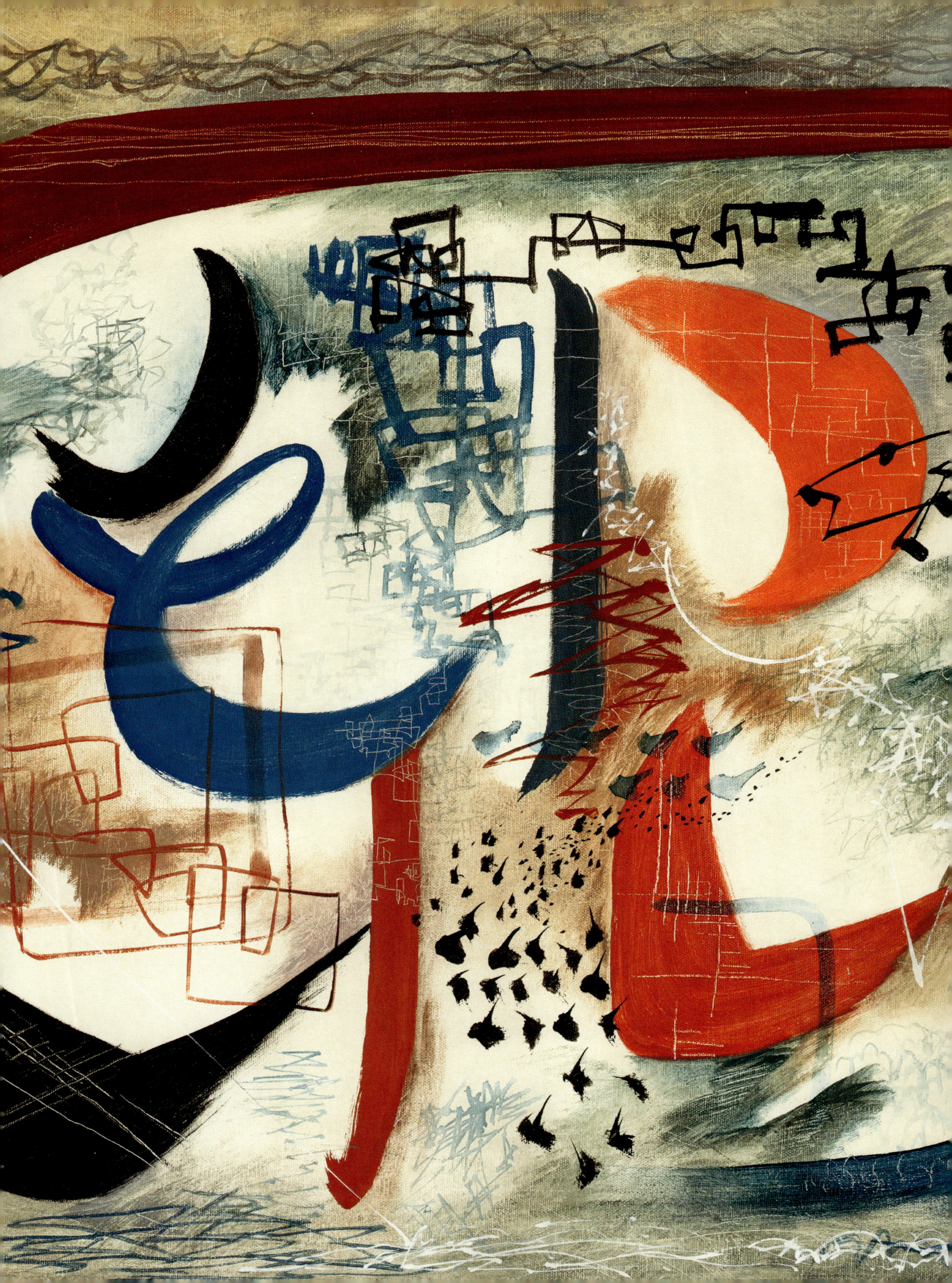

DONORS TO THE PUBLICATION

PLATINUM

4Culture
Paul Carlson & Shawn-Marie Hanson
Edmonds Arts Commission
Hugh and Jane Ferguson Foundation
Richard Hesik
Nancy Rothwell
Ron & Tina Tanemura Family Foundation
Tony Valenzuela, Group 44, in memory of Ian Osthus

GOLD

Thomas Barwick
Lindsey & Carolyn Echelbarger
Donald Hall
Ruth & Bill Ingham
Gwen & Steve Johnson
Julie Long
Bruce R. McCaw Family Foundation
Michael & Katherine Meeks
Michael & Danielle Mroczek
Jim & Mariette O'Donnell
Mary Olsen
Pamela Proske
Goro & Hatsune Tokita

SILVER

Sharon Archer & Don Eklund
Wayne Dodge & Lawrence Kreisman
Charles & Jeannie Gravenkemper
Lucy Hart
Maria Mackey
Lisa Sakura Nomura-Kidwell
Jean & Steve Pennington
Herb & Lucy Pruzan
Mel & Leena Sturman

Shopping Center, 1950
Detail of Fig. 4.11

BRONZE

David Aggerholm & Gwen Lundberg
Jan & Randy Holbrook
C. David Hughbanks
Christina Koons & James McIntire
Stephen Lacy
Mary & Sam Magill
Sharon & Ken Mattson
Alison & Dale Miller
Mary & Frank Montgomery
Ned & Joyce Turner
Robert & Laura Walls

FRIEND

Eloise Beachell & Robert D. Levin
Bette Bell
David Brewster & Mary Kay Sneeringer
Brenda & David Chamness
Jim Carraway
Susan Dixon
Patrick & Susan Dunn
Gerald & Elizabeth Finkel
Ron & Barbara Hammond
Jeff Howard
Naomi Joy & Albion Joy III
Karen & Lawrence Matsuda
Robert & Sylvana Rinehart
Judy Sambataro
Iyla Winterfeldt

EXHIBITION PARTNER:

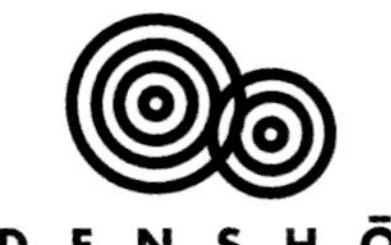

Cascadia Art Museum is grateful for the continued support from our community partners:

Hazel Miller Foundation
Walker Foundation

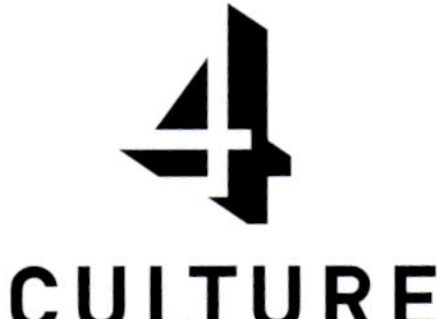

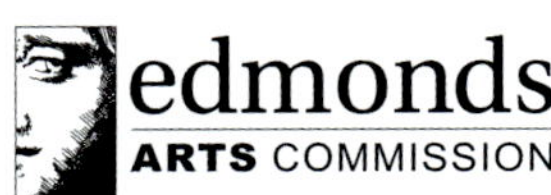

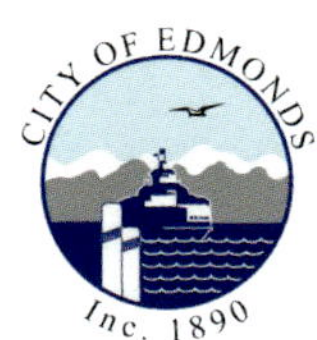

Kenjiro Nomura, American Modernist: An Issei Artist's Journey is published in conjunction with an exhibition of the same name, organized by Cascadia Art Museum and on view from October 22, 2021, to February 22, 2022.

This publication has received lead support from 4Culture, with additional support from the Hugh and Jane Ferguson Foundation.

The publication and the exhibition are funded in part by the City of Edmonds Arts Commission, with additional support from Nancy Rothwell, the Ron and Tina Tanemura Family Foundation, and many individual donors.

Denshō is Cascadia Art Museum's community partner for the combined project.

Cascadia Art Museum
190 Sunset Avenue South
Edmonds, WA 98020
cascadiaartmuseum.org

Distributed by University of Washington Press
uwapress.uw.edu

Library of Congress Control Number: 2021913181
ISBN: 9780998911236

Design: Phil Kovacevich
Editing: Jane Lichty
Proofreading: Carrie Wicks
Index: Susan Stone

Cover: *Puget Sound* (detail of fig. 2.5), ca. 1933
Oil on canvas, 19⅝ × 23¾ in.
Tacoma Art Museum, gift of Mr. and Mrs. Cyril A. Spinola, 1992.8

Frontispiece: Untitled (detail of fig. 4.20), 1952
Gouache on paper, 17¼ × 22¼ in.
Seattle Art Museum, gift of the Estate of Mr. Nomura, 60.87

P. iv: *Main Gate* (detail of fig. 3.11), 1942
Watercolor on paper, 19 × 24 in.
Tacoma Art Museum, George and Betty Nomura Collection, 2013.7.6

Back cover (also fig. 4.18): Kenjiro Nomura at easel, 1952
Photo: Charles Pearson
University of Washington Libraries, Special Collections, Pearson 5210-64A

Photography credits for works of art

Addison Gallery of American Art, Phillips Academy, Andover, MA/ Art Resource, NY: 2.19

Rob Fraser: 2.6

Tod Gangler: 1.14, 1.15, 1.16, 1.19, 1.21, 2.7, 2.8, 2.9, 2.14, 2.17, 3.5, 3.13, 3.25, 3.32, 3.35, 3.45, 4.5, 4.6, 4.9, 4.10, 4.11, 4.12, 4.13, 4.15, 4.16, 4.17, 4.21, 4.22, 4.23, 4.24, 4.29, M.1, M.2, M.4, M.7, M.8, M.9, M.10, M.14, M.16, M.17, M.18, M.19, M.20, M.24, M.25, M.26, M.27, M.28, M.29, M.30, M.31, M.32

Paul Macapia: 2.3, 4.25, M.24

Elizabeth Mann: 4.20, 4.26, 4.28

Richard Nicol: 2.2, 3.2, 3.6, 3.7, 3.8, 3.9, 3.10, 3.11, 3.20, 3.23, 3.26, 3.27, 3.30, 3.31, 3.34, 3.36, 3.37, 3.39, 3.42, 3.43, 3.45, M.15

Duncan Price: 3.4, 3.16, 3.19, 3.21, 3.28, 3.29, 3.33, 3.44

Doug Yaple: 2.5, 3.14, 3.24, 3.38